Dennis —
The most beloved
students, friends, and
now colleague.

With great affection and love

Richard Valentassi

THE MAKING OF THE SELF

THE MAKING

of the SELF

Ancient

and

Modern

Asceticism

Richard Valantasis

CASCADE *Books* · Eugene, Oregon

THE MAKING OF THE SELF
Ancient and Modern Asceticism

Cascade Books
A Division of Wipf and Stock Publishers
199 W. 8th Ave., Suite 3
Eugene, OR 97401

www.wipfandstock.com

ISBN 13: 978-1-55635-286-7

Cataloging-in-Publication data:

Valantasis, Richard
    The making of the self : ancient and modern asceticism / Richard Valantasis.

    xxii + 314 p. ; 23 cm.

    Includes bibliographical references.

    ISBN 13: 978-1-55635-286-7 (alk. paper)

    1. Asceticism. 2. Asceticism—History. 3. Asceticism—History—Early church, ca. 30–600. 4. Ascetics—Rome. I. Title.

BV5023 V35 2008

Manufactured in the U.S.A

For

Margaret R. Miles

who introduced me to the academic study of asceticism

and Douglas K. Bleyle

who enlivened and expanded my ascetical horizons

Contents

Preface

I WAS HARD-WIRED FOR ASCETICISM SINCE I GREW UP IN A GREEK Orthodox community in Canton, Ohio, which, in former generations, took the disciplined Christian life very seriously. Fasting, very long liturgies, vigils, abstinence of all sorts, and ritual cleansings all built the ascetical foundation upon which I lived my life. Then as an Episcopal priest now of nearly 35 years, I realized that the Book of Common Prayer with its regular cycle of daily prayer and weekly Eucharist created the structure for myself personally and the communities of which I was a member, to live the ascetical life. This hard-wiring for asceticism enabled me to explore the depth and riches of human striving as a priest and scholar alone and in the various academic and ecclesiastical communities in which I served. So it is not surprising that my work over these years have explored the expanse of ascetical theory and practice. This volume documents that lifelong passion and interest.

I have discovered that asceticism constitutes a human impulse. Something drives humans to dream of being a better person in a more healthy society and in a cosmos that holds promise of helping them to flourish. In dreaming of that wholesome state for self, society, and the cosmos, humans become dissatisfied with their lives, relationships, and connection to the cosmos. The dissatisfaction births the ascetical impulse. Asceticism reflects that attempt to live a different sort of life, to resist the tendency simply to live like all other people, and to branch out into selves defined by dreams for flourishing, not resting in the various selves our societies and mundane living present, but resisting that ease to branch into new directions. Asceticism also drives the desire to create new societies, healthier ways of relating to others, more just ways of connecting to those close-by and far away, as well as biological and constructed families that create a human ecology filled with grace, harmony, respect, sensitivity, and honor. The ascetic impulse also fuels the desire for repairing the physical environment in which humans live after years of abuse, pollution, deforestation, and profligate use of natural resources. Of course all these ascetic dreams of people, societies, and environments depend upon creating a wholesome human, social, and natural ecology that contests the dominant structures that hold dreamers back, or impose debilitating and limiting social structures, and abuse the physical environment. Resistance to those dominant sources begins in the ascetic impulse for personal, social, and cosmic transformation.

I argue that this ascetic impulse is nothing new. Throughout history ascetics have dreamed and resisted. In my work, that historical asceticism began with the Greek and Roman philosophers and Gnostic literature of the Nag Hammadi Library; it continued to early Christian writers. Historically, asceticism was not relegated to the Christian monasteries alone, but began long before Christianity. Asceticism developed in attempts by Greeks and Romans to transform the moral and spiritual status of the person and society and it expanded as many different kinds of Gnostics forged new contemplative ground for the embodied person. Christians seem to have connected quickly with their ancient philosophical counterparts to embrace the ascetical impulse as a permanent way of life and they engaged in vigorous debate with the Gnostics about the parameters of orthodox asceticism and contemplation. If anything, history proves that asceticism pervades the Western intellectual tradition. I have worked to bring this ascetical substratum to light in antiquity, while at the same time to open other people and movements to analysis through the lens of asceticism. My theory of asceticism, now more fully elaborated in these essays, allowed a broader view of the ascetic impulse in historical contexts as well as our postmodern world.

In discussions over the years, some of my critics have argued that according to my theory of asceticism *anything* can be ascetical. And to my critics I answer a resounding "Yes!" I have tried to open the space to analyze a wide assortment of behaviors through asceticism in order to understand how societies operate hegemonically and with those who resist. So body-builders, monks, gang members, environmentalists, community organizers—in short, anyone who resists in order to create new selves, different ways of socializing, and a cohesive way to relate to the physical world bespeaks the presence of an ascetical impulse. I have a hunch that the more asceticism in religious communities becomes submerged, that is, the more people limit asceticism to specific religious actions and groups of people in history, the more other forms of non-religiously specific asceticism emerge to fill the vacuum created by the submersion. The vigorous attention to the body, its health and transformation through exercise, emerged in postmodernity precisely at the point at which most churches completely ignored the ascetical practices that made religion vital, engaging, and transformative.

Asceticism, broadly defined as I describe it, opens the way to investigating difference, which has become a pervasive theme of postmodern critical theory. Asceticism's focus on resistance, on the difference created by a person's or community's self-definition in opposition to dominant social, religious, and political structures, opens the way to understanding the various means of personal and cultural transformation. To see the interplay of dominance and subversion within a person and within a society lays bare the contours of desire to change, to renew, to transform, to articulate in often dramatically different modes a way of life that fulfills that desire. By documenting the practices that articulate that difference, ascetical historians and theorists document the practices that articulate the fault lines within a person and society. The ascetical theory developed in these essays point the way to documenting that difference in whatever arena it may be found, wherever desire to be someone different and to live in a different sort of society with a different understanding of the way the world operates. Excavating difference through documenting subversive practices defines the ascetical task. And many of the essays that follow show how that has been accomplished in various historical contexts in order that scholars and religious practitioners today may extend that analysis into the social, religious, and political modes of postmodernity.

This connection between asceticism then and now, between history and contemporary society, is an important one. I have studied asceticism not only to understand the lives of historical people, but also to enrich the lives of people living in colleges and universities, churches, cities and towns, and nations today. I have used the historical sources not only to understand the dynamics of transformation in the past, but to understand and equip myself and others to understand the dynamics of transformation, resistance, and renewal in our own lives and societies today. As a priest-historian my focus always seems to bridge what happened then to what is happening now, so that, in the end, I can not only understand Roman ascetics, but also understand our contemporary ascetics like the

Branch Davidians in Waco, Texas, or the body-builders we all see at the gym, or even the mentally ill colleague struggling to create a self that can flourish and thrive through daily practices that lead to mental health. All these connect with the work of the monks in the desert, and the Roman moral philosophers, and the Gnostic writers as well. My theory of asceticism as it is developed in these essays tries to connect these events and to open them for analysis, scrutiny, and discernment.

It is precisely this desire to connect past and present that forced me to define asceticism more generally. If we restrict asceticism to specific practices like fasting, or sexual abstinence, or withdrawal from society, we so limit the arena that other performances are occluded. A restricted definition of asceticism allows us only to see the foreground of the social painting, whereas asceticism may also be seen in the background. By shifting the definition away from these specifically religious actions (fasting, chastity, withdrawal), it becomes possible to see in the foreground elements of ascetical activity otherwise occluded by a restrictive definition. I understand that not everyone is interested in connecting the past to the present in the same way, but for me it seemed such a logical and necessary move that I felt compelled to open the definition to the broadest perspective possible to account for our contemporary actions that seemed so ascetical at heart. Again, I suspect that the suppression of asceticism in religious contexts has led to the rise in secular ascetical activities to fill the void created by the impulse to define an alternative body, society, and cosmos.

In the end, however, it has been religious communities that most have benefited from this expansive definition of asceticism. Over the years I have taught in parishes, led retreats for clergy, conducted renewal programs for monasteries of men and women, supervised quiet days for seminarians and lay people, organized weekly meetings to study the scriptures in preparation for the Sunday Eucharist, and engaged actively in the life of the church—in every occasion this expansive definition of asceticism has opened new ways of living for searching religious folk and helped them to look at their own lives and the lives of those with whom they live. Asceticism broadly defined has enabled religious practitioners to renew their own lives and communities, to connect deeply and intimately with their own yearnings and desires to become someone more transparent to the presence of the divine, and to envision ways of living that transform and renew their communities, their societies, and their relationship with the physical universe. This alone has made it worthy of my effort at defining and studying asceticism. The benefits of this kind of study reach far beyond the academic journals, the seminary classroom, and the professional academic meetings to touch the lives of people living out their desires in a complex and often debilitating social and religious context. And it has been worth every minute of study and frustrating analysis and writing to make this available to those outside the academy and university.

So these essays stand as an ending and a beginning. The essays here collected bring together many specific studies as in a pointillist painting to present asceticism as an important instrument for understanding the past. It brings together many past studies as a kind of summary of my work. In that sense it brings to a close an era of my own research and writing. At the same time these essays represent a beginning. They open doors for analysis of historical and postmodern resistant performances that allow postmodern people to analyze, investigate, scrutinize, and transform aspect of self, society, and cosmos, and in the end, as the Roman philosophers would put it, to discern what is truly good (as opposed to what is merely an apparent good) and what is truly bad (as opposed to what is simply an apparent evil). It is my hope that just this sort of discernment about good and evil present in both the dominant context in which we live and in the resistant modes that respond to our deepest desires will begin a new phase in ascetical studies. For this beginning, I offer these essays here collected that have emerged from a hard-wired life of asceticism, a long priestly ministry, and a lifetime of historical study.

Acknowledgments

I HAVE BEEN SURROUNDED BY A "GREAT CLOUD OF WITNESSES" WHO have helped me to think, write, and theorize about asceticism over the past twenty-five years. Here I want simply to acknowledge those who have been consistent partners with me in my work. I would be remiss for not acknowledging the impetus to graduate study that the sisters of the Society of St. Margaret, an Anglican order of women monks, provided me early in my career. After the first years of my teaching and preaching as their Chaplain, they sent me off to Harvard to begin my study, arguing that I needed to systematize both historical and applied asceticism for the mutual benefit of scholars and practitioners. Without the practical context provided by the convent in those early years of my study, I would not have been able all these years to bridge the academy and the church as has been my passion. So the primacy of thanks goes to those many professed sisters and novices who pushed me to theorize and teach about the interior life of contemplative activists.

Following immediately upon the sisters' push, I owe a great debt to those priests and ministers around me who helped me to find practical expression for my study and who also guided my research and writing in unconventional directions. This begins with my wife, Janet Carlson, whose continual press for excellence and writing for the church has spurred me for these past nearly thirty-five years of our yoking. Janet has urged me to bridge church and academy, knowing that both contexts demand strenuous ascetical activity for the pursuit of excellence and the advancement of the religiously human condition. With Janet, Jennifer Phillips with whom I was co-rector at St. John's Bowdoin Street in Boston, Daniel Handschy who was first a student at Harvard and then a priestly colleague, and Karen Ullestad who began as a church musician but finally acceded to the call to minister through her own musical asceticism—all in their ways supported, challenged, engaged, tested, and criticized my work on asceticism and brought new avenues of research and writing.

In my academic life as a professor, many have held my hand as I worked through these ascetical issues, theories, and texts. When I write anything, these are the people who stand imaginatively around my desk and criticize, applaud, object, encourage, redirect, and respond with energy to my work. Vincent Wimbush, with whom for over a decade I worked to assemble a yearly colloquium on asceticism before the American Academy of Religion and Society of Biblical Literature annual meetings (how did we ever manage it?); James Goehring, whose own creative work on Egyptian monasticism has spurred me into new ways of conceptualizing the ascetical context; Teresa Shaw, whose insight and conviviality made studying these dusty old men both fun and challenging; Elizabeth Clark, who helped me get my theory of asceticism published in the first place and whose own work has opened new horizons for me; Clayton Jefford, who does not do asceticism but likes to hang out with ascetical types for interesting conversations and dinners at academic meetings; and Derek Krueger, a Byzantinist whose publishing continually reminded me of the larger ascetical context in which I myself was formed—all these continue to inhabit my social body as companions on the academic ascetical way. At Iliff School of Theology in Denver, Colorado, I had colleagues who, although not themselves interested in an asceticism that took them away from the dinner table, encouraged and supported me in my work: Pamela Eisenbaum, Mark George, and Jacob Kinnard were non-ascetical ascetics who read and responded to my work with enthusiasm and grace.

Among my friends whose asceticism primarily relates to intense and wonderful conversations usually with fine food and drink, I must acknowledge Delwin and Nancy Brown whose company refreshes and renews so that work becomes fun, and Robert and Victoria Sirota who over many years have been supportive colleagues in the work of transfiguration of the church and the world.

I would also like to thank those who have participated in a weekly experimental Eucharist in my home, first in Denver, then in Atlanta. The routine began as a simple experiment to test the thesis that simply breathing together in chanting and singing could become the basis of a renewed Christian community. The resultant community proved the thesis. In Denver, I thank especially Sara Rosenau, Catherine Volland, Gregory Robbins, Lucy McGuffey, Raymond Raney, George and Betsy

Hoover, Maryann O'Brien, Shelley Brown, Beth Taylor, Mark Miliotto, Steve Medema, Deb Trissel, Maggie Hammond, Katie and Lee Parker, Ann and Henry Jesse, John Taylor, Kevin Fletcher, Carrie Doehring, George Magnuson, Burt and Joanne Womack. In Atlanta, Elizabeth and Kees Schellingerhoudt and their children, Penny Chase, Kyle Tau, Alice Rose, Maria Artemis, Nancy Baxter, Justice Schunior, John Blevins, and Pat and Jerry Zeller. This experiment would not have been possible in either Denver or Atlanta without the community that spans both cities: Doug and Jennifer Bleyle, Linda Bailey, and Josephine Bernier. Their constancy further proved the depth of the reality of that common-breathing formation.

I would be remiss in not thanking a very recent working group on asceticism, although I am sure they would be surprised by my description of our common work as "ascetical." These are the people who have helped birth the Institute for Contemplative Living founded by Douglas Bleyle and myself. Corey Keyes of Emory University, Howard Bad Hand, Pedro Gonzales, and James Dumesnil of the High Star Sun Eagle Foundation have in recent months begun to revitalize my ascetical interests by expanding my work into the lives of non-academic and even non-church people. I am deeply indebted to their spiritual work and their support for future ascetical projects both academic and applied.

This book would not have been possible without the vision of my editor, K. C. Hanson at Wipf and Stock Publishers, and without the long-suffering and painstaking work of my wife Janet Carlson. Janet has reformatted all the footnotes, tracked down all my "whiches" that should have been "thats," and put together these essays into what is a beautiful book. It would not have been possible without her. So much of the editing of my own work over the years has passed through her red-pencil reading and come out the better for it.

I dedicate this book to two people who have had an enormous impact on my life. Margaret R. Miles introduced me to the study of asceticism. I remember clearly the first reading course I did with her as a "minister in the vicinity" while Chaplain to the sisters. She brought out all the old, dusty ascetics and made them come alive in my presence. Her critical appropriation and deep love for the ascetic masters, and her own writing about them, guided me into deeper and more profound love for them and like Origen to Gregory Thaumaturgos, implanted the divine spark into my soul so that I was compelled to study, write, and apply my knowledge for others. Without Margaret Miles's support I could not have made it as an academic. Similarly without Douglas K. Bleyle's eager and enthusiastic delving into my ascetical theory and writing, I would have considered my work on asceticism to be complete. But Doug insisted that I teach him asceticism, both as an academic pursuit and as a church discipline and then pushed me to articulate the convergence of asceticism and contemplation in the Christian traditions. When I thought I had said just about everything I needed to say, Doug has spurred new avenues of thinking and different ways of applying ascetical theory and practice. Margaret at the beginning of my career and Doug at the middle point (I refuse to say "end") have given me more than they can ever imagine. I am eternally grateful for their presence in my life.

Several of the chapters in this volume appeared in a variety of publications in earlier editions. The publishers and I are grateful for permissions to use this previously published materials.

1. "A Theory of the Social Function of Asceticism" first appeared in *Asceticism*, edited by Vincent L. Wimbush and Richard Valantasis, 544–52. New York: Oxford University Press, 1995. By permission of Oxford University Press, Inc.

2. "Constructions of Power in Asceticism" first appeared in *JAAR* 63 (1995) 775–821. Used with permission.

3. "Asceticism as a Sacred Marriage: Eastern and Western Theories" will also appear in *Sacred Marriages: The Divine-Human Sexual Metaphor from Sumer to Early Christianity*, edited by Martti Nissinen and Risto Uro. Winona Lake, IN: Eisenbrauns, 2008. Used with permission.

4. "Asceticism or Formation: Theorizing Asceticism after Nietzsche" first appeared in *The Subjective Eye: Essays on Art, Religion, and Gender in Honor of Margaret R. Miles*, edited by Richard Valantasis, Deborah Haynes, James Smith, and Janet Carlson, 157–75. Princeton Theological Monograph Series 59. Eugene, OR: Pickwick, 2006.

5. "A Theory of Asceticism, Revised" has not previously been published.

6. "Uncovering Adam's Esoteric Body" first appeared as "Adam's Body: Uncovering Esoteric Tradition in *The Apocryphon of John* and Origen's *Dialogue with Heraclides*" in *SecCent* 7 (1990) 150–62. Used with permission.

7. "Daemons and the Perfecting of the Monk's Body" first appeared as "Daemons and the Perfecting of the Monk's Body: Monastic Anthropology, Daemonology, and Asceticism" in *Semeia* 58 (1992) 47–79. Used with permission.

8. "Ascetical Withdrawal and the Second Letter of Basil the Great" first appeared as "The Stranger Within, the Stranger Without: Ascetical Withdrawal and the Second Letter of Basil the Great" in *Christianity and the Stranger: Historical Essays*, edited by Francis W. Nichols, 64–81. Atlanta: Scholars, 1995. Used with permission.

9. "Is the *Gospel of Thomas* Ascetical?" first appeared as "Is the *Gospel of Thomas* Ascetical?: Revisiting an Old Problem with a New Theory" in *JECS* 7 (1999) 55–81. Used with permission.

10. "Competing Ascetic Subjectivities in the Letter to the Galatians" first appeared in *Asceticism and the New Testament*, edited by Leif Vaage and Vincent L. Wimbush, 211–29. London: Routledge, 1999. Used with permission.

11. "Nag Hammadi and Asceticism: Theory and Practice" first appeared in *Studia Patristica* 35 (2000) 172–90. Used with permission from Peeters Publishers.

12. "Demons, Adversaries, Devils, Fisherman: the Asceticism of *Authoritative Teaching* in Roman Perspective" first appeared as "Demons, Adversaries, Devils, Fisherman: The Asceticism of *Authoritative Teaching* (NHL, VI, 3) in the Context of Roman Asceticism" in *JR* 81 (2001) 549–65. Used with permission from the University of Chicago Press.

13. "Musonius Rufus and Roman Ascetical Theory" first appeared in *GRBS* 40 (1999) 207–31. Used with permission.

Abbreviations

ACW	Ancient Christian Writers
ANRW	*Aufstieg und Niedergang der römischen Welt: Geschichte und Kultur Roms im Spiegel der neueren Forschung.* Edited by Hildegard Temporini. Berlin: de Gruyter, 1972–
APF	*Archiv für Papyrusforschung*
ASP	*American Studies in Papyrology*
BJRL	*Bulletin of the John Rylands University Library of Manchester*
CBQ	*Catholic Biblical Quarterly*
CH	*Church History*
CSCO	Corpus scriptorium christianorum orientalium
CWS	Classics of Western Spirituality
EEC	*Encyclopedia of Early Christianity.* 2nd ed. Edited by Everett Ferguson. New York: Garland, 1997
ER	*The Encyclopedia of Religion.* 16 vols. Edited by Mircea Eliade. New York: Macmillan, 1987
FRLANT	Forschungen zur Religion und Literatur des Alten und Neuen Testaments
GRBS	*Greek, Roman, and Byzantine Studies*
GTh	*Gospel of Thomas*
HDR	Harvard Dissertations in Religion
HR	*History of Religions*
HTR	*Harvard Theological Review*
Int	*Interpretation*
JAAR	*Journal of the American Academy of Religion*
JAC	*Jahrbuch für Antike und Christentum*
JBL	*Journal of Biblical Literature*

JECS	*Journal of Early Christian Studies*
JFSR	*Journal of Feminist Studies in Religion*
JR	*Journal of Religion*
JSOT	*Journal for the Study of the Old Testament*
JTS	*Journal of Theological Studies*
LCL	Loeb Classical Library
LTP	*Laval théologique et philosophique*
NHC	Nag Hammadi Codices
NHL or *NHLE*	*Nag Hammadi Library in English.* 3rd ed. Edited by James M. Robinson. San Francisco: HarperSanFrancisco, 1988
NHS	Nag Hammadi Studies
NovT	*Novum Testamentum*
NTS	*New Testament Studies*
OrChrAn	Orientalia Christiana Analecta
PG	Patrologia graeca
RE	*Realencyklopädie für protestantische Theologie und Kirche.* 3rd ed. 24 vols. Edited by Albert Hauck. Leipzig: Hinrichs, 1896–1913
REG	*Revue d'études Greques*
SAC	Studies in Antiquity and Christianity
SBL	Society of Biblical Literature
SBLDS	Society of Biblical Literature Dissertation Series
SBLSBS	Society of Biblical Literature Sources for Biblical Study
SecCent	*Second Century*
SHR	Studies in the History of Religions
StPatr	Studia patristica
STRev	*Sewanee Theological Review*
TDNT	*Theological Dictionary of the New Testament.* 10 vols. Edited by Gerhard Kittel and Gerhard Friedrich. Translated by Geoffrey Bromiley. Grand Rapids: Eerdmans, 1964–76
Teubner	Bibliotheca scriptorum graecorum et romanorum teubneriana
TJ	*Trinity Journal*
TJT	*Toronto Journal of Theology*
VC	*Vigiliae Christianae*

part one

THEORY

CHAPTER 1

A Theory of the
Social Function of Asceticism

OVER THE COURSE OF THE PAST SEVENTY YEARS OR MORE, THEORISTS IN the social sciences and the humanities have explored asceticism as a vital component of sociology, social history, and hermeneutics, while historians have been exploring the role of asceticism and the place of ascetics in the societies of Late Antiquity and the Western Middle Ages. The historical perspective has focused on the function of asceticism and the ascetic within the dominant social context, while the attention of the theorists has focused on it as an economic, social, political, and interpretative instrument within the larger cultural domain. Although at first glance the distinction seems minor, there is in fact a great difference in approach: the theorists understand asceticism as a large and pervasive cultural system, while the historians view asceticism as specific religious practices relating to social withdrawal, restriction of food, regulation of sexuality, and the formation of religious community. The larger cultural systems of the ascetical theorists locate asceticism at the center of cultural, social, and individual engagement in every sphere of cultural expression; the particular religious practices of the historian locate asceticism only in the religious or philosophical arenas.

Here I will present the ascetical theories of the three primary ascetical theorists of this century (Max Weber, Michel Foucault, and Geoffrey Harpham) and develop a theory of asceticism within which the social function of asceticism may be described. These three theorists represent a wide diversity of interests, from economic history and the sociology of religion to social history and literary theory. Although each succeeding

3

theorist has studied the work of the previous ones, the perspective on asceticism and the academic discourses of each have been significantly different. My own theory, presented below, will attempt to build on the contributions of each of these. I hope, thereby, to bridge the gap between ascetical theory and historical study.

WEBER, FOUCAULT, AND HARPHAM

Max Weber's theory of asceticism, developed early in the last century, treats asceticism as part of sociological theory and the history of economics. Weber's *The Protestant Ethic and the Spirit of Capitalism* developed the theory of inner-worldly asceticism as a means of understanding the emergence of capitalism. This initial exploration of asceticism explored the relationship between the development of the work force; the valuation of wealth and material good in the Protestant Reformation; the Protestant concept of a vocation to live in the world (as opposed to those Catholic monks who withdrew from the world); and the doctrine of predestination, which provided the opportunity for right conduct of life to prove that one is saved. In this economic study, Weber treats asceticism primarily as "methodically controlled and supervised" conduct.[1] Weber maintains that, for Protestants, this controlled conduct was directed specifically to living in the world, a world that consisted of daily living as the focus of Christian life and vocation. Asceticism, the controlled conduct, undertook, then, to remodel the world, so that Protestant ideals would be able to be achieved within it. The heart of the argument revolves about the remaking of the economic world through the development of theological principles that have been worked out in particular patterns of behavior. The asceticism of working in the world creates the work force, the kind of subjectivity necessary for the work force to function, and the theological justification for the sort of lifestyle to be lived.

Weber again addresses the theory of asceticism in his *Sociology of Religion*. Under the heading of paths to salvation, Weber links three elements of asceticism: the particular path of salvation, particular human conduct, and the means of training in that conduct. Moving from economics to the theory of the sociology of religion, Weber locates the methodically controlled behavior specifically within the teleological path toward salvation. The particular goal of salvation, the manner of

1. Weber, *Protestant Ethic*, 132.

achieving sanctification, emerges from a psychic and physical regimen of discipline aimed toward controlling and creating within a person an anti-instinctual response subordinated to the religious goal. Asceticism, here, is defined as "a methodical procedure for achieving religious salvation."[2] He identifies asceticism as either world-rejecting (that is, salvation achieved through withdrawal from the world) or inner-worldly (that is, salvation achieved through participation in the world while rejecting the world's institutions.

There is much about Weber's theories that is outmoded—his propensity for polarities, for example, between asceticism and mysticism, and between inner-worldly and world-rejecting. Yet they establish that asceticism has wider economic and political implications; that behaviors are at the heart of ascetical activity; that those behaviors are strongly regulated and directed toward specific goals; and that ascetic behaviors set out ways of relating to other people (as, for example, by creating a work force). The link, including the economic implications and orientations toward the world, of the three elements—identified as paths of salvation, human conduct, and the means of training in that conduct—hits at the heart of ascetical theory.

Michel Foucault explores the place of asceticism in the context of ethical formation. In an interview[3] in which he explained the project of his *History of Sexuality*, Foucault distinguished four aspects of what he called "the relationship to oneself": (1) the ethical substance (that is, the part of oneself that concerns moral conduct, the material with which ethics works); (2) the mode of subjection (that is, the mode that encourages or spurs people on to relate to their moral obligations, such as revelation or divine law); (3) asceticism, or self-forming activity (that is, the changes that one makes to oneself in order to become an ethical subject); and (4) the *telos* or goal (that is, the end toward which the ethics moves, the end result of ethical formation). Although Foucault identifies asceticism as one aspect of this process of ethical formation, he also views asceticism as the heart of the entire process of formation:

> No technique, no professional skill can be acquired without exercise; neither can one learn the art of living the *technē tou biou* without an *askēsis* which must be taken as a training of oneself

2. Weber, *Sociology of Religion*, 164.
3. Foucault, "Genealogy of Ethics."

> by oneself: this was one of the traditional principles to which the
> Pythagoreans, the Socratics, the Cynics had for a long time attrib-
> uted great importance.[4]

In the second volume of his *History of Sexuality*, titled *The Use of
Pleasure,* he further develops this perspective on asceticism. It is here that
Foucault distinguished between the set of rules of moral conduct itself;
the evaluation of the person based upon those rules; and the systems of
formation that enable one to be a subject acting according to those rules.[5]
These different ways of constructing oneself as a subject of moral action
differ according to the *telos* or the goal of the moral life that is the result
of moral formation. Foucault explains:

> There is no specific moral action that does not refer to a unified
> moral conduct; no moral conduct that does not call for the form-
> ing of oneself as an ethical subject; and no forming of the ethical
> subject without "modes of subjectivation" and "ascetics" or "prac-
> tices of the self" that supports them.[6]

Foucault's system, then, proposes a system of formation that involves a
goal of life encapsulated in a system of behavior, which requires formation through processes of subjectivation and ascetic practices.

Geoffrey Harpham develops a theory of asceticism in relation to
contemporary structuralists, poststructuralists, and postmodern theories of literary criticism and in conversation with Mikhail Mikhailovich
Bakhtin, Jacques Derrida, Michel Foucault, and other theorists of contemporary literary criticism. In his book, *The Ascetic Imperative in Culture
and Criticism*, he enlarges the arena of ascetical studies by exploring the
relationship of asceticism and culture. Harpham develops the theory of
asceticism as "the 'cultural' element in culture; it makes culture comparable, and is therefore one way of describing the common feature that
permits communication or understanding between cultures."[7] He views
asceticism as "the fundamental operating ground on which the particular
culture is overlaid."[8] Harpham's work directs attention from the merely
descriptive—whether of the literary strategies or of the ascetic's behav-

4. Foucault, *History of Sexuality*, 364.

5. Foucault, *Use of Pleasure*, 26.

6. Ibid., 28.

7. Harpham, *Ascetic Imperative*, xi.

8. Ibid.

ior—to the systems invoked to give meaning and to enable communication within a given culture. Harpham argues that asceticism is related to culture because asceticism is that which enables communication in a culture. He likens asceticism to the MS-DOS that enables programs to run on a computer: asceticism is the fundamental operating ground upon which culture is laid and because of which culture can function. Like Foucault, Harpham emphasizes the ethical nature of culture itself, arguing that there is an inherent level of self-denial necessary for a person to live within a culture so that the resistance to appetites and desires is at the heart of cultural integration and functioning. Asceticism, moreover, structures oppositions without collapsing them so that asceticism raises the issue of culture by creating the opposite, the anticulture. Asceticism, therefore, is always ambivalent, compromising the polarities it establishes.

Harpham defines asceticism in a tight sense as the asceticism of early Christianity, the historical ideology of a specific period and in a loose sense as "any act of self-denial undertaken as a strategy of empowerment or gratification." Central, therefore, to any ascetical agenda is resistance. Resistance is a structural part of desire itself, not imposed from outside it, and desire is always resisted from within, since without resistance there is no desire.

A THEORY OF ASCETICISM

My own theory of asceticism begins with the important factor that Harpham's orientation omits. He correctly asserts that the basis of ascetical activity is the cultural foundations that lie behind the particularities of a given culture, like MS-DOS, a particular computer operating system. However, the ascetical program relates not to interaction of the two systems (deep cultural structure and cultural expression) but to the integration of an individual person, and of groups of people, into the culture itself. At the center of ascetical activity is a self who, through behavioral changes, seeks to become a different person, a new self; to become a different person in new relationships; and to become a different person in a new society that forms a new culture. As this new self emerges (in relationship to itself, to others, to society, to the world), it masters the behaviors that enable it at once to deconstruct the old self and to construct the new. Asceticism, then, constructs both the old and the reformed self and the cultures in which these selves function: asceticism asserts the subject of behavioral change and transformation, while constructing and reconstructing the environment in which that subjectivity functions.

The relationship of this subjectivity to environment is the relationship of individual to culture. Asceticism links the two by enabling the integration of individual into culture. Through asceticism, integration into a culture occurs at every level of human existence: consciously and unconsciously; voluntarily and involuntarily; somatic and mental; emotional and intellectual; religious and secular. This means that asceticism functions as a system of cultural formation; it orients the person or group of people to the immediate cultural environment and to the unexpressed, but present, systems that underlie it. Until a person or a group of people is equipped or empowered to perform within a culture, the culture remains an esoteric system into which the person or group has not been initiated. Asceticism initiates a person or group into the cultural systems that enable communication; that equip the person or group for productive living within the culture; and that empower them to live within the culture. As the primary system of formation within a culture, asceticism unlocks the otherwise closed or invisible systems of communication and rhetorical production in a culture and hence intersects all the operative systems: larger cultural systems, social systems, and individual psychological systems.

This leads to my preliminary definition of asceticism. Asceticism may be defined as performances designed to inaugurate an alternative culture, to enable different social relations, and to create a new identity. This definition hangs on four elements: performances, culture, relationships, and subjectivity. I will explore each one in turn.

Performances

It is not difficult to notice from the history of asceticism that it involves the performance of certain acts: fasting, withdrawal from society, silence, physical prayer, and manual labor, to name just a few. These acts function as signifiers in a semiotic system, in that they carry meaning with the context of their performance: a particular performance such as fasting bears no inherent and self-evident meaning except that which is assigned it in the system.

The method of ascetical training resembles the workshop and rehearsal method for acquiring competence in theatrical performance. Richard Schechner describes this method in this way: "The task of the workshop is to deconstruct the ready-mades of individual behavior, texts, and cultural artifacts into strips of malleable behavior material; the work of the rehearsal is to reconstruct them into a new integral system: a performance."[9] The interiorizing and naturalizing of behavior, emotions, and every cultural expression through the deconstructive and reconstructive process, anterior to a convincing performance, emerges from the patterning the theatrical role in its world, with its peculiar systems, relationships, and psychology. The rigorous and systematic repatterning eventually enables the actor to enter and to be the character. Asceticism, with its goal of creating new persons through patterning of behavior, operates in a similar fashion. By systematic training and retraining, the ascetic becomes a different person molded to live in different culture, trained to relate to people in a different manner, psychologically motivated to live a different life. Through these performances, the ascetic, like the performer who becomes able to "experience as actual" anything imaginable,[10] can experience the goal of ascetical life as the transformed life.

These performances consist of learned and repeated activity and behaviors: the ascetic learns the techniques of asceticism by repeated activity, repeated prayer, consistently affirmed withdrawal, continuous silence, repeated physical acts of fasting, sleep deprivation, and manual labor. As these activities and behaviors are repeated, the ascetic masters them. This means that the activities and behaviors that are performed are eminently repeatable and that they can be learned, mastered, and repeated until the ascetic achieves a certain state or quality of life. In their repetition, these acts take on the appearance of verisimilitude; they become natural activities for the monk as perceived within the ascetic culture. The verisimilitude points toward the successful creation of a larger frame of reference and of meaning that supports the ascetic manner of living.

These performances, therefore, include an element of intentionality: the behaviors intend more than mere repetition and imitation of behavior; the behaviors displace attention from themselves to a larger referen-

---

9. Schechner, "Magnitudes of Performance," 345.
10. Ibid., 363.

tial arena, and their purpose relates at once to an alternative culture and to the potential of a new subjectivity.

Culture

Clifford Geertz explains that "Culture is the fabric of meaning in terms of which human beings interpret their experience and guide their action" and that culture is "an ordered system of meaning and of symbols in terms of which social interaction takes place."[11] Negatively described, asceticism breaks down the dominant culture through performances that aim toward establishing a countercultural or alternative cultural milieu. Positively described, the ascetic, like an actor learning to be a character in a play, lives in a new culture created through the careful repatterning of basic behaviors and relations.

The behavior shifts the center of the culture and creates an alternative culture around this new center. The performances force the construction of a culture in which such new behavior is normative. The heavy emphasis on the location of asceticism (withdrawal, monastery, desert, pilgrimage, pillar) articulates and creates the cultural occasion for a change in cultural venue. This new culture becomes the normal or normative or true culture for those whose performance initiates them to it.

It is not necessary that the alternative culture formed through asceticism oppose the dominant culture. The countercultural orientation need not indicate hostility or mutual exclusion. Cultures may coinhere, and an ascetic may participate in a number of different cultures simultaneously.

Moreover, communities may, like monasteries, create a new culture without individual members of that community knowing it. The intentionality does not always rest on the individual body but may reside with the corporate body.

Relationships

Culture defines the potential, the larger systems upon which humans can call in their living: culture becomes concrete at the level of social relationships. Within this broader cultural context, Geertz explains, there are the "actually existing network of social relations" and "the ongoing process of interactive behavior." Behavior invokes the systems laid out in the culture, while the culture makes available to an individual the parameters, direc-

11. Geertz. *Interpretation of Cultures*, 144.

tion, and action of social interaction. "Culture is the fabric of meaning in terms of which human beings interpret their experience and guide their action; social structure is the form that action takes."[12] The new culture is built upon two correlative elements—new social arrangements and new subjects capable of living in the culture. Cultures enable (or prohibit) certain kinds of social structures. A new culture, therefore, must define new and different ways of relating in order to differentiate itself from other cultures and other ways of relating.

Subjectivity

The goal of ascetic performance finds its fullest expression in the articulation and construction of a new subjectivity. Both performance and culture open potential space for the creation of an alternative or new subject.

The new subjectivity is the *skopos* (guardian) that calls for the behavior and the cultural milieu. There is an element of the intentional, the deliberate, the articulation of a new goal and a new understanding of subjectivity, toward which the person moves. This teleological element is crucial and central to understanding asceticism.

The ascetic subjectivity is multivalent and multicentered in that it bears by nature at least a two-way centeredness (the old person and the ascetically reconstructed person) and possibly more, since people may participate in a number of different coinherent cultures. The various locations of the ascetic subject (social/political, geographical, philosophical, psychic) articulate or represent other centers of the ascetic subject—centers from which the entire new culture may be organized. Therefore, the ascetical location duplicates the multivalency of the emerging subject's ascetical activity.

THE SOCIAL FUNCTION OF ASCETICISM

Within this definition, asceticism performs four major social functions. First, asceticism enables the person to function within the re-envisioned or re-created world. Through ritual, new social relations, different articulations of self and body, and through a variety of psychological transformations, the ascetic learns to live within another world. To "live as an angel"—the goal that Orthodox monks have set for themselves—means that through their asceticism monks are enabled to function "as angels"

12. Ibid.

from the beginning of their ascetical activity, or at least to begin to know what it means to "live as angels." Asceticism allows this life on the basis of a re-envisioned world.

Second, since so much of the ascetic culture relies upon narrative, biography, demonic and angelic psychology, as well as systems of theological anthropology and soteriology, asceticism provides the method for translating these theoretical and strategic concepts into patterns of behavior. The metaphoric presentation of the transfiguration of Antony in Athanasius's *Vita Antonii*, for example, does not explain how one goes about imitating Antony in order for the self to be transfigured. Asceticism patterns such theories and images into purposeful and systematic practices whose goal can be incrementally achieved. After a similar regimen of fasting, withdrawal, meditation, and conflict with demons, the ascetic may achieve the same goal as Antony, or, more precisely, the ascetic may achieve the state that a community understands as a correlative state defined by the literary presentation of Antony's life. Asceticism patterns and makes concrete such distant phenomena in purposeful behavioral patterns.

Third, the re-envisioning of the world and of human life in it requires intensive perceptual transformation. In order to achieve a different state, as visualized or pictorialized by a religion, there must be at the most basic perceptual level of the senses, and of perceptions and experience, a form of retraining geared toward the re-envisioned world. Asceticism provides the means for this retraining. It is at the level of ascetical performance that the ascetic experiences and perceives the world differently. The novice who enters a monastery must learn at the outset the differences between, for example, "eating in the world" and "eating in the monastery": both relate to food, but the signification of the food and its eating will differ, in referent and in content, from cultural domain to cultural domain. At this most basic level, asceticism retrains the senses and perceptions of the ascetic, a retraining based upon the theological culture and its articulated goals.

Fourth, asceticism provides the means through which other domains of knowledge and understanding can be incorporated into the re-envisioned world. Scientific, historical, doctrinal, sectarian, and other kinds of issues are translated through asceticism into the other conception of the world. A good example of this is the patristic genre of the

Hexameron,[13] a theological exposition of the days of creation, which uses the ascetical activity of exegesis to incorporate coeval scientific and medical information into the religious culture. Asceticism functions as a prism through which the light of other domains of knowledge are refracted into a new interpretative cultural environment. This refraction gives the old knowledge a new interpretative environment so that the context provides the frame of reference for understanding and meaning.

Asceticism operates through the goals that it sets up for organizing human mentation and behavior.[14] By positing a goal (or goals) toward which the individual or group is to progress as the highest good, or the more perfect state, or the most absorbed by the sacred, asceticism lays out the attaining of that goal through concrete patterning of behavior. Because asceticism operates at the level of behavior, behavior itself often becomes the focus of attention, yet the goal is generally not known in the specific behavior, but in the state or experience the behavior is designed to effect. The goal, however, expresses the particular culture's own peculiar systems; the ascetical practices systematize the procedure for movement into the culture; and the individual finds fulfillment and nurture in the integration into the highest aspiration expressed in the goal.

My definition of asceticism, then, locates the function of asceticism in the cultural, social, and psychological frames of a culture and its countercultures. Asceticism initiates the practitioner into the new culture and initiates the practitioner into the social and psychological systems that activate the culture. This theory of asceticism points our historical study of religious asceticism toward the exploration the larger cultural complex of meanings, relationships, and subjectivities that construct the ascetic and the ascetic's performances.

13. Basil the Great, Gregory of Nyssa, and Ambrose of Milan have written such expositions of the first six days of creation in *The Book of Genesis*.

14. Foucault, *Care of the Self*, 64–68.

CHAPTER 2

Constructions of Power in Asceticism

JAAR 995

> Abba Lot received Abba Joseph and said to him: "Abba, according to my ability I perform my order of prayer a little, my fast a little, the prayer and the meditation and the silence, and according to my ability the cleansing of my thoughts. What more remains, then, that I must perform?" When the old man arose, he stretched out his hands to heaven, and his fingers became as ten lamps of fire, and he said to him, "If you wish, become entirely as fire."[1]

THE SAYINGS OF THE CHRISTIAN DESERT MASTERS, A LITERATURE paradigmatic of Christian ascetical teaching, are filled with questions of power, empowerment, and the renunciation of power. Abba Lot inquires regarding the development of his own ascetical power through the performances of his daily order of prayer and his regimen of fasting, to which he adds his discipline of personal prayer, a practice of silence, and a routine to purify his thoughts. These performances empower the monk in the monastic way of living. In seeking out another, however, Lot, having the same title as the monk whom he intercepts ("Abba"), tacitly acknowledges that he is not fully empowered yet, and seeks advice. The advice given comes to him from another world: the more proficient (understand this to mean "the more powerful") of the two monks stretches out his fingers toward heaven and they become flames and he encour-

---

1. The narrative is about Abba Joseph of Panephis and is taken from the alphabetical collection of sayings of the desert masters. The text is Saying 7 and is taken from *Apophthegmata Agion Pateron,* 53. The translation is my own. Note that I have translated *poein* as "perform" to be consistent with the definition of asceticism that follows.

ages the less powerful monk to become totally aflame. Power infuses the discussion from beginning to end, and the interests in power encapsulate the constructions of power in all asceticism. But what kind of person can become entirely as fire? What kind of subjectivity does this imagine? In what kind of society would the goal of becoming living flame be acceptable or achievable? Why are they both treated as masters and yet there is a distinction made between them, and, at least by implication, one is greater and more powerful than the other? And who is the narrator whose invisible power seems omniscient, and from whence does this narrative power arise? These are all aspects of the construction of power in asceticism that catch the readers' attention.

This essay will explore these constructions of power in asceticism. I have three goals. First, I will explore current theories of power generally and as they might relate to asceticism. In this section I will survey the recent Anglo-American theorizing about the "Three Faces of Power," as well as present the theories of power by Thomas E. Wartenberg, Louis Althusser, Michel Foucault, Edith Wyschogrod, and the social semiotic theorists Robert Hodge and Gunther Kress, in order to establish a foundation for the intersection of power and asceticism. Second, I will offer definitions of both power and asceticism to frame my own discussion and to provide a basis of further discussion. Third, I will explore the constructions of power within that set of definitions by outlining some possible constructions of power within the theories presented, and by developing typologies based upon the kinds of constructions of power from a wide base of ascetic texts of the Greco-Roman period (Christianity, Gnosticism, Hermeticism, Neo-Platonism).

POWER IN RECENT THEORY

The theory of power has emerged as a central concern in a wide assortment of disciplines. Historians, political scientists, sociologists, anthropologists, feminists, theologians, and critical analysts from many other fields have explored the expression and meaning of power and powerlessness in society. Many of those theories have influenced the study of religion, but few have been applied to the study of asceticism. I begin, therefore, with the Anglo-American discussion of the "Three Faces of Power"; this is a foil to the more sophisticated and nuanced perspective on power that has emerged in recent years. I intend to map the gradual, but persistent, move from a naive conception of power (which mirrors a naive reading of asceticism and ascetical theory) in the debate about the "Three Faces of Power" toward the complex and rich theories of power (which inform a modern theory of asceticism and the historical realities of Greco-Roman and Late Antique asceticism) in recent theoretical writing.

The "Three Faces of Power"

The unmasking of the three faces of power shows the gradual awareness of the complexity of power in society. The debate about the three faces of power in Anglo-American scholarship begins with the articulation of the simple and naive concept that one social agent has power over another.[2] The first face of power (the work of Robert Dahl in response to C. Wright Mill's *The Power Elite*) conceives of power as a relationship in which the primary agent causes the secondary agent to act in a manner in which the latter would not otherwise act.[3] This conception of power has been described as one-dimensional in that it only looks at the surface of power relations as a measurable means of causality between two agents.[4] The second face of power (the work of Peter Bachrach and Morton Baratz in response to Dahl) criticizes the naivete of the first face and indicates that power also limits the exercise of power, so that the exercise of power requires both social interaction and the prevention of the exercise of power.[5] This face has been described as two-dimensional in that it includes both an expression of power and its hidden thwarting. The third face of power (a theoretical critique and reformulation by Steven Lukes) moves into a three-dimensional view of power, not only as causality in interaction, and causality in interaction with limitation, but to causality, limitations, and the question of each agent's interest. The exercise of power involves the influence of one agent over another contrary to the best interests of the receiving agent[6] so that the dominant agent could

2. Wartenberg, *Forms of Power*, 51–70.

3. Ibid., 51–56.

4. See Isaac, "Beyond the Three Faces of Power," 35–36.

5. Ibid., 37–38; Wartenberg, *Forms of Power*, 57–58.

6. Isaac, "Beyond the Three Faces of Power," 39–41.

convince the subordinate agent to do something that is really contrary to his or her own interests.[7]

It is surprising that so shallow and unsophisticated a perspective on power would sustain interest and conversation through so many years. To be sure, this debate has come under significant criticism by some of its participants. Isaac, in a realist vein, would prefer to see the social underpinning of power relations emphasized because he believes that social relationships structure behavior by distributing power in a particular way.[8] Others have noted particular important areas ignored by the debate: gender (Hartsock and Miller), race (Wartenberg in *Rethinking Power*), domination (Airaksinen), and oppression (Young). All these critiques of the three faces of power reject the more mechanistic and behavioral interpretation of power as a measurable and observable "power over" in favor of the more relational, social, and systemic aspects of power. Terence Ball[9] in particular has identified three specific challenges to the behavioral model: the communication critique that underscores the competence both to send a power message and to receive it; the realist critique that underscores the social structures inherent in the exercise of power; and the deconstructionist critique of Michel Foucault that moves the discussion of power away from repression and dominance to the exploration of the disciplinary and technological exercise of power and power's relationship to knowledge.[10]

As it stands, the three-faces debate would not be sufficient to analyze so typical an ascetic narrative as that with which this chapter began. The relationship of Abba Lot and Abba Joseph exhibits no external power of one ascetic over another, nor does it manifest any inherent limitations or prevention of the exercise of power, nor is there any intimation of activity that would be contrary to the benefit of either participant in the conversation. The ascetic power of this dialogue rests in the unexplored areas identified by the critics: in the monastic and desert social setting, in the rhetoric of communication, in the social arrangements among monastic ascetic practitioners, in the worldview that the monks share, and in the disciplinary and technological practices of the monks. The three-faces

7. Wartenberg, *Forms of Power*, 58–61.

8. Isaac, "Beyond the Three Faces of Power," 48–49.

9. Ball, "New Faces of Power."

10. For a critique of Foucault, see Spivak, "More on Power/Knowledge."

debate lacks the critical acuity to be able to analyze the power systems that are found there.

Thomas E. Wartenberg

The most fruitful advance in the three-faces debate was achieved by Thomas Wartenberg[11] who, through a thorough-going critique and re-orientation of the question of the "three faces" of power, has developed a "field theory of social power." Wartenberg begins with a basic distinction between two fundamental referents to power: power as "power-to" (syn-onymous with ability, capacity) and as "power-over" (in the sense of force, influence, might; synonymous with dominion). Laying aside the study of power-to, he develops a theory of power-over in socially hierarchical relationships, that is, in relationships that exhibit a social ordering.[12]

Wartenberg's theory locates the concept of power-over (henceforth called simply power) within the realm of intentional discourse: power is neither the possession of one agent alone, nor simply an element in-tervening in "discreet interactions between social agents."[13] This power discourse occurs in a social environment in which one social agent has power over another only when that agent "strategically constrains" the social environment (the environment of action and choosing) of the sub-ordinate agent. Wartenberg, therefore, constructs power as *articulated* because other systems of power are simultaneously present;[14] as *situated* in that power is socially and historically constituted by "peripheral social others"[15] who construct the relationship within society; and as *dynamic* in that power "exists as an ongoing but changing feature of society"[16] and as such has a temporal aspect as well as a negotiated social aspect.[17] These aspects of his theory of power-over constitute his critique of previous theorists: that power is involved with intention; that power is socially

---

11. Wartenberg, *Forms of Power.*
12. Ibid., 9–31.
13. Ibid., 64.
14. Ibid., 91–114.
15. Ibid., 141–61.
16. Ibid., 168.
17. Ibid., 163–83.

situated; and that power is dynamic in potentially drawing alternative social alignments to change the structure of power.[18]

These three points deserve closer attention. First, Wartenberg insists that an adequate conception of power must locate it "within the context of intentional human activities."[19] He believes that previous theorists have had a myopic, structural view of human agency[20] that limited the development of the theory of power essentially to a description of political power, rather than a general theory of power.[21] By shifting the discussion to the arena of intentional human activity as the locus for the understanding of a theory of power, Wartenberg emphasizes the *uses* of power. Power, he argues, may be intended either to dominate other people, the essentially negative construction of power found in modern theories,[22] or to transform them, as is evident in recent feminist positive appraisals of women's ways of exercising their power in relationships and family.[23]

Second, Wartenberg argues that power is always socially situated. Relationships always function within the range of social relationships posited in a society, and power relationships are just one kind of social relationship. Social groups thus construct power relationships and act as peripheral agents in the generation of a particular power relationship.[24] Wartenberg suggests that the emphasis on the dyad, power exercised in a two-agent relationship, which is the focus of the three-faces debate, only looks at one aspect of the social situation[25] and neglects to consider the socially situated context that constructs that relationship.[26] It is precisely the social context or environment as a social field that structures and conveys power to certain relationships.[27] This context is called an "agent's action-environment," which Wartenberg claims "specifies the structure within which an agent exists as a social actor. The actions that an agent engages in can be specified in terms of the options available to her in her

18. Ibid., 168–75.

19. Ibid., 163.

20. Ibid., 63–66.

21. Ibid., 3–8.

22. Ibid., 115–39.

23. Ibid., 183–222.

24. Ibid., 163.

25. Ibid., 142; and Wartenberg, *Rethinking Power*, 82.

26. Wartenberg, *Forms of Power*, 142; and *Rethinking Power*, 85.

27. Wartenberg, *Rethinking Power*, 85.

action-environment."[28] Wartenberg defines power, then, as the ability to exercise power over another agent "by affecting the circumstances within which the other agent acts and makes choices."[29] Within this definition of power there exists a threefold typology of power (force, coercion, and influence) depending upon the modality of its exercise.[30]

Finally, Wartenberg insists that power is dynamic, not static. Power has a temporal aspect in that it exists as an ongoing social phenomenon and perdures through any number of transformations. Power's dynamic evolves from its transitions and social arrangements, its shifting and moving from one agent to another in a social relationship and from one institution to another in society. But at the point at which power becomes articulated, immediately it posits and creates a struggle and resistance to it. Power is exercised in the dynamic environment of temporal change, social contestation, and transformation.[31]

Wartenberg's advancement of the theory of power moves toward more workable categories. His emphasis on the centrality of human intention, the constitutive role of social formation, and the interactive dynamic of power to transform and to invoke resistance provides a fuller contextualization of the theory of the exercise of power. Power, however, remains largely abstracted and objectified for Wartenberg: people exercise power; environments restrict the power of others to act; power invokes a contestation to its exercise. Wartenberg's theory of power maintains power as an objectified and disembodied force. Wartenberg's theory would expose some aspects of the power manifested in the dialogue of Abba Joseph and Abba Lot: Abba Joseph's intention to assist his fellow ascetic in his program of self-improvement and the dynamic power structures in desert monasticism. But the monastic conversation's construction of power would remain opaque. This may be the result of the critical decision by Wartenberg to put aside a crucial aspect of power, the "power-to," without which his concept of human agency and social discursivity lack substance and direction. There is power manifested in Abba Lot's desire to do more ascetical work, and this power is not related simply to social hierarchy and ordering, but to the capacity, the ability to become

28. Ibid., 79.
29. Ibid., 86.
30. Ibid., 90–114.
31. Ibid., 168.

someone greater. Without such data, the concept of power suffers and it fails to account for the structure and exercise of power in the monastic narrative.

Louis Althusser

The Marxist theorist Louis Althusser takes up the problem of disembodied power while explaining the embodied nature of power in social institutions. His theorizing represents a significant advancement for power theory. In analyzing capitalist power, Althusser differentiates between the public state power and the social institutions that support it.[32] The state power operates by repression whereas the private power operates through ideological structures.[33] No one may exercise state power, according to Althusser, without simultaneously controlling the supporting ideological structures.[34] The ideological structures constitute organized and powerful social institutions [schools, religious organizations, families, systems of communication, cultural associations and traditions][35] that function to construct "the imaginary relationship of individuals to the real conditions of existence"[36] precisely because they are material apparatuses, practices, and operations.[37] Historically the church and the family together were the primary ideological structures colluding to support state power, but in more recent history they have been supplanted by the school and the family in collusion,[38] especially since institutional schools take young children and train them with either knowledge wrapped in ruling ideology or pure ideology.[39]

It is the embodied reality of these apparatuses that commends Althusser's theories. For Althusser, both private and public systems of power have material reality, because they exist in material living conditions by fully embodied people. Power exists materially both in the person

---

32. Althusser, *Lenin and Philosophy*, 142–44.
33. Ibid., 145.
34. Ibid., 146.
35. Ibid., 143.
36. Ibid., 162.
37. Ibid., 165–66.
38. Ibid., 153–54.
39. Ibid., 155.

and in the person's social relationships with others.[40] Power, therefore, is a practice. Althusser writes: "We can assert the *primacy of practice* theoretically by showing that all levels of social existence are sites of distinct practices."[41] These material apparatuses are "constituted by a structure" combining three elements: the raw material, the means of production, and the "historical relations . . . in which it produces."[42] Even human conceptualization is materially produced: "In every case, the ideology of ideology thus recognizes, despite its imaginary distortion, that the 'ideas' of a human subject exist in his actions" and "*his ideas are his material actions inserted into material practices governed by material rituals which are themselves defined by the material ideological apparatus from which derive the ideas of that subject.*"[43] (emphasis his).

Althusser's theories address some of the significant issues in the opening narrative between Abba Lot and Abba Joseph. The conversation between the monks revolves about the production of a state of being ("becoming entirely as fire") that the specific performances (fasting, prayer, liturgy, meditation, silence, and the cleansing of thought) materially produce as the ideological structure "monasticism." The asceticism promulgated in the narrative consists of the raw material of embodied ascetics (food, conversation), the means of production (fasting, prayer, silence), and the historical context of the relationship (monasticism). Althusser's two primary contributions (the materiality of practice and the materiality of social institutions) move the discussion of power and asceticism significantly forward by emphasizing the effectiveness of material practices.

Michel Foucault

Building upon the Althusserian perspective and concurrent with the Anglo-American debate about the three faces of power, Michel Foucault took up the question of power in an influential series of studies of the prison, the clinic, and the history of sexuality. Foucault, along with both Wartenberg and Althusser, posits that power is relational and socially constructed, although he explores the resistance to power as a catalyst for

40. Althusser and Balibar, *Reading Capital,* 41–45.

41. Ibid., 58.

42. Ibid., 41.

43. Althusser, *Lenin and Philosophy,* 168.

exposing relationships of power.[44] Foucault insists that power relations are "rooted deep in the social nexus, not reconstituted 'above' society as a supplementary structure"[45] so that power cannot be distinguished or differentiated from the expression of power in society and in personal relationships.

Foucault defines power as the "delimitation of another's field of action,"[46] but in distinction to Wartenberg's proposition, Foucault emphasizes (in a more Althusserian vein) the formative aspect of power relations by arguing that power evidences itself in the governance of behavior and the restriction of possibilities. He says, "The exercise of power consists in guiding the possibility of conduct and putting in order the possible outcome."[47]

Foucault also argues that power relationships have specific objectives that must be analyzed in order to expose the power in the relationship.[48] The teleology of power expresses the central interest of power while also exposing the modality of its exercise. In addition to such objectives, Foucault identifies other aspects of power that are related and that need to be explored: systems of differentiations (class, gender, sexuality), the means of bringing power relations into being, the forms of institutionalization of power in relationships, and the degrees of rationalization needed to sustain the power.[49]

Foucault advances the discussion of power in three important linkings: the linking of power and subjectivity, of power and knowledge, and power and technologies. The linking of power and subjectivity revolves about two senses of the word "subject": first, subjectivity as being subject to someone else's control, or to be dependent upon another and second, subjectivity as the basis of one's own identity through conscious self-knowledge.[50] Within this duality of meanings, Foucault focuses on three modes of subjectivity: the speaking subject who is known by rhetoric and science; the differentiated subject who emerges from distinctions such

---

44. Foucault, "Afterword: The Subject and Power," 210, 217.

45. Ibid., 222.

46. Ibid., 220.

47. Ibid., 221.

48. Ibid., 223.

49. Ibid.

50. Ibid., 212.

as class, race, and gender; and the self that is turned into a subject by knowledge such as the subject produced by knowledge of one's sexuality, or of one's own medical situation.[51] Power permeates each of these modes of subjectivity because, as Foucault argues, in order for power to be exercised, the subject upon which power is exercised must always remain an objectified subject. Power cannot be exercised where there is no subjectivity, nor where the freedom of those subjects has been diminished.[52] The "careers, thoughts, and intentions of individual agents," however, do not manifest power, because power is not found *in* particular agents, nor do supra-individual "truths" manifest power, but rather power is manifested in these utterances as they are produced by agents in social settings.[53] Power and subjectivity are linked.

The linking of power and knowledge follows a similar pattern. For Foucault, power and knowledge are correlated, not power and falsity.[54] In distinction to the view that power is ideologically constructed to create false subjectivities and relationships, Foucault argues that since the subject already is a fiction, subjectivity is constructed within disciplines of knowledge.[55] These disciplines of knowledge indicate "according to artificially clear and decanted systems, the manner in which systems of objective finality and systems of communication and power can be welded together."[56] Power is exercised, then, in a block that includes the capacity of subjects, communication among them, and the power that communication and knowledge creates.

Foucault's discussion of the history of sexuality in which sex is transformed into discourse exemplifies this merging of power and knowledge. The discourse about sexuality, the "passing of everything having to do with sex through the endless mill of speech" began in the confessional practices of the early Church, developed in the monastery, and was imposed upon Christian faithful in the seventeenth century when the Church required the practice of the confessional for everyone.[57] Within

---

51. Ibid., 208.

52. Ibid., 220.

53. Gordon, "Afterward," 244.

54. Ibid., 237.

55. Ibid., 238.

56. Foucault, "Afterward: The Subject and Power," 219.

57. Foucault, *History of Sexuality, Volume 1*, 115–16. Elizabeth A. Clark ("Foucault, The Fathers, and Sex," 619–22) explains the problem that Foucault faced between the

this system knowledge of one's self, the construction of one's self as a sexual being, the subjection of that knowledge to the pastoral offices of the Church created the discourse that linked the power of sexuality with the knowledge of sexuality. Power and knowledge are linked.

The final linking is that of power and technologies, which will be taken up in two aspects: the technologies of self-formation and the technologies of social governance. Within the technologies of self-formation, Foucault distinguishes between the set of rules of moral conduct itself, the evaluation of the person based upon those rules, and the systems of formation that enable one to be a subject acting according to these rules.[58] Foucault thereby connects the moral system, the formation of moral subjectivity, and the practices that enable that subjectivity to emerge. He calls these connections "codes of behavior" and "forms of subjectivation."[59] Struggle and resistance, as aspects of power, support the creation of a subject. *Enkrateia* (self-control) in Late Antiquity, for example, implies an agonistic relationship with pleasure[60] in that the ascetic is to resist submitting herself to pleasure. *Enkrateia* is an agonistic relationship with oneself as well in that the pleasures are understood to be a part of her[61] and it is also an orientation toward victory over the self and the passion in the form of establishing a regime of governance over it.[62] The technologies of control are the technologies of power.

Within the realm of the larger social governance, the technologies of governance refers to the means of bringing power relations into being and the forms of institutionalization of these power relationships. This is the sort of analysis that Foucault presented in his works on the prison and on the clinic. There are three rationalities that operate in social technologies: first, the *strategies*, which both create and exploit possibilities in the field of social interaction; the *technologies* of specific discourses and "non-discursive social and institutional practices," which implement

---

writing of the first and second volumes of his *History of Sexuality*. The projection of the entire project back into Greek and Roman antiquity, as well as early Christianity, forced a significant reconsideration of the archeology of modern theories and practices of sexuality.

58. Foucault, *Use of Pleasure*, 26.

59. Ibid., 26–29.

60. Ibid., 65–66.

61. Ibid., 66–69.

62. Ibid., 69–70; see also Clark, "Foucault, The Fathers, and Sex," 631–34.

the strategies; and the *programs,* which organize the strategies and technologies and which suit the objective and the intention of the exercise of power to the specific person upon whom that power is exercised.[63] Power requires a program, which needs a technology and a strategy to exploit the possibility that the strategy creates for the exercise of power.[64] Power and technologies are linked.

Foucault could be called a modern-day ascetical theologian. Like Abba Joseph and Abba Lot, Foucault investigates the power of behavior initiated in particular technologies. The regimentation of the monks' ascetical practice mirrors Foucault's interest in the institutionalization of practical regimes as technologies that, for both ancient monastic ascetics and Foucault, relate to both self-formation ("becoming all flame") and governance (the institutionalized asceticism of desert monasticism). As Foucault explained, this behavioral perspective demands a different knowledge and subjectivity, a different manner of understanding human agency and activity so that "become all flame" would have cognitive value, and a new subjectivity that would enable the monk to pursue the human-become-flame status.

Edith Wyschogrod

If Foucault could be called a modern-day ascetical theologian, then Edith Wyschogrod could be called a modern-day theologian of renunciation. Wyschogrod's book *Saints and Postmodernism* has both asceticism and power as subthemes. Wyschogrod links the practice, the asceticism, of the saint's life oriented toward the alleviation of suffering, with the practices "through which the addressee is gathered into the narrative so as to extend and elaborate it with her/his own life."[65] The confluence of alterity, powerlessness and power marks the process whereby the saint becomes a saint through her practices. Wyschogrod's central point about the saint's power is significant: "*The power to bring about new moral configurations is authorized by the prior renunciation of power*"[66] (emphasis hers). The saint's influence, according to Wyschogrod, has three tiers: first, the renunciation of power, which enables the saint to exercise power; second,

---

63. Gordon, "Afterward," 246–48.
64. Ibid., 248–55.
65. Wyschogrod, *Saints and Postmodernism,* xxiii.
66. Ibid., 56.

the arena of power's pure possibility for the exercise of power in which the saint has the full spectrum of potential acts for alterity at her command; and third, the limited power of power-already-exercised in which the saint denies the pure possibility by choosing one action or mode of action.[67]

The social power of the saint resides in the saint's empowering of others to imitation through the exercise of power. Power, for the saint, however, is always a power oriented toward alterity, toward the command of the other, so that power and powerlessness are linked, not just by inversion, but by the empowerment of the saint through powerlessness, and by the imitation of the saint's powerless power by others. Imitation, alterity, powerlessness and power intertwine.

The saint also experiences the "powerlessness of destitution" in which power is the "dissemination or scattering of egoity," the stripping of the self before the Other.[68] This powerlessness constitutes an imperative of alterity: the power of the suffering of the Other empowers, motivates, and infiltrates the saint toward the renunciation of power that empowers the saint to action.[69]

Wyschogrod's postmodern perspective on asceticism emphasizes the constructive and transformative basis of renunciation. Renunciation and withdrawal stand at the center of monastic asceticism, but whereas Foucault would attend to the positivist meaning of monastic behavior, Wyschogrod attends to the empty spaces. Wyschogrod points to the renunciation that would enable Abba Lot to become "as fire," to the stripping of self through ascetical acts pointing toward an *alter ego* and to the ascetic imitation that enables Lot to mimic Joseph and become a saint. Ascetic renunciation, as Wyschogrod indicates, produces newly empowered saints: the negative constructs the different reality in which the ascetics live.

Social Semiotics: Robert Hodge and Gunther Kress

All of the theories of power presented to this point have progressed toward a more systematic analysis of the social dimension of power with a materialist understanding of social behavior and an incrementally

67. Ibid., 60.
68. Ibid., 98–99.
69. Ibid., 167–83.

more embodied presentation of power. Yet most of these theories, even Foucault's theory that attempts to avoid the problem, have tended to investigate power as one element among many in social arrangements. The final theory presented breaks down all divisions between power and society and systematically outlines the interrelationship of power and society. With the social semiotic theories of Robert Hodge and Gunther Kress, the exercise and manifestation of power and its social constructions merge, so that "solidarity is an effect of power just as power is an effect of solidarity."[70]

Social semiotics posits that communication, the complex "social structures and processes, messages and meanings," materially embedded in social conditions and problematized by "a multiplicity of visual, aural, behavioural and other codes," is a process of the production and reproduction of meaning that "exists in relationship to concrete subjects and objects, and is inexplicable except in terms of this set of relationships."[71] The construction of these social relationships hinges upon the creation or destruction of solidarity and exemplifies the modulation of power. Hodge and Kress describe the general theory in this way:

> Social semiotics treats all semiotic acts and processes as social acts and processes. What is at issue in social processes is the definition of social participants, relations, structures, processes, in terms of solidarity and in terms of power. Semiotic processes are means whereby these can be tested, reaffirmed, altered. Hence questions of power are always at issue, whether in the affirmation of solidarity or in the assertion of power; whether in the reproduction of a semiotic system or in a challenge to that system.[72]

Within social semiotic theory, the definition of the social expresses a construction of power; the exercise of power posits a social structure.

This merging of power and solidarity rests upon three theoretical points: ideology, logonomic systems, and the theory of transformations. An ideology in social semiotic theory is a contested version of the understanding of the world imposed by one group upon another.[73] Ideologies normally operate as complexes of ideologies and inherently describe a

70. Hodge and Kress, *Social Semiotics*, 39.

71. Ibid., vii, viii.

72. Ibid. 122.

73. Ibid. 3.

relationship involving power in a social setting. An ideological complex structures a relationship and sustains that relationship with respect to solidarity and to power, while at the same time "serving the interests of both dominant and subordinate. . . . Ideological complexes are constructed in order to constrain behavior by structuring the version of reality on which social action is based."[74]

Logonomic systems, the second point, are sets of rules that prescribe behavior both in their production and in their reception. Hodge and Kress define a logonomic system as "a set of rules prescribing the conditions for production and reception of meanings; which specify who can claim to initiate (produce, communicate) or know (receive, understand) meanings about what topics under what circumstances and with what modalities (how, when, why)."[75] These logonomic systems regulate the terms of producing and receiving messages by articulating the terms and conditions for the generation of meaning.

Transformations, the third point, articulate the changes in meaning over time and through space. Since semiotic theory tends only to observe and analyze synchronic phenomena, social semiotic theory accounts also for meanings as they are produced and received diachronically, as well as synchronically. "Every semiotic structure inevitably exists in space and time, and every semiotic process takes place in those dimensions."[76] A transformation is a "structural change, from structure A to structure B,"[77] The structures observed in transformations are those that semiotically connect "participants to each other and to the series of messages and meanings they produce."[78] The theory of linguistic transformations of W. Labov, which Hodge and Kress present, illustrates these structural changes over time. Labov's theory of transformations has five steps: first, there is a period of free variation in which new structures and new forms develop freely and without any constraint; second, these free variations are systematized and identified with a particular group; third, these variations take on meaning and become a group marker; fourth, the marker becomes systematized and generalized so that it is used by the group for

74. Ibid.
75. Ibid., 4.
76. Ibid., 163.
77. Ibid., 168.
78. Ibid.

self-identification and by those outside the group for group definition; fifth, the markers become exaggerated and become social markers as stereotypes, and form the basis of community prejudice.[79] These transformations, progressions of semiotic processes, mark the change of meanings over time and illustrate the simultaneous development of power with solidarity and solidarity with power both as an internal dynamic of the relationship of groups, and as a function of definition from without the relationship.

In addition to the general theory of social semiotics, other aspects of social semiotic theorizing have value for examining constructions of power in asceticism. In the first place, social semiotics theorizes that the context provides a primary arena of meaning. Meaning never exists outside a particular social context and domain. A domain is a site where a specific meaning of a specific group of people may be expected to prevail, so that such domains as school, work, monastery, road travel, family, and hermitage have certain rules and complexes of meaning within which certain people (teachers, laborers, monks, drivers, children, hermits) participate.[80] "Settings exert a coercive force on the meanings that can be produced or received within them"[81] so that communication rests solidly on the social and physical context in which it arises.[82] Bodies also become a locus of meaning by virtue of their placement in space, since spatial location indicates social status, and spatial location marks social power and its resistances.[83] The context of communication communicates.

Social semiotic theory also posits that definitions of reality are socially constructed. "Modality" describes the stance of participants toward semiotic systems that structure social relations, places, people, and other cultural values and places.[84] Agents either feel affinity or they lack affinity with the dominant structures in which they exist.[85] Modality points to the construction of knowledge systems so that people's attitudes toward phenomena around them, their modalities, construct such categories

79. Ibid., 184–85.
80. Ibid., 68–69.
81. Ibid., 68.
82. Ibid., 39.
83. Ibid., 52–59.
84. Ibid., 122.
85. Ibid., 123.

as "knowledge" and "facts." *Truth* emerges when participants accept the system of classification and structures;[86] that is, when their modality is positive; and *reality* emerges when that structure is perceived as secure, and, therefore, as capable of sustaining relationships and power.[87] Communities form around questions of definitions of truth and reality. Truth is not what is testable or objectively proven, but rather a function of the solidarity and power of a group. Either in affinity or by rejection of other versions of reality, a group creates solidarity and empowers itself either by rejecting alternative constructions or by constructing alternatives:

> The issue of truth is bound up inextricably with issues of power and solidarity in a specific group. Truth is thus mobilized and put to the test in every semiosic exchange. Difference thus becomes the primary motor of semiosis—different versions of reality to be resolved through semiosis, coalitions to be created, antagonisms to be overcome or prevented, or activated and declared. Because of the complex dialectic that surrounds difference, truth and reality have a double face and double function, as either an effect or a determinant of social relations.[88]

Questions of the construction of truth, reality, the modes of receiving and producing communication about truth and reality, form the basis of community, knowledge, and behaviors.

And finally, social semiotics develops a theory for training subjects for culture.[89] People are not assimilated into culture, they enter a complex process of initiation and formation in it. Children and immigrants learn a "multiplicity of complex processes of reaction, resistance, subversion, acquiescence and acceptance,"[90] which are interactive and dynamic processes of learning to receive and to produce messages. This process of cultural formation means that participants in a culture continually and constantly construct worlds of meaning about them, and that people, therefore, continually and constantly need to be empowered, or enabled, to enter into those communication strategies.

86. Ibid., 122.
87. Ibid., 122.
88. Ibid., 151.
89. Ibid., 240–60.
90. Ibid., 240.

Social semiotic theory brings a wealth of resources to the study of power and asceticism. The concept of the interconnection between solidarity and power defines the centrality of community as the basis of social semiotic activity and highlights the importance of ascetic community. Solidarity marks out a community in which meaning is constructed, while power defines the community both with respect to its interior dynamics and the community's relationship with those outside that communicating community. And Labov's theory in particular applies to the formation of ascetic communities: ascetic communities either create the literary and textual language that may be used by diverse people in diverse settings and different times for their ascetical benefit, or they create the interior language of the ascetic community that provides them with an identity and a structure of power. Semiotic theory and Labov underscore the ideological basis of the monks' conversation: their worldview contests the dominant perspective, and this contestation becomes visible in such logonomic systems as ascetic traditions of specific practices (such as fasting, rules of prayer), as the systems of monastic authority, and as the established hierarchy of spiritual achievement.

By raising the question of power and solidarity from the perspective of social formation, social semiotic theory provides the final element to this discussion of the theory of power in asceticism. The interception of the two ascetic masters takes place in the desert, in the smaller context of the locus for historic monasticism, and in the larger context of the fearful and dead space metaphorized by the lifelessness of the desert. In this context, a discursive encounter occurs: Abba Lot's question ("What more must I perform?") raises the possibility of his own life-transformation through his own ascetical growth and development. He stands at the crossroads where his formation as a member of this social group intersects all the practices and the logonomic systems, the discursive and communication patterns of his fellow monks, and the socially constraining circumstances of his location, manner of life, and relationship with Abba Joseph. But these social patterns are questions of power—power to become "entirely as fire," power to give and receive direction, power to live in a world in which such flaming digits are real and visible, and power to understand and construct a world in which such phenomena may be repeated and imitated.

After all the preceding exploration of power theory, the story appears to be much more complex. Indeed, the story of the two monks' encounter and the transfer of advice from the greater ascetic to the lesser may be viewed dyadically, but that is not enough. The social dynamic consists of more than a simple conversation between two ascetic agents. A complex construction of ascetic society lurks behind the apparently straightforward request for assistance, because there is, as the word "received" (*paralambanein*) suggests, a studied and determined distance between the two agents, which Abba Lot transgresses momentarily for the purpose of his further ascetical growth. The power to transgress social boundaries meets the power to teach a greater way. And that greater way, expressed in Abba Joseph's flaming digits, results from a process of continued formation (beyond what Abba Lot had already achieved) with its own program, strategies, and technologies as Foucault would recognize. Becoming "entirely as fire" defines such a program—a program that Wyschogrod would understand as the renunciation of power in order precisely to open the way toward other possibilities, other modes of powerlessness, diminished egoity, and empowered alterity. Ascetic communities, the churches, and the wider society, moreover, have defined and established their relationship (as Wartenberg would argue). But, as Hodge and Kress would maintain, Abba Lot and Abba Joseph function within a socially defined reality that many others would be unable to inhabit, whether Christian or otherwise, whether during their own time or ours, nor would other people necessarily be interested in entering their world. This reality is replete with ideologies and logonomic systems intended to train the monk for the fiery life achieved through such practices as prayer, fasting, withdrawal, meditation, and liturgy.

DEFINITIONS

From the analysis of the conversation between Abba Lot and Abba Joseph, which has served as the touchstone to the investigation of power theory, one might easily conclude that asceticism and power are closely related. Geoffrey Harpham, in a statement with which Wyschogrod would concur, defines asceticism as a process of empowerment: he claims that asceticism "refers to any act of self-denial undertaken as a strategy of empowerment or gratification."[91] For Harpham power, and its immediate condition and location in resistance, is at the heart of ascetical activity.[92]

91. Harpham, *Ascetic Imperative,* xiii.
92. Ibid., 231.

Given the preceding investigation, power may now be defined very simply. Jean Baker Miller defines power as "*the capacity to produce a change*—that is, to move anything from point A or state A to point B or state B."[93] Taken together with Foucault and Wartenberg's formulation, this definition may be further amplified to include the capacity to affect the productive environment of another. With regard to asceticism this simple definition addresses many of the issues raised above: the construction of reality and truth, which embraces a wide spectrum of intellectual, theological, literary, and political knowledge as well as specific ideological and logonomic frames; the social situation of asceticism in which the practice and teaching of the ascetic distinguishes itself from the practice and lives of the non-ascetic; the importance and centrality of practices and technologies to the ascetic program in which the practices at once construct power and modulate social concerns; the critical linking of solidarity/sociality with power as inverse descriptions of one another; and finally, the production of systems that support the ascetic's subjectivity, social relations, and symbolic universe. The capacity to change and the capacity to affect the productive environment of another subject (even when that "other subject" is simply a redefinition of one's own self) implicate a wide assortment of human activity. Ascetical power, then, produces the capacity for change and a capacity to affect the environment in which change is produced.

This definition of power mirrors the root meaning of the term "asceticism." In Western Antiquity, *askesis* referred to training for athletic events. The root metaphor of ascesis is taken from sport and connects the definition of power with the subjects' empowering training for success. "The Greek athlete, for example, subjected himself to systematic exercise or training in order to attain a goal of physical fitness."[94] The categories might be extended to include philosophical, ethical, and spiritual training as well, or any other training in virtue or in a more valued way of life."[95] The extended arenas for asceticism were transferred from physical development to "the development of the higher powers belonging to the spirit."[96] The ascetic endeavor involves the manipulation, regulation, and

93. Miller, "Women and Power," 241.
94. Kaelber, "Asceticism," 441. See also Hardman, *Ideals of Asceticism*, 1–5.
95. Ibid., 441.
96. Hardman, *Ideals of Asceticism*, 5.

renunciation of physical and spiritual power for a higher purpose. The ascetic "undertakes the regulation of his body and all its powers in all their use of those things for which they have an appetite; and his method consists largely of restriction, surrender, renunciation."[97] Kaelber's definition of asceticism confirms this:

> *asceticism* . . . may be defined as a voluntary, sustained, and at least partially systematic program of self-discipline and self-denial in which immediate, sensual, or profane gratifications are renounced in order to attain a higher spiritual state or a more thorough absorption in the sacred.[98]

But such definitions and explanations of asceticism, while furthering the understanding of the process, use specific ascetic activities to define the concept itself. Renunciation, self-discipline, self-denial, restriction, surrender—are all elements that are universal in scope and not limited only to religion or ethics. Others similar universal activities (such as fasting, sexual abstinence, poverty, withdrawal, both physical and mental pain[99] and sleep deprivation) may also characterize, but not define, asceticism. The attention to specific activities identifies asceticism too closely with particular activities and diverts attention from its more universal elements (as in Chadwick).

Asceticism indeed is a universal phenomenon. This universality, however, does not emerge simply from a universal human religious experience and practice, as some would argue,[100] because each of these universal practices (fasting, sexual continence, etc.) could have different and even contradictory meanings in various religious environments.[101] Nor does the universality of asceticism emerge simply from a universal set of ascetic assumptions: that asceticism involves a spiritual alterity;[102] or that asceticism values "spirit" over "body";[103] or that spiritual perfection

97. Ibid., 10.

98. Kaelber, "Asceticism," 441.

99. Ibid., 442.

100. Ibid., 442–43.

101. Ibid., 443.

102. Hardman, *Ideals of Asceticism*, 5; Kaelber, "Asceticism," 441; McGuckin, "Christian Asceticism."

103. Chadwick, Hardman.

requires withdrawal from and rejection of society.[104] Recent theorists, in addressing a sort of universal dimension of asceticism, have widened these narrow confines significantly. Max Weber treated asceticism as a "methodically controlled and supervised conduct"[105] that transformed economic reality. Indeed, Weber's *The Protestant Ethic and the Spirit of Capitalism* argued that the economic world was remade through the development of certain theological principles that were worked out in particular patterns of behavior. Later Geoffrey Harpham's *The Ascetic Imperative in Culture and Criticism*, while recognizing the more universal meaning of asceticism as any general strategy of empowerment, develops the historical ideology of asceticism as the primary instrument of cultural and hermeneutical transformation. These theorists point to the centrality of asceticism to a wide variety of cultural phenomena.

Asceticism relates to cultural formation. Harpham situates asceticism at the interchange of communication between cultures: he argues that "Asceticism is the 'cultural' element in culture; it makes culture comparable, and is therefore one way of describing the common feature that permits communication or understanding between cultures."[106] Harpham further maintains that "Asceticism *raises the issue* of culture by structuring an opposition between culture and its opposite"[107] (emphasis his). For Harpham, asceticism operates at the most fundamental level of cultural formation in the context of cultural diversity and resistance. The social semioticians Hodge and Kress develop methods for exploring this level of cultural communication and formation, arguing that members of a society must be initiated into the complex and varied systems of communication before they may become competent and empowered members of that society.[108] The disciplined activity of learning to communicate; of constructing a personal and social identity; of living in the complex social and political worlds; of creating theologies, philosophies, and cosmologies to validate these social roles; and of the training to become competent communicators within a society point toward a role for asceticism far more significant than previously imagined. This universal

104. Chadwick, "Ascetic Ideal," 8–14.
105. Weber, *Protestant Ethic*, 132.
106. Harpham, *Ascetic Imperative*, xi.
107. Ibid., xii.
108. Ibid., 240–60.

aspect of ascetical formation has one important limitation: asceticism as a particular formative practice begins to operate in the arenas of personal, social, and intellectual opposition. As Harpham especially has emphasized, asceticism begins to operate when an alternative to the social and religious givens is developed.

Three overarching topics serve to focus this formative aspect of ascetical discipline. First, asceticism involves the articulation and construction of a particular subjectivity that defines the sort of agencies and identities toward which the ascetic moves and away from which the ascetic withdraws. The ascetic develops a subjectivity alternative to the prescribed cultural subjectivity. This is evident from Jerome's biography "The Life of Paul the Hermit," which was written specifically to promulgate and model the ideal ascetic subject.[109] Paul, who was born into a socially entitled Egyptian family and was well educated, withdrew from that society during the Great Persecution to an isolated cave containing a date-palm tree and a water spring. In this isolation, Paul practiced his harsh asceticism, which Jerome eloquently describes. Even the great Antony visited him and confirmed this ascetic subjectivity and his rejection of his cultural expectations.

Second, asceticism involves as well the delimitation and restructuring of social relations both in the sense that the ascetic develops a restricted field of potential social arrangements, relationships, and encounters, and in the sense that these restrictions construct a particular (usually negative) attitude or modality toward other social groups and people. The ascetic develops an alternative set of social relationships usually defined in conflict to the dominant social arrangements. An example of the alternative social relations may be found in the description of the monk Theodore's life found in the Bohairic *Life of Pachomius* [110] Theodore's desire to be an ascetic led him from the practice of asceticism in his home, to collaborating with a group of other local people interested in living ascetically, and finally to a Pachomian monastery. Each of these arrangements satisfied his immediate needs, until finally he found a significant place in the Pachomian structure. Theodore, an educated person from a family of high social status, rejected his socio-political and ecclesiastical position for a life as a common monk. His rearrangement of his

109. See Harvey, "Jerome, *Life of Paul*," 357–59.
110. Goehring, "Theodore's Entry," 352–56.

social world required the total rejection of familial relationships so that even when the bishop of Sne arranged for Theodore's grieving mother to visit the son she considered lost, Theodore would only allow himself to be seen by her, thereby harshly denying any contact with himself.

Third, asceticism involves the construction of a symbolic universe capable of supporting these subjectivities and social relationships by producing and training ascetics in the logonomic, ideological, strategic, technological, and programmatic factors that enter into the construction of the ascetic's reality and truth. The ascetic validates the work to create a personal and social alternative by consciously developing an alternative symbolic universe.[111] The many ascetical treatises that articulate the *theory* of ascetical practice and theology function primarily as instruments for this validation. Philo's treatise "On the Contemplative Life," for example, consciously projects an alternative symbolic universe. The ascetic world presented by the Therapeutai redefines the classical tradition of the symposium by using its imagery and signification in an entirely new way, and it describes a style of contemplative life that cannot easily be located solidly in any known tradition in Judaism or Christianity.[112] Philo uses the meals, the fasting and prayer, the diet, and the ordering of the day around liturgy and contemplation as well as the social arrangement of the community to create an ascetical world that anyone searching after virtue would be encouraged to enter. Other treatises such as John Climacus's *The Ladder of Divine Ascent* and John Cassian's "Conferences" also explicitly develop the symbolic universe.

I offer, then, for the basis of the exploration of the constructions of power in asceticism, my own definition of asceticism. *Asceticism may be defined as performances within a dominant social environment intended to inaugurate a new subjectivity, different social relations, and an alternative symbolic universe.*[113] Subjectivity, social relations, and the symbolic uni-

111. Anne McGuire ("Virginity and Subversion," 239–58) has used Ricoeur's theory of the narrative world of a text to analyze the subversive gender constructions in the Nag Hammadi treatise *The Hypostasis of the Archons*. The narrative world serves as an invitation for the reader "to dwell in the imaginative world depicted in the text" (257). McGuire's article identifies an important instance in which the symbolic universe becomes decisive. The importance of narrative to asceticism has been explored by Harpham, *Ascetic Imperative*, 67–88 and Wyschogrod, *Saints and Postmodernism*, 6–13.

112. Corrington, "Philo," 134–36.

113. This definition replaces my own prior definitions. In a less articulated form it appears in my "Theory of the Social Function of Asceticism." See chapter 1, p. 8. The defi-

verse have been mentioned earlier in the exploration of theories of power and they, together with the opposition to a dominant social environment, will be explained more fully in the following section. Three aspects of this definition, however, need to be explored here as part of the definition of asceticism: performances, intention, and novelty.

Asceticism revolves about performances.[114] Richard Schechner defines a performance as "an activity done by an individual or group in the presence of and for another individual or group."[115] Performances are displayed actions, actions that become public because they take place before an audience. Audience here need not be defined narrowly, as Schechner describes:

> Even where audiences do not exist as such—some happenings, rituals, and play—the function of the audience persists: part of the performing group watches—is meant to watch—other parts of the performing group; or, as in some rituals, the implied audience is God, or some transcendent Other(s).[116]

Asceticism, with its elaborate systems of withdrawal and delimited arenas of social involvement, with its extensive regimes of eating and drinking and clearly defined regimes of meditation and prayer, which are carefully described in ascetic narratives[117] to make them imitable,[118] becomes performance. The world, the religious community, the other ascetics watch one another perform the ascetic life, and ascetics carefully watch themselves. In the case of the ascetic, particularly the solitary or hermit ascetic, the audience in fact may be the "other self," the deconstructed person, the thoroughly socialized being who is being rejected; or it may

---

nition was developed initially for the Modern Greek Seminar of the Center for Literary and Cultural Studies at Harvard: Margaret Alexiou and Michael Herzfeld offered critical advice that was taken so seriously that they would probably not recognize the definition now.

114. Patricia Cox Miller has also been using performance theory as a means of interpreting and understanding asceticism. She argues that the ascetic body is a "perceptual construct" that enables desert reporters to see in the emaciated body of the ascetic the emergent angelic body ("Desert Asceticism," 137–53). The ascetics assisted in this perception by their "performative visibility" in which the secret and invisible is made public and knowable (146–49).

115. Schechner, *Performance Theory,* 30.

116. Ibid.

117. Wyschogrod, *Saints and Postmodernism,* 6–16.

118. Harpham, *Ascetic Imperative,* 13–16.

be the new emergent person, the one who is the imaginary being who is being fashioned into existence by asceticism. Every kind of asceticism involves an audience (whether personal, social or divine) and, therefore, every asceticism becomes a performance.[119]

Performances involve specific actions. Schechner enumerates six performative genres: ritual, play, games, sports, dance, and music,[120] not in order to limit the purview, but to define what is central to theater. In the case of ascetics, there are some standard performances: food performances, sex performances (either by denial or fully engaged participation), social performances (either by rejection, full participation, or theatrical events and happenings), prayer and meditation performances, among others. These may come under the rubric of ritual, or ritualized activity, but there are sufficient explicit ritual behaviors among ascetics simply to define other ascetic activities as generalized performances. Most ascetic behaviors, codes of conduct, instruments of formation, and technologies have the aspect of performance, of displaying or acting. The regimens, again, do not need to be on display for other people; they may be on display for one's own self as a means of articulating a new subjectivity in opposition to the dominant subjectivity provided in a society.

Among ascetics, however, another sort of performance, not discussed by performance theorists, but addressed by other theorists,[121] emerges from the narratives and stories about ascetics. This textualized performance discusses the rigor, strictness, and steadfastness of the ascetic's life in order to idealize and dramatize the ascetic's efforts. Textualized performance constructs an imitable subject, an imitable performance. These textualized performances do not actually exist, but are created of the stuff of narrative and metaphor, precisely in order to set up the illusion of a reality to be imitated.[122] It sets the character, dramatizes the methods and regimes, it substantiates the fantasy, it performs the ascetical discipline in the mind.[123] Asceticism, then, becomes a highly complex performance genre.

119. See Miller, "Desert Asceticism," 138–39.

120. Schechner, *Performance Theory*, 6.

121. Wyschogrod, *Saints and Postmodernism*, 19–28; Harpham, *Ascetic Imperative*, 15–16.

122. Valantasis, *Spiritual Guides*, 147–55.

123. Miller, "Desert Asceticism," 146–48.

The question of intention as it relates to a definition of asceticism also warrants preliminary discussion. Intentionality finds expression in the modes of subjectivity, in the manner of structuring social relations, and in the explicit theological and metaphorical constructions of the symbolic universe. Since the ascetic constructs an alternative to the cultural givens, then the question of the goal, the intentions, the direction, the final product toward which the ascetic effort works becomes important. Why is an alternative subjectivity necessary? How will it come about? The conflict between cultural norm and ascetic reformation demands an articulated alternative, a goal toward which the ascetic performance aims. Goals are implicit in the concept of performance itself: according to Schechner, the subject of performance is "transformation: the startling ability of human beings to create themselves, to change, to become—for better or for worse—what they ordinarily are not."[124] The intentions call out and structure the performances by virtue of imaging or imagining a new self, capable of different social relations, and drawn to live in a different world. Asceticism does not simply reject other ways of living (that is the misconception denoted by the negative implications of the word "asceticism"), but rather asceticism rejects precisely in order to embrace another existence,[125] another way of living embodied in a new subjectivity, alternative social relations, and a new imaging of the universe. And this intentionality has power: power to create a new person, power to restructure society, power to revise the understanding of the universe.

And finally, asceticism involves novelty. The novel, the alternative, the new undergirds ascetic performances, not so much that every action is new, but that every action is one of the building elements to someone, something different. Asceticism may be described, then, as avant garde, by nature: it is "'what's in advance of'—a harbinger, an experimental prototype, the cutting edge."[126] Asceticism, however, is also by nature transgressive, because the new always emerges from the discounting of the common or accepted, or from the rejection of the socialized acceptable, in order to move toward something that at once rejects that priority to construct a novelty. Novelty makes asceticism attractive, desirable: the newness of the reconstructed self, society, and world creates the desire

124. Schechner, *Future of Ritual*, 1.
125. Miles, *Fullness of Life*, 134–54.
126. Schechner, *Future of Ritual*, 5.

that provides the energy and impetus for transformation and ascetical performance. This definition of asceticism as performances within a dominant social environment intended to inaugurate a new subjectivity, different social relations, and an alternative symbolic universe describes the novel, intentional, and performative aspect of asceticism. Ascetic performances revise the understanding of the self, society, and the universe by directing them intentionally toward an alternative mode of existence within a dominant environment.

CONSTRUCTIONS OF POWER IN ASCETICISM

It remains, now, to address the questions of power in ascetic subjectivities, ascetic social relations, and ascetic symbolic universes. Having problematized the theory of power in relationship to asceticism and the theory of asceticism in relationship to ascetical behavior, this discussion lays out typologies of ascetic subjectivities, the constructions of power in the concomitant social relations, and the theory of power in the conceptualized universe.

Power in Ascetic Subjectivity

Subjectivity in asceticism revolves about a duality: asceticism always operates between two subjectivitites, the one identified as the rejected subjectivity and the other articulated as the desired subjectivity. This subjective duality may be interpreted from two perspectives. From the ascetic's perspective, the only real, commanding subjectivity is that toward which the ascetic moves and for which the ascetic works.[127] This becomes evident from reading the sayings of the desert masters: while the warfare of the ascetic at once deconstructs the old self, learning to recognize its destructive socialization and practices, at the same time it posits a new subjectivity in the future; it is the *emergent* person, the victorious athlete who becomes visible in the fruits of ascetic labor. The articulated goals of ascetic labor, together with their constructions of social and religious categorizations, define that new person. Variously articulated within the Christian ascetic tradition, the categories and distinctions of human ambition and growth involve the following: angels, humans, daemons, those

---

127. For work and labor, see Wyschogrod, *Saints and Postmodernism,* 83–86.

who rise and fall, those who are stable and those who move about, the married and the single, and the encratites .[128]

From the perspective of the observer of the ascetic (whether ancient or modern), the ascetic appears as figured and constructed.[129] The ascetic subject becomes the encoded,[130] the figural, the literary subject. Narrative sources[131] best describe this perspective, as well as the proscriptive ascetical theological treatises in which the ascetic figures as the hero, the divine guide, the miracle-worker, the superhuman enemy of the Enemy. This figured subject elicits either positive or negative modalities from the observer depending upon the affinity experienced with the goal and direction of ascetical practice. To other ascetics, the starvation regimes emerge as positive signs of a real, truthful subject; but to a member of the dominant culture, the starvation only signifies sickness and delusion, the non-real and the lie about living.

These two perspectives on the ascetic subject mark the ascetic as an intermediary and evolving subject, a *tertium quid*. The ascetic participates fully neither in one subjectivity (the one left behind, but still being overcome) nor in the other subjectivity (the not-yet-present, but the one on the horizon), because the ascetic always moves between the deconstructed and the constructing identity, being held by the former while yearning for the latter. And the ascetic consequently appears always to be in transit, in process, in motion toward a new subjectivity. The early Christian monks, for example, experienced themselves as neither fully human, nor fully divine, as embodied angels, as disembodied humans, as living corpses, who lived in society and yet did not, who withdrew from society in order to create another so that at once they existed in a non-existence.[132]

This mediatory role, however, points not only to the ascetic subject and its environment, but also to the society at large. The ascetic mediates the array of subjectivities available in any given culture. The ascetic must know and understand the socially constructed options in order to withdraw from them and thus create a new subjectivity. The rejection

128. See "Daemons" chapter 7, pp. 138–42.

129. Miller, "Desert Asceticism," 137–43.

130. Wyschogrod, *Saints and Postmodernism,* 30.

131. See Harpham, *Ascetic Imperative,* 67–88.

132. See "Daemons," chapter 7, pp. 162–68.

of the dominant culture's forms of subjectivities marks the basis for the embracing of a culturally different identity, an alternative subjectivity. This process, therefore, provides the range of possible subjectivities in a given environment. Withdrawal opens the space for this new subject to exist, but its reference always relates at once to that which the new subjectivity has left behind and the goal toward which the ascetic aspires: to be a renunciant identifies by negation the state from which the ascetic has emerged while at the same time identifying the state toward which the asceticism is oriented.

The general discussion of the ascetic subject leads to the exploration of typologies. In my reading of a wide assortment of ascetic texts from Late Antiquity, I have identified five types of ascetic subjects.

The first type of ascetic subject is the *combative subject*. In this model, the deconstructed identity and its social and religious setting has such great power that the ascetic may only move from it toward another by constant warfare. The power of the old structure holds the power of the new being (personal, social, and religious), but cannot prevent its existence. While moving from one identity to another, the ascetic becomes powerful, manifests superabundant exterior power, and establishes an identity where power has been redefined.

The exemplar of the combative subject is Antony of Egypt as portrayed by Athanasius in the *Vita Antonii*. Strong opposites define Antony's transformation and his acquiring of virtue/power as an ascetic: the city and the desert, the outer desert and the inner desert, the monastery and the mountain, God and Satan, virtue and vice, angels and demons. Athanasius situates Antony in combat from the moment he enters the desert until his death. In the beginning, Antony fights with the demons and the model of his ascetic subjectivity revolves about his ability to withstand the demonic attacks, but in the discourse that Athanasius has Antony deliver in the middle of his hagiographical account, Antony positively develops this combat as the means of acquiring virtue, of gaining and possessing the immutable and permanent. The battle and conflict becomes the means of persevering and transforming the body into a subject capable of living virtuously. The power achieved through this combat manifests itself in right thinking (the final sections on Arianism, Neo-Platonism, Meletianism [*Vita Antonii* 68–77]), through miracles (see again the final section), and through the instruction of the wise philosophers by the uneducated ascetic [*Vita Antonii* 74–88]. Combat creates this type of ascetic subjectivity.

The second type of ascetic subject is the *integrative* model. In this type of subjectivity, the ascetic subject remains substantially the same as the socially constructed subject of the dominant culture, but through asceticism, or religious experiences, or initiations and ritual observances, or any other sort of planned exercise, the ascetic subject achieves a transformation or enlightenment that enhances and enriches the subject's life within the dominant culture. In the integrative model the emphasis remains on the development and maturing of the subject over a period of time, without a strong bifurcation of old and new subjectivities, without setting up a conflict between old and new identities, but while encouraging the growth and development of the subject into a more perceptive or aware mode of existence. The ascetic exercises provide a temporary, protective time, space, and set of relationships for personal integrative development. Power here emerges as empowerment, as the gradual unfolding of greater and greater access to exterior power and the gradual manifestation of divine or exterior power within.

The asceticism of the Nag Hammadi Hermetic document, *On the Eighth and the Ninth*, exemplifies this type of integrative ascetic subjectivity. In this treatise, the spiritual master and the disciple ritually withdraw in order to create a space in which the disciple may ascend intellectually and spiritually under the guidance and support of the master. In the process, the disciple becomes aware of the "brotherhood," the enlightened ones whom he joins, but the disciple does not receive instruction to leave society, or to live in any way other than as an enlightened one. Presumably, at the end of the initiation into the ninth, the disciple returns to assist others in their spiritual and intellectual development. The goal for the disciple remains integration, maturation, and continued religious development within an existing social structure. Power comes to the disciple through the ritualized processes and the relationship with the master, but remains with the disciple afterward. The disciple integrates and internalizes the power.

The *educative* model of ascetic subject constitutes the third type. The educative ascetical subject submits to the teaching of a master and by training and practices becomes adept through education. Learning structures the asceticism so that the teacher, the font of wisdom, transmits knowledge and understanding to the student, an empty vessel.

Knowledge/power passes from educator to student, from mind to mind, from God to the teacher to the student, until the student becomes empowered to be a teacher. Here power is located outside the emerging subject, in the teacher, and in the teacher's extraordinary powers and abilities. Only as the student submits to that exterior power does the student eventually become empowered, but in becoming empowered, the student actually has moved into becoming a teacher. As in the integrative model, the educational asceticism provides a temporary spatial, temporal, and intellectual environment for the education of the student—an environment that the student must leave in order to signify that the education has been completed.

Gregory Thaumaturgos's description of his teacher, Origen of Alexandria, exemplifies this type of asceticism. Gregory, yearning for education, studies under Origen. The treatise presents detailed descriptions of the subject matter for Gregory's education: philosophy, mathematics, music, theology, textual interpretation. But Origen mediates the knowledge, so that Gregory metaphorically describes Origen as a divine figure who has ascended to the height of religious experience and knowledge and has returned, divinized, to teach him the sacred knowledge. Gregory's emptiness, his lack of power, gradually dissipates as his relationship with his teacher transforms him from a mere human student, to a divinized and articulate (gnostic?) practitioner, and then to become a teacher himself when, as he puts it, he leaves the garden of paradise and must go forth, now fully empowered, into the world. The former subjectivity, the empty vessel and student, has been transformed by educational asceticism into a fully empowered and articulate teacher.

The fourth type of ascetic subject is the *pilgrim* who travels from place to place to construct a subjectivity transformed by the experience of not having a stable home or by the encounter with holy places and people. For the pilgrim, the environment defines subjectivity, so that as the pilgrim moves from place to place, from site to site, the contours of a new subjectivity emerge, and at the arrival at the pilgrim's goal, the subject emerges fully transformed. The unstable and changing condition of the pilgrim creates an environment free of the socialization of the dominant culture precisely to enable the creation and development of alternative perspectives. In this model power resides in some other place, in the movement toward that other place, and in the gradual empowerment of the pilgrim as the pilgrim moves toward full participation in an exterior power. The interior power may only happen when the exterior person has moved.

The *Acts of Peter and the Twelve Apostles* from the Nag Hammadi Library exemplifies this model. Peter and the apostles travel from their original destination (lost in the lacuna) to two other cities. At the first, called Habitation, they arrive as seekers, strangers, and travelers and meet the pearl merchant (and divine figure), Lithargoel. Lithargoel encourages them to come to his city, Nine Gates, and to receive the pearls that he is giving away freely. In order to travel they must renounce their possessions and learn to fast; in other words, these ascetical practices are a prerequisite to arrival at the merchant's city. "No man is able to go on that road, except one who has forsaken everything that he has and has fasted daily from stage to stage" (5:20–25). When they arrive at Nine Gates, they are empowered to return to the city of Habitation and to minister as physicians to the poor, after they discover that Jesus has been among them as Lithargoel and the physician.

In this model, the change in subjectivity is reflected in the altered understanding of the religious quest. Jesus has three different appearances to Peter and the twelve apostles, according to their understanding, level of asceticism, and empowerment for ministry: he is Lithargoel, the merchant in a strange city, freely displaying his pearls to the poor and giving them to Peter and the twelve; he is the physician at Nine Gates who heals the poor; he is Jesus Christ who commissions the apostles to return to Habitation and to commence a ministry of healing, as physicians, until the time that the poor can inherit for themselves the eternal habitation.

The fifth and final type of ascetic subject is the *revelatory subject*. In this type of ascetic subjectivity, a solitary awaits revelation or enlightenment. Waiting often constitutes the asceticism, while other ascetical activities (prayer, fasting, ablutions) may take place during the wait. The ascetic subject disappears before the awaited revelation, so that the revelation may indeed come to the seer. The ascetic experiences power as totally exterior and experiences the self as powerless before the revelation. The seer or receiver of the revelation does not necessarily have personal power, nor access to power, but rather the ascetic simply becomes an instrument, agent, or medium for the reception of power. Preparation for empowerment through various performances, therefore, constitutes this asceticism.

One exemplar for this type of ascetical subject is in the Nag Hammadi treatise *Allogenes*, in which the character Allogenes studies, learns, engages with spiritual guides until he must simply withdraw for a hundred years in order to await the revelation. After the revelation, Allogenes becomes empowered as a spiritual guide to lead the others in their asceticism.[133] A ritualized form of ascetical preparation is found in the *Hêkâlôt Rabbâtî*. Michael Swartz has argued that this ritual does not present "an exemplary way of life, but preparation for an extraordinary experience."[134] Here the fasting and the recitation of divine names cleanse the ascetic and prepare him for his revelation.

These types of ascetic subjectivities are intended to be suggestive, rather than exhaustive. These various subjectivities construct their power in the ascetic subjectivity in opposition to the dominant or received subjectivity of their social environments. The subjectivities set a variety of means for producing change; that is, they provide a wide assortment of methods of empowerment through the construction of another subjectivity. The ascetic subject exerts its power over other subjects' productive environment by simply positing another subject, moving to another geographical location, entering into a different relationship as with a teacher. The ascetic subject experiences and participates in those intersecting powers (capacity to change and capacity to affect the productive environment of another subject) according to the techniques of formation or asceticism inherent in the practices.

Power in Ascetic Social Relations

Constructions of power in ascetic social relations shifts the discussion both toward a definition of the type of society in which the ascetic lives and toward the social location of power within the dominant society, in the ascetic society, as well as in the relationship of the two. Here Hodge and Kress's linking of solidarity/sociality with power plays an important role in that the very creation of social relationships posits power (and its contestation) in a variety of ways.

In articulating the kinds of ascetic solidarity, the traditional Christian system differentiates social from solitary asceticism. Harpham has described this differentiation as a distinction between the socialized

133. Valantasis, *Spiritual Guides,* 105–45.
134. Swartz, *"Hêkâlôt Rabbâtî,"* 228–29.

orientation of coenobiticism, with its emphasis on defending oneself from error or mistake, and the transcendent power orientation of eremitism, which "goes on the offensive, seeking to embody and exercise supernatural power."[135] Harpham argues: "Eremites renounced the world; cenobites renounced themselves. Accordingly eremites gained themselves; and cenobites, through the monasteries that exerted their powerful influence until the Reformation, gained the world."[136] For Harpham, both the social and the solitary ascetic access power, but through different means: the eremites' power is transcendent and bestowed, the coenobite's power is socially constructed and political.

The coenobite constructs a new society, away from and in opposition to the dominant society, and lives with other ascetics, while the hermit constructs an inner society and lives with interior realities that resist the self as defined by the dominant society. Coenobitic ascetic communities renounce the power operative in the dominant society as false in favor of a more true and real, reconstructed, ascetic understanding of power. The hermit renounces all forms of social power in any society in order to battle with the interior powers in an interiorly and personally constructed society of one.[137]

This distinction locates the ascetic in society either as participant in the construction of an alternative society that has ongoing relations with the dominant society or as renunciant of society constructing an alternative interior society on the fringes of, or outside, the dominant society. Within ascetical language, this social construction refers to withdrawal (Greek: *anachoresis*). In some form or other, asceticism depends upon withdrawal to construct the environment in which ascetic performances may create new people. Withdrawal defines the *field* of choices and actions and relationships: it may be understood as demarcating the field of power by establishing clear, separative boundaries between the realms or regimes of power and thereby as enclosing or defining another field in which a particular construction of power operates.

Withdrawal, however, may be widely and variably constructed. There may be, as in the case of Plotinus as described by Porphyry in his "Life and Books of Plotinus," a withdrawal within community that also

135. Harpham, *Ascetic Imperative*, 22.
136. Ibid., 29.
137. "Daemons," chapter 7, pp. 162–68.

forms ascetic community: Plotinus withdraws mentally and noetically while continuing to work in his own immediate ascetic community and to play an important role in the larger society as well. Or, as in the variety of levels of withdrawal portrayed in the "Life of Antony," the monk withdraws to the desert to be alone, or to the desert to live with other monks, or to live with another monk as a trainer in asceticism, or to live alone as a solitary with other monks living in close proximity. The spectrum of society in Christian monastic literature moves from the complete solitary whose only society is the interior characterizations of his mental and physical impulses, to the monk who lives in community and who must learn to live with other ascetics in a redefined, ascetic society.

Withdrawal defines the arena of asceticism and the social body by creating the precise social space in which a subjectivity may be developed and an alternative social arrangement may be implemented. In defining the arena of subjective development and social relationship, withdrawal simultaneously constructs systems of power operative in that arena. The power field and the ascetic arena collude to create a complete society and the modalities of that collusion may be seen in the typologies of ascetic subjectivity.

The *combative subject* withdraws from the demands of the exterior society to wage a war on the interior society of demons, distractions, thoughts, impulses. The combative subject's asceticism orients itself toward the struggle for dominance among interior powers and tendencies, so that social power develops as interior struggle with demons' revelations. The physical withdrawal from society foregrounds the interior powers (both positive and negative) and backgrounds social powers (all negatively defined). The desire for real social relations with other people (as friends, lovers, companions, sex partners) is translated into a temptation that must be resisted. The power of social relations operates as an interior power and a site of resistance. The social withdrawal defines the arena as interior and the combat occurs within an interior society.

The *integrative subject* does not reject social relations and power; in fact, the power gained from ascetical integration bears great social value and enhances social power. The integrative subject locates power in the relationship of the initiant with the divine or ascetically more advanced figure. The relationship of guide to disciple constitutes a formative relationship in which the initiant develops and manifests power. This transference of power within this smaller relationship mirrors the initiant's empowerment in the dominant society. What happens formatively in the integrative relationship translates into enhanced social power. This may be articulated as the initiant joining a select group within the dominant society or as the achievement of a new social and political station. Here the withdrawal operates as a working site to social empowerment.[138]

The *educative subject* likewise maintains the social structures that empower teachers to teach and students to learn and that values educative empowerment as socially desirable. As in the integrative model, the student and teacher create an ascetic site in which the teacher transfers knowledge/power to the student. The virtual site of empowerment again mirrors the social empowerment emergent at the end of the educative process. Whereas the combative subject interiorizes society, the educative and integrative subjects create a temporary alternative ascetical society through which they attain social and religious status in the dominant society.[139]

The *pilgrim subject*, however, works with a bidirectional withdrawal: the pilgrim withdraws from one society in which the pilgrim has been socialized and habituated in order to withdraw toward, or to progress toward, another society that holds the promise of transformation and encounter with newness. Withdrawal for the pilgrim situates the asceticism: the withdrawal and the intermediary state becomes the asceticism that finds its completion only upon arrival. The social vagrant's social ambivalence, mobility, and itinerancy constructs a fluid society, and the pilgrim's active living in that fluid society constitutes the asceticism, until arrival at the pilgrim site completes the transformation. Social power, for the pilgrim, may develop among the others who are pilgrims, in the solidarity of others who are traveling the same spiritual and religious route, but that solidarity at once flattens social difference and subjects the pilgrim to the powerful attraction of the final destination. All power for the pilgrim, then, derives from the goal, and its affect upon the pilgrim.

The *revelatory subject*, like the pilgrim subject, moves away from society, but only as a means of creating a space for revelation. A revelatory subject withdraws from society in order to become a medium of revelation. The revelation relates to the society, as in a community that might grow up around a particular revelation, but the asceticism of awaiting

138. Valantasis, *Spiritual Guides,* 63–104.
139. Ibid., 13–33.

revelation requires temporary social withdrawal. The revelation constructs power for the revelatory subject, and the revelation (not usually
the revealer) retains social power.

This examination of power in ascetic social relations leads to four
general conclusions. First, the very concept of ascetic withdrawal posits
that social power is always contested. Two different societies, two different worlds compete for the definition, articulation, and modulation
of power. This contestation reveals the duality of power in asceticism, a
duality that revolves about the constellation of old world and new, old
person and new, old society and new, and the various ways in which different systems of power operate in each of these dual environments.

Second, this power duality implies that, since ascetic society remains
a society in transition, in movement between the renounced and the not-
yet emerged cultures, *in medias res*, ascetic power as well remains fluid,
transitory, dynamic, and fluctuating. No one system of power maintains
itself through the entire process of ascetical formation, because at each
point in ascetical progress, one power weakens as another grows, one
power system deconstructs as another comes into being gradually, almost
imperceptibly, in the performances aimed at once toward dishabituating
the old and creating the new.

Third, contrary to any theory of power, ascetic power maintains the
odd possibility of a system of power that operates and functions only
within one person; that is, ascetic power may be constructed non-dyadi-
cally and without social interaction. The existence of hermits and extreme
social renunciants enables the possibility of a system of power existing
and operating only within one person's mind and body. This potential for
a unique, unprecedented, and non-dyadic construction of ascetic social
power problematizes the social and subjective categories of current research in power theory.

Finally, the most influential power of all the ascetical constructions
of social power remains the power that does not yet exist or that is not
yet fully constructed or real. The social power of asceticism emerges from
the articulation and pursuit of a goal, an imaged final product of ascetical
performance. This non-existent power takes on power more and more
as the ascetic pursues the goal, but it commands greater power in non-
existence than in its existence: the goal as unrealized demands more

attention (another way of articulating power) than the power already spent.[140]

Power and the Symbolic Universe

The exploration of power in the ascetic symbolic universe must begin with the research of Peter Berger and Thomas Luckmann on the sociology of knowledge. Berger and Luckmann contend that "reality is socially constructed and that the sociology of knowledge must analyze the processes in which this occurs."[141] Basing their study on the everyday experience of living,[142] they described society as both objective[143] and subjective.[144] They maintain that the construction and the maintenance of the symbolic universe function with the objectified reality.[145] Since "(a)ll human activity is subject to habitualization,"[146] institutionalization follows naturally with the development of roles[147] and the sedimentation into tradition.[148] The function of the symbolic universe is to legitimate these habitualized and institutional practices.[149] Therefore, symbolic universes "are bodies of theoretical tradition that integrate different provinces of meaning and encompass the institutional order in a symbolic totality."[150] They function by signification, not by reference to everyday life.[151] "The symbolic universe is conceived of as the matrix of *all* socially objectivated and subjectively real meanings; the entire historic society and the entire biography of the individual are seen as events taking place *within* this universe."[152] Symbolic universes provide the context through which human experience may find meaning through the organization and articulation of the

---

140. See Wychogrod, *Saints and Postmodernism*, 56–58.

141. Berger and Luckmann, *Social Construction of Reality*, 1.

142. Ibid., 1–43.

143. Ibid., 45–118.

144. Ibid., 119–68.

145. Ibid., 85–118.

146. Ibid., 50.

147. Ibid., 67–74.

148. Ibid., 63–67.

149. Ibid., 85–88.

150. Ibid., 88.

151. Ibid., 89.

152. Ibid.

structures of meaning that legitimate human practice.[153] There are many machineries for maintaining the symbolic universe: experts,[154] mythology, theology, science, therapeutic practices among many others.[155]

Berger and Luckmann's theory, however, investigated the constructed reality of the dominant group in a society: it was the dominant symbolic universe that they described. With asceticism's orientation to a constructed reality opposing or resisting the dominant society's reality, their theory must be adjusted to account for the conscious development of an *alternative* reality. This is a complex process in ascetical societies. In the first place, because asceticism operates by performances, the symbolic universe evolves from realizations, rationalizations, and experiences articulated by the ascetic's own experiences as well as from the received traditions about those performances. This means, for example, that the traditional meaning carried by fasting within a given ascetical community may not necessarily be the significance of fasting of a particular ascetic's performance, as with a monastic woman suffering from anorexia nervosa living in a monastic house with strict rules of fasting based in the Christian tradition of monasticism.[156] The performances at the heart of ascetical activity demand that the meanings carried and supported by the ascetic community continually adapt to the immediate experience of ascetics operating either positively (by adoption) or negatively (by rejection) in a tradition.

The second adjustment to Berger and Luckmann's theory relates to the simultaneous presence of alternative realities at the heart of asceticism. Ascetic reality is by definition a resistant reality within a dominant system. This means that the ascetical symbolic universe always operates in the presence of other universes, and, therefore, it is always consciously developed and maintained as an opposing force. The need consciously to articulate the symbolic universe emerges from conflict and change. Conflict is the social dimension. Berger and Luckmann argue that a symbolic universe tends not to need to be legitimated until there is some problem with it.[157] The greatest problem results from the presence

153. Ibid., 90–95.
154. Ibid., 108–10.
155. Ibid., 101–5.
156. See Corrington, "Anorexia, Asceticism, and Autonomy."
157. Berger and Luckmann, *Social Construction of Reality,* 96–97.

of alternative or deviant symbolic universes shared by some group of people within a dominant world,[158] which in the case of ascetical communities, are explicitly developed. The existence of a group with an alternative symbolic universe calls forth repression of the alternative to stabilize the dominant perspective:[159] ascetical withdrawal invites social repression. The repression enables the dominant group to solidify power around its social institutions;[160] and assists the ascetical practitioner to justify its alternative. There is also a personal dimension. Berger and Luckmann argue that symbolic universes change because the people who embody them change. Since it is individuals who define the reality of their lives,[161] and since no individual is ever fully socialized,[162] change among and within individuals requires an adjustment of the understanding of the symbolic universe. Ascetic performances are organized around such change in subjectivity, in social relations, and in the total context of meaning production.

Within the definition of asceticism presented here, the need for articulating a symbolic universe becomes evident. The conflict at the heart of asceticism between a dominant and an emergent perspective involves a simultaneous adjustment of the symbolic universe. The new subjectivity and the alternative social relations not only emerge from resistance, but also create resistance, so that the conflict and redefinition of symbolic universe is inevitable. The new subjectivity and the alternative social arrangements also require legitimation. They both need to be made to fit into the entire picture of living, to explain and to enhance the emergent identity and society. The ascetic's goal, however, is not pluralism, as in Berger and Luckmann,[163] but an entirely alternative creation: the intent of asceticism demands precisely the development of different institutions and patterns of legitimation in opposition to what preceded. The construction of an alternative symbolic universe combines with the structural systems created by the ascetic's performance to create a conscious movement and institutional change. It amounts to an ideological con-

158. Ibid., 98.
159. Ibid., 99.
160. Ibid., 100.
161. Ibid., 107.
162. Ibid., 98.
163. Ibid., 110–15.

struction from outside the dominant structure as well as an institutional reformulation within an alternative society.

The ascetic symbolic universe legitimates the regimes of power in ascetic subjectivity and ascetic social relations. The ascetical performances, which always take place in an arena of conflict with the dominant structure, apply pressure to the ascetical universe simultaneously to define itself in opposition to the dominant universe and to create the context of meaning for the ascetic's life experience. The ascetic's universe continually makes reference to its rejection of and withdrawal from the dominant society. Its power is always a justification of an alternative power; its articulation empowers ascetical performance. The ascetic universe supports the new systems and provides depth, rationale, metaphoric analogues, and application to peripheral centers of knowledge (politics, anthropology, philosophy, cosmology, science).

The ascetic symbolic universe structures the various ideologies and their contestation, as well as developing the various logonomic systems operating in their alternative society. The relationship of various systems of power are explored, compared, and valorized in economic, political, diverse religious, educational, penal, and juridical regimes, which create the field in which performances take place, and this exploration takes place with the dominant social perspective clearly present. The symbolic universe publicizes the ascetic performance, creating the stage and backdrop and mediating the communication systems in order for a performance to create an alternative meaning.

Power, then, becomes a subject of the symbolic universe. Subjectivity and social relations address the question of power as an object within their various performances, because subjective power and social power remain peripheral to the performances creating a new subjectivity and a new society. Power remains "object" within those frames of reference in so far as the new subject and the new society do not directly address the theory of power in their performances. Within the symbolic universe, however, power becomes a subject in itself, which may be explored, defined, and analyzed theologically, juridically, sociologically, philosophically, politically, academically, and in every other disciplinary mode. Power, as a subject, may become a discourse. The understanding and interpretation of power changes when power becomes a subject of investigation, the subject of a discourse: it loses its relational and personal identity and becomes abstract, theoretical, objective. This aspect of power has predominated in the academic study of power theory.

Conclusions: Constructions of Power in Asceticism

In 1993 the American public was horrified as it watched the fiery end of the Branch Davidians in their compound in Waco, Texas. The Branch Davidians were an ascetic community (according to the definition given above): their performances revolved about the formation of a community defined in opposition both to other religious sects and to American secular culture as a whole; their tradition of biblical exegesis accentuated their apocalyptic understanding of their withdrawal and their special place in the spiritual history of the world; their social relations strengthened their bond with each other and their mutual dependence upon their leader, David Koresh; their community life, even in its most extreme militaristic orientation, was the real community in which the power of God was and would continue to be manifested not only for members of their community, but also for the whole world. Their performances, played out in the communication media (especially television), shocked the American public. Many people watching the dramatic and fiery outcome of the community's refusal to submit to the secular power of the government could not understand the power that the Branch Davidians exercised: observers could not comprehend the Branch Davidians' self-understanding and their ascetic experience in relation to their faith and to their leader; many were at a loss to sympathize with their forceful refusal to surrender; even the government's use of force baffled the extended television audience. But the Branch Davidians' ascetical formation had formed them, prepared them, initiated them, and even rehearsed them for just that most important moment in their individual and corporate lives.

The issue for the Branch Davidians, as it was for Abba Joseph and Abba Lot, was power—the power to "become entirely as fire." The parallels between these ancient ascetics and their modern successors are sobering, and yet both societies resulted from the conscious and deliberate construction of an alternative world opposing and resisting a dominant society. The above critique of power theory assembled an assortment of tools to assist in analyzing this complexity: the three faces of power debate reformulated by Wartenberg directs attention to the context and dynamic of power; Althusser draws attention to the material and ideological dimensions of ascetical power; Foucault points to the formational and technological aspects of ascetical power, especially as they constitute systems of self-formation; Wyschogrod underscores the value and centrality of the inversions and renunciations that construct power; and Hodge and Kress expand on Foucault's technologies to focus on the systems of social formation and communication that make this ascetical world functional.

The construction of power in asceticism advances the general discussion of the theory of power in a number of significant ways. First, ascetical power emerges precisely at the point of conflict, resistance, and opposition, so that the analysis of power begins at its encounter with a dominant power. Power cannot be understood as existing in isolation from the resistances of that power, or divorced from the technologies, ideologies, and structures that a subversive power creates to counter that power. Moreover, ascetical power strives for the construction of an entirely alternative world of subjects, social relations, and understandings. Ascetical opposition, like many of the oppositions operating in most societies in today's world, does not present itself as one option among many, but as *the* option for those capable of disciplined performance. And finally, ascetical power unmasks the material and performative aspect of power. The ascetic behavior performs the power: the ascetic's activities and thoughts, played out on a different social stage and in a different theatrical world, create that world with the people and relationships that the concrete practices embody.

By looking at the capacity for change and the capacity to affect the productive environment of another among those people whose performances within the dominant social environment inaugurate a new subjectivity, different social relations, and an alternative symbolic universe—that is, by looking at power and asceticism—this essay points to the value and necessity of exploring theories of power in religious phenomena and to the importance of theorists of power to consider religious manifestations of power in their theories. The Desert Fathers Lot and Joseph have as much in common with the Branch Davidians as with any other group in conflict with a dominant system, whether religious, politi-

cal, social, ideological, economic, educational, or juridical. The constructions of power in asceticism open a window to that powerful conflict.[164]

164. I would like to thank Vincent Wimbush and Walter Kaelber for inviting me to
write this paper as the focus of a panel discussion at the first meeting of the joint AAR
and SBL program "The Ascetic Impulse in Religious Life and Culture." Their comments,
and the critical comments of the panelists, have been taken seriously in the revision, even
though I did not always follow their direction. I must also acknowledge the assistance
of Teresa Shaw and James Goehring who read a draft and brought to the fore important
points about asceticism. Finally, I would like to acknowledge the *JAAR*'s anonymous
reader without whose disciplined response this paper would have been significantly
diminished.

CHAPTER 3

Asceticism as a Sacred Marriage

Eastern and Western Theories

SACRED MARRIAGE AND ASCETICISM HAVE BEEN JOINED IN SACRED UNION at least from the beginning of the Christian era. The union works in both directions: sacred marriage invokes ascetical discipline; asceticism metaphorizes its highest aspirations as a sacred marriage with the divine. The linking of the two, however, did not end in the early Christian period. As recently as 2000, Brian Livingstone, a survivor of the Branch Davidians in Waco, Texas, described the formative processes of this Seventh Day Adventist apocalyptic religious sect as a sacred marriage of the soul with the divine,[1] while invoking a tradition probably unknown to him of the alignment of asceticism and sacred marriage. Sacred marriage and asceticism remain complementary notions.

The conjoining of the two has perdured throughout the Christian tradition, especially in Eastern Christianity, but also in the Western mystical tradition. To this day in the Greek Orthodox tradition, for example, the faithful celebrate the ascetical sacred marriage in the liturgies of Holy Week in the Matins of the Bridegroom celebrated at the beginning of the new day on Monday, Tuesday, and Wednesday in churches throughout the world. The sixteenth-century Catholic mystics of Spain, John of the Cross and Teresa of Avila, worked the metaphor of sacred marriage and talked about the ascetical disciplines necessary to receive it.

Although the signifier, ascetical sacred marriage, remains constant throughout the ages, what it signifies shifts and changes from historical context to historical context, so that the same signifier points toward dif-

1. Fagan, "Mount Carmel."

ferent signifiés in a process of perpetual reinvention and rediscovery of meanings. The Branch Davidians in the twentieth century and Macarius the Egyptian in the fourth century used the same signifier to mean radically different things, all joined and made familiar by the invocation of the same language. The ascetical image both perdures and shifts in meaning throughout the Christian ages.

So what precisely is the connection between sacred marriage and asceticism? It is an important question. Something about the metaphor of marriage with the divine articulates the intimate union experienced by advanced ascetics in their quest for complete absorption into the divine. This chapter explores that articulated union in Eastern and Western asceticism by looking closely at the description of sacred marriage in two different ascetical systems. I will argue that in all asceticism, sacred marriage describes the apex of ascetical effort, complete absorption into the divine. I will explore Eastern and Western ascetical sacred marriage to prove this assertion.

Two different perspectives frame my argument: my own theory of asceticism, which I use as a lens for analyzing ascetical practices; and the writing of two Christian ascetical theologians, one Eastern and one Western. Adolphe Tanquerey (1854–1932), who published the definitive analysis of the ascetical and mystical life at the beginning of the twentieth century, represents the West, while Marcarius the Egyptian (300–390 C.E.), whose *Fifty Spiritual Homilies* instructed a wide assortment of Christians from ancient monks to John Wesley, represents the East. They each provide different points of reference for analyzing the ascetical use of sacred marriage by means of my own definition of asceticism.

I define asceticism as "performances within a dominant social environment intended to inaugurate a new subjectivity, different social relations, and an alternative symbolic universe."[2] My definition distinguishes between asceticism and formation proper, which revolves about the processes of training people for a role and function within a dominant society. Although Foucault and others call this kind of formation for living in the dominant society "asceticism," I think it is a misnomer, and should properly be called simply "formation."[3] Asceticism addresses the peculiar identity developed in order to differentiate the self from the dominant

2. See "Constructions of Power," chapter 2, pp. 14–59; definition on page 38.
3. See "Asceticism or Formation," chapter 4, pp. 80–100.

society, as in the root metaphor where an athlete prepared the body to compete in sport events precisely to excel in ways that the majority of people could not. Asceticism invokes alterity, difference, and newness in a way that subverts the subjectivities promulgated by the dominant society.

In contradistinction to those dominant subjectivities, the ascetic begins to act in public in such a way as to enact a decidedly different identity. Those enactments constitute a withdrawal from the dominant culture that enables the development of a new subjectivity, supported not only by different social relationships but also by the structures of a new symbolic universe, both of which make the enactment of a new subjectivity sustainable.

In this context, sacred marriage constitutes a particular identity. The metaphor and its attendant implications for personal and intimate relationship with the divine constitute a removal from the realm of the ordinary and socially known and an entrance into a new subjectivity now solely connected with the divine. On the scale of human identities and status, those married to God or united to God in a fixed state of union no longer resemble the majority of believers. The nuptial chamber is only for the elite, the perfect, the fully developed ascetic. An analysis of two different writers from two different eras and regions will support this hypothesis.

Tanquerey and Ascetic Sacred Marriage

Adolphe Tanquerey's *The Spiritual Life: A Treatise on Ascetical and Mystical Theology*, a magisterial work of the late-nineteenth century and translated and promulgated in the early-twentieth century, presents a complete and detailed analysis of the development of the soul as it advances ascetically toward mystical contemplation.[4] Tanquerey attempts to summarize and to systematize the entire tradition of ascetical and mystical theology. He both preserves and arbitrates the ascetical tradition in a succinct and exhaustive explication of the ascetical tradition. Within that larger frame Tanquerey treats sacred marriage as the apex of the religious life, the penultimate experience to the Beatific Vision, a vision that is beyond the

---

4. Tanquerey, *Spiritual Life*. Throughout his text, Tanquerey italicizes words and phrases important to his discussion. All the emphases in these quotations are his, not mine.

scope of both asceticism and mysticism since Tanquerey does not discuss
it in his treatise: "After so many purifications, the soul at last reaches that
calm and abiding union, called the *transforming union*, which seems to
be the final goal of the mystic union, the immediate preparation for the
Beatific Vision."[5] This union with God represents the culmination of a
lifetime of ascetical effort. The ascetic works diligently through the various stages of the religious life, through the various stages of purification
necessary to prepare the soul for union, and attempts to the best of the
ascetic's ability to be granted the transforming union.

But within the ascetical life degrees of union exist. Among the various degrees, spiritual marriage constitutes an exceptional and peculiar
relationship of seeker to the divine. Some degrees of union may be the
result of human effort, but spiritual marriage never results from the
ascetic's own efforts. Spiritual marriage comes only as a divine grace bestowed gratuitously upon select and specifically chosen ascetics:

> Again, it is God Who *determines* the *moment* and the *manner*, as
> well as the *duration* of contemplation. He alone puts the soul into
> the passive or mystic state seizing its faculties in order to act in
> them and through them, but always with the free consent of the
> will. This constitutes a sort of *divine possession*; and since God is
> the Sovereign Master of His Gifts, He intervenes when He wills
> and as He wills.[6]

Various degrees of contemplative union with God exist. These various
degrees achievable by human ascetical effort become the dominant perspective. These unions may be accomplished by any persevering ascetic.
But spiritual marriage functions outside that dominant kind of union.
Because it does not result from human effort, but comes from divine election, spiritual marriage exists as an alternative subjectivity, a reserved and
alternative ascetical identity beyond the reach of the majority of ascetics.

Tanquerey explains the exclusivity of spiritual marriage. He distinguishes the stage leading toward spiritual marriage from the natural
development of the soul in regular ascetic activity by careful differentiation between the results of ascetic's active and engaged work and the
passive and infused state of contemplation. A contemplation resulting
from discursive effort does exist, but such a contemplation differs sig-

5. Ibid., §1469, 691.
6. Ibid., §1388, 651.

nificantly from the contemplation of spiritual marriage. In fact, the two ways, acquired and infused contemplation, posit significantly different subjectivities, which form the basis for understanding the unique role of spiritual marriage in asceticism. Tanquerey compares the two subjectivities in this final section of his book, and distinguishes them through positing a number of different polarities, the first of which has already been mentioned: the polarity of activity for the ascetic and passivity for those selected by God for spiritual marriage. The normal goal of an ascetic's activity leads to a discursive contemplation, while those contemplative ascetics selected by God for union remain passive to the divine effort.

Another polarity relates to the manner of understanding truth. Those ascetics who achieve acquired contemplation come to understand reality through rational thinking, while the select contemplatives understand reality more intuitively and without effort:

> In contemplation God acts especially in what mystics call the *subtile point of the soul*, the *summit of the soul*, the *summit of the will* or *the inmost depth of the soul*. By this we must understand all that is loftiest in the intellect and the will; it is the intellect, not inasmuch as it reasons, but inasmuch as it perceives truth by a simple glance, under the influence of the higher gifts of understanding and of wisdom; it is the will in its simplest act, which is that of loving and of relishing things divine.[7]

The ratiocination of the earlier stages of the ascetical life gives way to the purer vision of God immediately and directly grasped by the mind without effort, but with a simple sight and unmediated apprehension. The earlier stages of rational analysis prepare the ascetic for an intuitive knowledge. The early ascetic practices lay the groundwork for a transformation. They assemble the (presumably subconscious) elements necessary for activating a (presumably conscious) intuitive sense of God.

The next polarity builds on the manner of apprehending truth: God infuses knowledge and love into the soul directly for those selected for union, while others acquire knowledge and love of God through their ascetical effort to cleanse the self and to acquire the virtues necessary for apprehending God. Tanquerey describes this phenomenon in this way:

> God produces at the same time *knowledge* and *love*. . . . By producing with us what are called *infused impressions* which, because

7. Ibid., §1389, 651.

they proceed from God, represent divine things in a more perfect
and more telling fashion; this is what occurs in some *visions* or
revelations.[8]

Because the ascetic remains passive to the divine revelations, God infuses
knowledge and love directly into the soul without any effort by the ascetic
and without any intermediary primarily through visions and self-revela-
tions. The ascetic cannot will the visions, nor develop the revelations;
God alone provides them irrespective of the work of the ascetic. Those
chosen for union understand and love God with an immediacy and an
unmediated comprehension denied to those who know God through acquired effort. Ascetic effort at the beginning and middle of the religious
life prepares the ascetic to receive these visions and revelations.

Tanquerey further explains the difference as one between the passive and infused knowledge of those destined for union as opposed to the
active discursive practices of the majority of ascetics:

> [The soul] is *passive* in this sense, that it is powerless to act on its
> own initiative as it did previously; at the moment of contempla-
> tion it can no longer employ its faculties in a discursive way; it is
> dependent upon a higher principle which governs it, which fas-
> tens its gaze, its mind and its heart upon the object of contempla-
> tion, makes it love and relish that object, suggests what it must do
> and imparts to it a powerful impulse to enable it to act.[9]

Tanquerey draws a firm and immovable line between discursive and
contemplative modalities. The contemplative modality moves decisively
beyond will and thought. In fact, the infused contemplative may never
return to discursive practice. The differentiation implies an ontological
difference effected by the divine in the soul of the contemplative destined
for union that can never be traversed:

> But there *must be no return to discursive meditation* once they
> have ascertained their inability to pray in that manner; they must
> keep their souls at rest, even though it may appear that they are
> doing nothing, and they must be content with a loving and peace-
> ful gaze on God.[10]

8. Ibid., §1390, 652.
9. Ibid., §1392, 653.
10. Ibid., §1433, 673.

The distinction and differentiation of these two subjectivities, one oriented toward acquired contemplation and the other to infused, remains an absolute barrier. One may not pass backwards from union to discourse, from infused to acquired methods of knowledge and love.

The final polarity contrasts direct experience of God with knowledge acquired through training. Tanquerey describes it in this way:

> This knowledge is very sanctifying, because it enables us to know by *experience*, what we had previously learned through reading or personal reflection, and because it makes us see at a glance what we had analyzed by successive acts of the mind.[11]

The demarcation of subjectivities revolves about the difference in identities that each manner of knowing articulates: one knows and learns by discursive and rational effort to understand, but the other knows and understands directly and intuitively that which others must learn by reading and reflection.

Tanquerey describes spiritual marriage as the final and permanent state of union with the divine. Taking his lead from St. Teresa of Avila, he distinguishes four degrees of union: quietude, full union, ecstatic union, and transforming union or spiritual marriage. The degrees, Tanquerey explains, describe the effects both temporal and physical on the person united to God: "The various degrees are marked by a greater and greater hold of God on the soul." He continues:

> 1. When He takes possession of the *subtile point of the soul*, letting the lower faculties and the senses free to exercise their natural activity, we have the *prayer of quiet*.
>
> 2. When He seizes *all the interior faculties*, leaving merely the exterior senses to their own activity, we have the *full union*.
>
> 3. If He takes possession at the same time of the interior faculties and of the exterior senses, we have *ecstatic union* (spiritual espousals).
>
> 4. Lastly, once He extends His hold over all the internal and external faculties and this, no longer in a transitory manner, but in a *stable* and *permanent* fashion, we have the *spiritual marriage*."[12]

11. Ibid., §1403, 659.
12 Ibid., §1419, 666.

All four degrees describe states of union, but stability and permanence differentiate a general union with God from spiritual marriage. Spiritual marriage consists of a perpetual state of union with the divine when God has taken possession of all the faculties both interior and exterior, as well as the senses, permanently and perpetually so that no reversal to a prior state of being is any longer possible. The difference between spiritual espousal to God, the third degree, and spiritual marriage rests precisely on the question of the permanent state of union: espousal has periods when the union does not manifest itself, while marriage manifests union continually and without interruption.

Tanquerey situates spiritual marriage as the final and highest state for the ascetic and the mystic. But spiritual marriage remains the gift to only a few. The majority of ascetics and seekers find themselves in the realm of acquired grace and contemplation, which come to the ascetic as a result of the ascetic's own effort at purification from sin and development of the virtues of the spiritual life. According to Tanquerey, an ascetic cannot will or develop an infused contemplative state, but can only achieve an acquired contemplation, which differs in both stature and status from infused contemplation. Since infused contemplation relates only to a few, it creates a sort of hierarchy of spiritual status, the culmination of which the tradition articulates as a spiritual marriage, a permanent and stable union with God. In essence, this spiritual marriage, and every other degree of union as well, suggests an ontological divide between those who know by discursive thought and those who know by direct experience. The difference in ways of knowing God describes a difference between two kinds of people, two identities in relationship to God, two distinct subjectivities.

Macarius the Egyptian

Macarius the Egyptian, perhaps the most influential of Eastern Christian ascetical authors both in the East and in the West in antiquity as well as through the ages, also develops an ascetical spiritual marriage in his *Fifty Spiritual Homilies*.[13] At the base of his concept of the spiritual marriage lies two different types of people, two subjectivities developed out of an

13. I am here using *Pseudo-Macarius: Fifty Spiritual Homilies and the Great Letter*. The Greek text upon which Maloney translates is that of J. P. Migne, *Patrologia Graeca* 34:449–822. I will refer to the Homily and paragraph number as well as the page number in Maloney's translation.

exegesis of the wise and foolish virgins of Matthew 25:1–13. The normal subjectivity, the one provided by the world and represented by the foolish virgins, remains divorced from the divine and enmeshed in worldly affairs:

> The other foolish ones, however, content with their own nature, did not watch nor did they betake themselves to receive "the oil of gladness" (Ps. 45:7) in their vessels. But still in their flesh, they fell into a deep sleep through negligence, inattentiveness, laziness, and ignorance or even through considering themselves justified. Because of this they were excluded from the bridal chamber of the kingdom because they were unable to please the heavenly Bridegroom. Bound by ties of the world and by earthly love, they did not offer all their love and devotion to the heavenly Spouse nor did they carry with them the oil.[14]

The foolish by nature take the path of least resistance. Their fleshly and embodied state lulls them into a sort of stupefaction with regard to things heavenly, and they make no effort toward sanctification or toward love of the heavenly spouse. These foolish virgins remain in their particularly animal state:

> But other souls, who remain on the level of their own nature, crawl along the ground with their earthly thoughts. They think only in a human way. Their mind lives only on the earthly level. And still they are convinced in their own thought that they look to the Bridegroom and that they are adorned with the perfections of a carnal justification. But in reality they have not been born of the Spirit from above (Jn 3:3) and have not accepted the oil of gladness.[15]

Macarius describes the "natural" human, the person who lives only in and through the body without attention to the higher or loftier aspects of human existence, the aspects that join human to the divine and to the spiritual. This natural person receives no regeneration by the divine, resides in a stupefied state of worldly concern, exists in a basically animal-like existence of crawling on the earth, remains concerned with earthly and worldly realities alone, and through laziness and inattention refuses to engage with the ascetical struggle toward perfection. This is the natural

14. Macarius, *Spiritual Homilies* 4:6, 52.
15. Ibid., 53.

state, the dominant subjectivity of those who do not struggle by asceticism to be transformed.

Macarius compares this natural person to a supernatural person, the preferred ascetical subjectivity that leads toward spiritual marriage with the divine. Macarius emphasizes that this supernatural person does not conform in any way to the natural person and that the supernatural person in fact far exceeds the status and position of the natural:

> Take, for example, the five prudent and vigilant virgins (Mt 25:1–13). They enthusiastically had taken in the vessels of their heart the oil of the supernatural grace of the Spirit—a thing not conformable to their nature. For this reason they were able to enter together with the Bridegroom into the heavenly bridal chamber.[16]

Macarius posits this supernatural person as an alternative to the natural. Macarius reserves entry to the bridal chamber only for those who received spiritual empowerment from God. This spiritual and supernatural empowerment distinguishes between the natural and the supernatural person. The supernatural person orients the self completely toward things divine and seeks earnestly the sanctification offered by the divine spouse:

> But the souls who seek the sanctification of the Spirit, which is a thing that lies beyond natural power, are completely bound with their whole love to the Lord. There they walk; there they pray; there they focus their thoughts, ignoring all other things. For this reason they are considered worthy to receive the oil of divine grace and without any failure they succeed in passing to life for they have been accepted by and found greatly pleasing to the spiritual Bridegroom.[17]

While the natural person orients self entirely to the world and the flesh, the supernatural person orients self entirely to the Lord and to things divine. These supernatural persons literally live in heaven, in the divine realm, and concentrate all their efforts on the sanctification that their search guarantees for them. Macarius understands this supernatural subjectivity as ontologically distinct and opposite to the natural subjectivity.

16. Ibid., 4:6, 52.
17. Ibid.

Macarius presents spiritual marriage as a dramatic regeneration and renewal of the supernatural person by God. Macarius describes that regeneration as both a purification and adornment:

> Take the example of a king who would find a certain poor maiden, dressed in rags. He would not be ashamed, but he would take away her dirty rags and would wash off her blackness. He would adorn her in elegant clothes and maker her a partner of the king. He would give her a place at his table and share with her a banquet. Thus also the Lord found the wounded soul that was stricken. He gave it medicine and removed the black garments and the shame of evil and he clothed it with royal, heavenly garments, those of the Godhead, all shining and glorious. And he placed a crown upon it and made it his partner at the royal table unto joy and gladness.[18]

The regeneration and adornment prepare the supernatural person to become partner to the king and to become a partaker of the heavenly banquet. God, the divine king, effects the ontological change from natural to supernatural person. The ascetic receives this ontological change passively and gradually such that God prepares the natural person for transformation to a supernatural person by a process of cleansing and adornment. The marriage metaphor signifies not simply a change in status and stature, but also a complete remaking of the person, a total transformation from something unclean, sick, and unworthy to something beautified, healed, and worthy of high regard by the king.

This regeneration results in a complete reorientation of the self away from things of the world and toward divine things. This becomes most evident in the sanctified person's prayer:

> One kneels down in prayer and at once his heart is filled with the power of God. And his soul exults in the Lord as a bride with the bridegroom according to that which Isaiah the Prophet said: "As the bridegroom will take delight in the bride, so the Lord will take delight in thee" (Is 62:5). It happens that he is the whole day occupied by work and can give himself to prayer for only an hour. The interior man is caught up with prayer and plunged into the infinite depths of that other world with great sweetness. His whole mind as a result is lifted up and caught up in that region where he sojourns. In that time his thoughts of earthly cares recede into

18. Ibid., 27:3, 175.

oblivion because now his thoughts are filled and held captivated by divine and heavenly things, by the infinite and incomprehensible, by wonderful things that escape human expressions, so that for that one hour he ardently desires and says: "Would that my soul might pass over with my prayer."[19]

Even while engaged with the daily work and concerns, the spiritual person's mind enters heaven and dwells there. Even for the one hour of prayer, while the outward person remains engaged in labor, the interior person persists in prayer and meditation. The divine has seized and captured the mind of the seeker to a degree that defies logic and understanding and remains mysterious, ineffable, and spectacular.

Macarius further metaphorizes this spiritual state as an imprinting of the divine image upon the soul, which gives the soul value and function. Again Macarius contrasts the natural person, the one described in this analogy as a corpse, and the supernatural person, described here as a golden coin bearing the divine image:

Just as in the case of the golden coin, if it does not receive the imprint of the king's image, it does not reach the marketplace nor is it stored up in the royal treasuries, but it is discarded, so also the soul, if it does not have the image of the heavenly Spirit in the ineffable light, namely, Christ, stamped on it, it is not useful for the treasuries above and is cast out by the merchants of the kingdom, the Apostles. For also he who was invited and yet did not wear the wedding garment was cast out as a stranger into the alien darkness for not wearing the heavenly image. This is the mark and sign of the Lord stamped upon souls, being the Spirit of the ineffable light. And as a cadaver is useless and completely of no good to those of a given place, and so they carry it outside the city and bury it, so also the soul which does not bear the heavenly image of the divine light, the life of the soul, is rejected and completely cast off. For a dead soul is of no profit to that city of the saints, since it does not bear the radiant and divine Spirit. For just as in the world the soul is the life of the body, so also in the eternal and heavenly world the life of the soul is the Spirit of the Godhead.[20]

Macarius contrasts the dead corpse of the natural person who does not relate to God to the truly living and spiritual person upon whom the Spirit

19. Ibid., 8:1, 81.
20. Ibid., 30:5, 191–92.

has imprinted the divine image. The two contrasted subjectivities could not be more clearly defined or contrasted—one fully alive and supernatural, the other dead and natural. The election to the divine status, the election to receive the divine imprint, distinguishes the two subjectivities.

For Macarius spiritual marriage results from human longing and effort. Unlike Tanquerey's theorizing, Macarius's distinction between the two subjectivities does not relate to acquired or infused contemplation, but to the effort of the will to respond to a deeply implanted desire for God. By responding to their own desire for God, ascetics "daily perceive in themselves that they are spiritually progressing toward their spiritual Bridegroom."[21] Through ascetical effort, those who yearn begin to live in the supernatural state that enables them to experience the mysteries and revelations of the Beloved:

> Having been wounded by the desire for Heaven and thirsting for the justice of virtues, they await the illumination of the Spirit with the greatest insatiable longing. And should they be considered worthy to receive through their faith knowledge of divine mysteries or to be made participators of the happiness of heavenly grace, they still do not put their trust in themselves, regarding themselves as somebody. But the more they are considered worthy to receive spiritual gifts, the more diligently do they seek them with an insatiable desire. The more they perceive themselves advancing in spiritual perfection, the more do they hunger and thirst for a greater share of and increase in grace.[22]

Macarius assumes a curious mixture of human effort and divine grace. The ascetic experiences the longing for union implicit in ascetical activity, but then passively awaits illumination. The ascetic's efforts prepare the way by making the ascetic worthy of divine grace, yet they cannot effect the sanctification itself apart from the divine initiative. The mere fact of ascetic effort creates the desire for spiritual gifts and the longing for greater and greater degrees of sanctification. This combination of intense activity to prepare for the bestowing of divine grace is what makes the process curious: sanctification is simultaneously actively pursued and passively achieved.

21. Ibid., 10:1, 88.
22. Ibid.

Nevertheless, sanctification demands serious effort. The transformation of the self from the dead corpse to the living, spiritual person comes only with significant toil and dedication over a long period of time:

> For one to reach this level is not a matter of a single act guaranteeing immediate results nor is it attained without testing. But through labors and many trials, through a long period of time and much striving, with testing and various temptations such a person receives spiritual growth and increase, reaching even to the perfect level of freedom from passions so that, courageously and with great effort enduring every temptation with which it is attacked by evil forces, he attains the greatest honors and spiritual gifts and heavenly riches.[23]

The ascetic expends significant labor in order to achieve sanctification and to be worthy of spiritual marriage, which comes not gratuitously to a few, but which anyone willing to struggle may achieve.

The yearning spurs on greater and greater effort in order to attain to the mystery known in perfection. The ascetic's efforts lead to sanctification, communion, union, spiritual marriage with the heavenly Bridegroom:

> But daily he perseveres in prayer with a hungering and a thirst in faith and love. He has an insatiable desire for the mysteries of grace and for every virtue. He is wounded with love for the heavenly Spirit, having a burning desire for the heavenly Bridegroom through grace which he always possesses within himself. This stirs him to desire perfectly to be regarded as worthy to enter into the mystical and awesome communion with him in the sanctification of the Spirit.[24]

The combination of yearning and effort, on the one hand, and communion and mystic knowledge on the other, defines the spiritual marriage, the state of sanctified union of soul with Christ that characterizes the spiritual marriage. Macarius explains how this union occurs:

> The face of the soul is unveiled and it gazes with fixed eyes upon the heavenly Bridegroom, face to face, in a spiritual and ineffable light. Such a person mingles with him with full certitude of faith, becoming conformed to his death. He always hopes with the

23. Ibid., 10:5, 90.
24. Ibid., 10:4, 89.

greatest desire to yearn to die for Christ. He certainly and completely believes that he will obtain liberation from his sins and
dark passions through the Spirit, so that, purified by the Spirit in
soul and body, he may become a pure vessel to receive the heavenly unction and become a worthy habitation for the heavenly
and true King, Christ. And then such a person is considered worthy of heavenly life, having become a pure dwelling place for the
Holy Spirit.[25]

The union becomes complete as the sanctified person, the bride, transforms the self from mere body and drudgery into a pure instrument of
the Spirit capable of uniting with the divine Bridegroom in mystic communion. The union advances through the process of gradual sanctification effected through the ascetic's labor.

Repeatedly, however, Macarius describes the process of election to
spiritual marriage as initiated by God. The ascetic's efforts respond to a
divine initiative:

Take the example of a certain, very wealthy man, a noble king.
He sets his eyes on a poor woman who possesses nothing other
than her own being. He falls in love with her and wishes to take
her as his spouse and wife. If she bestows on him all kindness and
continues to show love for him, behold, that poor and indigent
woman, who possessed nothing, now becomes the lady of the
house of all the possessions of her husband.[26]

Macarius completes the analogy:

So also a person whom Christ, the heavenly Spouse, has asked
to be his bride in a mystical and divine fellowship. Such a one
has tasted the heavenly riches and ought with great diligence to
strive sincerely to please the Bridegroom, Christ. This person
ought faithfully to fulfill the service entrusted by the Spirit so as
to please God in all things and never to grieve the Spirit in any
matter.[27]

Spiritual marriage thus suggests a mutuality of work—the Bridegroom selects and loves a spouse far beneath him in stature and perfection, while the bride strives more and more to rise to the position

25. Ibid., 89–90.
26. Ibid., 15:1, 108.
27. Ibid., 15:2, 108.

granted by the Bridegroom and to manifest the divine status bestowed both through the bride's own effort and through the work of the Spirit in perfection.

The mutuality of relationship between Bridegroom and bride bestows upon the bride all the possessions of the bridegroom: "In the things around us, everything that belongs to the spouse belongs to the bride as well. So also everything that belongs to the Lord, no matter how much it is, he entrusts to you."[28] Conjugal union founds this mutuality of relationship. Macarius relates that:

> Those who have been deemed worthy . . . to be reborn by the Holy Spirit from above, and who have within themselves Christ, illuminating and bringing them rest. . . . are like a spouse who enjoys conjugal union with her bridegroom in divine resting.[29]

And in order to be sure the nature of this spiritual conjugal union invokes the most vivid of carnal union, Macarius explains the union in this way:

> Those things spoken of here concerning the workings of the Spirit belong to the level of those who are not far from perfection. Those various manifestations of grace that we spoke of, even though they are expressed differently, still they act on such persons in a progression, one operation following another. Finally, when a person reaches the perfection of the Spirit, then it becomes all light, all eye, all spirit, all joy, all repose, all happiness, all love, all compassion, all goodness and kindness. As in the bottom of the sea, a stone is everywhere surrounded by water, so such persons as these are totally penetrated by the Holy Spirit. They become like to Christ, putting on the virtues of the power of the Spirit with a constancy. They interiorly become faultless and spotless and pure.[30]

The language of penetration, together with the ecstatic description of the relationship confirm the intimacy and immediacy of the union, while at the same time describing the way that the two become one, bestowing the gifts and graces of the bridegroom upon the bride. In explaining the yearning of Mary, versus the work of her sister Martha (Lk 10:42), Macarius writes:

28. Ibid., 16:13, 135.
29. Ibid., 18:7, 144.
30. Ibid., 18:10, 145.

> Oh, the intensity of the love of the Lord's Spirit that moves power-
> fully toward the spotless Bridegroom! Oh, what a concentration
> of desire in the soul toward God the Word! Oh, what intimate
> communion of the bride with the heavenly Bridegroom! Imitate
> her, O child, imitate her . . . .[31]

Macarius portrays the spiritual marriage as complete union and as intense longing and desire. Macarius develops every aspect of the metaphor of spiritual marriage, including the physical conjugal acts of desire
and coitus.

One passage in particular summarizes all the arguments made about
spiritual marriage in the Macarian sermons:

> For God desired to have fellowship with the human soul and es-
> poused it to himself as the spouse of the King and he purified it
> from sordidness. Washing it, he makes it bright from its black-
> ness and its shame and gives life to it from its condition of death,
> and he heals it of its brokenness and brings it peace, reconciling
> its enmity. For even though it is a creature, it has been espoused
> as bride to the Son of the King. And by his very own power God
> receives the soul, little by little changing it until he has increased
> it with his own increase, for he stretches the soul and leads it to
> an infinite and unmeasurable increase, until it becomes the bride,
> spotless and worthy of him. First he begets the soul in himself and
> increases it through himself, until it reaches the perfect measure
> of his love. For he, being a perfect Bridegroom, takes it as a perfect
> spouse into the holy and mystical and unblemished union of mar-
> riage. And then it reigns with him unto endless ages. Amen.[32]

Spiritual marriage begins in the divine bridegroom's love for the human
soul, which the bridegroom nurtures and reforms until it is perfect. As
the bride becomes more perfect, partly through her own effort and partly
through the gracious work of the bridegroom, she unites more and more
to her bridegroom and begins to reflect the bridegroom's own love and
devotion more perfectly. In the end the bride will reign as a perfect mate
to the divine bridegroom.

31. Ibid., 25:8–9, 163.
32. Ibid., 47:17, 238.

Conclusions

Tanquerey and Macarius as representatives of the ascetical tradition describe sacred marriage as the apex and culmination of the religious life. They construct an elite subjectivity marked by complete union with the divine. Both stipulate that, although the ascetic constructs that subjectivity over a long period of time and through rigorous ascetical performances, the divinity enacts the union itself gratuitously.

The way each describes that sacred marriage differs, however. The Western concept emphasizes the passivity of the ascetic to mystic union, the infused state of contemplation of and knowledge of God, the intuitive as opposed to the discursive knowledge of the truth, and the permanence and stability of the state of union characterized by spiritual marriage. The Western view clearly articulates an ontological difference between the subjectivity oriented toward discourse and that subject to infused knowledge and intuitive perception.

The Eastern ascetical tradition prefers to speak in terms of natural and supernatural subjectivities. The natural subjectivity must work to transform the self into a supernatural one. The supernatural person passively receives spiritual graces toward which the ascetic's effort has been aiming. The supernatural person receives an imprint of the divinity that marks them as permanently transformed and regenerated by spiritual marriage. The Eastern tradition, in marked contrast to the Western, affirms the ability to achieve union through ascetic effort that creates both longing and desire for union. Such longing and desire results in a complete union, a communion and mystical knowledge of God in which God penetrates the very being of the ascetic to effect union.

The descriptions of spiritual marriage differ in both ascetical systems, but they overlap and agree on the essentials. Spiritual marriage articulates the culmination and apex of the ascetical life. It signifies a new subjectivity, one now marked by its intense identification and absorption into the divine.

I used these two exemplary figures as a means to test my hypothesis about the ascetical dimension to sacred marriage. Fortunately my hypothesis is not without precedent. In 1979 Richard Horsley wrote an article that grasped the deep connection between the *hieros gamos* and asceticism.[33] His article examined the role of Sophia, the Wisdom of God, in an

33. Horsley, "Spiritual Marriage."

ascetical relationship that enjoined celibacy for the ascetic. The exclusive intimacy between Sophia, or the goddess Isis among others, properly required complete fidelity and absolute faithfulness to the divine spouse. Horsley captured the essence and spirit of both Tanquerey and Macarius in their different understandings of the ascetical dimension of spiritual marriage. Horsley's article stopped at the question of celibacy and completely overlooked the ascetical performances necessary to achieve or to receive that union.

But even so Horsley was writing against the grain. For many years in the history of religions the study of the union or marriage of a human with a divinity revolved about the issue of the relationship of physical coitus to spiritual union. Richard Reitzenstein's *Hellenistic Mystery-Religions* set the parameters for such a discussion when he explained such love-unions as rooted in the Egyptian cultic practice for begetting the Pharaoh from a divinity, which in turn metonymically referred to the initiative action that gave birth to the divinity within the person. Reitzenstein located the *hieros gamos* in the initiatory practice of mystery religions.[34] And that is where the conversation remained for many years.

In more recent years, this mystery-religions orientation became most evident in the discussion of the nuptial chamber sacrament of *The Gospel of Philip*. Scholars debated the relationship of conjugal coitus with spiritual union and regeneration in the sacramental theology of the *Gospel*. Some argued for physical marriage as a prerequisite to the spiritual marriage in the bridal chamber sacrament;[35] others argued that the nuptial chamber referred to an eschatological regeneration;[36] still others argued for the complete rejection of marital and physical coitus in favor of spiritual union and marriage.[37] All argued that the nuptial chamber constituted an initiatory rite into a mystery religion.[38]

34. Reitzenstein, *Hellenistic Mystery-Religions*, 310–19.

35. Buckley, "Cult-mystery in the *Gospel of Philip*," 569–81.

36. Grant, "Mystery of Marriage," 129–40. Grant argued that the nuptial chamber anticipated the eschatological union. He also argued that marriage constituted an archetype of salvation in this sacramental system. He maintained that the *Gospel* perhaps confused physical and spiritual union.

37. Segelberg, "The Coptic-Gnostic Gospel," 189–200.

38. For a brief overview of the state of the question as it regards 1 Corinthians 7, see Peters, "Spiritual Marriage." For a listing and study of *hieros gamos* in earlier Greek literature see Klinz, *Hieros Gamos*.

Given my examination of Tanquerey and Macarius, this history-of-religions framing of the context and meaning of spiritual marriage as initiation into a mystery religion seems misleading. In the Western Christian tradition, spiritual marriage with the divine constitutes a spiritual regeneration that follows upon strenuous, vigorous, and intentional ascetic activity over a long period of time. Spiritual marriage does indeed initiate a person into the sacred mysteries of the divine, not as an isolated and inaugural event, but as the culmination of a lifetime of ascetical effort. Spiritual marriage initiates a union that culminates, rather than inaugurates, an ascetical agenda of self-transformation that constructs an identity, a subjectivity, capable of being united to God in order to experience mystic union, intuitive knowledge, and a new identity stamped with the divine image. The ascetical dimension to the *hieros gamos* gives meaning and substance to an otherwise easily misunderstood and misrepresented metaphor for the complete transformation of the ascetic, the inauguration of a new subjectivity completely oriented toward and united with the divine.

CHAPTER 4

Asceticism or Formation

Theorizing Asceticism after Nietzsche

THE WORD "ASCETICISM" IS NOT A COMMON PART OF POPULAR OR SCHOL-
arly discourse.[1] It conjures for many the ancient and medieval practices
intended to mortify the body. Mortification, or the punishment of the
body, might require lice-infested hair shirts worn in secret next to the
body, or intense fasting and the rejection of the pleasures of food and
drink, or abstinence from sexual pleasure and the rejection of marriage
with its attendant sexual engagement, or the rejection of society and the
pleasures of normal social relations in favor of dark caves and isolated
monasteries in some remote site in Egypt or Syria. These practices are
indeed ascetical, but when viewed as isolated practices they tell only part
of the story.

In order to get to the heart of an ascetical discipline, one must ask
questions about the intent or the purpose or the goal of a practice. To
what end does an ascetic wear a hair shirt? What kind of body does fasting fashion? What kind of intimacy does chastity construct? What kind

1. I owe my academic interest in asceticism to Margaret Miles. Her lectures on the
history of Christian thought at Harvard always attended to asceticism and the body, and
as a clergyperson just taking courses, I was hooked. Margaret Miles opened to me a
world of study—gender, critical theory, historical theology, the arts—that transformed
for me the study of asceticism from the arid religious practices of the past into living traditions that challenged and enhanced living. The publication of her book on asceticism,
Fullness of Life: Historical Foundations for a New Asceticism, not only put asceticism on
the academic agenda, it launched me into ascetical studies for my entire academic career.
Margaret Miles has moved on to other studies and issues, but I have stayed the ascetical
course. It is an honor to dedicate this latest incursion into historical and cultural perspectives on asceticism to the woman whose presence and writing inspired it.

of society is created by withdrawal from normal social relationships? The ascetic practices always connect to some larger purpose, to a wider conception of human existence or human potential, to a different understanding of society and world. The goal of the practice relates to creating this different person, whose life (at least in the common understanding of asceticism) depends on discomfort, renunciation, and withdrawal to create a more holy or more perfect person. This chapter explores the wider context for ascetical theorizing by distinguishing formation from asceticism as a basis for developing an alternative genealogy for the study of asceticism in the postmodern world. The distinction between formation and asceticism, as well as the new genealogy for the current interest in ascetical studies, both depend upon the development of a subjectivity in a specific context.

Both formation and asceticism posit the construction and reconstruction of the subject: formation constructs a subject for the dominant society or culture, while asceticism constructs one for an alternative and subversive society or culture. Let me begin with the ascetic. The ascetic performs the emerging subversive subjectivity in specific practices. When a person decides to wear a lice-infested hair shirt next to the body, that person chooses to redefine the self. There is some intimation that the person not wearing the hair shirt is less desirable, or less acceptable, or (in more theological language) less holy than the person who chooses to wear the hair shirt. The decision to engage in the ascetical activity immediately posits two identities, two different ways of articulating a subjectivity: the first identity, the received subjectivity that does not require a hair shirt, is a given in the society in which the person lives; the second person, an emergent subjectivity, imagines that through the wearing of a hair shirt a different person will emerge, a person significantly more improved than the received identity of the majority of people among whom the ascetic lives. Ascetical practice relates to the process of defining a new person in opposition to a received and normative subjectivity promulgated in any social and cultural context. Formation relates to the process of developing a subjectivity capable of functioning within the dominant society. The presence of two subjectivities, one given in a society and one contrary to the given, points to two different systems toward which a subjectivity orients itself. The practices constitutive of the dominant subjectivity

I term formation, those of the subversive or alternative society, I term asceticism.[2]

The early part of the twenty-first century eagerly engaged the important question of alternative subjectivities. The creation of an alternative identity in a wider culture perceived as being at odds with the dominant society became a hallmark of the times. The evidence for the pervasiveness of the ascetical context of the twentieth century may be amassed simply by listing some of the important movements whose aims were to construct alternative identities within the dominant culture: Black power, the feminist movement, gay activism, libertarian communities, right-wing Christian separatists, religious and political communes, the ecology movement, and the many ethnic movements that promulgate the development of a counter-cultural Chicano/a, Asian, Pacific Rim, or Native American identity in the United States. And there are many others. Each of these groups or movements find themselves caught between the two subjectivities—one received from the wider cultural context and one developed in opposition to that dominant subjectivity in order to articulate or define an alternative way of living.

The twenty-first century, bathed as it is in the blood of the clashing of various subjectivities, must address the questions of the relationship of conflicting conceptualizations and enactments of the self. Pluralism, which is the ability of many diverse people to live together harmoniously, depends upon the capacity for diverse people to create and sustain identities at variance with each other, but also identities who can live together. Religious pluralism demands that various religious identities cohere in a social and political environment without either losing the distinctiveness of their own identity or creating some identity that belongs to no one person in particular. Asceticism, which I present here as the practices that create these alternative identities, stands at the heart of pluralist religious, social, and political life.

The postmodern context, however, needs to recognize the difference between training for the dominant society and training in subversive identities. Asceticism, the creation of an alternative identity, must be distinguished from formation, the creation of an identity equipped to function in the dominant society. That is the first step. Then, based on that

2. For a more complete explanation of my theory of asceticism see "Constructions of Power in Asceticism," chapter 2, pp. 14–59.

distinction, I propose a new genealogy for the postmodern attention to asceticism that picks up other strands of the twentieth- and twenty-first-century phenomena based upon the construction of alternative subjectivities. That genealogy begins with two literary figures (Kazantzakis and Genet) and ends with two religious movements (the Branch Davidians and the human bombs of September 11).

FORMATION OR ASCETICISM

The following incident describes a formative process. On the eve of July 1 in Greece, the beginning of the feast of the dual saints of healing, Cosmas and Damian, who are called the "Holy No-Silver Ones" (ὁι ἅγιοι αναάργυροι)—because, according to the popular legend, they never asked for payment as did the secular healers of their day—the Greek Orthodox community on the island of Paros in the Kyklades gathers for a festival evening, at a remote and no-longer inhabited monastery perched high above the village on a mountain top. The festival begins with vespers followed by a community supper and concludes the next morning at sunrise with the celebration of the Eucharist. The little chapel, normally dark and deserted (although always well-kept and clean) is decorated for the occasion: the icons on the walls are garlanded as they were in pre-Christian antiquity with red and white carnations; embroidered and crocheted white cloths are hung below each large icon to cover the old wood of the icon screen; the brass hanging lamps are cleaned of their year's accumulation of olive oil; the candlestands are cleaned and prepared to receive the beeswax candles of the hundreds of pilgrims who will come for the celebration. At vespers, the tiny chapel is packed with worshippers. Hundreds of candles illumine the space and make seeing in the otherwise dark chapel possible. On a small table in the middle of the cramped space stand five enormous loaves of bread (at least two feet in diameter) that will be blessed during vespers and distributed to the assembly after the service. The vesper service itself begins about 9:30 p.m. (although it is announced for about 8:00 p.m.), and it continues until just about midnight.

Unless one has some understanding of Orthodox religious ethos, this event would remain troublesome, boring, long, and without any apparent logic. Once the participant learns some of the traditions associated with the festival, however, the celebration becomes clearer. Those traditions include the inauguration of a two-day festival with vespers on the eve of the saints' day, the blessing of loaves at the vespers as part of the commemoration of the biblical feeding (of the Israelites in the desert and of the five thousand by Jesus) and as an act of communal thanksgiving to God for sustenance and blessing, and the commonly known fact that Greeks normally do not even think about eating their dinner until about midnight. Supplied with this information, the outsider then begins to understand the festival: it coheres and displays the community's corporate sense of religious identity. Festivals are carefully planned and orchestrated events celebrating the spirituality of the community.

Various systems of formation exist for a group to communicate the systems necessary to understand and participate in its corporate life. The Parian islanders, reared in an environment of festival celebrations, learn these systems from their earliest youth through their lifelong participation. Knowing something of the religious environment from Greek Orthodox practice in the United States where I was born, I could quickly pick up the particularities and nuances peculiar to the customs practiced in Greece more generally, to Paros more specifically, and to this specific festival on the feast of the dual saints Cosmas and Damian more concretely. A tourist unfamiliar with Greek culture would probably neither know about the festival (the tourist would need to be familiar not only with the Greek Orthodox kalendar of saints, but also with the names of local shrines and monasteries on the island), nor would the tourist understand the various elements of the customary festival of a feast day (the festival would look like a late-night picnic delayed by a church service).

To those who have knowledge either as an insider or even as an outsider, the practices and traditions of the community bear witness that various systems of formation do indeed exist. A person must undergo a process of formation in order to understand and to participate in a cultural event. Those processes of formation are not always self-evident. Michel Foucault (1926–1984), more than any other theorist of the postmodern era, has explored and documented the formational systems, both visible and submerged, that enable members of a society to be constituted as a subject of that society. But what Foucault describes as "asceticism" is perhaps best called "formation." Foucault's study of the "care of the self" in the Greco-Roman period explored the means by which predominantly entitled male members of a society cultivated themselves in order to develop for themselves a mode of being consistent with the societal norms in which they lived. Foucault's concept of the care of the self "is what one might call an ascetical practice, giving the word 'ascetical' a very general meaning, that is to say, not in the sense of abnegation but that of an exercise of self upon self by which one tries to work out, to transform one's self and to attain a certain mode of being."[3] What Foucault here calls asceticism ought more properly to be called cultural or social formation. The systems engaged in the care for the self are systems that enabled the entitled males of the Greek and Roman period to form themselves as significant parts of the dominant society by acquiring "the knowledge of a certain number of rules of conduct or of principles which are at the same time truths and regulations. To care for self is to fit one's self out with these truths."[4]

The social formation that motivated these Romans revolved about the development of a socially acceptable *ethos*. Foucault defines that ethos as "the deportment and the way to behave. It was the subject's mode of being and a certain manner of acting visible to others." This ethos, Foucault argued, is directly related to the dominant social world in that "*Ethos* implies also a relation with others to the extent that care for self renders one competent to occupy a place in the city, in the community or in inter-individual relationships which are proper—whether it be to exercise a magistracy or to have friendly relationships."[5] In Foucault's thought, the care of the self aligns the person with a role and function in the dominant society. The wider context for the construction of an identity holds great importance: it is one thing to be trained to become part of the dominant culture and entirely a different thing to construct an identity to subvert that culture. Since some practices orient the person toward the society and other practices orient a person against that dominant society, the distinction between formation and asceticism becomes essential. The distinction here is between exercises and practices intended to integrate a person into the dominant society (formation) and exercises and practices intended to create a subjectivity alternative and subversive to the dominant structure (asceticism). Foucault develops a theory of formation. This chapter explores the basis for a theory of asceticism.

3. Foucault, "Ethic of Care for the Self," 2.
4. Ibid., 5.
5. Ibid., 6.

The distinction between formation and asceticism is one that, curiously enough, an important and influential source for Foucault articulated. Friedrich Nietzsche (1844–1900), beginning his third "Untimely Meditation" entitled *Schopenhauer as Educator*[6] with a similar excursion into a tourist's visit to a different land, articulates a distinction between the lazy person who accepts his socialization into the common mass culture and the liberated person who strikes out free from the constraints of custom to construct his own identity. Nietzsche characterizes the lazy person as one who acts "(f)rom fear of his neighbor, who demands conventionality and cloaks himself with it" and who is constrained "to think and to act like a member of a herd" with "indolence, inertia, in short that tendency to laziness." This lazy person remains "fettered by the chains of fear and convention." In contrast to this person is the "youthful soul" who understands the conventionality as far distant from its true self because "its liberation gives it a presentiment of the measure of happiness allotted it from all eternity." This liberated person "knows quite well that, being unique, he will be in the world only once and that no imaginable chance will for a second time gather together into a unity so strangely variegated an assortment as he is."[7] This youthful person constructs the way proper only to the individual—singular, unique, unfettered, and far distant from the person society constructs for itself; Nietzsche instructs this youthful soul:

> Let the youthful soul look back on the life with the question: what have you truly loved up to now, what has drawn your soul aloft, what has mastered it and at the same time blessed it? Set up these revered objects before you and perhaps their nature and their sequence will give you a law, the fundamental law of your own true self. Compare these objects one with another, see how one completes, expands, surpasses, transfigures another, how they constitute a stepladder upon which you have clambered up to yourself as you are now; for your true nature lies, not concealed deep within you, but immeasurably high above you, or at least above that which you usually take yourself to be.[8]

Nietzsche draws a stark contrast between the person formed by the dominant social paradigm for the mass culture, the person whose primary

6. Nietzsche, "Untimely Meditations," 125–94.
7. Ibid., 127.
8. Ibid., 129.

identity is provided by the social convention of the day and the other person who actively subverts that conventional formation to develop a self that actualizes the unique qualities and interests and gifts of an identity no longer constrained by convention or society. Nietzsche has framed an issue central to twentieth- and twenty-first-century people: the differentiation between formation and asceticism. Nietzsche's lazy person's training properly should be termed formation and his "youthful soul's" alternative, asceticism.

The differentiation of formation and asceticism is crucial for understanding the construction of both ancient and postmodern identities. Formation orients itself toward dominance; asceticism orients itself to alterity and subversion. Formation, the primary means whereby a person becomes a functioning member of a dominant group or society includes such systems as etiquette, social propriety, participation in ceremonial events and activities, as well as other customary practices. Members of a group are socialized, integrated, taught various appropriate behaviors and modes of thinking, and molded into a person capable of seamlessly participating in the life of the group. These groups may be of a wide variety including political, recreational, religious, educational, and civic, among many others.

A Genealogy of Ascetical Studies

If one does not include Foucault among the ascetical theorists of the twentieth century, then how did asceticism come to the fore of academic and public life? Four particular phenomena in the twentieth century, two literary and two political, seems to have thrust asceticism into modern and postmodern life. The first phenomenon is the ascetical exercises of Nikos Kazantzakis (1883–1957), who in 1922–23 created the first post-Eastern-Christian, secular ascetical theology. Kazantzakis, writing during a period of clashing cultures, political structures, and intellectual foment, promulgated an ascetical discipline intended to create a new and different understanding of modern identity precisely to address the problems of modern existence.

The second phenomenon of my genealogy revolves about the novels and plays of Jean Genet (1910–86), who translated Western ascetical practice into gay life, and from gay life, it found its way into French critical theory, including the work of Roland Barthes (1915–80) and Foucault.

Genet connected his efforts at defining a new identity to the Black Power movement in the United States, the gay activist movements in Europe, and the Palestinian effort to maintain a subversive identity in the context of the creation of the State of Israel. Genet's literary identities provided the context for the exploration of ascetical identity in the midst of seriously conflicted modern identities.

The third event of my genealogy is more recent: the Branch Davidians in Waco, Texas. The Branch Davidians brought alternative religious identity to the fore of American attention. Their religious alterity, linked with their libertarian political views and their apocalyptic religious beliefs and practices, at once condemned normative American values and practices and showed that some Americans were willing to risk everything to live by a different set of rules. Their alternative subjectivity ultimately resulted in their willingness to train themselves to become "all fire," a tradition with ancient roots among the Egyptian desert monks.[9]

The fourth event in my genealogy is even more recent, the Muslim "martyr heroes" who were trained to turn themselves and their fellow passengers into human bombs in the terrorist attack on the United States on September 11, 2001. These human bombs, when they practiced the identity for which they had so carefully been trained, became an effective display of the extent to which alternative religious and political practices contend with dominant subjectivities in order to assert their differences. Kazantzakis and Genet, though literary leaders of their generation, have been intellectually marginalized, especially as regards their ascetic teaching, but the Branch Davidians and the September 11 terrorists have captivated global attention in an unprecedented way. I contend that just as these four events forced me to think carefully about asceticism, so also these four elements conspire to force Western people to understand asceticism.

Nikos Kazantzakis

In the latter part of the twentieth century, the Western world came to know Nikos Kazantzakis primarily through the cinematic renditions of two of his most influential novels, *The Last Temptation of Christ*, which presented a view of Christ's own emergence as a Savior often against

9. See the story of Abba Lot and Abba Joseph in "Constructions of Power," chapter 2, p. 14.

his own will, and *Zorba the Greek*, which dramatized the character that became quintessentially "the Greek man" struggling against an interior and exterior Fate. The dramatic characterizations of Jesus, Paul, Mary Magdalene, Zorba, and the many other characters, both major and minor, in these novels and films attracted the attention of artistic leaders and the imagination of the general public.

Kazantzakis based his characterization on a specific theory of asceticism that he had developed early in his career. In 1922–23 Kazantzakis produced the first post-Christian ascetical theology in his book entitled *ΑΣΚΗΤΙΚΗ: Salvatores Dei*, which has been translated into English as *The Saviors of God: Spiritual Exercises*.[10] His ascetical work became a centerpiece, perhaps more appropriately a manifesto, for his philosophical, theological, political, and literary productions because each of his subsequent works presents various aspects of the theories and practices advocated in his ascetical theology. Kazantzakis considered his ascetical theology central to his intellectual, political, literary, and spiritual projects, but it has remained largely unknown.

Significantly, Kazantzakis wrote a post-Christian ascetical theology. Being nurtured in a highly ascetical religious environment of the Greek Orthodox Church in Crete, and having spent formative time living among the ascetics of Mount Athos, Kazantzakis nonetheless rejected Christianity as the primary conduit of ascetical behavior. For Kazantzakis asceticism provided the means to transubstantiate the flesh, to transform materiality into spirit.[11] His post-Christian ascetical theology moved to-

10. The Greek edition is *ΑΣΚΗΤΙΚΗ: Salvatores Dei*; the English translation, *The Saviors of God: Spiritual Exercises*. When he wrote the book in 1922–23, Kazantzakis originally entitled the work with the Latin "*Salvatores Dei*" followed by the Greek feminine adjective form of the adjective "ascetical." When he revised the book, however, he inverted the Latin and Greek titles. The use of the adjectival form implies that it is intended to be either "the ascetical theology" or "the ascetical book," as both "theology" and "book" are feminine in Greek.

11. Bien, *Kazantzakis*, 34–38. Bien argues that this concept was one taken from the work of Henri Bergson with whom Kazantzakis studied in Paris. The very mystical concept, according to Bien, resonated with Kazantzakis's own intellectual formulations. To my mind, the concept agrees to a great extent with the long tradition of transformation of self evident in the Greek ascetical tradition. Bergson provided the Western conceptual frame, but Orthodoxy provided the substance for the concept. The word "transubstantiation," however, is the Western Christian term for the transformation of the elements of the Eucharist (bread and wine) into the Body of Christ (body and blood) through the prayers of the priest at the Eucharist. Eastern Christian eucharistic theology places more stress on the invocation of the Holy Spirit over the gifts, which is commonly called

ward the founding of a new religious perspective resonant with all the currents of the period between the World Wars by combining in various ways Marxism, Communist theory and practice, radical Greek identity, the philosophy of Nietzsche, the teaching of Bergson, and readings in Buddhism. It was written as a post-Christian response to the rise of nationalism, the fall of the Ottoman Empire (and the consequent creation of modern Turkey), the spread of Communism in Eastern Europe, and the modern critical intellectual climate of Germany and France. Kazantzakis understood that the new world order, and the new ways of thinking about personality, society, and politics, required a different understanding of subjectivity. According to Kazantzakis, the world could not survive without a drastic reordering of the role and significance of individual effort in order to advance the human state to the next level of its evolution. His ascetical theology provided a scheme for this reordering of self, society, and the symbolic universe. His vision was prophetic for the beginning of the twenty-first century.

The center of Kazantzakis's ascetical agenda revolves about the "super-human struggle" (ο υπερανθρωπινός αγώνα).[12] Based on an understanding of the evolution of material culture toward some spiritual end, Kazantzakis understood human endeavor as the propelling agent that could force evolution to its next logical step. His ascetical program included five states: preparation (η προετοιμασιά); the walk along the road, or the march (η πορεία); the vision (το όραμα); practice (η πράχη); and silence (η σιγή). Further elaboration of his ascetical system need not detain us here.[13] What is important is that Kazantzakis developed and articulated a full ascetical system as a response to the significant changes in the society around him. That ascetical system recognized the important role of the transformation of an individual subjectivity as the means whereby further social and political development could occur.

Kazantzakis lived at the perimeter, on the boundary (this is an important image for him taken from the Byzantine figure Digenes Akritis) of many worlds: Eastern and Western philosophy, Ottoman and modern political structures, Eastern Christianity and Western, agricultural life and

---

"consubstantiation." Kazantzakis blends Eastern and Western traditions in his emphasis on the transubstantiation of flesh into spirit.

12. Kazantzakis, *Saviors of God*, 55; Greek text, 19.

13. For a full description and analysis of Kazantzakis's system, see Bien, *Kazantzakis*, 67–78.

industrial society, among many others. It is precisely this sense of being neither one nor the other that led him to articulate an ascetical theology. His goal was to provide a conceptual frame for people, including himself, to move forward amidst remarkably divergent systems of power and in the midst of dramatic social and political changes. The old structures that nurtured him in the West, in his youth, no longer could sustain themselves. Some new way of living, of being an agent in the world, of forming social alliances and families, and of conceptualizing the meaning and significance of the cosmos was necessary. For Kazantzakis, these new things begin and end in human transformation, in the creation of a subjectivity capable of carrying self, society, and world to a new level of spiritual and political awareness. Kazantzakis's instinct toward asceticism, probably arising in his border experience as an Eastern Orthodox-trained intellect engaged in Western philosophy, put the question of formation on the modern agenda. Although we know his asceticism primarily through the characters he developed to dramatize his ascetical theory, we have nonetheless been invited into an ascetical world that has held our fascination.

Jean Genet

In contrast to Kazantzakis's move toward a post-Christian ascetical theological system, Jean Genet took up the question of the construction of a new subjectivity in literature that invoked Catholic Christianity. Genet opened new possibilities for experiencing new subjectivities by taking the reader into the minds and experiences of characters (often with autobiographical referents) who display their ability to create new identities out of the often harmful elements of their true lives.

Genet's own ascetical formation has two formative loci.[14] First, he was raised as a foundling placed into a foster family in rural village of Alligny-en-Morvan. Rural life for the Regnier family revolved about the local Roman Catholic parish where Genet was a chorister and acolyte and where Genet was baptized, received a Catholic religious education, and received his first communion. This youthful formation in the rituals, practices, festivals, and music of the church resonates throughout Genet's novels. His characters take on religious significance (one queen in *Our Lady of the Flowers*[15] is called "First Communion," while another, "Divine,"

---

14. I base this section on the superb biography by Edmund White, *Genet*.

15. Genet, *Our Lady of the Flowers*.

"rises at cock's crow to go to communion, the Quite-Repentant"); char-acters even observe traditional ascetical disciplines in a completely gay context (the narrator relates: "Now, the fact is that Divine wore next to her skin a clinging hair shirt, unsuspected by Darling and the clients").[16] Genet applies his religious experience and his formative ascetical prac-tices to the life of his gay characters.

The second locus of Genet's own ascetical formation took place at Mettray, an agricultural reformatory for young offenders of the law. Mettray's program of reformation revolved about the rigorous monas-tic-style regimen of hard work, enforced religious training, and harsh discipline for those breaking the rules, in an all-male environment. This ascetical and severely disciplined life fused with the Roman Catholic religious asceticism of his youth to produce a uniquely gay asceticism modeled on ecclesiastical practices but applied in an entirely different context of male homosexuality.

Genet's asceticism revolved about a program to enact a gay identity, or more properly gay identities, in the context of a gay community. His characters act out their gay life, referring to each other in the feminine (a process that is enhanced by the narrator at various points by provid-ing the masculine birth names of his characters when they are brought into court), revealing their inner thoughts and especially their sexual desires, and living out their lives in the context of male homosexual love, prostitution, transvestitism, and society. In the process, Genet creates a gay culture, parallel to the heterosexual dominant society in France, but entirely subversive of it. This gay world that he creates resonates with the vibrancy of a subversive (and often dangerous) counterculture in which male homosexuals dominate and in which the male-female roles of the dominant French culture have been translated into the pimp-queen and into the active and passive members of gay coupling. The world in which these gay characters live does not correlate with the one into which they were born, but one into which they must be initiated by living in the subversive gay community and modeling themselves on the elder queens of the community. They follow a sort of monastic novitiate training to learn the precise practices—how to live as a queen, how to cross-dress, how to create the gestures that at once invoke feminine but bespeak gay

16. Ibid.

signification and context, how to greet one another, how to relate to one's pimp; in short, a complete novitiate training in gay culture and life.

Genet accomplishes his ascetical agenda in his novels and plays by piecing together what Richard Schechner, the performance theorist, calls "malleable bits of experience."[17] In writing Genet's biography, Edmund White repeatedly shows how Genet refracts events or elements of his life in the life, character, gestures, and events of his characters. Genet does not produce simple and plain autobiography because each of the elements seems to be changed, adjusted, refracted and in that process breaks away from the real events of his life into the fictive elements in the construction of a character. Genet creates identity out of malleable bits of experience refracted through past, present, and imaginary time. In so constructing his characters, Genet employs an ascetical modality in a literary endeavor intended to create a gay identity quite distinct from the dominant heterosexual identity assumed in French society. Genet's queens function in the context of a totalizing gay community with its own gay worldview. By employing this ascetical modality Genet transforms the traditional religious ascetical practices of his youth into the exercises, experiences, and metaphors of a completely secularized and subversive gay identity, society, and culture.

It can easily and generally be concluded that the middle of the twentieth century witnessed the emergence of a wide assortment of subversive and alternative identities, social configurations, and conflicting worldviews. I need only point to the sexual revolution of the sixties, the emergence of the feminist movement in the seventies and eighties, and the radicalized (especially in response to the AIDS pandemic) gay activist movement of the nineties. All of these movements tended toward the construction of alternative subjectivities within a dominant society against which they defined themselves, building alternative societies and cultures that would sustain their new identity, and developing divergent understandings of the symbolic universe to support their new identities. They were all in one form or another, ascetical movements. Jean Genet provided a significant starting point in the literary scene for the construction of such alternative subjectivities.

17. Schechner, "Magnitudes of Performance," 363.

The Branch Davidians

Alternative subjectivities in the twentieth century did not remain the province of philosophical, literary, or sexual radicals. Conservative religious groups also began to form intentionally ascetic communities. The Branch Davidians of Waco, Texas, provide an exemplar of such communities. The Branch Davidians move our genealogy out of the intellectual and literary world into the arena of religious politics.

On February 28, 1993, when the agents of the Alcohol, Tobacco, and Firearms division of the Federal Bureau of Investigation began their standoff with the Branch Davidians at their community center at Waco, the United States awakened to the existence of radically conservative Christian ascetical communities within its own borders. The standoff ended on April 19, 1993, when the confrontation erupted into violence and the community buildings of the Branch Davidians burst into flames killing eighty-six people, among whom were seventeen children. The Branch Davidians went nobly and fearlessly to their deaths, with only nine surviving members of the Waco community (excepting those who had been released during the standoff).

In every way, the Branch Davidians were an ascetic community. Their community was formed in opposition to the dominant religious and political culture around them in the United States and throughout the world. They held apocalyptic views of the end-times, metaphorized as a fiery ordeal in the tradition of the biblical book of the Revelation of John, views affirmed by their biblical interpretation and that led them to withdrawal from society to a sacred place apart. Their status as the elect who could rightly perceive and understand God (in contradistinction to all others) supported their living a common life of intense biblical study, common belongings, corporate meals, and mutual support and love. Their community was organized around the messianic self-understanding of their leader, who had adopted the religious name David Koresh. Their common life, focused as it was on David Koresh, organized itself as a religious militia prepared to join God in the destruction of the evil forces of the universe, an army prepared to join in the fiery ordeal that would end the beastly power of the United States and the evil governmental forces of the world. They were prepared to jump into the fiery ordeal in order to assist God in the establishment of a theocratic world government, the reign of God on earth under God's own messiah, David Koresh.

Little is known of the interior workings of this community. There is no evidence of a written rule of life nor a description of their daily life. Most of the surviving evidence revolves about biblical interpretation, the teaching of which became the central corporate act of their communal living as evidenced in the large number of transcribed tapes available from their regular bible study classes. Livingstone Fagan, one of those released from the community during the standoff, has provided a precious insight into the theory of formation operative among the Branch Davidians in an appendix to a larger biblical-interpretative piece entitled, "Intuition—The Emerging Soul."[18] Fagan describes the goal of the process as the ability "to think God's thoughts after Him, the Source of true Judgment." This ability to assimilate and to appropriate God's thinking is tied to the developing of the person, here called the "fledgling soul," that emerges from "intuition—the combined effect of the senses and seed of judgment of the fledgling soul." Intuition, together with the development of "conscience" enables and empowers one to think God's thoughts. Fagan's argument follows in this way:

> By themselves our thoughts are really ethereal labels attached to the feelings (processes and objects) of our senses. True thoughts begin with intuition and, with the aid of conscience, mature into judgments. Such judgments form the basis for true (correct) thinking, producing its corresponding thoughts. At each level—feelings, intuition, judgments, thinking—a new phase of consciousness emerges. In the light of each development, the understanding of the preceding level is completed. Becoming situated in true thinking, the soul is ready for birth.[19]

What Fagan describes here is the development of a totally new person whose soul is birthed through a process of formation. That formation consists of the reformation of thinking or thought according to a system that has been deemed "true," presumably in opposition to the false thoughts completely oriented to the senses or the physical world. The oppositions here are telling: fledgling soul versus mature, sensual versus divine thinking, lower levels of judgment versus higher levels. Intuition guides the person toward the mature, divine, and higher life that produces a new birth, a new person, a new subjectivity capable of thinking

18. Fagan, "Mount Carmel."
19. Ibid.

God's thoughts. In the process of being guided toward that new birth, the conscience of the person develops more fully, creating a new consciousness. This is a process gradually intended completely to reform the subjectivity of the believer.

Fagan emphasizes that the process is a complete program. It cannot be stopped before the complete transformation of the person:

> The importance of conscience in this process cannot be underestimated. It is like the umbilical cord of the developing child in the womb. The fledgling's link [sic] to the soul of the universe from which it is nourished and takes its form. Cut prior to maturity, and the soul fails of coming to birth. It dies and ultimately returns to nothing. As with a soul, so with a nation.[20]

Two issues emerge as central here. The first is that without the formation found in the community of believers, a person cannot thrive. Without the formation available in the community, the fledgling is doomed to death. Wisdom, salvation, health, vitality flow only from the ascetical formation and practices within the community. The second issue, more striking, is the linking of the microcosmic soul's fate with the macrocosmic fate of the nation. This innocuous-seeming comment, almost a simple addendum, indicates that there is a larger and more social component to this formative process. This is not a process intended simply to create spiritually reborn people, it is also a process intended to create a spiritually renewed nation. The ascetical disciplines at the microcosmic level create simultaneously a nation and a culture (they would probably call it a "world") at the macrocosmic level. The individual identity connects directly to a specific social environment and to a specific understanding of the goal and purpose of human existence articulated in the community's theology.

Finally, Fagan connects this understanding of human spiritual identity and the construction of a new world order to the biblical interpretation so familiar as a practice in the community:

> The matured soul combines thinking and its corresponding thoughts, the one male and the other female. The perfect image of god. At the birthing they are placed in separate forms, and are one, completely in touch with every aspect of each other. Perfectly mated. This is God's ideal of marriage, of which Adam and Eve

20. Ibid.

in their innocence were an example. His being formed first was an object less[on] in order. Her being the more beautiful, it was necessary for her to be formed from living substance, rather than raw dust. The majesty of femininity. This ideal has been blighted by sin and has degenerated to what we have today. The plan of salvation incorporates its restoration. Of a truth, the soul is created from nothing, coming via dust. In the Kingdom of God we are born perfectly mated.[21]

Here Fagan provides us with the theological rationale for the whole system emergent from an interpretation of the purpose of human existence in the first two chapters of Genesis. The system of formation, so non-biblical in its language and metaphor, becomes biblical because it is identified with the proper understanding of Adam and Eve's creation in Genesis. Chillingly, the metaphor of marriage opens the possibility of sexual abuse of women and children by the messianic figure, but the metaphor becomes naturalized in the interpretative process so that the concepts of restoration, of perfect mating, of a divided whole (presumably brought together in coitus), of the image of God all flow logically and properly from their biblical interpretation. Fagan claims that he merely explains the deeper meaning of scripture. This deeper level of understanding, however, provides the glue to all the other elements of the formative process. It is the creation of a symbolic universe that sustains the alternative subjectivity and gives depth and meaning to the construction of an alternative society or nation.

What ended in the fiery ordeal at the Branch Davidian community center in Waco was the logical conclusion to an intensive and complete ascetical formation. The members of that community were trained to become living warriors, willing to die in the heavenly conflagration that was to befall this sinful and evil world. David Koresh trained and equipped his religious community to become living fires, living flames that were intended to birth a new nation, a new era, a new Kingdom of God.

The Terrorists of September 11, 2001

It is but a short jump from becoming a living flame inaugurating the Kingdom to becoming a human bomb in honor of God. I began writing this essay in the aftermath of the September 11, 2001 bombing of the

21. Ibid.

World Trade Center buildings in New York, the Pentagon in Washington, D.C., and the destruction of the airplane in Pennsylvania, and during the intense fighting between Israel and the Palestinian Authority in Spring, 2002. After the terrorist attacks on American soil, the nature of American identity, power, and self-awareness—so long lived as dominant and unquestionably supreme—shifted weight permanently in the face of what have been called "martyr heroes" of the jihad. These human bombs provide the fourth political, social, and cultural event that has put asceticism on the (post)modern agenda.

In an article, Nasra Hassan[22] reported on the training of *shaheed batal* (martyr heroes) of the Palestinian uprising against Israel. Her account, without ever mentioning the word or the concept, relates an ascetical regime for young men to train themselves not only to become human bombs, but also to become martyrs for the cause of the holy war. The training in martyrdom,[23] as Hassan reports them, revolved about a nexus of important elements: the promise of immediate entrance into Paradise upon their self-imposed death; a "constant state of worship" as one of the martyrs-in-training described it; the attractiveness of a spiritually uplifting project; the close support of a cell of people (*al khaliyya al istishhadiyya*, [martyrdom cell]), whose life acquires an intensity based on a common holy calling; the love for the holy scriptures that gives contours and depth to the actions of the martyrs; the fame and blessing bestowed upon the family and community of the martyr; the clear sense of a calling—by clerics indirectly or from Allah directly—to a holy office and offering; and finally, the joy of knowing that there will be victory over the enemies of Islam. The young men selected for this office are carefully trained. The religious guides employ videos of exemplars of martyrs that model behavior, attitudes, and postures as they prepare themselves for their sacrifice. The guides reinforce such visual imagery with recitation and memorization of the qur'anic passages that justify and glorify their mission while emphasizing the rewards of their sacrifice on behalf of Allah. Recited questions and responses that train the mind in new ways of thinking of themselves and their world reinforce the learning and help the martyrs-in-training to image themselves in their chosen vocation.

22. Hassan, "An Arsenal of Believers."

23. See also Bruce Lincoln, *Holy Terrors*. Lincoln includes a translation of the letter, copies of which each 9/11 terrorist had in his possession, that provided the theology and instructions to them.

Signs and posters glorifying previous martyrs and their successes provide visual and verbal support from the religious and secular community around them to encourage the martyrs in their preparation (even though members of the community do not know specifically who those being trained are). And, of course, the profound sense of oppression from the enemy both in their personal experience and in the indoctrination of the martyrs' guides grounds their determination to become martyrs. This sense of oppression of the dominant society provides the greatest impetus and drives the martyrs-in-training to overcome their fear of death—and more importantly, fear of failure—through the exercise of their religious strength and determination. It is a complete ascetical formation provided to youths willing to accept the community's call to fight the holy war.

What emerges from Hassan's description is a classic ascetical system. The new subjectivity, immersed as it is in passages from the Qur'an, emerges as a result of specific training and specific individual and corporate practices. That new identity stands in stark contrast not only to the infidel identity and society, but also to other Muslim people and groups. The new subjectivity, to become a living bomb, belongs to a select group of religiously elect who constitute an elite religious society. The process of constructing that identity resembles that of the Branch Davidians, the gay people of Genet's novels, and the ascetical theology of Kazantzakis. These are Kazantzakis's superhumans who transfigure materiality through their efforts and who transform their own bodily existence into a holy, fiery presence.

THEORIZING ASCETICISM AFTER NIETZSCHE

By moving forward from Nietzsche's initial differentiation in *Schopenhauer as Educator* between the lazy person, blindly being constructed as a person of his age, and the youthful soul, energetically defining himself from within himself and rejecting the inherited societal norms, this essay has pursued Nietzsche's youthful soul into the ascetical construction of subjectivities opposing the dominant culture. I have argued that what characterizes validly ascetical activity is precisely this creation of an alternative identity in the face of a dominant and given social identity. The other side of the equation, Nietzsche's lazy person and Foucault's self-formed person, being oriented toward the dominant culture and their ability to function within it seamlessly, consists not of asceticism, but of formation. Formation prepares people to participate in the dominant society by equipping them with the requisite tools. Foucault's theories, exciting as they are, apply not to asceticism but to social formation, and that among primarily elite and entitled males in ancient society.

Once Foucault and his theory have been displaced from the discussion of asceticism proper, then the pursuit of a genealogy of subversive identity construction may begin anew. That genealogy, beginning with Nietzsche's youthful soul and moving through the undercurrents of the next two centuries' social and intellectual movements, emerges as an interesting combination of philosophical, literary, religious, and political movements. The genealogy develops through the expression of an undercurrent of subversive identities: Kazantzakis's superhuman, Genet's queens, David Koresh's fiery community, and the human bombs of September 11. Although these events are not necessarily directly related to one another, they form a progression from theory, to literary imagination, to community life that explains how many of the movements of the twentieth century created their alternative subjectivities. The interaction of theory and practice among the various subversive movements—feminists, people of color, ethnic groups, religious communes, ecological advocates, animal rights protagonists, to name just a few—locates them precisely in this ascetical stream, and not the formational one. These movements oppose the dominant culture and perspectives of their time in order to create something new, a new identity, different communities, and structures of meaning to support them in their new life. These movements fill in the genealogy from Nietzsche to September 11, providing ample proof that ascetic subjectivities will emerge to counter the hegemony of a dominant perspective.

The Feast of the Holy No-Silver Ones in Paros with which I began this chapter takes place in a monastery. The monks of the monastery were ascetics—they withdrew from society in order to construct a new identity in God. The people attending the festival, however, received formation, cultural information and practices to enable them to enter the dominant life of the Greek society of which the Church is a part and to enjoy the riches of hegemony. These two perspectives, formation and asceticism, stand as related and yet very different processes. Each orients itself in radically different ways to the dominant culture and each forges new subjectivities in response to that dominant culture, but each constructs its identities in decidedly different ways.

CHAPTER 5

A Theory of Asceticism, Revised

IN 1995 I PUBLISHED AN INITIAL DEFINITION OF ASCETICISM AS "PERFOR-
mances within a dominant social environment intended to inaugurate a
new subjectivity, different social relations, and an alternative symbolic
universe."[1] That definition centers on a few very basic concepts: that asceticism creates a new subjectivity through specific performances and
practices; that the new subjectivity distinguishes itself from other dominant subjectivities made available in a social or religious context; that the
subjectivity operates in a new social environment that supports the new
subjectivity; that the subjectivity demands a rethinking or reorganization of the understanding of the way the physical and spiritual universe
operates; and finally, that the new subjectivity emerges from actions,
performances, and other instantiated practices that bring it into being. I
intended that the definition remain broadly applicable to a wide variety
of human activity.

Over the years since 1995, through conversations and further research and consideration, that definition has basically remained applicable both to historical and to contemporary ascetical studies, but has
needed further elaboration and refinement. This refined reflection of
what constitutes asceticism may now be defined in this way:

> Asceticism consists of any performance resistant to an externally
> projected or subjectively experienced dominant social or religious
> context specifically intended (almost as a cognitive impulse) and
> purposefully performed in order to inaugurate a new and alterna-
> tive subjectivity. This new subjectivity may be understood both

1. See chapter 2, pp. 14–59, "Constructions of Power in Asceticism"; definition on
page 38.

inter-subjectively (those people and events constituting the social self of the individual) and intra-subjectively (those with whom the agent interacts beyond the individual social body). Social relationships must be transformed in order to support the new and alternative subjectivity. The symbolic universe or construction of reality must be adapted and changed in order to explain and sustain the resistant subjectivity.

This essay explores asceticism from this more expansive description, based on my earlier definition, in order to advance the discussion of ascetical theory and practice in scholarly, intellectual, and social discourse.

My understanding of asceticism distinguishes it from the broader concept of "formation" or enculturation. Formation aims to enculturate individuals into dominant social or political systems; it aims literally to inform them of the way of living in a particular setting, to conform individuals to a communal standard, to reform patterns of behavior deemed unacceptable, and to form cohesion within the social group. Asceticism, on the other hand, aims to resist dominant givens. Asceticism constructs itself as alternative, perhaps subversively so, to a perceived or real dominant context. Enculturation lacks the sense of resistance and orients itself to the incorporation of an individual or a group into an acknowledged group. Asceticism, however, always defines itself as resistant or withdrawn from a perceived or a real dominant context. My theory, then, relates to the way resistant people or groups relate to larger social, religious, and political communities. Another way of looking at this is to say that enculturation looks to erase difference, while asceticism intends to create difference. It is precisely in the articulation of difference that asceticism comes to the fore.[2] This short description of my understanding of asceticism, however, makes clear that some aspects of my theory demand further exploration, expansion, elaboration, and clarification. And the theory needs to be elaborated in an essay devoted to the theory itself. These supplements to the articles already in circulation that describe my

2. See chapter 4, pp. 80–100, where I argue the distinction between formation for living in the dominant society and asceticism that contests the dominant context. In further reflection, I have adopted the language of enculturation rather than formation for the training for living in the dominant context.

theory arise from conversations and responses over the years,[3] and from the critical work of my students over the past few years.[4]

RESISTANT SUBJECTIVITY

The heart of my theory of asceticism resides in the creation of an alternative subjectivity through intentional performances.[5] I have chosen the term "subjectivity" specifically because the ascetic creates more than a basic social identity or role, an articulated self, a persona, or a personality: the ascetic constructs an entirely new agency capable of functioning in a different and resistant way to the dominant culture that defines identity, personality, and social functions from hegemonic power.[6] In the popular mind and in most ascetical scholarship, specific actions such as fasting, or sexual abstinence, or sleep deprivation, or standing on a pillar for weeks (or years) on end, constitute the ascetic without attention to the effect of the action on the subjective make-up of the person. In my theory, the central factor of asceticism does not revolve about these specific acts (fasting, sexual renunciation, withdrawal from society) per se, but upon an intentional creation, recreation, or redefinition of a subjectivity, which constitutes the construction of an agent capable of functioning in a particular social, political, or religious environment in contradistinction to dominant or hegemonic environments.[7] This fashioning, or refashioning, or redefinition of the alternative subjectivity defines asceticism. The

3. I would like to acknowledge in particular the class at Iliff School of Theology taught by Professor Jacob Kinnard entitled "Asceticism and Monasticism" in the Spring quarter, 2006. Kinnard's attention to matters of theory and the students' engaging criticism have brought many issues to the fore. This essay would not have been possible without their contribution. I would also like to acknowledge the doctoral seminar at Emory's Graduate Division of Religion, "Asceticism in History and Theory," in Fall, 2006.

4. This work took place at Iliff School of Theology in Denver, Colorado. I mention here in particular the work of Douglas K. Bleyle who has been working on a theory of corporate asceticism based on my theory and whose conversations over the past two years have directed me to see needed nuances to my theory. I also acknowledge the contribution in discussions and papers of Dennis Haugh, Derek Selznick, Lucy McGuffy, and Sara Rosenau.

5. Couze Venn (see *Occidentalism*) has provided the stimulus to this discussion of subjectivity.

6. Post-colonial theory informs this aspect of my ascetical theory. See Bhabha, *Location of Culture*, 57–93.

7. I am obviously deeply indebted to Michel Foucault for the foundation of this theory of subjectivity and its relationship to asceticism. See Foucault, *Hermeneutics*, 413–89.

performances inaugurating that alternative subjectivity depend upon the kind of subjectivity the ascetic intends to inaugurate. No particular performances constitute in themselves ascetical activity; only performances intending to inaugurate a new, resistant subjectivity may properly be classified as ascetical.

Two perspectives on subjectivity in general will advance the understanding of asceticism: intra-subjectivity and inter-subjectivity. Inter-subjectivity refers to those people and events constituting the social self of the individual.[8] The social self invokes parents, extended family relatives, influential teachers, destructive relationships, and all the other personal and situational factors a person experiences from birth onwards that become constitutive of the individual's particular way of living, thinking, emoting, and understanding. And these formative experiences, both good and bad, both positively and negatively formational, dwell in the person's body or psyche so as to constitute a social body of many people and circumstances that inhere in the individual person's locus of living.[9] The intra-subjectivity, the second perspective, consists of those with whom the inter-subjective agent interacts beyond the individual social body. The inter-subjective person brings the social body, the inter-subjective community that constitutes the self, into relationship with other intra-subjectivities. The inter- and intra-subjectivity, then, constitutes a very complex understanding of an authorized agent. In fact, the subjectivity really exists as a locus, a location, where many divergent, distinct, and yet interrelated elements cohere to constitute a subject.

Both the inter- and the intra-subjectivity problematize asceticism to a great degree, because what constitutes the singular "subject" involves many more presences than a psychologically defined unitive subjectivity allows. But the ascetic situation remains even more complex. The ascetic subject, both inter- and intra-subjectively understood, resists the dominant subjectivity in a very dynamic way. As the ascetic performs the new, resistant subjectivity, it seems as though three interrelated and yet distinct subjectivities cohere within the ascetic subject: (1) a rejected

8. Couze Venn writes "that the entanglement of subjectivities and identities means that every subject exists as a relation to an other or to others, that is, every subject is intricated in an inter-subjective web." Venn, *Occidentalism*, 42. For a brilliant exploration of the dynamic of inter-subjectivity, see Butler, *Giving an Account of Oneself.*

9. For a more complete exposition and definition of the social body and the corporate body as well, see my "Praying the Bodies."

subjectivity understood as the dominant subjectivity from which the ascetic wishes to withdraw and against which the ascetic struggles; (2) a subjectivity not yet fully realized that constitutes the new subjectivity that the ascetic intends to actualize; and (3) an in-between subjectivity that fluctuates between the two as a work in progress. Couze Venn describes this subjectivity in this way:

> I am indicating a sense of temporality in which we live the now as a movement from a becoming-past to a coming-towards so that the consciousness of the present always leaches into the memory of the having-been and the anticipation of a to-come. The point, basically, is that temporality is a fundamental dimension of being.[10]

Ascetics articulate this temporality of subjectivity in the process of their reformation of their own subjectivity. The whole time that these three subjectivities function, the inter-subjectivity expands and develops in ways of integrating different elements. For example, the ascetic may incorporate the image of Antony, the great Egyptian ascetic, into the inter-subjective self in order to appropriate the particular way that Antony lived out the ascetic life as the ideal articulation of the goal of the new subjectivity.[11] Likewise, intra-subjectively, the ascetic may associate with a community of people dedicated to particular ways of living out the ascetical life in order to sustain and support a particular way of articulating and developing the new, resistant ascetic subjectivity. Examples of such communities would include a monastery, a Catholic Worker community, or an association of body-builders, each with their own perspectives on the ideal ascetic subjectivity. Both inter- and intra-subjectivity operate within the ascetical system as part of the complex process of inaugurating a new, resistant, ascetic subjectivity.

My focus on a subjectivity distinct from received dominant and socially mandated subjectivities highlights the complex interaction of subjectivities in a society. The resistance, or contrary relationship to the dominant context, distinguishes ascetical activity from activity intended simply to enculturate a person or community into the dominant social

---

10. Venn, *Occidentalism*, 41. See also Bhabha, *Location of Culture*, 10.

11. Gavin Flood understands this process as a performance and instantiation, if not embodied replication, of tradition. See *Ascetic Self*, 8–13, 179; specifically, on Antony and the Christian desert monastic tradition, see 144–74.

setting. This means that a rite of passage of a young person into the adult community does not in itself constitute an ascetical performance. What makes a performance ascetical (rather than enculturative) depends upon the intention of the performer or performers to resist, to contradict, to defy, or to define the self in opposition to the dominant social context. When ascetics take on that contrary intention, the performances become ascetical. Without that contrary intention, the performances remain non-ascetical or enculturative.

The resistance to the perceived dominant perspective may be characterized as outright resistance, crisis, or dissatisfaction.[12] Resistance, that is, runs along a very wide spectrum.[13] The obvious and most direct form of resistance is outright rejection of a dominant pattern. Monastic withdrawal from society functions as this form of resistance, as does the intense resistance of libertarians to government control. Crisis describes not so much an intentional rejection, but a withdrawal or resistance that comes about from the breakdown in systems around the ascetic. The ascetic desires a new subjectivity because circumstances in an ascetic's life shift and change in such a way that necessitate new directions, new understandings, or different modalities of existence that operate in an alternative conception of reality. Crisis has less direct agency than resistance and dissatisfaction, because crisis relates primarily to experienced circumstances. Catholic Worker communities, for example, respond to the economic injustices in post-industrial society to form ascetical communities that in their own practice and mission create an alternative. Dissatisfaction describes the sense that a person acquires when the subjectivity and mode of living no longer satisfy. The ascetic looks at the contours of his or her life and decides that the life as it is currently lived does not fulfill and does not represent the true self of the ascetic, so the ascetic sets out to create an alternative. Here, as in outright resistance, agency operates to a significant degree. These three terms, however, do not exhaust the possibilities. Resistance operates on a very fluid spectrum that encourages diverse ways of withdrawing and resisting in order to bring about a new subjectivity.[14]

12. I owe the concept and use of the term "crisis" to Thomas Fabisiak, which he used in a seminar discussion at Emory University, Fall, 2006.

13. Geoffrey Galt Harpham defines all asceticism primarily as strategies of resistance; see his Ascetic Imperative, 3–18.

14. On resistance and narrative see Harpham, Ascetic Imperative, 45–66.

The resistant subjectivity must be communicable, that is, the alternative subjectivity must articulate a difference that is in fact communicated to the dominant context.[15] This is the function of ascetic performance: to articulate and communicate ascetic difference.[16] Ascetic resistant performance, precisely as performance, underscores the public nature and the practical activity in a public venue that distinguishes asceticism from other religious phenomena such as piety and devotion, as well as from other social phenomena such as psychological psychoses and anti-social behavior. In order properly to resist, ascetics must have an audience; their alternative subjectivity makes sense only as it displays for self and others the difference between dominant and ascetical subjectivities. That public scrutiny may exist at a number of different levels: the ascetic's own display of difference; the difference articulated within ascetic communities; difference created by performances intended to differentiate ascetic from dominant subjectivity; or simply a performance intended to be observed by God alone. In this way, the ascetic always remains implicated in the various social contexts in which the ascetic operates because those social contexts provide the necessary public display of difference.

POWER AND ASCETIC DYNAMISM

This performed resistant relationship of ascetical person or community to the dominant context suggests an interplay of power. The interrelationship of subjectivities, with the ascetical resistance to the dominant subjectivities, plots the modulation of power within a society while at the same time describing the fault lines of social groupings and relationships within a given society.[17] The ascetic exposes the existing power structures of the dominant society that demarcate the subjectivities licit in the dominant world, while at the same time exercising power to create an alternative to those dominant subjectivities and structures of power. Ascetic alterity, that is, reveals the underlying systems of identity formation and of instruments for creating social solidarity. These power dy-

15. Flood connects the public nature of the ascetic subject to the ritual performance of a cultural memory, that is, the ascetic makes public and visible the culture's memory of tradition; *Ascetic Self*, 7, 212–31.

16. In this section, I am indebted to performance theory; see chapter 2, pp. 39–40.

17. These issues of the modulation of power and the creation of solidarity emerge from social semiotic theory; see Hodge and Kress, *Social Semiotics*, 1–12; and Van Leeuwen, *Introducing Social Semiotics*, 160–77.

namics, both for the ascetic and the world that the ascetic rejects, find their justification in their construction of reality, their symbolic universe. The ascetic's activity, then, begins to change the understanding of reality by reconstructing reality for the ascetic in order to substantiate the ascetic's alternative subjectivity. The alternative subjectivity thus demands that every other aspect of the ascetic's life shift and adjust to the creation of the new person: social relationships, understanding of science and politics, and the nature of the self itself change in order for the new subjectivity to become a reality.

The relationship between ascetics (whether individual or communal) to the dominant social and political context is dynamic, not static. In any given social setting "dominance" exists as a shifting and changing structure. In other words, no one "dominant" structure functions statically in relationship to the ascetic person or community.[18] "Dominant contexts" comprise an amalgam of various institutions and concepts against which the ascetic person or community defines itself; dominance is subjectively articulated. So the ascetic's resistance to dominance changes in relationship to the ascetic's discernment about the debilitating effect of the dominant amalgam, while at the same time the dominant amalgam shifts and changes in relationship to various factors relating both to those groups who contest its dominance (both ascetical and non-ascetical) and to the circumstances of the exercise of its hegemony. So the ascetic renounces according to the shifting dominant structures as perceived and articulated by the ascetic, and the dominant structures mutate according to the necessities of its hegemony in response to the public resistance of the ascetic. The ascetic person or community relates dynamically to a dynamic construction of dominance. The dynamic relationship displays increments of fluidity and adjustment.

THE INTERIOR DYNAMIC

The ascetic's withdrawal from and renunciation of the dominant context, then, also develops dynamically. The ascetic must continually adapt the performances leading to the articulation and instantiation of an alterna-

18. I am indebted to Douglas K. Bleyle's paper "The Ascetical Corporate Body" (unpublished) for the corporate dimensions to the construction of a communal ascetic subjectivity. Bleyle uses the theory of revitalization developed by F. C. Anthony Wallace to explain the mutual interaction and transformation that occurs between dominant culture and the ascetical minority and resistant communities.

tive subjectivity by reference to a continually shifting set of dominant structures. As the ascetic discerns the contours of dominance against which the ascetic defines the personal or corporate subjectivity, the ascetic adjusts the performances creating an alternative. Novelty, then, does not represent a novelty based on something entirely new or unique, but a novelty based on a new adaptation of renunciation and withdrawal reflecting the realities of the shifting dominant structure and reflecting as well the incremental progress of the ascetic toward realizing the imagined, alternative subjectivity. The performances relate to a dynamic shift in understanding the ascetic subjectivity as it defines itself in relationship to the mutating structures of dominance and to the ascetic's own success in gradually instantiating the new subjectivity. The ascetic continually refines the contours of the subjectivity in relationship to the rejected dominant structures. The interior dynamic of the formation of a subjectivity defies static understandings; the ascetic self dynamically defines and redefines its goal, its vision of a new subjectivity, in a subtle process that responds to the perceived nuances of change within the dominant context. The new, then, emerges as something incrementally small, something beginning as a small shift in performance responding to subtle changes in hegemonic structures.[19] The new subjectivity finds its articulation in a dynamic of definition and redefinition of the ascetic goal for the subjectivity in slight alterations of performance to accommodate the changes perceived in the rejected structures. The novelty, thus, is not something necessarily without precedent, but simply initial adjustments in conceptualization responding to the mutations in the dominant context.

AGENCY AND EMPOWERMENT

The novelty, however, progresses deliberately so that asceticism must be intentional: a person does not "fall into" asceticism by accident or become an unintentional ascetic, because asceticism operates by an intention to inaugurate a new subjectivity in contrast or opposition to the dominant subjectivities available in any particular context.[20] The example that

19. I am relying here on Hodge and Kress's description of W. Labov's theory of linguistic transformation. See Hodge and Kress, *Social Semiotics*, 184–86.

20. I am indebted to Jacob Kinnard for this observation. See also Flood's description of Simone Weil's asceticism, which takes on even the most common daily activities as intentional asceticism, in Flood, *Ascetic Self*, 37–63.

comes to mind is that of a student who matriculates at a school with a very specific and clearly articulated ideology that opposes the structures of the dominant society. By the mere fact of matriculating, the student does not become an ascetic. In order to become an ascetic, that student must intentionally, and with clear self-awareness, take on the performance of that ideology as a means of transforming or reconstructing the student's subjectivity. The student may matriculate while not functioning as an agent of the ideology, but through intentional adoption of the practices that instantiate the ideology, the student becomes an ascetical agent intentionally performing an alternative subjectivity. The ascetic, that is, must become an agent of the ascetical action and cannot remain passive to its forces. The active intention of the ascetic to inaugurate a new subjectivity demands a level of commitment to change and transformation that necessitates active pursuit of the ascetical goal.

I would argue the same for an ascetical community.[21] One does not become an ascetic merely by joining an ascetical community. Not all monks in a monastery live as ascetics. What constitutes communal ascetic agency must begin with an intention by the individual to conform to the communal practices.[22] A number of practices might fulfill the need for intentional adoption of communal norms: an intention to follow the rules of the ascetical community as a means of personal transformation; the intentional adoption of the community's pious practices in order to reformulate the self; the adoption of personal practices that translate the corporate subjectivity into personal self-reformation. As each individual takes on the ascetical regulations and practices of the ascetical community, the communal agency emerges. The ascetic community, moreover, sets forth communal practices intended to promote the alternative corporate subjectivity. These communal practices consist of rituals, liturgies,

21. In a doctoral seminar at Emory University, Chris Durante, a graduate student from Georgia State University, articulated a theory for the creation of a corporate subjectivity through three stages: the formation of a self, then a collective subjectivity, and finally a corporate subjectivity. The collective self described simply the people forming a group, like a football team, that has specific goals and interests, but remain isolated individuals. The corporate subjectivity, however, experiences the self and the world through the group's identity and worldview, like the members of a specific religious order.

22. Flood identifies this process primarily through rituals, *Ascetic Self*, 211–34; Harpham locates this process in hagiography and the narrative construction of identity based on historical or imaginary precedents, *Ascetic Imperative*, 67–88. Both ritual and hagiography play important roles in the formation of a corporate, ascetic subjectivity.

patterns of eating and socializing, systems of communal prayer (even when ascetics pray those in private), signifying systems that instantiate the communal understanding of the world, and other practices developed by the community to teach and to transmit the communal ascetical system to the community.

The ascetic and the ascetical community both constitute themselves as active agents capable of recreating themselves as different individuals or communities, capable of acting in a manner confronting the hegemony of the dominant structures, of actively engaging in the creation of alternative ways of socializing and gathering in solidarity with each other in opposition to dominant modes of social relationships, and of recreating the understanding of the symbolic universe, the cosmos, in order to accommodate this new agency. The ascetic agency, then, empowers the ascetic to perform in such a way as to exercise resistant agency. The ascetic performances not only create an alternative subjectivity, but they create at the same time a subversive energy and power that drive the ascetic individual or community to act against the grain of the dominant structures that surround the ascetic. This is indeed an empowered agency.

Although ascetic agency empowers, another sort of ascetic power emerges from this understanding of ascetic agency. The dissonant performances by ascetics, precisely in their rejection of dominant structures, plunge the ascetic into the spotlight of resistance. The alternative ascetic way of living marks a clear line between dominant world and ascetic world. The line between dominant and ascetic articulates an interrelated and interconnected system of power. The dominant context, accustomed as it usually is to its own dominance, experiences the ascetic resistance as a challenge to its hegemony and authority. Ascetics become a threat to the maintenance of power systems against which they define themselves. At the same time, the ascetic person or community, in rejecting the power of the dominant context, assume a contrasting center of alternative power that strengthens the internal cohesion of the ascetic or the ascetic community. By resisting the power of the dominant context, ascetics amass power for themselves, a power that enables them successfully to resist and to create an alternative subjectivity (both individual and corporate) with an alternative social structure, which has its own internal systems of power defined in opposition to the dominant systems of power.

INTENTION AND THE GOAL OF ASCETICAL PERFORMANCE

At a number of points in this discussion the question of intention arises: asceticism exists only where a clear and articulated individual or corporate intention operates. That intention, however, does not necessarily have specific content, because the intention simply rests with the goal of instantiating by incremental degrees an individual or corporate subjectivity that challenges the subjectivities of the dominant context. The intent, then, simply resides with the articulated end of creating an alternative subjectivity.

This simple intent, however, reveals a complex process of setting goals that direct and substantiate the intention. In formulating the alternative subjectivity, ascetics project for themselves a specific goal, an end-product, a vision of the new subjectivity. The intention to create an alternative subjectivity must have an image that guides and directs the actions and performances intended to incarnate the transformed subjectivity. It is the goal that determines the particular practices of ascetics.[23] That goal, however, exists in a constant state of flux, because ascetics revise the goal continually as they make progress toward achieving it. In discerning their advancement toward the new subjectivity, ascetics evaluate their own status in relationship to the goal and the status of the goal in relationship to the ascetics' capacity for instantiating the new subjectivity. That new subjectivity, moreover, shifts and changes as it encounters two other contexts: first, the adaptation that the dominant context has made to the ascetical resistance and second, the resistive adaptation that ascetics must make in relationship to the dominant context. A dynamic mutual exchange operates between the ascetic individual and community and the dominant context.[24] In other words, ascetics formulate their goals not statically, but dynamically as ascetics advance toward them and as they change in relationship to the dominant context and to the specific individual and corporate ascetical advances. The dominant context changes as well in relationship to the ascetic person or community's shifting goals so that the exchange between dominant and ascetical community remains mutual.

23. Flood, *Ascetic Self*, 178–81.

24. I rely here on Douglas Bleyle's description of the continual mutual exchange between the dominant and the resistant community in his unpublished paper, "The Ascetical Corporate Body."

As ascetics refine and redefine their goals, projecting a constantly more articulate and generative image or vision of the alternative subjectivity (both individual and corporate), they must also revise their performances whose intention is to inaugurate or instantiate that newly revised subjectivity. Just as ascetics adjust the goal, so must they adjust also the performances to achieve the goal. Ascetics practice discernment about both the goal and the means to the goal, the performances, and that discernment leads to continual revision and precision regarding the performances capable of instantiating the new subjectivity as it shifts and changes in the lives of the ascetics and the mutations in the dominant context.

The dynamic of ascetical revision both regarding the goal and the performances resembles the responses and imaging taking place within a constant flow of new information about ascetic self, ascetic community, and dominant non-ascetical context. That constant flow demands that ascetics gather an impermanent image in order to make sense of their resistant selves and their alternative communities in relationship to a flow of activity that moves in a contrary direction. Gathering information from that flow of information, ascetics project an image of the alternative subjectivity and imagine a set of performances that will lead them toward instantiating it. Pursuing the image for a while, the flow of information begins to disrupt the direction, forcing ascetics again to re-evaluate their status and the effectiveness of their performances, and they project a revised goal with reconsidered and reconfigured performances. This process happens subtly and endlessly in the minute and incremental progress of ascetic individual and communities toward their transformation. But the process is marked not by static performances and static understandings of progress, but by a dynamic that continually refines the categories of performance and goal as it moves incrementally toward the image of the new subjectivity.

REFLECTIONS ON A THEORY OF ASCETICISM

This revised theory of asceticism forges new ground for a theory of asceticism usable by both historians and postmodern scholars. The conceptualizing of the ascetic subject expands now to include both the intra- and inter-subjectivity resistant to dominant structures. This more complex understanding of the ascetic subject opens the way to a more sophisticated understanding of the nature of the dominant modes against which an ascetic struggles as well as a more complicated understanding of the process of internalizing both dominant modes and ascetic redefinitions of self, society, and cosmos. The ascetic subject is one intimately interconnected with the self understood now to embrace a wide variety of relationships that become part of the resistance and the articulation of a new subjectivity. This expanded view of subjectivity reflects current critical theorizing about the individual and social nature of the postmodern self, while at the same time articulating patterns of ascetical self-definition resonant with historical articulations and theories in history.

The expanded understanding of the self also explains the interior dynamic of ascetical struggle. Coinherent in the ascetical self stand three interconnected selves that relate to one another in the performative redefinition of subjectivity: the rejected self that reflects the ready-made and given self provided by the dominant context, the emergent self that begins to move away from the hegemonic modes of being toward something new, and the not-yet-fully-existent self that envisions a new self now fully transformed and redefined. The dynamic interconnection of these three selves, embodied in specific ascetical performances moving toward the goal of the envisioned new self, define the context of ascetical activity. The careful scrutiny of all three coinherent selves leads to the revision and transformation of the person and makes ascetical progress possible.

Ascetical progress emerges from this interior dynamic relationship of coinherent selves. Progress begins with the desire to resist the dominant modes of being, and that resistance itself functions along a spectrum that includes simple dissatisfaction, social or religious crisis, or a desire openly and directly to resist dominant modes. There is no one simple way of beginning the ascetical road toward progress, but many ways that might lead an ascetic to resist in order to move toward an alternative understanding of self, society, and the cosmos.

Tracking progress, discerning the debilitating effects of dominant modes of behavior and living, maps out the contours of power and authority in a given context. The ascetic struggle lays open the effects of dominant and given modes of living on the human and social spirit. What the ascetic resists shows the fault lines of dominance and hegemony. What the ascetic strives to achieve, moreover, shows the possibilities for renewal and transformation, the opportunities for growth and progress, possible through the articulation of difference. The individual's or community's goal shows the potential that comes from visionary, resistant dreaming. Ascetical progress, then, reveals the complex systems and dynamics of power operating in a given context and opens those systems to evaluation, discernment, and transformation. Without the ascetics these power dynamics are difficult to see; the ascetic makes them visible through their contestation while at the same time opening new avenues for the articulation of power and authority in a given culture. Real discernment, I would argue, can only emerge from analyzing ascetical desire and progress; real understandings of social, political, and religious power only result from looking at those places where ascetics resist dominance and hegemony. Ascetic progress makes this discernment possible not only in the arena of power, but also in every arena of human personal and corporate agency.

Ascetical performances must, therefore, always be communicable, that is to say, ascetical performances must always be communicated in ways understood both with the ascetical resistance and within the dominant and hegemonic context. Ascetic performances cannot communicate idiosyncratically and in ways only understood by the individual ascetic person or community. Ascetic performances always begin to speak in the language and symbols of the dominant context, even as they begin to articulate something new and different, something alternative and transformative of the dominant. This communicability makes sense of both the vision of the emergent self and the systems against which the ascetic struggles. It is an important aspect of ascetical struggle and progress. Even a hermit like Antony, walled up so many years in the interior desert of Egypt, had an impact far wider than the immediate circle of his associations: his life communicated to others the new goal and the destructiveness of the old ways of living at once to those who knew him, to those who wrote and published his life in antiquity, and to those who read about it today.

Another way of articulating this is to say that the communicability of ascetical performances is revelatory. Ascetics reveal the inner workings and effects of dominant structures. They open to analysis and discernment the social, religious, political, and personal dynamics operative at any particular point in time, and they reveal the way those dynamics affect the person, the religious community, the society at large, and the physical environment. Ascetic communication reveals both the actual and the potential, both the lived reality and the possible new realities, and both the limits of the old and the expectation of the new.

All that has been said of the individual ascetic applies as well to ascetic communities. Even hermits do not live alone: they have a network of people around them, a community that supports and sustains them, as well as a community for whom the ascetic performs his transformation. This relational network in asceticism suggests that the individual always functions within a social and cosmic context. But ascetical communities also exist. Communities envision together new ways of being a person, new ways of relating to others and to the world in which they live. Corporate entities also desire, form ascetical intention, resist, dream of new possibilities, and envision performances that will bring them into reality through corporate effort. Just as individuals have ascetic agency and intention, so do communities.

It is always interesting to watch individual and communal agency performing new individual and communal subjectivity. The progress toward the goal seems never to be direct, but rather seems to meander through many different paths to reach the goal. There seems to exist a kind of ascetic chaos theory operating for individuals and community. Progress happens for them as they envision a resistant goal. Moving toward that goal, they evaluate the effectiveness of the performances and the result of their effort, and they adjust performances to accommodate their progress. Moving forward, thus, moves along a path directly until the evaluation demands reformulation of the performances and the progress refines the understanding of the goal. Temporary steps taken along a well-defined path find themselves thrust into the chaos resulting from discernment and evaluation. The chaos then leads to further refinement of the goal, new performances, and different understandings of the interior and social dynamic of growth. In turn the process begins again. Ascetic growth emerges from this dynamic formation and reformation of performances in relationship to an ever-refined ascetic goal. This makes studying asceticism interesting, because it is not a simple progression through a specified performance, but rather a complex process of growth through continual refinement and redefinition of both performance and end result. Asceticism, it seems, never stands still, nor does it ever stay in the same place, nor does it use only proven performances to achieve its goals.

part two

CHRISTIAN ASCETICISM

CHAPTER 6

Uncovering Adam's Esoteric Body

IT IS NOT UNUSUAL TO FIND SPECULATION IN THE SECOND AND THIRD centuries regarding the creation of human being.[1] It seems that the creation of the world in Genesis was the starting point for exploration into both cosmology and anthropology. The subject of this paper, however, is not the exegesis of Genesis 1 and 2, but a derivative topic: the formation of Adam's body. Quite by accident, while working on both Sethian Gnosticism and Origen at the same time, I realized that in two texts alone (at least so far) there was a discussion of the formation of the parts of Adam's body. There is no reason to think that these texts are related, or that one has any dependence on the other, so the differences and similarities of interpretations of what seems to be the same tradition regarding the formation of Adam's body were noteworthy.

The first text is *The Apocryphon of John*, where the discussion of the formation of Adam's body takes place in the context of an exegesis of Genesis 1:26. The second text is the middle section of Origen's *Dialogue with Heraclides,* where the discussion relates to the exegesis of Leviticus 17:11 ("the soul is the blood"). In both of these contexts there is a concern for describing the formation of the human body by listing various body parts. Each body part, in turn, is given an abstract quality or an ascetical significance. It seems likely that this represents a tradition of interpretation that is not necessarily related to the exegesis of Genesis 1:26, but rather to an independent tradition regarding Adam's body. The nature of the material, moreover, seems to point to an esoteric tradition of interpretation.

1. In thanksgiving for George MacRae, SJ.

The purposes of this chapter are to present an exegesis of the traditions of the formation of Adam's body in *The Apocryphon of John* and in Origen's *Dialogue with Heraclides*, then to compare them so as to discover the manner in which these traditions were functioning in different environments, and finally to speculate regarding the means of uncovering esoteric tradition.

APOCRYPHON OF JOHN

The Apocryphon of John (ApJohn) exists in four manuscripts and in two versions: two manuscripts contain the shorter version (Codex Berolinensis 8502 [BG] and Nag Hammadi Codex III [CG III, 1]) and two the longer version (CG 11,1 and IV,1).[2] The shorter version seems on form-critical grounds to be the earlier and to date from the second century with editorial expansions, which continued until the longer version was formed. A comparison of the longer with the shorter version shows the manner in which an earlier revelation dialogue was expanded to produce a very complex text.

The section of revelation dialogue that presents Adam's body begins in BG 8502 at line 45.1 with the statement and question regarding the Mother's agitation, and it ends at 52.12 with the creation of the woman. There are five parts to the structure of the pericope:

(1) The correction of the Mother's error [45.1–47.15]

(2) The forming of Adam [47.16–49.9]

(3) The creation of soul-substances [49.10–50.14]

(4) The raising of Adam [50.15–51.20]

(5) The demotion of Adam [52.1–52.18]

I will argue that section three is an interpolation into an earlier mythology and that the speculation regarding the psychic Adam was a later, esoteric expansion of an originally bipartite anthropology into a tripartite.

2. The translation of *The Apocryphon of John*, the shorter version, is that found in Foerster: *Gnosis*. There is another translation of the shorter version in Grant: *Gnosticism*. For a comparison of the two versions see Krause and Labib: *Die Drei Versionen des Apokryphon des Johannes* For the Coptic text, see Till and Schenke: *Die Gnostischen Schriften*.

The first section presents the mythological explication of the formation of Adam in direct response to the issue at hand in the revelation dialogue material. The dialogue concerns the occasion for the Mother's agitation: the formation of Adam soteriologically rectifies the Mother's error.

> "The Mother now began to be agitated, knowing her deficiency, since her consort had not concurred with her when she was degraded from her perfection." But I said: "Christ, what does 'be agitated' mean?" He smiled and said: "Do you think that it is as Moses said, 'over the waters?' No, but she saw the wickedness and the apostasy which would attach to her son. She repented, and as she went to and fro in the darkness of ignorance she began to be ashamed and did not dare to return, but went to and fro. Her going and coming is 'to be agitated.' Now when the Self-willed had received a power from the Mother, he was ignorant of a multitude which are superior to his mother. For he thought of his mother that she alone existed. He saw the great multitude of angels which he had created, and exalted himself above them. But when the Mother recognized that the abortion of darkness was not perfect, because her consort had not concurred with her, she repented (and) wept bitterly. He heard the prayer of her repentance, and the brethren prayed for her. The holy invisible spirit assented. Now when the invisible spirit assented, he poured upon her a spirit from the perfection. Her consort came down to her in order to put right her deficiency through a Pronoia, and she was not brought up to her own aeon, but because of the great ignorance which had become manifest in her she is in the nonad until she puts right her deficiency. A voice came to her: 'Man exists, and the Son of man.'" (45.1—47.15)

The Mother's self-will led the holy invisible spirit to send his spirit upon her and to send her a consort. This redemptive act is a providential one: the soteriology demands that the self-will of the Mother be rectified by the Spirit's providence, i.e., that Adam must undo the work of Ialdaboath. The creation of humanity has a positive and salvific role: Man becomes the agent of salvation in that what was originally done in error now is part of the Spirit's Pronoia. This positive role of humanity answers the question regarding the Mother's agitation and, therefore, seems to be a part of the revelation dialogue and the earliest stratum of the text.

The second section describes the archons' formation of Adam in the context of Ialdaboath's confusion. The archons are not portrayed as performing a negative deed: they are carrying out the task as part of redemption.

> The first archon, Ialdaboath, heard it (and) thought that the voice [came from his mother]. The holy perfect Father, the first man, [taught] him in the form of a man. The blessed one revealed to them his face. And the whole archon company of the seven powers assented. They saw in the water the likeness of the image. They said to one another: "Let us make a man after the image of God and his likeness." They created out of themselves and all their powers. They moulded out of themselves a creature, and each one of the [powers] [created out of its] power [a soul]. They created it after the image which they had seen; in imitation of him who exists from the beginning, the perfect Man. They said: "Let us call him Adam, that his name and his power may become for us light." (47.16–49.9)

The exegesis of Genesis 1:26 insists that the archons are copying an image that they see in the water—this certainly implies that it is a *physical* image that they are copying: the image is the physical image of the "holy perfect Father" who used it to teach Ialdabaoth. The Father was "in the form of a man," and the archons' physical creation, Man, imitates that divine image and likeness of the Father. All of these details point to a very positive, soteriological role for Man's body, even though it was created by the archons out of themselves.

The third section presents the creation of soul-substances by the "powers" and "angels."

> And the powers began from below. The first is Divinity, a bone-soul; the second is Lordship, a sinew-soul; the third is fire, a flesh-soul; the fourth is Pronoia, a marrow-soul, and the whole structure of the body; the fifth is the Kingdom, a [blood-] soul; the sixth is Insight, a skin-soul; the seventh is Wisdom, a hair-soul. And they adorned the whole body. And their angels stood by them. (They created out of the souls), which had first been prepared by the powers, the soul-substance, the arrangement of the limbs (and) the joints. And they created the whole body, which was fitted together by the multitude of angels which I have already mentioned. (49.10—51.14)

The active characters change in this section. The "archons" of the previous section have become "powers" in this section, and the "angels" mentioned in 46.6–7 as Ialdabaoth's creations are doing the actual work of putting the body together. This seems to indicate that we are to identify the work of archons with the work of the powers and that of the angels. It blurs the clarity of the creative process that has just been described. Since the creation has already been presented, this section with its change of characters and expansion of the process seems to be an interpolation.

The soteriological motivation of the material from the revelation dialogue, moreover, seems no longer to be a concern. There has been a shift from a focus on the *function* of the creation of Man to a focus on *the body itself*. The parts of the body are enumerated, given an abstract quality, and identified with a soul-substance—none of these elements are related to the soteriology of the myth. Adam's body had become a subject for speculation on its own, and it has been interpolated into the text at this point to extend the significance of the creation of humanity. The fourth section presents the raising of Adam.

> And it lay for a long time without moving, since the seven powers were not able to raise it up, nor were the 360 angels who fitted together [the joints. The Mother wanted to recover again] the power which she had given to the archon in compulsive desire. She came in innocence and prayed the Father of the All, whose mercy is great, and the God of light. He sent, by a holy decree, the Self-originate and the four lights in the form of angels of the first archon. They gave him advice, so that they might bring out of him the power of the Mother. They said to him: "Breathe into his face something of the spirit that is in you, and the thing will raise itself up." And he breathed into it of his spirit—which is the power of the Mother—into the body, and it moved at [once]. (50.15—51.20)

The creation of Man resulted in an inert body. The soteriology demands that the spirit be removed from the erroneous Ialdabaoth to the new creation. This is accomplished through the will and design of the Father. The Mother's spirit is no longer trapped in the error of her self-will, and the Father's will has been accomplished. The creation of Man was the medium for the restoration of the Mother's fall. Adam's body parts do not play any role in this restoration, and, therefore, they are not apparently related to the soteriological aspect of the myth.

The fifth section presents the demotion of Adam as a result of the archons' jealousy.

> [And] immediately [the rest of the] powers became jealous, because it came into being from them all and they gave to the man the powers which derive from them; and he bore the souls of the seven powers and their abilities. His understanding became far stronger than all of them, (stronger) than the first archon. But they recognized that he was free from wickedness, since he was more clever than they and had come into the light. They took him and brought him down to the regions beneath all matter. (52.1—52.18)

The archons became jealous because their creation, although derivative from them, has been given greater power. There is no specific reference to the soul-substances or the parts of the body—but only reference to the fact of a derivative creation. This jealousy is the means whereby the myth may be continued: it becomes the motivation for the oration of Zoe in the next section of the myth. The soteriological myth, then, becomes: the Mother falls through her own self-willing and bears a son; the Father wishes to rectify the Mother's error; he sends the spirit to produce a licit son by the Mother into whom the spirit in the fallen son will be put in order to release the Mother's spirit from bondage. By combining the physical image of the Father (*sōma*) and the Mother's spirit (*pneuma*), the human being restores the Mother's self-willed error. The formation of Adam's body by the powers, however, does not fit the soteriological perspective of the remainder of the pericope. The myth relates the somatic and pneumatic aspect of the creation of Man, while the powers and the angels add the psychic. Each part of the body is given a different psyche:

First	Divinity	bone-soul
Second	Goodness	sinew-soul
Third	Fire	flesh-soul
Fourth	Providence	marrow-soul
Fifth	Kingdom	blood-soul
Sixth	Understanding	head-soul
Seventh	Wisdom	hair-soul

The mythic structure only requires the existence of a body. The body parts do not relate either in order or qualities to the soteriology or to the anthropology of the myth. It seems as though this section is an independent piece of tradition. If this is so, then the mythic element should be able to stand without this interpolation; it does, in fact, seem to do so. Here is my reconstruction:

> They moulded out of themselves a creature, and each one of the [powers] [created out of its] power [a soul]. They created it after the image which they had seen; in imitation of him who exists from the beginning, the perfect Man. They said, "Let us call him Adam, that his name and his power may become for us light." . . . And it lay for a long time without moving, since the seven powers were not able to raise it up. . . . The Mother wanted to recover again the power which she had given to the archon in compulsive behavior . . . etc.

The parts of the body can be deleted without any change in the myth or in the structure of the section.

There is really no clue given in the listing of abstract qualities and soul-substances as to their significance or meaning. That the elements are numerically sequential indicates that there is some sort of progression from one to seven, but the nature and purpose of that progression is unexplained. There also may be a movement from the inner (bone-soul) to the outer (hair-soul), but that too is left unexplained. We are simply not given any clue as to the purpose, setting, or significance of the list except that it is placed in the context of the salvation myth of the Sethian Gnostics.

Although it may seem somewhat speculative, there is one clue that may indicate the function of the listing of the parts. That clue is the statement that forms the point at which the parts are included in the text: "Let us call him Adam, that his name and his power may become for us light." Adam's name and power are a light: he is functioning as a guide. It is possible that Adam is the guide for Gnostics and that the soul-substances are a kind of index of body-parts that the Gnostic manipulates in order to achieve certain ascetical states (divinity, understanding, wisdom; but fire?). Adam in his psychic dimension guides the Gnostic toward the inner (divine) and fundamental (bone-soul) person.

What is clear, however, is that originally the anthropology of the myth of the Mother was bipartite (*sōma* and *pneuma*) and that it functions well and reasonable as that. The addition, through the interpolation, of *psyche* creates a tripartite anthropology. This is rather surprising because it causes the distinction between Ialdabaoth and Adam to be diminished. They both resulted from the Mother, one licitly, one illicitly; they both had the Mother's spirit within them; they both functioned within the myth as important primordial personalities. Their significance arises, then, entirely in their role in the soteriological myth of the Mother's restoration. There is no indication of a negative attitude toward creation, body, or the sphere of created elements.

The inclusion of the parts of Adam's body with the abstract qualities and soul-substances may reflect an esoteric or magical understanding of the nature of human existence. Certainly the longer version continues at this point in the text to insert esoteric and magical material of a similar nature related to parts of the body: parts of the body are identified with particular creative powers (CG 11,1. 15:29ff.), the rulers of the seven senses (17:29ff.), the four elements (18:2ff.), and the human emotional structure (18:15ff.). The longer version seems more interested in the "psychological" dynamic of human existence, while the interpolation in the shorter version can be characterized as more ascetically oriented.

DIALOGUE WITH HERACLIDES[3]

There are only a few places where Origen discusses the issue of "is the soul the blood?"[4] They are notably in *De principiis* II. 8.1 and 2 and in the *Dialogue with Heraclides*.[5] Only in the *Dialogue* is there any reference to the formation of Adam's body. All other references discuss the creation of Adam, or the relationship of soul to body, but not through the medium of the parts of Adam's body.

The *Dialogue*[6] is a most unusual patristic work because it is a transcript of an actual meeting, which took place probably in Arabia sometime

3. My thanks to the Patristica Bostoniensis for their helpful discussion of this section of my paper, and especially to the Rev. Lloyd Patterson and The Rt. Rev. Demetrios Trakatellis. The final product, with all its arguments and conclusions, however, is entirely my own responsibility.

4. See *Biblia Patristica*.

5. There are not many places extant in the literature of the period that parallel the enumeration of body parts. The only serious possibility is Philo's *Questions and Answers on Genesis* II. 17, where Noah's ark is modeled on the parts of the human body and assigned some allegorical significance.

6. The Greek text of the *Dialogue* is that of Scherer, *Entretien d'Origene*. There is an English translation by Henry Chadwick, which I am using throughout this paper. See Chadwick, *Alexandrian Christianity*, 437–55.

between 239 and 244 CE.[7] Origen was brought into Arabia to evaluate the orthodoxy of a local bishop. The *Dialogue* takes up three separate issues: the faith of Bishop Heraclides, a question concerning the soul, and finally a discussion about immortality. It is the second issue, which is discussed at more length than the others, that relates to our discussion of Adam's body.

The structure of the argument in the second section of the *Dialogue* reveals an intricate concern. It is not written as a treatise, nor is it a piece of work that has been thoroughly reworked: it is a dialogue in which the argument is primarily verbal, and hence less literarily structured. There are three major segments: a lengthy preliminary argument, the discussion of the formation of the human being, and a conclusion. The outline of the argument would be:

I. Preliminary argument [144–54]
   A. Dionysius asks the question
   B. Definition of the problem
   C. The key to understanding it
   D. Creation of the human being in image
   E. Origen's disclaimers
   F. An exhortation to transformation
   G. Summary of the introductory material
   H. Further disclaimers

II. The creation of the human being [154–64]
   A. Creation in the image
   B. The inward and outward human being
   C. The parts of the body

III. The Conclusion of the Argument [164–66]

This outline shows that the weight of the argument is really on the preliminary material and it seems somewhat defensive. Clearly Origen senses that the question needs careful articulation and definition.[8] The definition of the problem is related to passages of scripture, but not exegetically:

7. Nautin, *Origene*, 388–89.

8. It might be suggested that Origen is simply playing to the crowds as a great city preacher and teacher appearing in a rural environment. The great length, however, that Origen takes to organize and define the problem seems to indicate that he wants the question articulated very carefully and deliberately: he is dealing with a Gnostic or at

Accordingly, the question posed by the beloved Dionysius forces our hand. I shall first set out the passages which trouble them, lest any one of them be omitted, and by God's permission we will answer each one of them in accordance with your request. The disturbing passage is as follows: "The soul of all flesh is blood" (Lev 17:11–12). This text has terribly distressed those who have not understood it. Also, "Ye shall not eat the soul with the flesh; pay strict heed to see that you eat no blood; ye shall not eat the soul with the flesh" (Deut 12:23). The disturbing text is this one. For the other distressing texts are far less emphatic in expressing the idea suggested here. (144–46)

The difficulty is not in the interpretation of the texts, but in the anthropological significance of that interpretation. The key to understanding those texts rests in an abstract principle.

For my part according to my measure of understanding, and praying for assistance in reading the divine words (for we are in need of help lest our minds should conceive ideas diverging from the truth), I have found that incorporeal things are given the same names as all the corporeal things, so that just as corporeal things apply to the outer man, those which are given the same names as corporeal things apply to the inner man. The Bible says that man is two men: "For if our outward man perish, yet our inward man is renewed day by day," and "I rejoice in the law of God after the inward man" (2 Cor 4:16 and Rom 7:22). These two men the apostle everywhere shows to be distinct. In my judgment he would not have ventured to invent this notion out of his own head, but rather said this because he had clearly understood statements in the Scriptures which are obscurely expressed. (146)

The key to understanding the argument is twofold: to understand that there is a correlation between the inner and the outer human being, and that this also correlates to the inward and outward human being of the Pauline writings. Once this key has been given, then the interpretation of the creation of Adam follows.

Some people imagine that there is a mere repetition when in the story of the creation of the world after the creation of man we read "God took dust of the earth and formed man" (Gen 2:7). The cor-

---

least an esoteric doctrine from which he wishes to distance himself publicly. It is a serious question that Origen takes seriously and that he answers carefully.

ollary of this interpretation is that it is the body which is the part "after the image" (Gen 1:26), and that God is given a human form or that the form of God is shaped like the human body. But we are not so crazy as to say either that God is composed of a superior and an inferior element so that that which is in his image is like him in both elements, which constitute God in his completeness, or that that which is in his image consisted rather in the inferior part and not in the superior. (146–48)

There then follows two rather long disclaimers: one negative and the other positive. The negative disclaimer is a topos about not giving sacred material to those who are unworthy. The positive topos is a call to purity to receive right doctrine. These disclaimers are followed by an extensive exhortation that the listener be transformed. This call to transformation implies that a person is able to change nature to be "changed from being a swine to being a man," or that repentance effects a real change in a person's being. Such repentance is, in fact, necessary for receiving the orthodox teaching regarding the blood and the soul. It is here that the defensive tone of the argument becomes most obvious.

The summary of the preliminary material presents in short order all elements of the argument. It is a very curious sort of exposition that has been going on: exhortation, the abstract key to the argument, the question itself are all a very peculiar preface to the actual explanation. Origen's brief summary of his argument is this:

Since it is our task to speak about man, and to inquire whether the soul of man is not blood and since this subject required us to discuss in detail the doctrine of the two men and as we have come to a mysterious subject [*logon mystikon*], I beseech you that you do not cause me to be accused of casting pearls before swine, of throwing holy things to the dogs, of flinging divine things to serpents, of giving the serpent a share in the tree of life. That I may avoid this accusation, be transformed, put off evil, quarrelling, wrath, strife, anger, division of opinion, that there may not be any further schisms among you but that "you may be firmly established in the same mind and the same judgment" (1 Cor 1:10). (152)

The discussion seems to revolve about two aspects of the discussion of "is the soul the blood?": first, the *logos mystikos* of the two men; and second, the exhortation to avoid evil and to be united in order that Origen not be accused. It does seem peculiar that Origen describes the doctrine as a *logos mystikos*: there can be no doubt that in Origen's mind the argument is characterized as esoteric or secretive. The esoteric nature of the material is further emphasized by the hortatory sections. The teaching is intended for the few, the worthy, and the select, and it cannot be taken lightly. The key to this esoteric doctrine is the discourse concerning the two men.

This leads directly to the explanation of the creation of the human being: there is the Adam "in the image" and the hylic Adam. This represents a strictly bifurcated hylic (made of earth) and eikonic (made in the image) human being.

> At the creation of man, then, there was first created the man that is "after the image," in whom there was nothing material. He who is in the image is not made out of matter. "And God said, Let us make man in our image and likeness, and let them have dominion" and so on. And when God made man he did not take dust of the earth, as he did the second time, but he made him in the image of God. That that which is in the image of God is understood as immaterial and superior to all corporeal existence not only by Moses but also by the apostle is shown by his words as follows: "Putting off the old man with his deeds and putting on the new which is renewed in the knowledge of him who created him" (Col 3:9). (154)

This bifurcated human being leads to the doctrine of the two men that allows there to be relationship between them.

> Therefore in each one of us there are two men. Why does Scripture say that the soul of all flesh is blood? It is a great problem. Just as the outward man has the same name as the inward man, so also this is true of his members, so that one may say that every member of the outward man has a name corresponding to what is true of the inward man. (154)

It is the same name that holds together the eikonic and hylic human being, and the name allows a human being to move from the hylic to the eikonic part of his being. The parts of the body are then listed with their correlative significances. The correlation is developed by references to scriptural passages, so that each bodily part has an inner and an outer meaning (an eikonic and a hylic meaning), as well as an inner an outer significance, which is developed through the scriptural proof-text. The parts of the body relate mostly to the senses (eyes, ears, nostrils, taste [tongue], hands [touch]) although there are also the fine parts, the heart, and the hairs.

The conclusion of the argument rests on the correlation between hylic blood and the eikonic soul. Just as the blood enlivens the body, so does the soul enliven the inner human.

> Thus you have all the parts of the visible body in the inner man. Do not doubt, then, concerning the blood also because it has the same name as physical blood, like the other members of the body. It is that which belongs to the inner man. . . . if one comprehends what the soul is, and that it belongs to the inner man, and that it is in that part there is the element which is "in the image," it is clear that Paul was right when he said: "For it were better to depart and to be with Christ" (Phil 1:23) (164)

This conclusion brings us back to the beginning of the argument: the blood is the vital power of the soul. The soul is the blood, and therefore at death the body does not contain the soul.

The argument of this section of the *Dialogue* presents a bipartite hylic and eikonic anthropology. It is interesting that the anthropology is not explained in the traditional language of body and soul (found in *ApJohn*), nor is there any reference to the psychic dimension of humanity. This doctrine also is presented with polemical overtones: the identity of the eikonic human with the physical image of God (accepted in *ApJohn*) is rejected without discussion. The relationship of inner/outer, hylic/eikonic is through an esoteric doctrine of the two men. This doctrine permits the identification of one part with the other, a movement from the hylic body to the eikonic being. This movement through the identification of physical to spiritual elements seems to have an ascetical orientation. By moving beyond the outer, the hylic, a human being is able to progress to the image of God, to the eikonic level of existence. The ascetical orientation is further supported by the hortatory material and the focus on transformation and repentance.

GENERAL COMPARISONS AND CONCLUSIONS

There seems to have been some common intellectual tradition of anthropological speculation about the formation of Adam in the image of God. Originally this anthropology was totally bipartite as it remained in

Origen's *Dialogue*, but was changed in *ApJohn* with the addition of the psychic parts of Adam's body. In *ApJohn* this speculation takes place in a mythological system wherein the parts of the body are merely enumerated with their abstract quality. In Origen this speculation takes place in a philosophical environment in which the psychological and spiritual key to understanding the relationship of the inner to the outer parts is set forth.

The tradition itself seems to have had a recognizable form which, in fact, derives from the exegesis and commentary on the phrase "in the image." This phrase is the heart of the form:

(1) the formation of Adam in the image

(2) the elaboration of the body parts

(3) the spiritualization of the body parts

In these texts there may be three stages in the development of this traditional form. First, the original level of the exegesis in *ApJohn* was a mythological exegesis of the creation of Adam. Second, the soteriological myth was expanded in *ApJohn* with a section that speculated on the body parts and applied theological, ascetical significance to those parts. Third, Origen takes that same esoteric tradition and reinterprets it so that the distinction is made between inner and outer bodily significances. The history of the tradition is, thus, from (1) the mythic powers who create Adam, to (2) the speculation on the body parts, and finally, to (3) the reinterpretation toward inner/outer body parts.

The life-situation, or function, of the form, judging from its attestation in Origen, is in personal asceticism. Cynic and Stoic asceticism consisted of practices for the development of virtue and elimination of vice. Christian asceticism, developing from there, posited a spiritual or pneumatic state superior to the physical, which was to be made manifest in the physical life. Christian asceticism became thus a transformative asceticism.[9] Both Origen and *ApJohn* are presenting the means to that

9. The classical example of this is chronologically later in Cassian's *Institutes*, where he discusses the eight principal faults. The vivid description of the physical phenomena and manifestations of the fault are intended to assist the ascetic to recognize the fault in its most concrete manifestations. The objective, then, became the transformation of that fault in the physical life so that it reflects the divine virtue. The physical level is intended to assist in transformation or reformation of life.

transformative asceticism. The teaching is such that ascetical theological categories are tied to body parts so that by focusing on a body part, attainment of an ascetical ideal correlative to that body part is made possible. If an ascetic knows the *key*, he may achieve the ascetical goal. By its nature such teaching would not be appropriate to the general public. Origen's hesitance to give the information would then be logical: such a *mystikos logos* is only for those who are in training to know. It can then be surmised that this form not only functioned in personal asceticism, but also in an esoteric environment.

The distinction between exoteric and esoteric thought is an important one. Exoteric thought or teaching is one that is intended to be appropriated by anyone. It is, hence, an open system that employs language in the traditional manner, using the commonly understood meaning and usage of words. It is thus directed at the broadest base of communication, and it is founded upon the use of reason to facilitate understanding and upon rational discourse as the educational norm. The object of exoteric thought is to communicate so as to pass on information, or convince, or please.

Esoteric thought, on the other hand, is by its nature a closed system. Language is used in a special way and is directed to the few, a select group of initiates or knowledgeable people who are given the key to the special language so that they and only they can understand. A key is necessary to understanding the system. This happens because the relationship of elements (symbol to referent, or concept to concept) is not one that grows out of the inherent meanings of the words or common use of language, but is an assigned or more arbitrary relationship of parts. The access to the system is limited.

The formation of Adam's body in *ApJohn* clearly is an esoteric system. Origen, however, is caught in the process of making an esoteric system exoteric: he is giving away the key to the system and is thus opening it for anyone to understand. It is this opening that gives us an entry into the ascetical nature of the material in *ApJohn*, and helps us to discover what is the nature of the speculation found there. Although this one traditional form is found in two very different environments, the uncovering of Adam's body helps us to understand the asceticism and speculation of the second and third centuries and to see the continuance of a bipartite anthropology in speculative, esoteric environments.

CHAPTER 7

Daemons and the Perfecting of the Monk's Body[1]

THE PROBLEM—DAEMONS

DAEMONS[2] ARE UBIQUITOUS CHARACTERS IN MONASTIC LITERATURE BE-cause monastic formation revolves about a struggle with them. Without the daemons, there could be no progress in the monastic life since progress begins when the daemons attack and succeeds by the monk's activity in their defeat. *Askesis*, the metaphor chosen by the monks to describe their formation, itself implies such athletic contending with opponents: the metaphor requires some "contender" for its completion.

Our knowledge and understanding of daemons, however, emerges from a conflation of a number of discourses that include daemons. In addition to monastic ascetical daemonology,[3] studies of daemons inter-

---

1. This paper has received the benefit of comments from two different groups: the Ascetic Behavior in Greco-Roman Antiquity research project of the Institute for Antiquity and Christianity (special thanks to Vincent Wimbush, Elizabeth Castelli, Elizabeth Clark, Gail Paterson Corrington, Karen Jo Torjesen, and Kathleen O'Brien Wicker); and a joint symposium on "Daemons in Greek Culture" at the American Philological Association and the Modern Greek Studies Association (special thanks to Charles Stewart, Michael Herzfeld, and Elaine Pagels). Two individuals also read and critiqued the paper: Professor Margaret Miles and Professor Bernadette Brooten, then both at Harvard Divinity School. Alas, what remains written here is my own responsibility.

2. This article intends, as the title indicates, to define monastic daemonology by constructing a separate semantic field for the monastic usage of the word "demon." In order to differentiate this monastic semantic field from others in the "demon" group and in order to avoid the tendency readily to assume that every concept of "demon" is the same, I have retained an older spelling for the word, namely "daemon" (Greek: *daimōn*).

3. See Harpham, *Ascetic Imperative*.

sect with studies of evil. The history of theodicy,[4] witchcraft, and magic[5] includes daemons as major characters, while contemporary Jungian psychology[6] and Christian healing[7]—themselves relating to ancient texts—have emphasized the daemonic aspect of human illness and recovery. Moreover, daemons are part of the philosophical and theological discourse of antiquity, which developed sophisticated daemonic theories to explain both cosmology and the human constitution.[8] Finally, daemons have been incorporated into the mythic narrative structures (both biblical and cultural) of the primordial fall of human beings from an original good state as well as into the various narratives about Satan, the Devil, Lucifer, and fallen angels.[9] Each of these three sorts of discourses construct a peripheral daemonology and these peripheral constructions are then applied to monastic asceticism. In monastic ascetical literature, daemons seem to be different from all of these, but the interrelationship of daemons and monks in ascetical living remains problematic and difficult to isolate. The following saying of Amma Theodora illustrates this complexity:

> And again she said: "Not asceticism, neither vigils nor all sorts of toil, saves, except genuine humility. For there was a certain anchorite who drove out daemons (*apelaynōn daimonas*). And he examined them: 'By what means do you come out (*en tini exerchesthai*) By fasting?' And they said, 'We neither eat nor drink.' 'By vigils?' And they said, 'We do not sleep.' 'By withdrawal?' And they said, 'We dwell in the desert.' 'So by what means do you come out?' And they said, 'Nothing, except humility, conquers us.' Know that humility is conqueror of the daemons."[10]

In this interaction it is clear that the daemons and the monks have a geographical relationship since they both live in the desert. They both also practice the same ascetical discipline: withdrawal from society, limiting of food and drink, and vigils. That the daemons and the monks converse,

4. See Russell, *Devil, Satan, Lucifer,* and *Prince of Darkness.*

5. See Kelly, *Devil, Demonology and Witchcraft.*

6. See Jung, "Foreword to Werblowsky's 'Lucifer and Prometheus.'"

7. See Kelsey, *Healing and Christianity* and *Discernment.*

8. See Dobbs, *Pagan and Christian,* chapter 2; Burkert, *Greek Religion,* 179–81; and Ferguson, *Backgrounds,* 184–86 and 361–62.

9. See Foerster, "*Daimōn.*

10. Theodora. *To Gerontikon ētoi apophthegmata agiōn gerontōn,* Saying 6.

and that the daemons are a subject of conversation among monks, indicates that they have a social relationship in which they converse with each other honestly and with respect. But they are locked in a discourse of power: daemons, despite their ascetical agility and proficiency, may be made "to come out from" (*exerchomai*) the monk who has the capacity to expel them (*apolaynō*) by having achieved "humility," and so the contest is between the daemons' advantage while within the monk, and the monk's advantage developed through asceticism.

For Amma Theodora, and in monastic literature generally, three systems interrelate: the system defining the "monk" as a category superior to "human being"; the system defining the daemons and their ethical signification; and the system explaining the relationship of monk and daemons in the ascetical life.

The monk (both as giver and receiver of ascetical teaching), however, is the invisible character in this dialogue. In our modem thinking (which we have projected onto the past), monks are simply "human beings" who live a particular "lifestyle." We assume that there exists an objective category "human being" that has perdured throughout all history, so that what a sixth-century monk means by "body" or "person" is the same as our contemporary understanding of human personality.[11] We also assume that this universal "human being" moves into different totally exterior and independent social situations in which the "body" remains the same and only its accidental circumstances change.[12] Daemons have, then, been understood simply as a form of "primitive" psychology and the discussion of daemons in ascetic literature as the means of communicating primitive psychological insights about eternal, and historically non-determined, "psychological realities."[13] Scholars have only recently begun to explore the social construction of human embodiment and personality. It is generally recognized now that the "body," as well as the "person," is a social construction whose signification is neither given nor transparent. Monastic literature differentiates between "human being" and "monk." Although the monks often discuss the signification and condition of their being a "human being," they categorize themselves as "humans becoming angels" or "divine beings" or any number of similar

11. See Haraway, "Biopolitics of Postmodern Bodies," 3–43 and Geertz, "Impact of the Concept of Culture," 33–54.

12. Michie, *Flesh Made Word*, 3–11 and 124–50; Rousselle, *Porneia*, 1–62.

13. See Nouwen, *Way of the Heart*; and Jones, *Soul Making*.

descriptions. They experience themselves outside the primary category "human." The socially constructed concept "human being" becomes in a monastic culture, "monk," and we cannot presume that the cultural signification and meaning of "monk" and "human" were the same.

This study will address each of these three categories of experience— monk, daemon, and asceticism—as complex metaphoric systems.[14] The foundation for understanding daemons in monastic asceticism is monastic anthropology. The first part of this study will attempt to construct the cultural systems that undergird the monk's own understanding of the body by noting what functions and meanings are assigned to the human body as distinct from other bodies (angelic and daemonic, animal), by tabulating the events that occur in and around the body, and by noting the kinds of socialized bodies available in the culture (married, virgin, celibate, cenobitic).

The daemonic forces operate within the framework of monastic anthropology. The second part of this study will gather information about daemons: their characteristics, origin, functions, social organizations, social relationships, and effects upon human beings.

Monastic asceticism employs an anthropology and a daemonology in a program of self-improvement. The third part of this study will explore monastic asceticism as a metaphorical system of perfection through daemonic transformation, which constitutes the transformation and perfection of the monk's body.

---

14. I have chosen three primary monastic texts, representing three different perspectives on the subject: the first is John Climacus, *Ladder of Divine Ascent* and the English translation is a revised translation of the earlier translation of Archimandrite Lazarus Moore by the monks of Holy Transfiguration Monastery based upon "the edition of Sophronius Eremites, Constantinope, 1883, and . . . Migne, *Patrologia Graeca*, volume 88. . . . [and] a ninth=century manuscript (No. 421) from Mt. Sinai" (xviii)—the paragraph numbers here refer to Moore's numeration. The second text is Pseudo-Athanasius, *Life and Activity of the Holy and Blessed Teacher Syncletica*; there is an English translation by Castelli in Wimbush, *Ascetic Behavior*, 265–311; the translation here, however, is my own adaptation. The third is Maximus the Confessor, *Ascetic Discourse*; the English translation used throughout this paper is by Polycarp Sherwood. See also the translation by George C. Berthold. The translation of *Apocryphon of John* is that of Frederik Wisse in Robinson, *Nag Hammadi Library in English*, 104–23. Climacus's *Ladder* represents a late sixth- or early seventh-century handbook of monastic formation; Syncletica's *Life* is a mid fifth-century instructional biography; and Maximus the Confessor's *Discourse* is a seventh-century exposition of the ascetical life.

MONASTIC ANTHROPOLOGY

The Social Body

Recent studies of pagan and Christian *anachōrēsis* have accustomed us to think in social categories when defining the monk's life.[15] Peter Brown has demonstrated that the body in Late Antiquity belonged to society and the city and, therefore, was inscribed with political responsibility:[16] "If their little world was not to come to an end for lack of citizens, they must reproduce it, every generation, by marriage, intercourse and the begetting and rearing of children."[17] I would contend not that the body belonged to society or that it primarily bore social significance (as does Brown), but rather that the monk's body consisted of all its social relationships. The body itself was defined by its social environment. What to our mind is a "scientific," or medically defined, body engaged in social relationships was for the monks a series of different social bodies defined by the social environment in which those bodies lived. The society, developed from the intricate relations of socially embodied people, belonged to the body, not the body to society. Such an observation is critical to understanding the next section on monastic anthropology because what we would call the scientific body also consisted of a social and communal dimension.

The socialized body of the monk becomes even more complex in its social dimension. Even though the monk claimed to have withdrawn from society, political life, and even the church,[18] the monk's self-defini-tion was based upon a complex system of social distinctions involving the monk's differentiation between human beings, monks, angels, dae-mons, other types of human being, and other manners of social life. The monk, thus, creates a social identity by defining the self in relation to other creatures (angels and daemons), as well as by defining the social self in relation to other social groups (the married, the chaste, city-dwellers, desert-dwellers, the coenobium). Each of these two foci of self-definition (other creatures and other social groups) will be taken up serially.

15. See Fowden, "Pagan Holy Man," 33–59 and Kirschner, "Vocation of Holiness," 105–24.

16. Brown, *Body and Society,* 5–36.

17. Ibid., 7.

18. Brown, *Body and Society,* 213–84.

Self-definition in Relation to Other Creatures

The monk's social definition rests on a primary and fundamental distinction between angels, daemons and human beings. The differentiation of one from the other revolves about two essential categories: those creatures who are capable of falling (*piptō*); those creatures who are capable of rising up (*anistēmi, egeirō*):

> It is the property of angels . . . not to fall, and even, as some say, it is quite impossible for them to fall. It is the property of men to fall and to rise again as often as this may happen. But it is the property of devils (*daimonōn*), and devils alone, not to rise once they have fallen.[19]

Both the capacity to fall and the capacity to rise are based on two interlocking assumptions: the priority of higher over lower, and of stability over movement.[20] The ability to ascend or be raised up determines an ascending hierarchy in which the human being functions in an intermediate state between daemons and angels, sharing with daemons the ability to fall, and exhibiting a capacity for rising upward toward those beings who cannot fall. The solidarity between the fallen beings (humans and daemons) masks the particular status of angels who neither fall, nor do they consequently need to rise again. Human movability highlights the immovability of both daemons (who cannot rise) and angels (who do not fall). Humanity, here, is that creature capable of falling, like the daemons, and capable of rising toward the higher creatures, the angels.[21]

Mirroring the distinction between angel, human, and daemon is a distinction made about kinds of human being. Human beings are categorized by their ability to live virtuously: those who are evil, those who are a mixture of evil and good, and those who are good. Such categorizations of evil, mixed, and good are frequent in ascetic literature (both monastic and gnostic). There is a long tradition of distinction between the psychic and the pneumatic person: e.g., 1 Cor 3:1–4 and also people categorized as hylic, psychic, and pneumatic; e.g., both the structure of the

19. Climacus, *Ladder* Step IV; Moore #31, PG 696D.

20. Williams, "Stability, 819–29"; and idem, *Immoveable Race*.

21. It is not, however, a strict demarcation according to ontological status, or a chain of being. In a chain, the body is connected only to the lower realms, while the mind or soul is connected to the higher. Both overlap in the person. But for the monk, the body is perfected, not simply linked to the lower nature or rejected. See argument below.

scriptures and their implied readership in *The Letter to Flora*.[22] Pseudo-Athanasius presents Syncletica as teaching the following anthropological distinctions:

> There are three classes of opinions (*treis gnōmōn ideai*) about human life (*kata ton tōn anthrōpōn bion*]) of which the first is [a life] of consummate evil (*tēs akrotatēs kakias*), and the second [a life] of a sort of middling state in that it looks out toward both while participating in one of the two, and the third, led toward greatness of contemplation (*eis megethos theōrias achtheisa*) not only holds herself together but also attempts to lead by hand those who are in the rear ranks. So the evil human beings, living among the inferior ones, all the more produce the increase of dreadful things, and the middling ones attempt to escape the undisciplined, fearing the same thing, lest again they be drawn down by them, for they are still like a child of the virtues, and the third, having vigorous minds and strong resolution, live together with and have converse with the common people, desiring to save them.[23]

In this reversed hierarchy, from highest evil to the greatest contemplation, the monk categorizes humans ethically and by their influence on others: the categories distinguish goodness/virtue, evil/vice, contemplation/dreadfulness, vigorous and weak minds, positive and negative effects on others. The vigorously minded and strongly willed contemplatives both provide for themselves and attempt to draw others with them from the middle, mixed category. The evil ones also attempt to drag the middle down with them. The ones in the middle are drawn from one to the other. All these beings are capable of activity and motion appropriate to the level of their ethical development.

Self-definition in Relation to Social Groups

In addition to the above categories of human being in relation to other beings, there are also classes of people in relation to whom the monk defines the self. The first distinction is between the "two classes" who were created to inhabit the earth: the married, whose function is to produce children, and the chaste, who were to live like angels. Both classes were called to holiness, but in different ways. This distinction is further refined

22. Epiphanius, *Panarion* 33.3.1—33.7.10; text in Layton, *Gnostic Scriptures*, 306–15. See also Pagels, *Johannine Gospel*; and Rudolph, *Gnosis*, 88–113.

23. Syncletica, *Life*, 71.

when it defines the categories within chastity as the anchorites, the en-cratites, and those who live a moderate married life.[24] In an exegesis of the parable of the sower, Syncletica distinguishes three degrees of life: those who reap the hundredfold are those who live "our own profession" (*to hemeteron epaggelma*), which must be the monastic life; the sixtyfold are "the ranks of the self-controlled" (*to tōn egkratōn tagma*); the thirty-fold are "those who live with control over sensual desires" (*tōn sōphronōs biountōn*). She argues that it is better to progress from the control of de-sire to self-control, and then to the monastic life, and not in the reverse order (Syncletica, *Life*, 23).

The social body of the human being moves continually away from social entanglement and activity into solitude and quiet, which becomes the ultimate goal of human existence. The progression moves from "mar-ried and physically engaged" to "married and chaste," then to "chaste and living with other chaste people," and ending with "chaste and solitary"; and it is valued as the progression from the lesser to the greater. Progress for humanity moves toward a nonsocial, solitary state:

> Just as the fetuses inside their womb, maturing from inferior food and life, are brought because of this to a greater security (*sōtēria*), so also, the righteous withdraw from the ways of the world for the higher journey.[25]

This withdrawal recalls the steady life of the angels in the earlier narrative about the fall and movement.

In marked contrast to our modern experience of body as bounded and limited, this monastic conception of a human being's social body is noticeably unbounded and fluid. Rising and falling between angels and daemons, and moving alternately toward the various polarities of virtues and vices, contemplation and licentiousness, social and sexual engage-ment and solitude, a human being has no fixed central point, no prede-termined limits. The immovable boundaries of angels and daemons not only highlight the extremely movable and tenuous life of humans who struggle in both virtuous and contemplative arenas, they also provide a vast and fluid environment in which human beings are to function.

24. See Clark, "Devil's Gateway," 23–94 and "John Chrysostom," 265–90; Pagels, "Politics of Paradise," 67–99; Wicker, "Ethopian Moses," 329–48.

25. Syncletica, *Life*, 91.

From within these various social distinctions (angel/human/dae-mon, good/mixed/evil, chaste/married), the monk emerges as a still more precise refinement. The monastic human being lives the angelic life on earth. This is a commonplace in monastic literature. Maximus the Confessor writes: "He that loves God leads an angelic life on earth, fasting and keeping watches, singing the psalter and praying, and always think-ing good of everyone" (First Century, 1.42). John Climacus's famous definition states: "Monasticism is an angelic order and state achieved in an earthly and soiled body."[26] The monk functions as an embodied angel who must through asceticism struggle not to fall, not to be dragged into evil, not to be lured into licentiousness. Conversely the monk, by devel-oping in virtue, training the mind in contemplation, and rising each time there is a fall, lives the life of an angel on earth. The monk does not leave the fluid human state, nor does the monk find respite from activity and movement, but rather the angelic life as a goal gives direction and mean-ing to the ascetical struggle. The social body of the human being finds its highest aspiration in the life of an angel, a monk, who lives alone, having withdrawn more and more from the lower strata of social relations and being more and more oriented toward those above.

The Material Body of the Monk

The two social self-definitions of the monk lead directly to questions regarding the monk's view of the material body. Classic monastic an-thropology understands the body as the arena for struggle. Although the daemons suggest that mortification of the flesh simply weakens it and wears it out unnecessarily, the strong monk recognizes that true spiritual strength and holiness are to be found in the punishment of the body. For example, Climacus writes:

> Let no one, when he is young, listen to his enemies, the demons, when they say to him: 'Do not wear out your flesh, lest you make it sick and weak.' For you will scarcely find anyone, especially in the present generation, who is determined to mortify his flesh, although he might deprive himself of many pleasant dishes. The aim of this demon is to make our very entrance into the stadi-

26. Climacus, *Ladder,* Step I. 4; Moore #4, 4.

um lax and negligent, and then make the end correspond to the beginning.[27]

And Syncletica teaches:

> For neither is the devil (*diabolos*) prohibited by his first evil; but rather he also suggests change to the soul. And he subscribes that our ruling mind (is) a flower of nature, and that as the body is dissolved, even the soul will be destroyed. All these things he suggests to us so that the soul might be destroyed through negligence.[28]

The monastic body, thus has become the athletic stadium for training toward victory through asceticism.

Since the body is an ascetical environment, the monk does not despise the body: it is too important a part of the monk's asceticism. Syncletica teaches that the gradual weakening of the body is advantageous:

> Let us not be distressed that because of the weakness and the striking of the body we are not able to stand for prayer or to sing with our voices: all these things are completed for the destruction of desires. For both fasting and sleeping on the ground have been made a law for us because of our most base pleasures. So if sickness has dulled them, the labor is redundant. Why do I say redundant? For just as by some greater and stronger drug, the death-dealing symptoms are put to rest by the sickness. And this is the great ascesis: to persevere in sicknesses and to send up thanksgiving hymns to the stronger. Have we been deprived of our eyes? Let us not suffer with disgust, for we have lost the organs of insatiate desire, but with the interior eyes we reflect the glory of the Lord. Have we become deaf? Let us give thanks that we have completely lost the vain hearing. Have we suffered with our hands? But we have the interior ones to prepare for the battle against the enemy. Does sickness totally conquer the body? But the health of the interior person will increase more.[29]

Here it does not matter whether passive sickness or active ascetic practice diminishes the body because the effect is the same. The body contains desires that are to be destroyed; the body enjoys pleasures that must be quieted; the body has eyes and ears and other sense organs that must be

---

27. Climacus, *Ladder*, Step I, PG 641; Moore, #24, 10.

28. Syncletica, *Life*, 88.

29. Ibid., 99.

oriented toward God alone. As a result the monk's body, thus sanctified by ascetic practice or sickness, becomes a healing agent to other monks: Syncletica's wounded body cured her disciples.[30]

Syncletica's body was, by virtue of her extreme illness, made the arena of her struggle. She suffered horrible sicknesses,[31] which completely consumed her: she seems to have had lung cancer, which eventually spread to her mouth. Her death, however, is not characterized as victory over the sick and decaying body, but as transformation, perfection, *in the body*:

> So, for three months she contended (*enathleō*) against this trial (*agōn*). With divine power her whole body was supported (*parakrateō*), for the things which contributed toward its continuance had been diminished. Therefore, starvation (*atrophia*) was present, for how was she able to partake of victuals while such putrefaction and stench prevailed? Even sleep, being smitten by her sufferings, withdrew from her. When the boundary of her victory and her crown was near, she beheld visions and attendants of angels (*aggelōn epistasias*), and (hosts of) holy virgins encouraging her ascension (*anodon*) and (she beheld) illuminations of ineffable light and the place of paradise. And after the spectacle of these things, as if it happened for herself, she announced to those arriving that they should bear themselves nobly and not belittle the present time.[32]

The present, the time in her body, witnessed her transformation into an angelic being. In her body, with its now spiritualized sense organs and its dispassion toward food and sleep, she became that for which she had striven through asceticism. The passions at rest, she is without nourishment or sleep, and made capable of living the angelic life.

The monk simultaneously experiences the body as friend, ascetic arena, instrument of glorification, vessel of nature; and as foe, tyrant, and object for mastery.[33] Climacus, at the very center of his ascetical scheme, portrays the monk as addressing his body:

> What is this mystery in me? What is the meaning of this blending (*synkrasis*) of body and soul? How am I constituted as a friend

30. Ibid., 110 and 107. Also see Brown, *Cult of the Saints*.

31. Syncletica, *Life*, 106–13.

32. Ibid., 112–13.

33. See Harpham, *Ascetic Imperative*, 19–44.

and foe to myself? Tell me, tell me, my yoke-fellow, my nature (*physis*), for I shall not ask anyone else in order to learn about you. How am I to remain unwounded by you? How can I avoid the danger of my nature? For I have already made a vow to Christ to wage war against you. How am I to overcome your tyranny? For I am resolved to be your master.[34]

The body is highly problematized, not simply rejected. The flesh, in turn, responds to the monk:

> And the flesh might say in reply to its soul: "I shall never tell you anything which you do not know equally well, but only of things of which we both have knowledge (*gnōsis*). I have my father within me—self-love. The fire which I experience from without comes from humouring me and from general comfort. The fire which burns within and the movement of thoughts come from past ease and bygone deeds. Having conceived, I give birth to sins; and they, when born, in turn beget death by despair. If you clearly know the profound weakness which is both you and me, you have bound my hands. If you starve your appetite, you have bound my feet from going further. If you take the yoke of obedience, you have thrown off my yoke. If you obtain humility, you have cut off my head."[35]

The body, conceiving through outward comfort and interior thoughts, produces sin that in turn begets despair and causes death. The bodily response to the bodily conception of sin and death is physical fasting and mental obedience. The body remains the origin of the human problem, the means to its remedy, and the environment of its final victory.

The physical body contains within itself the stimulus both to sin and to ascetical correction. For the monk, the daemons must be connected intimately to the body, and this connection is developed and preserved as part of the esoteric tradition of monastic asceticism. In "Adam's Body," I argued that there was speculation regarding the ascetical significance of the formation of the body observable in the various formations of Adam's body in *The Apocryphon of John* and in the discussion of "is the soul the blood" in Origen's *Dialogue with Heraclides*.[36] I further argued that Origen was in the process of making explicit the esoteric key to this knowledge. I

34. Climacus, *Ladder*, Step XV, PG 904A–B; Moore, #89, 120.
35. Climacus, *Ladder*, Step XV, PG 904A–B; Moore, #90, 120.
36. See "Uncovering Adam's Esoteric Body," chapter 6, pp. 119–33.

maintain that such speculation on the ascetical significance of the formation of the material body continued to be a part of the monastic ascetic
teaching and that it continued to be taught not as part of the *praktika*,
but as part of the *gnostica* of monastic instruction.[37] Evidence for such
a continued speculation is found in Evagrius Ponticus's *Ad Melaniam* as
well as in his *Gnosticus* and his *Kephalaia Gnostica*.[38] Subsequent monastic texts, under the pressure of the Origenist condemnation or out of a
tradition of keeping secret such gnostic speculations, have suppressed the
teaching on bodily formation and transformation, while at the same time
keeping and continuing to teach the connection between bodily manipulation and the development of ascetical virtue. The clearest (and most
straightforward) presentation of this speculation on the creation of the
body comes from the earliest example in *The Apocryphon of John*, which I
will use here to explore the systems underlying the monk's understanding
of the body.

In *The Apocryphon of John*, three bodies are created: the first is the
spiritual body of Adamas; the second is the primordial Adam created by
the daemons and angels who must trick Ialdabaoth into breathing life
into the inert body; the third is the purely material body created as a
parody by the jealous powers.[39] The creation of three bodies (one spiritual, one psychic and one hylic) reflects an interest in clearly distinguishing hierarchies of being from the spiritual to the physical. However, if
we avoid judgment on such categorization of bodies, we find interesting
descriptions of the method of creation of each body. The creation of the
"natural body" bears the greatest signification in relation to conceptual
systems that may underlie the monastic tradition of the formation of the
monastic body:

> This is the number of the angels: together they are 365. They all
> worked on it until, limb for limb, the natural and the material
> body was completed by them. Now there are other ones in charge

37. See Dechow, *Dogma*, 297–347.

38. See Clark, "New Perspective," 145–62; and O'Laughlin, "Origenism."

39. On the body in gnostic speculation, see the superb article by Williams, "Divine
Image," 141, who writes: "It is striking how frequently Gnostic mythology actually brings
in the human anatomy—and especially the sexual anatomy. It is as though many Gnostics
saw in the body not only an intimation, a reflection, of a divine Human identity, but a
kind of map of reality." I especially wish to thank Elaine Pagels for her help in clarifying
this section of the paper.

over the remaining passions whom I did not mention to you. But if you wish to know them, it is written in the book of Zoroaster. And all the angels and demons worked until they had constructed the natural body. And their product was completely inactive and motionless for a long time.[40]

The daemons and the angels create the natural body of which the passions are a part, and they rule over the passions. Such an understanding complements the monastic view of the body in which the body, as an athletic arena, is the environment for the control of the passions and desires as well as the arena for living the angelic life. The connection between vices, passions, and daemons in *The Apocryphon of John* further resonates with the monastic description of bodily asceticism, ethical development, and daemonic warfare:

> The four chief demons are: Ephememphi who belongs to pleasure, Yoko who belongs to desire, Nenentophni who belongs to grief, Blaomen who belongs to fear. And the mother of them all is Aesthesis-Ouch-Epi-Ptoe. And from the four demons passions came forth. And from grief (came) envy, jealousy, distress, trouble, pain, callousness, anxiety, mourning, etc. And from pleasure much wickedness arises, and empty pride, and similar things. And from desire (comes) anger, wrath, and bitterness, and bitter passion, and unsatedness, and similar things. And from fear (comes) dread, fawning, agony and shame. All of these are like useful things as well as evil things. But the insight into their true character is Anaro, who is the head of the material soul, for it belongs with the seven senses, Ouch-Epi-Ptoe.[41]

The body was a complex society inhabited by daemons and angels and whose parts were ruled by them. The four chief passions (pleasure, desire, grief, and fear), which the four named chief daemons manifest, are not by nature evil; they are neutral elements indigenous to bodily existence. The passions naturally form a part of the body, so living with the passions requires careful observation and a diagnostics of the body, as Climacus explains:

> As bodily fever is one thing, but the causes of this are not one but many, so also the boiling up of anger and the movement of our

---

40. *ApJohn* 19:2–14.

41. Ibid., 18:2—19:1; see also Syncletica, *Life*, 85 and 96.

> other passions have many and various causes. That is why it is im-
> possible to prescribe one identical rule for them. Instead, I would
> rather suggest that each of those who are sick should most care-
> fully seek out his own particular cure. The first step in the cure
> should be the diagnosis of the cause of each disease; for when this
> is discovered, the patients will get the right cure from God's care
> and from their spiritual physicians. And so, for instance, those
> who wish to join us in the Lord should enter the spiritual tribunal
> that lies before us, and there they should test themselves some-
> what concerning the abovementioned passions or their causes.[42]

The same kinds of passions that *The Apocryphon of John* describe as neutral are described by the monks as negative. The monk must discern and
confront the passions in order to master them: the monk must capture
each passion through vigilance, fasting, mental prayer and thereby gain
mastery over them through knowledge.

This mastery over the body and its passions, the hallmark of achieving the angelic and solitary life, results from rendering the body as
a corpse, or, in other words, from the "mortification" of the body. The
monk's body, already experienced as a community of angelic and daemonic elements in conflict, must be so stilled that it is, for every purpose,
dead. Syncletica teaches this in its most stark reality:

> For our profession (*epaggelma*) is nothing other than the renun-
> ciation of life (*apotagē biou*), the practice of death (*meletē thana-
> tou*). Therefore just as the dead do not operate in the body, so
> neither do we.[43]

Even though the renunciation of life constitutes the mortification of the
body, the body nonetheless manifests the angelic life. Climacus describes
the embodied life of the monk in this way:

> At the gate of your heart place strict and unsleeping guards.
> Restrain your unrestrainable mind within your active body.
> Amidst the actions and movements of your limbs, practice noetic
> stillness (*hesychia*.) And most paradoxical of all, in the midst of
> commotion, be unmoved in soul. Curb your tongue which rages
> to leap into arguments. Seventy times seven in the day wrestle
> with this tyrant. Fix your mind to your soul as to the wood of
> the cross, to be struck like an anvil with blow upon blow of the

42. Climacus, *Ladder*, Step VIII, PG 833C–D; Moore, #29, 85–86.
43. Syncletica, *Life*, 76.

hammers, to be mocked, abused, ridiculed and wronged, without being in the least crushed or broken, but continuing to be quite calm and immovable.[44]

The angelic life, manifested in the body, emerges from the control of the body and of bodily movements.

The monk's mind (*nous*) plays such a major part that it has become the most critical human faculty. The mind, as in Climacus's description above, may remain still when the body is active. Conversely, the mind may remain active when the body is still. Climacus explains that the mind continues to wage the war against the daemons even when the body is at rest:

> When we are lying in bed, let us be especially sober and vigilant, because then our mind without our body struggles with the demons, and if it [sc. the mind] is found to be fond of delight (*philēdonos*), it readily becomes a traitor.[45]

The mind reorients the monk from a concern with the body and its passions to the things of the soul: the mind, under the influence of prayer, turns the monk's attention toward God. The mind divinizes the monk's body. Maximus explains the process:

> Thoughts are directed to things. Now, of things some are sense-perceptible, some mental. The mind, then, tarrying with these things, carries about with itself thoughts of them; but the grace of prayer joins the mind to God, and joining to God withdraws it from every thought. Then the mind, associating only with Him, becomes God-like.[46]

The monk's body engages in a complex process of control: the body contains within itself the daemonic and the angelic elements that rule it, so the body must be mortified. The process of mortification relies upon the distinction, minimally, between the sense-perceptible and the mental. The mind subdues the body in prayer and ascetical activity and begins to be rid of the images and thoughts that turn the monk away from God. The mind, through further prayer, becomes oriented toward God and becomes God-like in the bodily state. The monk's progress both begins

44. Climacus, *Ladder*, Step IV, PG 700B–D; Moore # 36, 35

45. Ibid., PG 889C–D, Step XV; Moore [slightly altered] # 53, 112.

46. Maximus, *Ascetic Life*, #24, 116.

and ends in the body: in the beginning the body consists of the society of daemons, angels, and body parts; in the end, the body is subdued, still, and solitary in its union with God.

This conceptual model of the monk's body makes the body a living metaphor of the desert: the monastic body, withdrawn from social life, far from social engagement and politics has become a desert, a solitary body, punished by the environment. Like the desert, the body is even inhabited by daemons.

Monastic Daemonology

Although the daemons function within the sphere of the monk's corporeal and social body, they are discussed as though they were purely exterior forces whose impact was experienced interiorly. In fact, the daemons are the only constant companion for a monk who has withdrawn from the world. Monastic daemonology will be explored under three categories: the daemon's characteristics; the daemon's manner of interaction with the monks; and the methods in daemonic warfare.

The Daemon's Characteristics

John Climacus described the daemons as "strong; they never sleep; they are incorporeal and invisible."[47] Daemons are lighter than the human body, being capable of flying suspended in the air. Their ability to float enables them to see what is about to happen before humans can see it; they appear, therefore, to be able to predict the future, even though this is simply the result of their lighter bodily construction.[48]

Daemons are "spirits" (*pneumata*),[49] who rule everywhere except in heaven. Climacus relates the following daemonic self-revelation:

> At last, when flogged, they said: "We have neither beginning nor birth, for we are progenitors and parents of all the passions. Contrition of heart that is born of obedience is our real enemy; we cannot bear to be subject to anyone; that is why we fell from Heaven, though we had authority there. In brief, we are the parents of all that opposes humility; for everything which furthers humility, opposes us. We hold sway everywhere, save in heaven,

47. Climacus, *Ladder*, Step I, PG 641; Moore, #24, 9–10.
48. Ibid., Step IV, PG 672; Moore # 28, 19–20.
49. Ibid., PG 712A–B; Moore, #69, 42.

so where will you run from our presence? We often accompany dishonours, and obedience, and freedom from anger, and lack of resentment, and service. Our offspring are the falls of spiritual men: anger, calumny, spite, irritability, shouting, blasphemy, hypocrisy, hatred, envy, disputation, self-will and disobedience. There is only one thing in which we have no power to meddle; and we shall tell you this, for we cannot bear your blows: If you keep up a sincere condemnation of yourself before the Lord, you can count us as weak as a cobweb. For pride's saddle-horse, as you see, is vainglory, on which I am mounted."[50]

The daemons reveal that they are without beginning or origin (*archē*) and without birth (*gennesis*). Their unbegotten and unoriginate state has enabled them to be the "progenitors and parents of all the passions." The daemons, still in this confession, state that they fell from heaven where they had authority, so they cannot bear to be subject to anyone. Pride, therefore, is their chief weapon. Daemons are prevalent: they function everywhere and no one can hide from them. Their children are the vices that cause spiritual people to fall: "anger, calumny, spite, irritability, shouting, blasphemy, hypocrisy, hatred, envy, disputation, self-will and disobedience." Only when the monk acquires the virtue of humility can they be defeated.

Climacus's description echoes the description of the relationship of daemons to passion in *The Apocryphon of John*.[51] The daemons, themselves unoriginate yet fallen, have conceived all the evil passions, and those passions, woven into the monk's body, have become the community in which the monk will grow into humility.[52] Such a community presents no easy way; some monks even expressed a preference for the easier contest with the brethren in the community than for the daemonic warfare of more spiritual powers precisely because it was a more difficult warfare with a more formidable set of opponents. John Climacus explains:

50. Ibid., Step XXIII, PG 896C–D; Moore, #37, 141–42.

51. *ApJohn*, 18:2–19:1.

52. It is peculiar that the connection of daemons and the passions, at least in *Apocryphon of John*, comes about in the creation of the primordial Adam, the higher Adam, not the material Adam created later by the jealous powers. Even if we (or the monks of the monastic tradition) did not identify the monastic "angelic life" with the "primordial Adam" of the gnostic tradition, although the correlation is striking, the passions and the struggle centering on the passions for both the monks and *Apocryphon of John* signify a higher form of life than the material.

> I must not fail to adorn the crown of this step with this emerald. Once I started a discussion on stillness with some of the most experienced elders in the community. With a smile on their faces and in jovial mood, they said to me in a friendly way: "We, Father John, being material, live a material life, preferring to wage war according to the measure of our weakness, and considering it better to struggle with men, who are sometimes fierce and sometimes repentant, than with the demons who are continually raging and up in arms against us."[53]

The daemons, then, in their ruling everywhere except in heaven, rule also in the monk's body. It is their character to incite the passions and thereby to set the stage for the monk's progress: the daemons employ their cunning specifically to entrap or preclude the monk's successful combat with the particular passions that present that monk with the greatest difficulty. In this capacity, the daemons determine the form and content of ascetical activity. The daemons preserve their rule, while the monk, in order to encourage ascetical activity, characterizes the daemons as "other," "foe," "the enemy," "the adversaries."

The monks describe the daemons as an invisible army. For the monks the daemons are highly organized, hierarchical, and combative forces whose primary purpose is to destroy the monk's virtue. Climacus explains:

> We ought to consider whether our spiritual enemies have not each their own proper task to fulfill when drawn up in battle array against us, just as in a visible war. Surprising to say, they certainly have. When I thought about those who were tempted, I observed that falls were of varying seriousness. He that hath ears to hear, let him hear.[54]

From the monk's perspective, the daemons wage a well-conceived battle by attacking in ways the monk would least expect:

> The devil often has the habit, especially in warring against ascetics and those leading the solitary life, of using all his force, all his zeal, all his cunning, all his intrigue, all his ingenuity and purpose, to assail them by means of what is unnatural, and not by what is natural. Therefore, ascetics coming into contact with women, and

---

53. Climacus, *Ladder*, Step IV, PG 700B; Moore, Step 4, #35, 35.
54. Ibid., Step XV, PG 885A; Moore XV, #28, 107.

not in any way tempted either by desire or thought, have sometimes regarded themselves as already blessed, not knowing, poor things, that where a worse downfall had been prepared for them, there was no need of the lesser one.[55]

In warfare, the daemons systematically undermine the monks' ability to live dispassionately and quietly by creating for them a false dispassion and quiet.

The fact, however, that daemons and monks are locked in such intimate conflict and mutual knowledge confirms that their relationship is primary. Those monks who live in community do battle primarily with other members of the community: their battle field develops in the natural course of trying to become "perfect" in the context of community living. The hesychast, the monk achieving passionlessness and who represents the higher form of life, the life toward which the monks aspire, battles the daemons. The communal life, explored as a secondary level of monastic life, prepares the monk for the "higher" life of the solitary hesychast. The monastic life progresses then from community living to solitary life, from fellowship with brothers and sisters to the constant companionship of the daemons:

> Those living in stillness (*hesychia*) subject to a father have only demons working against them. But those living in a community struggle with demons and human beings. The former, being always under the eyes of the master, keep his commands more strictly; but the latter, on account of his absence, break them to some extent. However, those who are zealous and industrious more than make up for this failing by enduring collisions and knocks, and win double crowns.[56]

Their mutual companionship cannot always be characterized as antagonistic. The monks do not understand daemons to be "evil" or "evil forces" that the monks must reject. The monk's companionship with the daemons is one of growth-oriented antagonism. Consider this description of a conversation:

> One who had the gift of sight told me what he had seen. "Once," he said, "when I was sitting in an assembly, the demon of vainglory and the demon of pride came and sat beside me, one on

55. Ibid., PG 885B; Moore #29, 107–8.
56. Ibid., Step IV, PG 712C; Moore, #76, 43.

either side. The one poked me in the side with the finger of vainglory and urged me to relate some vision of labour which I had
done in the desert. But as soon as I had shaken him off, saying:
'Let them be turned back and confounded that desire evils for
me' [Ps. 39:20], then the demon on my left at once said in my ear:
'Well done, well done, you have become great by conquering my
shameless mother.' Turning to him, I made apt use of the rest of
the verse and said: 'Let them be turned back straightway in shame
that say unto me: Well done! well done!' And to my question:
'How is vainglory the mother of pride?' he replied: 'Praises exalt
and puff one up; and when the soul is exalted, then pride seizes it,
lifts it up to heaven and casts it down to the abyss.'"[57]

This conversation highlights the nature and import of the relationship:
the daemons constantly interact with the monk in order to force the
monk's spiritual growth. Without the presence of the monk's striving,
the daemons would be perceived as friendly: it is precisely the monk's
striving that constructs the daemons negatively. Since the monks have
left their normal habitat to live in the natural habitat of the daemons, the
conflict between monks and daemons has as much to do with the conflict
between natural geographical spheres of influence as with the presence of
mutually adversarial companions:

> As we have said before, some people in hermitages suffer far more
> severe attacks from the enemy. And no wonder! For the demons
> haunt such places, since the Lord in His care for our salvation has
> driven them into the deserts and the abyss. Demons of fornica-
> tion cruelly assail the hesychast in order to drive him back into
> the world, as having received no benefit from the desert. Demons
> keep away from us when we are living in the world that we may
> go on staying among worldly minded people because we are not
> attacked there. Hence we should realize that the place in which we
> are attacked is the one in which we are certainly waging bitter war
> on the enemy; for if we ourselves are not waging war, the enemy
> is found to be our friend.[58]

This relationship does not describe a confrontation between good and
evil (to any degree) but rather a kind of circumstantial adversarial companionship. The circumstances revolve about the natural geographical

---

57. Ibid., Step XXII, PG 953C–D; Moore, #35, 136.
58. Ibid., Step XV, PG 893A–B; Moore, #62, 113–14.

spheres of habitation, the body's natural relationship with its parts, and the monk's desire to transform the body into some sort of angelic body. Ironically, the monk lives in the daemons' world in order to get free of the body (which the daemons have helped to create): the monk's goal is to live as a corpse, or as an angel, both of which seem to result in the same transformation. The daemons, already bodiless, hover over the monk in order to restrain the monk's transformation and to maintain control both over the monk's body and the geographical terrain in which they rule.

The Daemons' Interaction with the Monks

These descriptions of the daemons as simultaneously friend and enemy, natural companion and supernatural enemy, lead directly to the discussion of the nature of the interaction between monks and daemons. The ambiguous companionship of monk and daemon provides the context for their equally peculiar manner of relation. The daemons strive to thwart the monk's ascetical transformation[59] through both exterior bodily and interior mental attacks:

> It is necessary, therefore, always to be vigilant (*grēgorein*). For he fights through external matters and subdues through internal thoughts (*logismōn*). And he does much more through the internal, for by night and in the course of the day he draws near immaterially.[60]

The daemons do not attack directly, but prefer to overcome monks because they are found to be negligent or because they (experiencing an increment of success) have been discovered to be arrogant:

> A twofold fear is placed on you: either [a fear] lest you return to the former things through negligence when the enemy attacks you; or [a fear] lest you shall be tripped while running. For our enemy the devil (*diabolos*) either draws one to himself from behind at whatever time he sees that the soul is slow and sluggish, or, when it seems to be excellent and patient of toil toward ascesis, he enters afterward subtly and covertly by means of arrogance, and in this way, he destroys the soul together with the person.[61]

59. See, e.g., Climacus, *Ladder*, Step VII, PG 816C; Moore, #68, 80.
60. Syncletica, *Life*, 28.
61. Ibid., 49.

The daemons' attacks, moreover, consistently move from interior to exterior, from one set of vices to another, shifting the arena of the monks' attention and practice:

> And what were his first traps? Clearly [they were] gluttony, love of pleasures, fornication. These spirits especially happen at the more youthful ages. Greed, covetousness and things like them follow after these. So the struggling soul, when it survives these passions, supposing that it might rule the stomach, when also it might leap over the pleasures of the belly with dignity, when it might despise money, then, from all quarters the malicious one, perplexed, subjects undisciplined movement upon the soul.[62]

Since the daemons set traps for ensnaring monks, the monks must constantly remain vigilant. This cycle of entrapment and vigilance defines the primary manner of their relating. The monks' vigilance, consequently, must become increasingly more sophisticated with ascetical progress because the daemons customize their assault to the weakness of each individual monk:

> The adversary (*ho enantios*) sets this rationale before those who turn from worldly wisdom to the solitary life, for the devil (*diabolos*) who is sensible about evil things places traps for human nature. To some he persists through [their] despair, and he draws some down through vanity, and he buries others because of their love of money. For, like a death-dealing doctor, he brings poisons to humans. And one person he destroys through the liver, bringing him the toxin of desire; another he makes wounded in the heart, fastening his temper to anger; and he dulls the authoritative power of some, either wrapping them with ignorance, or twisting them through useless learning.[63]

Each of these vices evolves from the three primary daemonic origins of all vices: the first is bodily pleasure, the second is psychic desire and the third is a grief that mixes both bodily and psychic elements. These principal monastic faults, which reflect the listing in *ApJohn* 18:2—19:1, define for the daemons the principal areas of monastic weakness while providing for the monks the foundational areas for vigilance of body and psyche:

62. Ibid.
63. Ibid., 85.

There are three principal heads of the enemy, from which all evil descends: desire, pleasure, grief. These depend one upon the other, and one follows from the other: it is possible moderately to rule over pleasure, but it is impossible [to rule over] desire. For the former (that is, the one) regarding pleasure is accomplished through the body, but the latter arises from the soul. But grief is constructed from both of them. So do not allow desire to function and you will disperse the remaining things.[64]

The monks' vigilance focuses on desire, while the daemons may attack from a wide spectrum of the passions derivative from desire.

Practicing a sort of impish delight in trapping monks, daemons employ a variety of techniques. The daemons use the monks' memory to remind them of family and to suggest their families' grief at their withdrawal:

After our renunciation, when the demons inflame our hearts by reminding us of our parents and brethren, then let us arm ourselves against them with prayer, and let us inflame ourselves with the remembrance of the eternal fire, so that by reminding ourselves of this, we may quench the untimely fire of our heart. If anyone thinks he is without attachment to some object, but is grieved at its loss, then he is completely deceiving himself.[65]

Or they may transform themselves into angels or martyrs and suggest that the monk is in communion with them:

Demons often transform themselves into angels of light and take the form of martyrs, and make it appear to us during sleep that we are in communication with them. Then, when we wake up, they plunge us into unholy joy and conceit. But you can detect their deceit by this very fact. For angels reveal torments, judgments and separations; and when we wake up we find that we are trembling and sad. As soon as we begin to believe the demons in dreams, then they make sport of us when we are awake too. He who believes in dreams is completely inexperienced. But he who distrusts all dreams is a wise man. Only believe dreams that warn you of torments and judgments. But if despair afflicts you, then such dreams are also from the demons.[66]

64. Ibid., 96.
65. Climacus, *Ladder*, Step II, PG, 657; Moore, #10 and 11, 13–14.
66. Ibid., Step IV, PG 672A–B; Moore, #29, 20.

The daemons may also depart from the monk to deceive the monk into thinking that the warfare has ended:

> And we ought not to forget, my friends, that the wicked demons sometimes suddenly leave us, so that we may neglect our strong passions as of little importance, and then become incurably sick.[67]

Or contrarily, the daemons may suggest as warfare the very ascetical practice that will increase the monk's most problematic passion and lead to a fall:

> If we are observant, we shall see that many irritable people are practicing vigils, fasts and stillness. For the aim of the demons is to suggest to them, under the pretext of repentance and mourning, just what is likely to increase their passion.[68]

The daemons push the monk to sin, and when the monk cannot be provoked to the intended sin, the daemons then lead the monk to another sin—judgment of others who have sinned:

> The demons, murderers as they are, push us into sin. Or if they fail to do this, they get us to pass judgment on those who are sinning, so that they may defile us with the stain which we ourselves are condemning in another.[69]

Finally, the daemons suggest means for the monk to experiment carefully with sins while using either the memory of sinful acts to defeat the monk or the monk's ignorance of sin to encourage sinful experimentation:

> The snake of sensuality is many-faced. In those who are inexperienced in sin, he sows the thought of making one trial and then stopping. But this crafty creature incites those who have tried this to fresh trial through the remembrance of their sin. Many inexperienced people feel no conflict in themselves simply because they do not know what is bad; and the experienced, because they know this abomination, suffer disquiet and struggle. But often the opposite of this also happens.[70]

67. Ibid., Step VIII, PG, 829A; Moore #9, 82; see also Step XXVI, PG 1025C; Moore #61, 170.

68. Ibid., Step VIII, PG 832C–D; Moore, #21, 84.

69. Ibid., Step X, PG 848C; Moore, #11, 91.

70. Ibid., Step XV, PG 896A; Moore, #68, 115.

Each of these daemonic methods relies upon an appearance of propriety and an inversion of expectation and reality:

> During temptation, I have felt that this wolf was producing incomprehensible joy, tears and consolation in my soul, but I was really being deceived, when I so childishly thought to have fruit from this and not harm.[71]

The daemons entrap the monk, using every means to keep the monk linked to the passions:

> Let us watch and see (for perhaps in season, we may void gall by bitterness) which of the demons uplift us, which cast us down, which harden, which comfort, which darken, which pretend to communicate enlightenment to us, which make us slothful, which make us cunning, which make us sad, and which cheerful.[72]

With such constant and ever-changing daemonic possibilities, the monks must constantly and consistently be aware of themselves and vigilant against further surprising attacks.

The daemons' companionship with the monk provides them with information about the monk's weakness while at the same time developing the monk's ability to discern the tricks of the adversary. The monk gains self-mastery and self-knowledge because the daemons provide constant and ever more subtle opportunities for self-examination, self-control, and self-understanding. Without the daemons, the monks would not be able to advance or to achieve their goals. The more subtle the daemonic attack, the greater the monks' achievement.

Methods in Daemonic Warfare

Five methods are discernible in the descriptions by monks of their warfare with the daemons. I have organized these methods to move from the most concrete and embodied concerns to the more ethereal.

In the first method, the daemons attempt to preserve the monks' social body as a socially engaged body. In this initial phase of the monastic life, the monks' memories of family are enflamed by the daemons during waking hours,[73] and during sleep the daemons "try to disturb us

---

71. Ibid., PG888 D; Moore, #42, 110.

72. Ibid., Step XXVI, PG 1073C: Moore, #184, 191.

73. Ibid., Step II, PG 657, Moore #10 and 11, 13–14.

with dreams, representing to us that our relatives are either grieving or dying, or are held captive for our sake and are destitute."[74] The monastic life cannot be lived without a withdrawal both from the social body and from the physical, so the monks initially attack the social body, rendering the physical incapacitated in the next method.

In the second method of warfare the daemons attack the monks' physical body:

> The daemon battles with those in obedience, sometimes to de-file them with bodily pollutions, and make them hardhearted, and sometimes to make them more agitated than usual. At other times, he makes them dry and barren, sluggish in prayer, drowsy and benighted, in order to tear them away from their struggle by making them think they have gained nothing by their obedi-ence, but are only backsliding. For he does not allow them time to reflect that often the providential withdrawal of our imagined goods or blessings leads us to the deepest humility.[75]

The daemons attempt to thwart the monks' mental prayer and concentra-tion, which are the means of achieving mastery over the daemons, "[f]or by distractions, the daemons aim to bring our prayer to nothing."[76] It is only through mental activity and prayer that the monk is capable of mas-tering the body and the daemons: "Be concentrated (*synnous*) without self-display, withdrawn into your heart. For the demons fear concentra-tion as thieves fear dogs."[77] The pure body of the monk makes God rejoice and the defiled monastic body makes the daemons rejoice:

> The Lord, being incorruptible and incorporeal, rejoices in the pu-rity and incorruptibility of our body. But nothing gives such joy to the demons, some say, as the stench (*dysōdia*) of fornication; and no other passion so gladdens them as the defilement of the body.[78]

---

74. Ibid., Step IV, PG 669B–C; Moore #27, 19.

75. Ibid., PG 708B; Moore, #58, 40

76. Ibid., Step IV, PG 717A; Moore, #101, 46; see also Step V, PG 777C–D; Moore, #29–30, 64; and in relation to accidie, Step XIII; PG 860B–C; Moore #8, 96.

77. Ibid., Step VII, PG 805A; Moore, #15, 72.

78. Ibid., Step XV, PG 888B; Moore, #35, 109.

These attacks on the monk's body intend to force the monk back into society, into marriage, sexual relations, familial responsibility. The first two methods mirror one another.

In the third method of warfare, daemons wage mental warfare. The daemons attempt to weaken the monk's mind using a number of techniques. First, they attack using the memory so that the remembrance of sin might discourage the monk and lead to a fall.[79] Next they will "darken the mind" of the monk "and then they will suggest whatever they like."[80] The daemons fill the minds of the inexperienced with impossible goals and those of the experienced with images of hospitality and ministry that will distract them from their immediate pursuit.[81] In Climacus there is even a tabulation of a new mental trick called the "flick of the mind" (*pararrhipismon noos*), which particularly distresses the monk:

> Amongst the more precise and discerning Fathers, there is mention of a still more subtle notion, something which some of them call a flick of the mind (*pararrhipismon noos*). This is its characteristic: without passage of time, without word or image, it instantaneously introduces the passion to the victim. There is nothing swifter or more indiscernible among spirits. It manifests itself in the soul by a simple remembrance, which is instantaneous, independent, inapprehensible, and, in some cases, even unknown to the person himself. If anyone, therefore, with the help of mourning has been able to detect such a subtlety, he can explain to us how it is possible for a soul, by the eye alone, by a mere glance, or the touch of the hand, or the hearing of a song, without any notion or thought, to commit a definite sin of impurity.[82]

By manipulating the monk's mind, the daemons disable the monk's ability both to understand and to resist the daemonic warfare.

Method four is related to the mental warfare: it is the presentation to the monks of fantasies that they have achieved a high status[83] and that they no longer need to be concerned about their spiritual progress.[84] These fantasies appeal directly to the monks' arrogance and pride, and

79. Ibid., PG 896A; Moore, #68, 115.
80. Ibid., PG 901A; Moore, #81, 119.
81. Ibid., Step IV, PG 725B; Moore, #118, 52.
82. Ibid., Step XV, PG 897B–C; Moore #75, 116–17.
83. Ibid., Step IV, PG 708B–C, Moore, #59, 40.
84. Ibid., Step XV, PG 885B; Moore #29, 107–8.

cause serious falls. The daemons even achieve this by withdrawing from the monk, bringing a temporary end to the warfare, which in turn creates the image that the monk has already arrived at perfection, or the angelic life, or the communion of angels and martyrs.

In the final, fifth method of warfare, the daemons become angels of light. They become what the monks most deeply desire to see and to be, so that the monks, believing that they have received visions and prophesies and that they are a part of the gloriously transformed angels on earth, are deceived and fall even further.[85] Toward the end of his *Ladder*, Climacus writes:

> When the demon of pride gets a foothold in his servants, he appears to them either in sleep or in a waking vision, as though in the form of a holy angel or some martyr, and gives them a revelation of mysteries, or a free bestowal of spiritual gifts, so that these unfortunates may be deceived and completely lose their wits.[86]

At this level, the monks remain vulnerable to the most deceptive of attacks, so their discernment and subtle understanding of themselves and of the daemons' work is crucial to their success.

Monastic daemonology, as it has been developed here, revolves about an intense relationship between monks and the daemons that rules over the monks' bodies and that also regulates the development of virtue for the monks through a constant process of testing. In this monastic daemonology monks and daemons are companions in the ascetic way.

Monastic Asceticism

From the perspective of monastic anthropology and monastic daemonology, it is now possible to discuss monastic asceticism. Without the conception of the social body of the human being and the physical body of the monk, and without the creative role of daemons in the body's passions, monastic ascetic activity may be thought to have "produced some star ascetic athletes, whose achievements in devising ever more eccentric tortures for their own bodies might seem to have eclipsed all competition in body renunciation."[87] But once the monk's ascetical activity is located

---

85. Ibid., Step IV, PG 672A–B; Moore #29, 20.
86. Ibid., Step XXIII, PG 968C–D; Moore, #19, 140.
87. Williams, "Divine Image," 129.

in the body (both social and material), and once the monk's development is understood to occur through the bodily control of bodily functions materialized as daemons, then monastic asceticism becomes significantly embodied and its goal that of experiencing in the body the most profound quiet and communion with God.

Monastic asceticism, then, is *not* other-worldly asceticism. The monk receives reward for ascetical labor in this world, in the body, in the society of monks and angels:

> You see how in loosing every band of wickedness from our hearts and in undoing every knot of contracts forced for grudges, and in hastening to do good for our neighbor with our whole soul—you see how we are illumined with the light of knowledge, and freed from the disgrace of passions, and filled with every virtue; and are illumined by God's glory and freed from every ignorance; and praying for things after Christ's mind, we are heard and shall have God with us continually and are filled with godly desire.[88]

Monastics aim to become gods, to be deified[89] by their ascetical labor:

> Therefore let us give ourselves entirely to the Lord, that we may receive Him again entire. Let us become gods through Him, for on that account He became man, who is by nature God and Master. Let us obey Him and He will without trouble vindicate us against our enemies.[90]

This goal is consistent and expressed in various monastic literatures in remarkably similar language. The monk's body becomes divine by mastering the passions and the crafty daemons who rule them. This mastery perfects the body in virtue and brings the monk to an illuminating knowledge of God while transporting the monk into an immediate communion with God.[91] The goal of the monastic life, and the end of ascetical activity, is the perfecting of the monk's body.

Asceticism manages the perfecting of the monk's body. Asceticism, however, is a metaphor because it uses a concept taken from sports to explain a religious way of life. As a metaphor, asceticism explains the monk's experience through the experience of an athlete training for a

88. Maximus, *Ascetic Discourse*, #41, 133.

89. See Valantasis, "Eastern Church's Theme," 89–101.

90. Maximus, *Ascetic Discourse*, #43, 134.

91. See Valantasis, *Spiritual Guides*, 13–33.

contest: both the monk and the athlete must train, must carefully develop and regulate their bodily functions, must take into account the competition, and must pursue vigorously the victorious prize.

The metaphorical structure in monastic asceticism, however, is even more complex because "monastic asceticism" employs two other sophisticated metaphoric systems, viz. the "monk" and "daemons." The monk defines a complex social and religious relocation of the body and its relationship to angels and God by means of a particular social isolation and withdrawal. That is, the monk defines the transformation of body and its relationships, which the monk experiences by talking about systems of withdrawal from society and body. Daemons are personifications of human experience used to explain the complex relationship between the parts of the body, the body's desires and activities, and the natural resistance to bodily change in the development of virtue. Each one of these systems (monastic anthropology, monastic daemonology, and monastic asceticism) are metaphorical because each explains some aspect of the monastic life by reference to another system of knowledge.

The literary study of metaphor, however, has treated metaphor primarily as rhetorical device and embellishment, and therefore has on the whole not seriously considered metaphor to be central to either culture or experience. And yet in monastic ascetical culture, metaphors creatively connect particular physical experience, general culture and understanding, and spiritual education.

The recent work of George Lakoff and Mark Johnson on metaphor develops a useful, experientially based system of understanding, of which metaphor is one element. They argue that the human body, the physical and cultural environment in which human beings live, structures human experience.

> Recurrent experience leads to the formation of categories, which are experiential gestalts with those natural dimensions. Such gestalts define coherence in our experience . . . [Direct human understanding occurs when human experience is perceived] directly from interaction with and in our environment. . . . We understand experience metaphorically when we use a gestalt from one domain of experience to structure experience in another domain.[92]

92. Lakoff and Johnson, *Metaphors*, 230.

Both asceticism and daemonology are metaphoric systems in which the metaphor organizes and communicates the experience of the monk: the activity of the daemon is a metaphor because it is a gestalt from one domain used to organize and explain the monastic experience.

The identification of these systems as metaphoric redirects our attention. The daemons, even in monastic literature, have been incorporated into a complex system of interrelated narratives:

(1) about the Fall of human beings (either in Gnostic speculation or in Christian and Jewish exegesis of Genesis 1–3); or

(2) about the warfare resulting from the fall of angels who become devils with an army of daemons;

(3) about the fall of human beings through the sin of Adam and Eve and their expulsion from paradise, which has necessitated a divine savior; or

(4) about the identification of the Christian with the warfare reminiscent of Jesus' warfare with the devil in the desert as a form of the imitation of Christ.

These narratives disguise the fact that the monastic ascetical systems really concern the monk's experience and perfection of the body through withdrawal, because these narratives each direct attention to the historical sequences (body in society, body out of society, body fighting daemons in the desert like Jesus, body victorious in resisting devil, body crowned with victory). In monastic asceticism, however, the primary motivation to fight daemons relates not to the imitation of Christ, or to the myth of redemption or rising from a Fall, or any other narrative, but to the perfecting of the monk's body.

Monastic asceticism is *not* a personal appropriation and undoing of a Fall narrative, but the writing in life, in the world, in the body, of transformative practices aimed at perfecting and divinizing the body. The distinction between various types of asceticism may relate, then, not so much to the ascetical practices themselves, or to the physical manipulation of the body for the production of a divinized body, but rather to the narrative structures that give meaning to these practices by placing them within an interpretive frame. It is conceivable that the difference between the asceticism of certain Gnostic groups (termed by ecclesiastical authority as "heretical") and the asceticism of the monks (termed "orthodox") relates not to the understanding and working of the body, but to the narratives to which each assigns the significance of their ascetic practice. The narratives about daemonic warfare indicate whether or not the ascetical practices are considered dualistic. The emergent catholic church, for example, deemed the asceticism of the Sethian and Valentinian gnostics who developed a complex mythological structure and narrative, as "heretical;" and "gnostic" ascetics disparaged the lack of perception on the parts of "orthodox" practitioners. Both groups shared similar methods of asceticism, related conceptions of the formation of the body, correlative understandings of the relationship of corporeality to virtue, and practically identical formulations of the goal of ascetical activity. The monks aspire to the divinization of the body identified as the corpse, the hylic body. The various narratives about the formation and redemption of the body locate the body that is being perfected. For those ascetics (gnostic or monastic) who wished to preserve a strict delimitation between body and spirit in their narratives, this perfectible body was definitely not the hylic body that the jealous powers created, but the psychic and the pneumatic body that the daemons and angels constructed and into which the life-breath was breathed. For the monks discussed in this paper, however, all of these bodies are collapsed into one: the body from the Fall narrative, the angelic body, the hylic body meet in the monk; it is that monk's body that will be divinized.

The monk's body by definition is a withdrawn body, a body removed from its normal social environment and placed in what is experienced as an hostile environment. Asceticism, then, must take into account the body (here including those body parts ruled by the daemons) and the environment in which that body must live. A series of (at least) four withdrawals or changes in environment perfects the monk's body: withdrawal from family and society; entrance into a community; withdrawal from community to a hermitage; living in the angelic body. Each withdrawal or change in environment creates an altered awareness of the body and its functions (both socially and physically). By controlling the body at each of these stages, the monk becomes knowledgeable about the body and the environment, acquiring more sophisticated knowledge about the complex interactions of social body, physical body, and environment.

The monk first withdraws from family and society to begin a strict regimen of fasting, sleep deprivation, and mental prayer. The monk gains mastery over the body's need for nourishment and rest, while at the same time being weaned from the body's need for pleasure and sexual enjoyment and from the person's need for companionship. The first two methods of daemonic warfare (the daemonic attack on the social and physical body of the monk) occur during this initial stage. The environment is defined primarily by where it is not: it is not a familiar setting, but foreign space.

The second stage is a withdrawal into community, or an entrance into monastic community. Here the close proximity of community forces the monk to become aware of the psycho-physical responses to incarceration, as well as the effect of the passions emergent from close living. The passions (particularly anger, and others that emerge from a loss of self-will and self-regulation) emerge as the center of the struggle. The monk must learn, by obedience and humility, to blend with the community. The monk's body must voluntarily become a member of another social body by controlling the will and the drive to control. In this stage the development of social virtues and the learning of mental prayer and concentration in the midst of community constitute the daemon's third stage of warfare.

In the next stage, the monk withdraws from the community to a hermitage, from companionship to the solitary life. The monk enters the most intimate relationship with the body, recognizing and mastering the most persistent of bodily reactions manifested as daemonic warfare. In this body the monk masters both the voluntary and the involuntary bodily functions, learning to still the body and to bring bodily activity to its most quiescent state. The daemons' attack concentrates on the creation of fantasies and images of perfection, so that the monk is deceived into thinking that this body is the final state. The subtle body knowledge that emerges becomes increasingly sophisticated.

The final stage is the monk's body at rest, the angelic or divinized body. The monk must practice great discernment, because in the prior stage the daemons suggest this victory. But when it happens, it is evident and visible in the body. Antony the Great, Syncletica, the great monks of the desert tradition, all experienced this final victory. The monk's body, stilled, unmoved, dried out, unaffected by passion, turns all of its sensual and physical attention toward God.

The function of the daemons in each of these stages remains the same. Daemons expose both the voluntary and involuntary, natural and unnatural, bodily responses in reaction to each *new* environment in which the body is made to function on its way to perfection. The body does not remain the same in each stage; it changes in each stage. The change in body explains the change in the kind of daemonic warfare. Since the daemons rule the passions, and each environment brings out a different passionate response (i.e., bodily response), the body undergoes social and physical transformation at each stage. The daemons assist the monk to transform that new body in each of its environments. This transformation by daemonic manipulation enables the perfecting of the monk's body.

Each person's body is unique, each daemonic structure is unique, and therefore there can be no universal system for every person to follow in order to become perfect. Every monk must follow the unique way that that particular monk's body requires. The customizing of daemonic attacks discussed here actually signifies the recognition of great diversity among people's constitutions. Since the body is not, as we would perceive it, simply an object with bones, sinews, organs, muscles, tissues, etc., but a creation by angels and daemons who imbue the body with its passions, each passionate and embodied creation is different and different sorts of asceticism are necessary for each one. And if each body is different, each body in each different environment becomes equally diverse and equally in need of particular ascetic activity. Both the material and the social bodies of the monks are subject to ascetical activity.

The daemons enable the monk to construct the monk's new body through the ascetical activity that the presence of the daemons and passions necessitates. The monk, working through the various stages of his bodily transformation, gradually stills the body. The communion of monk with other people, family, other monks, gradually becomes a communion only with the daemons, and finally becomes a communion only with God. The monk's various bodies culminate in the perfect, divinized body. And so the initial distinction between daemon, human, angel, must be adjusted to accommodate one other socialized body, the divinized body of the monk. Because of the daemons' work, the perfected body of the monk hovers above the daemonic and the human, and below the angelic, resting and still and divine.

CHAPTER 8

Ascetical Withdrawal and the
Second Letter of Basil the Great

THERE IS A CERTAIN POETIC JUSTICE TO LINKING ASCETICISM AND strangeness.[1] Asceticism is a strange subject, an arena of behavior and theology difficult to comprehend, a set of attitudes strangely peculiar, unusually renunciative, weirdly denunciatory of other ways of living, peculiarly estranged from the dominant culture from which the ascetic withdraws.[2] Strangeness and asceticism go hand in hand; indeed, asceticism defines a set of systems marked by both becoming a stranger within oneself and becoming a stranger within society. This essay explores the ascetic's creation of the stranger within and the stranger without, the interior stranger constructed of withdrawal from the normative personality within a culture, the exterior stranger created by withdrawal from the normative relationships of the dominant society.

1. This essay grew out of two lectures given at two different times. The original lecture was presented to the Modem Greek Literature section of the Center for Literary and Cultural Studies at Harvard University under the graceful leadership of Professor Margaret Alexiou. The final form of the lecture was presented at Mary Washington University where Professor James Goehring and many students debated with me about the implications of these theories. The final form here, unfortunately, may not always reflect the valuable criticism I received at both institutions, but I gratefully acknowledge their intellectual hospitality.

2. Recently many scholars have turned their attention to the study of asceticism. This present study emerges from collaborative work on Asceticism in the Greco-Roman Society Group of the Society for Biblical Literature. That group has published the following significant works: *Ascetic Behavior in Greco-Roman Antiquity* (edited by Vincent L. Wimbush); volumes 57 and 58 (1992) of *Semeia* whose general theme was *Discursive Formations, Ascetic Piety and the Interpretation of Early Christian Literature*; and *Asceticism,* edited by Vincent Wimbush and Richard Valantasis.

I would like to pursue this stranger within and stranger without in a number of different ways. First, by telling a true story about a pilgrim monk who stayed in the same place, an estranged person by culture and vocation whose estrangement was manifest and clear. Second, I will analyze the stranger within and the stranger without through a brief discussion of a theory of asceticism. Third, I would like to explore the development of ascetical theology as a theology of the stranger from a letter of *the* ascetical theologian of the Eastern Church, Basil the Great, Bishop of Caesarea (c. 330–79). Fourth, and finally, I would like to draw some conclusions (both historical and theological) from this construction of asceticism.

THE ESTRANGED MONK WHO STAYED IN ONE PLACE

While traveling on a Greek island a number of years ago, I heard of a monk, Jacob, who was a former Anglican priest now living as a monk in an Orthodox cenobitic community. Being interested in monastic asceticism in the Christian East, I went to see him. When I arrived at the monastery to ask about him, however, the guest master pointed in another direction, to either a church near the cemetery, or to what seemed to be an abandoned monastery on the next mountain. I searched for him first at the cemetery, knowing that in monastic tradition there would be no reason that a person could not pray and live there. Not finding him, I began the long trek in the morning heat to the next mountain.

When I finally made it to the small church complex, I knocked at the door. No one answered. I knocked again. Still silence. Then at the third knock, the monk poked his head out the window above the door and asked what I wanted. When I asked for him by name, he said that he would allow me to enter, explaining that normally he does not admit visitors except those who seem to have serious business, and since I knew his name, I must have had a serious intent. He looked very much like an Orthodox monk, dressed as he was in a monastic habit dirty from manual labor, face bearded and head covered with a small cap. His Greek pronunciation, however, betrayed his British origins.

After showing me to his chapel to pray, and after giving me a short tour of the monastery where he lived as a hermit, we settled in his common room and the monk began, in response to my initial questions about him, to relate the story of his life. His spiritual pilgrimage began at a theological school of a British university during the First World War. He was part of a small movement within the Anglican communion that sought union with the Roman Catholic Church and acknowledgment of the Catholic basis of Anglican holy orders, because the Anglican communion could not (according to followers of this movement at least) provide the connection to the primitive Church, either in purity of doctrine, continuity of orders, or catholicity of orientation. After his ordination to the priesthood in the Church of England, the young priest took up his first parochial position and continued intensive study of Roman Catholic dogma and practice, ostensibly to institute Roman Catholic practice, ritual, and doctrine into his local parish, but, in actuality, in anticipation of being received into the Roman Catholic Church. During this curacy, he visited a Benedictine monastery in France, for he was also interested in exploring his vocation as a monk in the Roman Catholic Church.

While in France, however, he met some people newly converted to Greek Orthodox Christianity, who introduced him to the liturgy and theology of the Orthodox Church. His long fascination with the Roman Catholic Church began to wane. He was no longer convinced that the Roman Catholic Church retained the pure and clear apostolic doctrine and practice that he sought. What he yearned for seemed to be fully present only in Eastern Orthodox Christianity. Gradually he was drawn more and more into the Orthodox Church. Eventually he was chrismated, and then received as a novice into the monastery where he ultimately took on the great and holy schema (vesture) of a monk.

The monastery into which he was received as a novice had a reputation for strict observance of the monastic life, for significant intellectual and spiritual work by the abbot and the monks, and for receptivity to non-Greeks and non-Orthodox for theological dialogue and debate. It was an obvious place for him to be.

In this illustrious monastery, Jacob, after rigorous training in the religious life and detailed study of Orthodox faith and practice, became disillusioned with the manner of life there. After many years of complaint to the abbot and his fellow monks about their manner of life and their liturgical practice, the monk could no longer contain his dismay. His desire for purity and literal observance of the monastic rules needed to be addressed.

Some background about Orthodox ascetical practice is necessary here. Fasting in the Eastern Orthodox Church, and especially in monasteries, consists of limiting both the quantity and the kinds of food that can be eaten.[3] On days of strict fasting, the monk (and other devout Orthodox Christians) do not eat anything until after Vespers (late afternoon, usually about 3:30 p.m.). On normal fasting days, meals may be taken at the normal times. Orthodox fasting rules have various levels of restriction. Most days restrict meat and dairy products; other days restrict meat, dairy products, fish, and wine; some days there is also a restriction of oil, or of oil and wine. Each day of the year is graded as to the manner of observing the fast. Monasteries regularly observe the strict fast as a norm, while devout Orthodox lay people restrict the fast to Wednesdays and Fridays throughout the year, the fast before the Nativity of the Lord (from about November 29 until Christmas), the fast of Great Lent (the forty days before Easter), the fast of the Dormition of the Theotokos (August 1 through 14), and other specified days throughout the year.

Since meals are connected with the monastic horarium, that is, since the breaking of the fast is determined by the singing of Vespers, the monks at this monastery, and at many other Orthodox monasteries including Mount Athos, have adjusted their monastic horarium so that all of the offices are sung at one time throughout the night.[4] Arising at about 2:30 a.m., the monks chant the Night Office, Matins, Lauds, the Little Hours (Prime, Terce, Sext, and None), and Vespers so that the entire sequence of offices is usually completed by sunrise or a little later. This means that, Vespers having been completed, the monks may eat their meal, and then proceed to a full day of work and solitary prayer until Compline and sleep. This practice meant that the correlation between the actual setting of the sun and the monastic office of Vespers to be sung as the sun was setting was disrupted. No longer was there a correlation between the hours of the day and the monastic office.

The monk living at the hermitage did not like the disruption. He preferred to have the symbolism of the office match the actual time of day. He wanted the offices to correlate to the actual rising of the sun and the hours of the day, Vespers to follow at its proper time in the late afternoon, and to break the fast only at the appointed time after Vespers.

3. These directions are given to Orthodox Christians in the ecclesiastical calendar, *The Church Kalendar*.

4. These adjustments are not necessarily accepted by all Orthodox parishes and monasteries. The Russian tradition, at least, gathers the offices into three "aggregates" to be recited at sunset, sunrise, and midday. See Kovalchuk, *Abridged Typicon*, 36–74.

So Jacob asked for permission to live alone as a hermit in order to fulfill the full complement of monastic offices in their chronological sequence and to fulfill the monastic fast strictly according to the ancient monastic traditions. This withdrawal was the only way he could imagine coming to the true life of a monk living according to the ancient and pure monastic way. Living alone and chanting the monastic offices alone, he could insure that they would be done properly and in accordance with the ancient monastic ways.

THEORY OF ASCETICISM

This story serves as the basis for exploring a theory of asceticism[5] through which I wish to interpret Jacob and his relationship to his monastic community. Asceticism revolves about the creation of a new identity. A person begins ascetical practices precisely in order to become someone else, to become a different kind or quality of person. Newness of personality marks the ascetic impulse. Jacob was searching for a new identity, first in his vocation as an Anglican priest; then through his interest in Roman Catholicism; subsequently in his reception into the Greek Orthodox Church and his acceptances in the monastic life; and eventually in his life as a hermit. In each one of these situations, Jacob sought to become a new person, a more authentic person, a more enlivened person.

This new personality, however, does not operate in a vacuum. In order to become a new person through ascetical practices, the person must also restructure social relations and recreate the cultural universe in which the person lives. In other words, the ascetic must leave behind the old person in order to become a new person, and that "leaving behind" includes the intricate social relationships that support the old way of life in favor of new social relations that support the new way of life.[6] The ascetic must put aside the old way of looking at the world, the old culture and must create a new culture. Jacob did both of these things. In leaving England, in visiting France, in rejecting Western society, Jacob created a free space in which Eastern monks and Eastern culture would

5. The following is an early articulation of my theory of asceticism. For continuing work, see my "Theory of the Social Function of Asceticism," chapter 1, pp. 3–13. Also see the significant theoretical analysis of asceticism in Harpham, *Ascetic Imperative*.

6. This observation is based upon the primary insight of Max Weber. As an historian of economics and as a sociologist, Weber has opened the ascetical to its social and economic implications. See *Protestant Ethic*.

support and enhance his new personality. But the monks of the monastery, although culturally connected to the Greek people living outside the monastery, had also left the normative social relationships of their families, villages, and nation in order to enter the monastery. They too left the mundane world of their Greek culture to enter a cultural world defined by the centrality of their religious vocations.

So asceticism may be defined as practices intended to inaugurate a new personality, to develop new social relationships, and to support these by the articulation of a new culture, a new worldview.[7] The foundation of all ascetical practice revolves about a series of withdrawals, from old conditioning of personality, from old, intricate, social relations, from an old understanding of the world. In other words, there can be no asceticism, no new personality, no new social relations, no newly articulated worldview, without first becoming a stranger to the old. Becoming a stranger, therefore, stands at the heart of ascetic activity. The stranger within defines the person who withdraws from the familiarity of an already defined personality to move toward a new definition of personality. The stranger without defines the person who has withdrawn from society in order to create a different sort of society, and withdrawn from the world, as normally understood, in order to enter a new world.

The complex interaction of these elements of my theory, however, becomes clearer in a further exploration of Jacob's relationship with his community. At each level of these descriptions (personal, social, cultural) our hermit monk had become proficient at the cultural practices without becoming fully acculturated. Jacob entered the monastic life while never really becoming a part of it—he remained a stranger. He clearly had mastered the theology and literary tradition of Orthodox monks both through reading and through intellectual training; these traditions defined the cultural world of the Eastern Orthodox monks. He had also become proficient at the monastic discipline (prayer, fasting, reading, manual labor, corporate prayer) through his own training as a monk and through many years of practice. In short the monk had become proficient in and a master of the practices and social relationships of the monk, without fully assimilating some of their cultural elements. Jacob's estrangement from the community articulates this.

7. The contours of this discussion may be (naively) dependent upon the anthropologist Clifford Geertz, *Interpretation of Cultures*, 144.

The difference between this monk and his brothers did not relate to questions of proper actions or proper ascetical practice—for they agreed about the form and content of those activities—but rather to questions of the construction of the monastic culture. The hermit monk Jacob needed and valued a literal correlation between the hours of the day and the times of the monastic hours. Lauds was to be chanted as the sun rose. Vespers was chanted toward the end of the day. The other brothers neither needed nor valued such a literal correlation. Their world and its time were constructed of the liturgies that determined them, not by the course of the sun through the day. One worldview was literal, the other figurative.[8] They were differently constructed understandings and, therefore, different religious cultures, for at the basis of the division were elements essential to the interpretation of all other monastic activity—ascetical, liturgical, spiritual, and secular. Since the cultural perspectives differed, the practices that make such a plan of life emotionally accessible and satisfying were not correlative. The emotional appropriation could not happen for the hermit monk. The cultural transfer had not been complete and the hermit monk never was able to fully enter his brothers' culture. Jacob, at many levels, would always remain a stranger to his community.

Jacob, however, was not at a disadvantage in his remaining a stranger, because even the community defined itself as a stranger to the wider culture, the wider world, in which the community found itself and from which the community withdrew. The center of ascetic behavior embraces a series of estrangements signified by a series of withdrawals.[9] Jacob withdrew from his world to join the monastic world. Then he withdrew from the monastic community to become a hermit. The rest of the community would view this series of withdrawals as a deepening conversion, as a calling toward more sanctified living. To the community's eyes, Jacob was simply progressing normally, even though his personal estrangement began in a different culture and centered on different kinds of issues. To become a monk means precisely to become a stranger, first to the world at large, and then even to other monastic practitioners. To understand this process of continually becoming a stranger within oneself and from society we turn now to Orthodox ascetical theology.

8. This difference is fully explored in the metaphor theory of Lakoff and Johnson, *Metaphors*; see especially 3–10.

9. For a fuller account of this process, see "Daemons and the Perfecting of the Monk's Body, chapter 7, pp. 134–68.

The Case of Basil's Second Letter

Basil of Caesarea plays a central and critical role in the discussion of religious formation through asceticism, and his influence persists today. His writings belong to the foundational documents of Christian asceticism and of Orthodox monasticism. His famous second letter to his friend and fellow bishop Gregory of Nazianzus (329–89), written about 358,[10] provides a concise summary of Basil's ascetical theology and encapsulates the ascetical culture that Basil wished to promulgate. For this essay Basil's letter provides a testing site for the dynamics of ascetical theory presented above.

Cultural Level

At the basis of Basil's ascetical theology rests the preference of a new world over the common world. Basil posits a blissful or blessed state "which counts all the things of this earth as nothing compared with the promised bliss which is in store for us," and which, he submits, is the norm of human life. This blissful world or state contrasts negatively with the problematized world that only leads to mental and spiritual distraction, because "man's mind when distracted by his countless worldly cares cannot focus itself distinctly on the truth." The blessed state may be characterized in a number of different ways: entrance into the heavenly court, transformation into a living temple of God, filling the memory with God. These all relate to the existence of another world, a more blessed world, which is the destiny for human beings. As destiny, however, that blessed world does not naturally reveal itself to the common world, which is filled with trouble, distractions, disturbances, and the remnants of distraction and the distracted self. Escape from this world, withdrawal from society, and the recreation of the self constitute the means of entering this blissful world.

Entrance into this world requires withdrawal from city, society, and from self. The goal of withdrawal is to contemplate God. A myth informs both the withdrawal and the contemplation of God. The soul, when it is undistracted by worldly cares, naturally ascends toward contemplation of God and receives an illumination that enables the soul to forget its own nature and thus it is no longer able to be drawn away from contem-

10. The text and most of the following translations from this letter (unless otherwise noted) are found in *St. Basil: The Letters*.

plation and illumination; this contemplation and illumination orient the soul to the development of virtuous living. Prayer, scripture study, pious asceticism, create this tranquility of mind, which characterizes both the illuminated state and the goal of withdrawal. This transformation of the soul by contemplation and illumination reconstructs and reconstitutes the soul—a soul no longer distracted and weighed down by the lower nature, but one oriented toward the memory of God and the tranquility of contemplation. By becoming a stranger to the common and normative world, the ascetic begins the process of self-transformation and renewal.

Social Level

Social relations are at once problematized and idealized. The positive goal of "withdrawal" finds its definition in a series of privations that characterize the ascetic's estrangement.

> The withdrawal from the world is not somatically to be outside it, but rather to sever the sympathy of the soul towards the body and to become cityless, homeless, possessionless, friendless, propertyless, without means of living, without business activity, without converse with other humans, and ignorant of human teaching.

The marking of this "withdrawal" is through the privative. This withdrawal also means the reception into the heart of "impressions of the divine teaching."

Involvement in social and business relations hinders the activity of the ascetic and impedes progress toward the supernatural goal by implicating the soul in distracting and complicating systems. Only by becoming a stranger to family, friends, business, wisdom, and all other socially normative activities may the ascetic achieve the highest teaching, the divine state.

Consistent with this problematization of social relationships, marital and familial relationships present particular problems. Both in the desire for marriage, children, and a household in which to nurture a family, and in the actual marriage relationship, rearing of children and management of a household, family destroys tranquility. Such relationships bind the ascetic to the matters of the lower nature of human being and prevent the soul from its natural ascent to God and toward contemplation. The ascetic, therefore, must become a stranger to family and even the desire for family.

The ascetic develops a different set of relationships to replace the old, rejected relations. These idealized relationships encouraged in Basil's system revolve about the culturally defined higher or spiritual aspect of human existence. Ascetics form spiritual community. This is the intent of the letter to Gregory: that he might be persuaded to live the ascetic life in community. The community, oriented toward tranquility and the contemplation of God, structures relationships so as to assist the soul in its ascent. This community also includes the society of scriptural models. One by one, the masters of the religious life (Jesus; Joseph, the lover of chastity; Job, the teacher of fortitude; David, the warrior and hymnodist; Moses, the strong advocate against idolatry) become active members of the community through meditation, imitation, and godly converse. And, of course, there are the angels and the heavenly chorus with whom the ascetic sings the divine hymns. These relationships with other human beings, with biblical archetypes, and with heavenly beings reformulate the nature of society and reconstitute society now only in relation to ascetical goals. While becoming a stranger to normative social relations, the ascetic becomes friends of biblical figures, angels, and God. The new society implicates the ascetic in the same way that the negative relationships of the old society did, but now in relation to the proper goal and higher aspect of human being.

Again, at the social level, the ascetic recreates and redefines the self. The self created in social solitude, unlearns habits acquired in the world for relating, and learns a manner of conversation consistent with the new divine and heavenly society in which the ascetic lives. The physical location of the ascetic mirrors the new self. It is far from social intercourse, far from distractions and interruptions, conducive to contemplation, and peopled only with sympathetic others of similar bent.

Personal Level

The seriousness of becoming a stranger within and a stranger without is most evident at the personal level. The negative aspects of estrangement are most pronounced at the level of personal integration and behavior. Asceticism appears as mostly negative behavioral injunctions, the negative aspects of becoming a stranger. Despite leaving the city, Basil describes himself as unable to leave his own self, since even in his solitude he carries about with him the interior disorders and disturbances that were present in the city. Even though he is a stranger without, Basil finds the creation of the interior stranger to be the most difficult. This is the central behavioral problem: to still this interior dialogue and to fill the mind rather with the memory of God. This quietude emerges from a re-training of the mind and the self, like the training of the eye not to shift its gaze sporadically, but to focus its attention on only one thing. The mind, like the eye, needs to be focused. The interior stranger emerges from the intense concentration on God alone.

The beginning of that focusing occurs in the renunciation of mar-riage, family, and household, and the renunciation as well of the desire for them. This renunciation is mirrored in flight from the world and withdrawal into a life of social privation. In this altered environment, the soul may be reconceptualized and understood anew, so that the old pat-terns of behavior and reaction may be broken and new patterns inscribed on the ascetic's life. Through solitude, and assisted by liturgical and cor-porate prayer, the old ways are erased and new ones created. Through solitude and the fellowship of others living this higher life, the tongue, eyes, ears, and lips are turned away from their lower functions and reori-ented toward the steady concentration upon God.

This new person, capable of contemplating God, stranger to the world while friend of saints and angels, finds new practices to fill the void created by stillness. The ascetic's new personality orients self toward positive practices that enhance the new personality. The study of scrip-ture opens up the new world. After study of scripture, prayer re-envisions God and orients the ascetic to the new world that emerges as the memory of God fills the mind with nothing but God. Other practices, such as the careful regulation of conversation, attention to simplicity, functional ves-ture, limited and healthy food, and moderate sleep, assist in the process of ascent by enacting in the body the reorientation toward the spiritual, the modulation of the self, which is necessary for the vision of God. The stranger within and the stranger without gradually becomes a friend of God.

TWO SETS OF CONCLUSIONS

The story of Jacob as well as Basil's ascetical theology, has underscored the complex relationship of the familiar and the strange, the old and the new. The process of becoming a stranger to the normative culture becomes the means of becoming a participant in another world and another society, while also becoming the basis of a new personality. But why become a stranger within and a stranger without? What is the social value of withdrawal? What is the social function of asceticism? This leads to two different kinds of conclusions. The first is about the historical rhetoric of Basil's letter; the second is about the method of remaking modern society.

First, I will address the historical conclusions about Basil's ascetical theology.[11] Basil's letter probably does not address Basil's own biography, or even that of his fellow bishop Gregory, because they both were actively involved in the life of the Church and in its theological development. Basil promulgates, however, a life that both Hellene and Christian could understand. Although there may be some modeling of the withdrawn philosophical life on that of the monks of the Egyptian and Palestinian deserts, Basil's description does not resonate with the literatures and models developed in desert monasticism.[12] Rather, Basil's monastic culture resonates fully with the sort of philosophically based asceticism found in Greco-Roman philosophical circles.[13] Basil's description of his withdrawn life could provide the rule of living that is implicit in Porphyry's *Life of Plotinus* and the *Order of His Works*; Basil's myth of the soul rising to contemplation parallels that of Plotinus in his *Enneads*. The image of the contemplative life of undistracted attention to God, as well as the vision of the continuous delving into the mysteries of God, find their theoretical explication in Gregory Thaumaturgus' *Oration to Origen*. Basil's intertextual field lay primarily with the images of Platonic community refracted through Plotinus and Porphyry and with the images of Christian gnosticism refracted through Origen's ascetic writings and those of Gregory Thaumaturgus. These texts, together with the Jewish *On the Contemplative Life* of Philo of Alexandria, provide the primary reference points for Basil's philosophical and ascetical life. Basil applies the pan-religious cultural phenomenon of ascetic withdrawal for contemplation to the ascetical life of the Christian. His strategy was to apply

11. Many historians have studied asceticism in historical context. See Brown, *Body and Society*, especially 210–338; Clark, *Ascetic Piety;* and Harvey, *Asceticism and Society in Crisis.*

12. For a description, see Rousseau, *Pachomius.*

13. See Meredith, "Asceticism—Christian and Greek." For the Christian perspective alone see Rousseau, *Ascetics, Authority, and the Church.*

the "Hellenic" or "Roman" to Christian intellectual life. Philosophical and religious movements outside Christianity were, through ascetical practices, integrated into Christian practice. Basil christianizes foreign practice by creating a Christian philosophical and ascetical life of withdrawal for contemplation, comparable to that of other philosophical and ascetic communities of Late Antiquity.

In the days following the Emperor Constantine, Christianity moved from a persecuted to an imperial religion.[14] The writers of the fourth-century Church, responding to the shift in religious attitudes and religion, consciously began to create a Christian culture.[15] Emperor Julian's attempt to discredit and displace that Christian culture stands as proof of the vitality and speed of this cultivation of a universal culture.[16] Likewise, Julian's attempt to reinstitute the philosophical asceticism of Hellenic culture as the means of displacing Christian influence also speaks of the centrality of asceticism to that cultural agenda.

Patristic religious writing aimed at creating a Christian culture whose theological battles were a screen against which the contours and geography of that Christian culture were projected. Fighting Gnostics, Manichaeans, and other religious organizations that were outside the Church, as well as fighting heretical doctrinal and ascetical movements within the Church, the early writers of the Christian era developed an acceptable cultural milieu through argumentation. These battles were not simply theological arguments, but elements in the construction of a worldview, the foundation of the new culture.

The creation of this new culture, with its new understanding of human personality, social relations, and cultural dynamics, was a complex ascetical activity. The new Christian culture begins in the estrangement from the old Roman culture. The withdrawal creates the space in which a new culture may be founded. So at first, all the old Roman culture is marked as "stranger" and rejected, but gradually the most effective elements of that society are translated into the Christian culture. The cultural stranger must also become a friend of God. And this is what Basil is doing. The best of the estranged culture is transferred into the Christian faith, reconciling the most prized aspects of the older culture with the

14. For an extensive discussion, see Frend, *Rise of Christianity,* 439–517.

15. See Fox, *Pagans and Christians,* especially 21–23.

16. See Bowersock, *Julian the Apostate,* 5–65.

new creation in Christianity. By being transferred into Christianity, however, the old cultural systems of contemplation become, like the ascetic, something new. The new context, the new symbolic systems, the new social relations create a different meaning in a different environment. In historical terms, this ascetical project of the early Church became precisely the instrument of cultural, social, and psychological redefinition and reorientation, and simultaneously the means of ascribing new meaning and interpretations to common cultural realities. Historically, asceticism, by claiming the reality of being a stranger to the old cultural way of living, created the means whereby the old could be remade into something new.

This is the historical conclusion to my presentation on the stranger within and the stranger without in ascetical theory and in Basil of Caesarea's second letter. There is also a conclusion regarding contemporary life. I learned a great deal from talking with the monk Jacob—much about him, but even more about myself, American culture, cultural myopia, and frustrations with the world as it exists. Jacob and most ascetics shed light on the world they have left. The ascetic illuminates the dynamics of the world by holding up a light at its edges.

Jacob the ascetic speaks to us, not of becoming a stranger in order to baptize the old culture into the new (as Basil did), but of the possibility, through personal formation, of transforming our own lives, our relationships, our world. Jacob directs our attention to the power of transformation.

At the personal level, Jacob always sought out the strange, the foreign, the different, as the place precisely where he might more directly find God. From the cultured sophistication of English university life, Jacob ended up as an unwashed, bearded, fasting, poorly clothed monk in a small hermitage on a Greek island. His transformation led him directly into difference, into the strange. We, however, fear the different. We are xenophobic, fearers of the strange. So we learn instead to create homogenous communities of similar people—where the "we" may signify a very diverse set of possibilities: Muslim fundamentalist, Christian liberal, Vietnamese Buddhist, Indian Hindu, American Indian. Our society has yet to be transformed into a society capable of including wide diversity and difference. Ascetics teach us that we are all strangers, we are all strange, we are all on the outside looking in, and, therefore, that we are all called to the performances that bring us into closer contact with the other, the stranger, the different, so that we may be transformed and find our rest, as Jacob did. By embracing the stranger, we become a friend.

Jacob also speaks to us in our modern times about the transformation of society. This British convert to Eastern Orthodox Christianity called the rest of his community (and ours) to task for unfaithfulness to our highest ideals. Although we modern Western people speak of ourselves as peaceable people, we continue to construct the normative relationship of people around violence. Our cities are filled with armies of youths, equipped with the weapons of destruction, using them to destroy those perceived as their enemies. Our churches violently attack each other for disagreement about values. Our government violently enters other countries to inflict upon them a peace to our liking. Our national Congress fights and bickers continually, without ending the sort of bureaucratic stalemate that our continued progress and corporate health depend on. Our weapons are words, drugs, guns, abusive patterns, slurs, sound bites, characterizations, dishonest speaking, and disrespect. We are a violent people who speak of ourselves as peaceable, inviting, loving, and kind. The ascetic points a way for each one of us to withdraw from the world of violence, and to construct, through the reformation of each individual life, a society of peace.

And finally, the ascetic points to the transformation of the world. The ascetic points to the universality of the need for transformation, of the movement from estrangement to friendship, of the transformation of violence into peace. Everyone everywhere in the world must undertake an ascetical transformation. Standing on the edge of society, the ascetic shows the rest of us the interconnectedness of all things: ascetic with non-ascetic, rich with poor, Indian with African, American with Bosnian, Muslim with Christian with animist. Everything around us interconnects and forms a unity with everything else. We are both part of the transformation and part of the need for transformation, part of the problem and part of the solution, part of the violence in the cities and part of the poverty in the country, part of the bickering in Washington and part of the peacemaking in Palestine, part of the Hezbollah and part of the Serbian Christians. The ascetic speaks from the edge of society. No matter how we withdraw, no matter how we define ourselves and our social relations and our world, no matter where and who we are, ultimately, we can never be a stranger within or a stranger without. There is no such thing as an estrangement, there is no such person as a stranger. We are all, both within and without, whether we know it or ignore it, ascetics forming ourselves into a new people, into a new society, into a newly understood world.

CHAPTER 9

Is the *Gospel of Thomas* Ascetical?

IT IS TIME FOR REEVALUATING THE CATEGORIES THAT SCHOLARS HAVE used to classify the religious literature of the Greco-Roman and Late Antique world. Michael Williams, in his magisterial book *Rethinking "Gnosticism": An Argument for Dismantling a Dubious Category*, began the process of serious reappraisal by challenging the modern construct "gnosticism." He argues that the modern construction of historical gnosticism does not adequately explain the literature generally classified as gnostic and that this categorical insufficiency demands alternative ways of studying and understanding the diverse religious movements of the period.[1] My study of asceticism, although independent of Williams's work, continues that reexamination of categories using the specific case of the *Gospel of Thomas* and its classification as an ascetical text.

Since the very early years after the discovery of the *Gospel of Thomas*, some scholars almost instinctively have sought to interpret it as ascetical. Asceticism as a category explained some of the *Gospel's* peculiar sayings, or resonated with the exoticism of the geographical location of its discovery so close to a Pachomian monastery, or accounted for the way that this *Gospel* and other Sayings Gospels differ from their narrative counterparts. Something about the *Gospel of Thomas* seemed to demand that it be classified as ascetical. The argument for its ascetical orientation, however, has never received clear articulation nor found wide acceptance. There seems not to be sufficient internal evidence to argue categorically for its ascetical orientation, and yet the denial of any ascetical interest in the text somehow leaves the *Gospel* insufficiently explained.

1. See Williams, *Rethinking "Gnosticism"* throughout and especially the conclusions on 263–66.

This paper will revisit the nagging problem of the ascetical dimension of the *Gospel of Thomas* from a new perspective. I intend first to examine the main scholarly approaches to the question in order to understand the failure of previous attempts to classify the *Gospel* as ascetical. Then I will suggest a new direction for understanding the general principles of asceticism in order to provide a new understanding of asceticism itself and to open the *Gospel of Thomas* to a new reading. Finally, I will apply a new theory of asceticism to the *Gospel* in order to understand precisely the manner in which the *Gospel of Thomas* is ascetical. In this way I will visit an old problem with a new theory.

Previous Scholarly Approaches

Scholars explore the question of the asceticism of the *Gospel of Thomas* under a few broadly defined questions: Does the *Gospel* contain the themes understood by them to be "ascetical"? Is the *Gospel* "ascetical" or simply "gnostic" (where those categories are seen to be mutually exclusive)? Does the *Gospel* conform to the style of asceticism prevalent in the postulated geographical location in which the *Gospel* arose? Each of these strategies presumes that the question of the asceticism of the *Gospel* depends upon the conformity of the *Gospel*'s content to a modern construction of asceticism. These scholars engage in a circular argument in that they develop an image of asceticism, then compare the *Gospel* to that image. The image constructed relates to the overarching themes, the polarity gnosticism/asceticism, or the style of asceticism peculiar to a particular geographical region.

Scholars have reached diametrically opposite conclusions about the asceticism based upon the presence (or absence) of ascetical themes in the *Gospel*. W. H. C. Frend[2] presents the most consistent argument for the ascetical thematization of the *Gospel* by arguing that the *Gospel* promulgates an "advance toward spiritual perfection through the practice of ascetic virtues and repentance"[3] and displays a "stress on the attainment of perfection through complete sexual abnegation."[4] He identifies these virtues as "childlikeness, singleness and simplicity, abstinence, and world-

2. I am basing this summary on his article "Gospel of Thomas: Is Rehabilitation Possible?"

3. Ibid., 16.

4. Ibid., 17.

renunciation"[5] as well as "continuous prayer, fasting, and continence."[6] Jean-Daniel Kaestli summarizes the negative ascetical dimension of the *Gospel* as its renunciation of wealth, family, and sexuality.[7] The scholars who assume a late second-century date for the *Gospel of Thomas* identify the ascetical propensities of the *Gospel* with the second-century sectarians[8] called the Encratites (*enkrateia* means self-control or continence), whose dualistic theology denigrated the physical dimension of earthly existence including marriage and the use of wine in the Eucharist.[9] On the other side of this argument, Jorunn Jacobsen Buckley argues that the *Gospel* "seems quite uninterested in asceticism" because "sexual abstinence, prohibition of procreation and marriage are never mentioned in the *Gospel*."[10] In fact, Buckley's observation is correct: these traditional themes of renunciation find very little direct reference in this *Gospel*.[11] The thematic approach does not allow for a definitive description of the *Gospel* as ascetical simply because the *Gospel* contains very few (if any) direct reference to ascetical themes or subjects as they have traditionally been described.

The second means of establishing the ascetical nature of the *Gospel of Thomas* begins with a strict bifurcation of two categories: asceticism

5. Ibid., 15.

6. Ibid., 17. Frend lists these latter virtues as consistent with the sexual renunciation of Jewish-Christians like the Nazirite James, and he aligns this variety of cultural asceticism with the content of the *Gospel of Thomas*.

7. He argues this in the context of laying out a number of theological elements of the *Gospel of Thomas* in Kaestli, "L'Evangile de Thomas," 394. Marvin Meyer similarly argues that the ascetical orientation of the *Gospel* provides the basis for its attitude toward sex and sexuality. See Meyer, "Making Mary Male," 554–56.

8. Michael Williams, *Rethinking "Gnosticism,"* 29–53 has called into question the scholarly propensity to create such sectarian movements on the basis of modern scholarly reconstructions.

9. On the Encratites, see Stander, "Encratites," 370–71 and Gasparro, "Asceticism and Anthropology," 127–46.

10. Buckley, "Interpretation of Logion 114," 270. See also her *Female Fault*, 84–104. Stevan L. Davies also argues that "Thomas, in its aversion to fasting and lack of interest in marriage, contradicts encratism." See *Gospel of Thomas and Christian Wisdom*, 22.

11. Saying 14 specifically rejects the traditional ascetic and pious acts of praying, fasting, and giving alms. The theme of singularity (Sayings 4, 11, 16, 49, 75, 106) does not necessarily imply the rejection of marriage, but it certainly does suggest an alternative construction of subjectivity. See my *Gospel of Thomas*, 10–12. I will address the ascetical nature of these sayings below.

and gnosticism.[12] When they are established as mutually exclusive, the *Gospel* must fit into one or the other. Since the *Gospel* does not have any of the attributes of fully developed second-century gnosticism,[13] scholars using this approach argue that it then must be ascetical. Gilles Quispel maintains the strict bifurcation of the categories in arguing that the *Gospel of Thomas*'s orientation toward singleness is not gnostic, but encratite in a Syrian tradition.[14] Quispel argues that the *Gospel* manifests a strict encratite predilection for celibacy and the rejection of marriage.[15] Others argue that although the *Gospel* remains ascetical, it represents a stage of asceticism moving toward fully developed gnosticism.[16] Cyril Richardson, for example, contends that the categories themselves are not necessarily mutually exclusive, but that the *Gospel* is definitely encratite moving toward gnosticism. He maintains that the *Gospel*'s three main anxieties (death, movement, and sexual incompleteness) "are overcome by the troubling and mysterious realization of the self as of heavenly origin," which is a process with "practical results" that require the initiate's life "to be marked by sexual abstention, poverty, aloneness, uninvolvement and freedom from ceremonial rules."[17] Kaestli holds that the asceticism of the *Gospel* articulates the practical consequence of a gnostic discovery of the self.[18] This approach remains difficult because the cat-

12. Even the perceptive work of Michael Williams (*Rethinking "Gnosticism,"* 139–88) reflects the persistence of old patterns. Williams does not question that asceticism relates primarily to the issues of procreation and marriage, and he subsumes asceticism under the category "ethics" and places it in contrast to "libertinism." Although his argument does not promote the polarity gnosticism/asceticism, his contrast of "asceticism" to "libertinism" under the rubric of "ethics" takes the discussion again far afield. Asceticism must first be understood on its own before it can be contrasted to or subsumed under other categories.

13. The scholarly consensus in fact argues that the *Gospel* reflects a wisdom genre moving toward the fully developed gnosticism of a later period. See Koester, *Ancient Christian Gospels,* 75–128 and Cameron, "*Gospel of Thomas*," 381–92.

14. See Quispel, "Gnosticism," 65–85; see also his "*Gospel of Thomas* Revisited," 218–66, especially 254–59 where he unsuccessfully lays out the argument for an encratite source for the *Gospel*.

15. Quispel, "L'Évangile selon Thomas," 35–52; more discussion of this article will follow below.

16. Or vice versa: Oscar Cullman ("Gospel of Thomas," 426) argued that "the last editor was a Gnostic with strong encratitic tendency."

17. Richardson, "Gospel of Thomas," 71.

18. Kaestli, "L'Évangile de Thomas," 375–96.

egories themselves resist definition.[19] The relationship of gnosticism and asceticism also eludes precise articulation.[20] In the end, to argue that the *Gospel* is ascetical and not gnostic, or ascetical moving toward gnostic, or gnostic moving toward ascetical, does not adequately account for the complexity of the texts and the sayings contained in it or for its themes, content, or direction.[21]

The third means used to explore the ascetical dimension of the *Gospel of Thomas* revolves about the postulate that the *Gospel* was formulated in Syria and, therefore, that the *Gospel* manifests ascetical interests and practices peculiar to Syriac asceticism. Sidney Griffith, writing on the early history of Syrian monasticism, centers early Syrian asceticism on three primary elements: the theology of the solitary who has a special relationship to the Son of God and who imitates Christ in the community; the community of those solitaries who represented restored paradise; and (more marginally) the mourners who were penitents living the hermetic life.[22] Quispel argues that the *Gospel of Thomas* stands as an encratite text with a pronounced predilection for celibacy and for those who renounce marriage; this model of asceticism arose in Edessa in Syria, and therefore the theology of Thomas emerged from the Syriac encratite tradition.[23] Michel Desjardins even uses the evidence of the ascetic orientation, especially regarding a "longing for androgyny, unity and the celibate state," as the best evidence that the *Gospel* has a "Syrian provenance."[24]

19. Williams, *Rethinking "Gnosticism,"* 29–53. Ernst Bammel ("Rest and Rule," 88–90) uses yet other categories and locates Saying 2 in a pre-gnostic Jewish tradition because the concept of striving with wonder does not seem particularly gnostic.

20. This issue receives careful attention by Williams, *Rethinking "Gnosticism,"* 139–88.

21. Gärtner (*Theology*, 12.) goes so far as to write "that the term 'Gnosticism' and 'Gnostic' are used here without further definition to denote all those syncretistic streams in the early Church which differed from the main traditions, being dominated by a different idea of God, a different concept of the world and man (sic), and a different teaching on the Saviour, and which finally led to a split with the Church."

22. Griffith, "Asceticism in the Church of Syria," 220–45. This article corrects some misconceptions about early Syrian asceticism promulgated by the widely influential *History of Asceticism in the Syrian Orient* by Arthur Vööbus.

23. Quispel, "L'Évangile selon Thomas," 39. In this article Quispel argues for a Jewish-Christian origin for Christian asceticism that precedes even the Syrian models of asceticism. This view has not found wide acceptance.

24. Desjardins, "Where was the *Gospel of Thomas* Written?" 126. He is using the evidence to establish Antioch and not Edessa as the site of production of the *Gospel*.

Although the scholarly consensus locates the geographical matrix for the *Gospel of Thomas* in Syria, that location does not account fully for theological propensities of the *Gospel*. Griffith does not cite the *Gospel of Thomas* as a major source for the description of Syrian asceticism and monasticism, but does refer to the later Odes of Solomon and the Acts of Judas Thomas as "foundational documents."[25] The *Gospel of Thomas* composed probably around 100–110 C.E. or earlier provides the earliest evidence for Syriac asceticism organized around the theme of solitude and celibacy.[26] In the end, explaining the *Gospel* by its origins in a specific geographical and theological environment does not sufficiently address the issues.

All three of these strategies for exploring the ascetical dimension of the *Gospel of Thomas* fail to convince. The process of constructing precise early Christian themes, movements, and geographical theologies does not permit either a close and accurate reading of the text of the *Gospel of Thomas* itself or a fully articulated understanding of the cultural frames used to interpret the *Gospel*. That process remains a circular one with no clear explanation of the text. In addition, the question of the dating of the *Gospel* intrudes. If it is assumed that the *Gospel of Thomas* is a late second-century text, then it is possible that the *Gospel* could be associated with late second-century encratic and gnostic movements because the evidence points toward the full emergence of such theological sects during that time. But if the *Gospel of Thomas* is dated to the turn of the second century or earlier, then those movements have not yet emerged and the *Gospel* remains an anomaly. Some other means of assessing the ascetical dimensions of the *Gospel* must emerge to provide clarity; the rest of this paper will explore other avenues.

GENERAL PRINCIPLES OF ASCETICISM

Most scholars who have considered the question of the asceticism of the *Gospel of Thomas* begin with a negative description: asceticism consists of specific practices of self-denial with respect to food, sexual expression, and social relations. For them the presence of these renunciatory prac-

---

25. On the texts basic to understanding in the Syrian tradition, see Griffith, "Asceticism in the Church of Syria," 220–23.

26. On the various approaches to the dating of the *Gospel of Thomas* and my justification for the first decade of the second century, see my *Gospel of Thomas*, 12–21.

tices indicates the ascetical dimension of the text. The argument about asceticism, then, revolves about the ability of the scholar to prove the presence or absence of those practices in the text. This constitutes a narrow understanding of asceticism.

Asceticism may also be understood in a positive sense. In discussing the asceticism of Clement of Alexandria, Margaret Miles describes asceticism as the spiritual disciplines that "require effort and concentration" for the gradual improvement of the individual's life. She writes that asceticism involves "the choice to stop temporarily the outflow of the soul's attention and affection to the objects of the physical world, and to turn this attention and affection to one's connection with 'divine power and grace.'"[27] At an international conference on asceticism, Kallistos Ware also addressed the positive dimension of asceticism as a challenge to the traditionally negative understanding. In explaining the positive strain of both *anachoresis* (withdrawal) and *enkrateia* (self-mastery), he insisted that asceticism might be understood as "transfiguration rather than mortification" such that any human being, not simply an elite corps of renunciants, might practice it.[28]

This positive understanding of asceticism revolves about the intentional reformation of the self through specific practices. The presence or absence of an agenda to reformulate or refashion the self provides the key to whether (or not) a text is ascetical. That ascetical refashioning of the self consists of two simultaneous movements: a rejection of the existent self and the conditions for its maintenance and a positive movement toward the construction of a new self and the conditions for its survival. That goal of achieving a refashioned self organizes and galvanizes the energy for the reconstruction of the self. That emergent self, even though clearly demarcated from the renounced self in the mind of the ascetic, exists as a developing and fluctuating status as the new self comes into being.

The *Gospel of Thomas* clearly promulgates a refashioned self. Scholars have recognized this for a long while, although this promulgation of a new self has been understood as pointing to a gnostic milieu. Helmut Koester, for example, maintains that the focus of this *Gospel* "is the formation, not of a community, but of the individual."[29] R. McL. Wilson articulated it in

27. Miles, *Fullness of Life*, 44–45.

28. Ware, "Way of the Ascetics," 13. The international conference was held at Union Theological Seminary in New York City, April 1993.

29. Koester, "Story of the Johannine Tradition," 21. Gregory Riley concurs with

this way: "The Kingdom ... has been allegorized into an expression of the spiritual state of the Gnostic. It is by coming to a knowledge of himself, of his own true nature, that a man (sic) finds the knowledge of the Father and of the Kingdom."[30] Buckley maintains that the *Gospel* espouses a mythology of restoring the seeker to the unity Adam lost in Paradise.[31] The orientation of the *Gospel* toward refashioning the self, regardless of the particular categories under which it has been analyzed, stands generally acknowledged.

The articulation of the insufficiency of a given self provides the starting point for understanding the *Gospel of Thomas* as an ascetical text. Saying 67 relates: "Jesus said, 'If one who knows the all still feels a personal deficiency, he is completely deficient.'"[32] The saying describes two selves in a chronological sequence moving from "still feel(ing) a personal deficiency" toward "know(ing) the all" confidently. It exemplifies the two movements: it rejects those who experience deficiency in their knowledge, and it advocates a self fully confident of its knowledge of the all. Other sayings confirm this articulation of two selves, one rejected and one emergent. Saying 3 metaphorizes those who do not know themselves as "dwell(ing) in poverty" and in fact becoming "that poverty"; while those who know themselves will both be known by others and "realize that it is you who are the sons of the living father." Saying 47 emphasizes the incompatibility of these selves:

> Jesus said, "It is impossible for a man to mount two horses or to stretch two bows. And it is impossible for a servant to serve two masters; otherwise, he will honor the one and treat the other contemptuously. No man drinks old wine and immediately desires to drink new wine. And new wine is not put into old wineskins, lest they burst; nor is old wine put into a new wineskin, lest it

Koester who "sees the GTh as recommending 'radical encratism' with a Gnostic orientation as standard behavior for the individual disciple, a viewpoint which does considerable justice to its content as a whole" (Riley, "*Gospel of Thomas* in Recent Scholarship," 229). Although I do not agree with Riley or Koester about the gnostic orientation of the *Gospel* or the manner in which encratism is identified with asceticism, I agree that the *Gospel* orients itself to the development and articulation of individual behavior. For further elaboration on these themes, see my *Gospel of Thomas*, 1–27.

30. Wilson, *Studies*, 25.

31. Buckley, *Female Fault*, 84–104.

32. I use throughout the translation of the *Gospel of Thomas* by Thomas O. Lambdin, *Nag Hamadi Codex II*, 2–7.

spoil. An old patch is not sewn onto a new garment, because a tear would result."[33]

The two conflicting selves compete for the attention of the seeker, because they remain incompatible: the old and the new cannot coexist without ruining each other, causing rupture and discord, or being ripped apart. This articulation of two selves, one rejected and one sought after, provides the strongest evidence for the ascetical orientation of the *Gospel of Thomas*. The asceticism relies not so much on the specific renunciatory practices, but rather on the articulation of a newly fashioned self: one inconsistent with the past, one confidently knowing the all, one new and sufficiently different from the old to be spoiled by contact with it. This dynamic struggle of selves reveals the ascetical orientation of the text. It does not matter here whether the new self is gnostic or whether the practices align with modern understandings of encratism. Only the positive agenda for creating a newly refashioned self in conflict with the old self matters in describing the *Gospel* as ascetical.

This understanding of the asceticism of the *Gospel of Thomas* enables an ironic reading of some of its problematic texts. When certain renunciatory acts relating to eating, sexual expression, and social relations defined asceticism, the argument could be made (as it was by Buckley[34]) that the *Gospel* rejected asceticism because it rejected traditional ascetically pious acts. Saying 14 provides the clearest example:

> Jesus said to them, "If you fast, you will give rise to sin for yourselves; and if you pray, you will be condemned; and if you give alms, you will do harm to your spirits. When you go into any land and walk about in the districts, if they receive you, eat what they will set before you, and heal the sick among them. For what goes into your mouth will not defile you, but that which issues from your mouth—it is that which will defile you."

This saying overturns the traditional categories of ascetical piety, namely fasting, prayer, alms, and care about ritual purity. When those particular acts define asceticism, the *Gospel of Thomas* cannot be considered asceti-

---

33. See my *Gospel of Thomas*, 123–24. The existence of these sayings in the Synoptic Sayings Source Q indicates that the ascetical orientation of some of these sayings may perhaps emerge from the earliest level of the Jesus movement. That argument, however, cannot be fully developed here.

34. Buckley, "Interpretation of Logion 114," 245–72.

cal because it rejects them. However, when these acts become associated with the old self, the rejected self, then the renunciation of pious acts becomes part of the construction of a new identity no longer requiring the traditional pious acts. The positive understanding of asceticism enables these renunciatory acts to fulfill a positive function in creating a new kind of person. They are, therefore, strongly indicative of an ascetical orientation of the *Gospel*.

As a starting point, the ascetical dimension of the *Gospel of Thomas* depends not upon specific renunciatory patterns, but upon a positive agenda of refashioning the self. The *Gospel of Thomas* refashions the self by forcing the seeker to choose between the old self and the new (old wine in new wineskins), by positively characterizing the new self as confident and knowledgeable about the all while negatively characterizing the old self as deficient and poor. This description enables a clearly positive answer to the question "Is the *Gospel of Thomas* Ascetical?", but much more can be said. Further explanation, however, demands further refinement of the understanding of asceticism.

A Theory of Asceticism

The contest of two selves, as evident in the *Gospel of Thomas* and many other ascetical texts, provided me the starting point for a theory of asceticism.[35] I define asceticism as "performances within a dominant social environment intended to inaugurate a new subjectivity, different social relations, and an alternative symbolic universe."[36] This definition simply points to the central elements of asceticism: performances, an intentionally new identity, redefined social relationships, and a reconstituted symbolic universe. Asceticism refers to the practices that inaugurate a new identity in the context of a received identity. Social relationships support and maintain both the old and the new identity, and, therefore, they must be changed from old patterns to new ones to enable a new subjectivity to develop. Likewise, intricate systems of belief and understanding (the symbolic universe) authenticate both the old and the new identity, and, therefore, they too must be reconstructed in order to authorize the

35. I develop this theory most fully in chapter 2, "Constructions of Power," pp. 14–59, but here I am also relying heavily on chapter 1, "Theory of the Social Function of Asceticism," pp. 3–13.

36. Chapter 2, "Constructions of Power," p. 38.

new identity. All of these transformations (as Kallistos Ware[37] calls them) focus, however, on specific, often insignificant, actions or practices that form the heart of asceticism.

Borrowing from performance theory in theater, I locate asceticism in intentional performances.[38] No particular action in itself constitutes an ascetical one, but the intention of specific actions to create an alternative identity within a larger social or religious setting does. The shift in definition from particular actions to intentional actions with a clear objective makes a significant difference in the reading of an ascetical text like the *Gospel of Thomas*. The *Gospel* need not exhibit the "encratite" behaviors of fasting, sexual renunciation, or limited social engagement to be understood as ascetical.[39] These themes, not often present in the *Gospel*, do not advance understanding because they remain merely descriptive of its content. Rather, it is the question of the intentional refashioning of an identity that marks the text as ascetical. By exploring the contours of the new identity and the means (performances) set out to achieve it, interpreters move from mere description to the unfolding of the social and religious dynamic promulgated in the text. Moreover, asceticism, precisely because of its basis in performances, remains a public activity because the new identity (as any identity) remains a public and social phenomenon. Therefore, ascetic performances display for public notice the clear distinction between the old person and the new or emergent one, and the ascetical text provides the clue both to the manner of the development of the new identity and to the contours of that identity in the face of a more dominant or socially acceptable one.

37. Ware, "Way of the Ascetics," 8–12.

38. In addition to chapter 1, "Theory of the Social Function of Asceticism," pp. 3–13, see Miller, "Desert Asceticism," 137–53. On performance theory, see Schechner, "Magnitudes of Performance," 144.

39. This more universal impulse toward asceticism was explored at a 1993 international conference on asceticism. That discussion has been transcribed as "Practices and Meanings of Asceticism in Contemporary Religious Life and Culture"; see Wimbush and Valantasis, *Asceticism*, 588–606. Peter Van Ness argues this particularly well in his comments during this discussion, "Asceticism in Philosophical and Cultural-Critical Perspective," idem, 589–93.

Performances

When understood from the perspective of this performative theory of asceticism, the *Gospel of Thomas* exhibits a strong ascetical orientation. The manifold performances promulgated by the *Gospel* bespeak a complex refashioning of the self. These intentional performances may be organized into three different types: performances oriented toward discovery, performances relating to social relationships, and performances shaping attitudes toward living in the world. These specific performances become the basis for articulating the subjectivity envisioned in the *Gospel*.

The performances oriented toward discovery play a primary role in the *Gospel*. This discovery operates at a number of different levels beginning simply with the injunction to seek: "Seek and you will find" (Saying 92). Saying 94 exemplifies this simple process ("He who seeks will find, and [he who knocks] will be let in") and even guarantees the seeker an increment of success. In yet another description, Saying 1 guides the seeker to "find the interpretation of these sayings" in order "not [to] experience death." This search for interpretation becomes the hallmark of the seeker and it finds further elaboration throughout the collection of sayings. Saying 2 in the Coptic version exemplifies a more complex structuring of the injunction to seek and discover, describing the search as a complex interlocking process:

> Jesus said, "Let him who seeks continue seeking until he finds. When he finds, he will become troubled. When he becomes troubled, he will be astonished, and he will rule over the all."

The Greek version complicates the process even further because its final element is rest: "And [once he has ruled], he will [attain rest]." Clearly, these sayings envision a person whose life orients itself to seeking and finding on a spectrum from a very simple process to a very complex one.

The performances oriented toward discovery do not function only at a general level, but they also have a very specific referent in a particular relationship with the living Jesus. Jesus pronounces all the sayings in this *Gospel*. The persistent beginning of the vast majority of sayings with "Jesus said" finds explicit statement in the Prologue: "These are the secret sayings which the living Jesus spoke." The discovery promulgated relates to an encounter and engagement with the living Jesus. Through this engagement with Jesus in the sayings, the seeker strives to reconstruct the self. Saying 59 relates: "Jesus said, 'Take heed of the living one while you are alive, lest you die and seek to see him and be unable to do so.'"[40] This seeking defines human, earthly life with its attention to Jesus in daily life; it is not oriented toward life after death. The performative search both defines the actions of the seeker and engages the seeker in transformative relationship with Jesus.

The injunction to discovery that is focused on an engagement with the living Jesus[41] has very high stakes. The subjectivities of both Jesus and the discoverer change as a result of these performances. Saying 108 makes this theology explicit:

> Jesus said, "He who will drink from my mouth will become like me. I myself shall become he, and the things that are hidden will be revealed to him."

This saying advances two different descriptions of the relationship. The seeker will become "like" Jesus by drinking from his mouth. The seeker's engagement with the sayings and the speaker of the sayings are both metaphorized as Jesus' "mouth," and this "mouth" eventually transforms the seeker into a likeness of Jesus. In the second description of the relationship, Jesus becomes the seeker and that identification enables the seeker to receive the revelation of hidden things. These relationships are not equal because Jesus "becomes" the seeker while the seeker simply comes to resemble Jesus,[42] but they do indicate the intensity of engagement and mutual involvement envisioned in the injunctions to seek and to discover.

The second group of performances regulates social relationships.[43] The family social grouping receives consistent attention in the *Gospel* un-

---

40. The asceticism of this *Gospel* does not relate to a future time of fulfillment but to an immediate contact and presence with the living Jesus whose commanding words are the basis of a new form of living. This is a slight variation on the "realized eschatology" of the *Gospel*. See Patterson, *Gospel of Thomas and Jesus*, 208–14.

41. On the important and unique role Jesus plays in this *Gospel*, see Kaestli, "L'Évangile de Thomas," 380 and 390.

42. This represents a further refinement of the analysis of this saying I presented in *Gospel of Thomas*, 188–89.

43. Stephen J. Patterson, applying Gerd Theissen's theories, provides a good description of the social history of the movement in his *Gospel of Thomas and Jesus*, 121–57.

der the dual aspects of rejection and reconstruction. Saying 55 presents the renunciatory aspect directly:

> Jesus said, "Whoever does not hate his father and his mother cannot become a disciple to me. And whoever does not hate his brothers and sisters and take up his cross in my way will not be worthy of me."

This is strong and definitive language with little ambiguity about its intent. The biological family of father, mother, brothers, and sisters must be hated in order that one becomes a disciple of Jesus. This saying rejects categorically the fundamental relationships structured by the family. At the same time, Saying 99 retains the category "family" with new and alternative signification:

> The disciples said to him, "Your brothers and your mother are standing outside." He said to them, "Those here who do the will of my father are my brothers and my mother. It is they who will enter the kingdom of my father."

While implying that members of the biological family remain outside the kingdom, this saying restructures "family" around those obedient to the will of Jesus' father. This restructuring of family around the will of the father reflects a pattern of reconstructed "family" imitative of Jesus. Saying 101 displays these connections between Jesus and the reorganizing of social relationships:

> <Jesus said,> "Whoever does not hate his [father] and his mother as I do cannot become a [disciple] to me. And whoever does [not] love his [father and] his mother as I do cannot become a [disciple to] me. For my mother [. . .], but [my] true [mother] gave me life.

Again, the new social arrangement begins with hatred modeled on Jesus' hatred for biological family with a simultaneous redefinition of family based on discipleship. This saying also portrays two different identities emergent from two different mothers: one identity issues from "my mother"; the other identity, described as life-giving, arises from "my true mother" (if the lacuna in the text does indeed provide a negative contrasting example). The social relationships connect directly to the contest of the two identities; new patterns of identity evolve from the different set of social relationships. These sayings articulate a redefinition of new social relationships based on the renunciation of the biological family, the redefinition of the family, and the alternative social identities envisioned in the new social arrangements.

The reconstruction of the family provides only one (albeit the most pervasive) aspect of the performative creation of a new identity through redefined social relationships. There are others. One saying (Saying 95) restructures economic relationship by encouraging the seekers to lend money to people who cannot repay it.[44] Such behaviors undermine the very fabric of hierarchical and economic social structures while simultaneously redefining the nature of economic relationships around a freedom from concern about making and losing of money. In a strategy simply dismissive of basic elements of human daily existence, Saying 36 warns the seekers not to worry about either food or clothing. Again, this lack of worry at once undermines elements of normal social relationship while thematizing freedom for the seeker. Saying 86 valorizes the concept that the son of man has "no place to lay his head and rest" as exemplary for the seeker; this homelessness completes a pattern of embracing persecution, hunger, and rejection as a blessing (Sayings 68 and 69). Saying 31 encourages the seeker to find a true identity and a fulfilling relationship with those who are outside one's familiar communities.[45] The most dramatic restructuring of social relations, and perhaps the most bizarre, remains the parabolic injunction in Saying 98 that the seeker practice his murderous actions at home on the wall to test whether he is able to kill a powerful person:

> Jesus said, "The kingdom of the father is like a certain man who wanted to kill a powerful man. In his own house he drew his sword and stuck it into the wall in order to find out whether his hand could carry through. Then he slew the powerful man."

The fundamental social relationships have been significantly revised in order to inaugurate new social patterns organizing power, economics, the propriety of clothes, the ordering of the day to meals, social stability, and many other aspects of quotidian existence.

The restructuring of the family remains one element in a consistent pattern to redefine and reorganize social relationships. The alternative

---

44. See Patterson, *God of Jesus*, 104–6.

45. Patterson, *Gospel of Thomas and Jesus*, 121–57 provides the best description of the social theology of the *Gospel of Thomas*.

identity depends upon such social redefinitions to enable it to thrive. Correlatively, the new social arrangements call into existence a new identity capable of living them out. These ascetical performances remain highly interdependent as elements within an intentional system of refor- mation of self. Thus the restructuring of the family and other examples of restructuring life become a consistent pattern to redefine and reorganize social relationships linked to a newly fashioned self. The new identity calls forth new social relationships and those new relationships in turn provide a social location for that identity to exist.

The third group of performances set forth a particular way of under- standing the world. Lack of interest and investment characterize the most pervasive attitude toward the world.[46] Saying 42 expresses this simply and clearly: "Become passersby." The seeker need not reject the world, but simply acknowledge that the world does not merit the seeker's attention. The same bifurcation of old and new identities finds expression in the way the seeker ought to live in the world envisioned by these sayings. Sayings 47, cited above, argues for a clear choice because of the impossibility of mounting two horses or stretching two bows or serving two masters. The seeker's life in the mundane world resembles the spoilage resulting from putting old wine into new wineskins, or the damage resulting from put- ting new wine into old wineskins, or the rip resulting from sewing an old patch onto a new garment. These metaphors reinforce the danger of living in the world as new agents and they warn the seekers to recognize at once the new identity they have attained and the destructiveness to their new identity that the world with its old patterns occasions. The two worlds stand side by side, the world within the community of seekers and that one without. The hearer of these sayings may live safely only in one, the one created by the seekers, and cannot live in both because each world demands different actions and attitudes. The two worlds cannot be mixed without detriment, so it is best to become a passerby to the mundane and common world.

The mundane world receives harsh characterization. The *Gospel of Thomas* understands the world as a corpse: "Whoever has come to understand the world has found (only) corpse and whoever has found a corpse is superior to the world" (Saying 56). The discovery and under-

46. On social orientation, see Patterson, *Gospel of Thomas and Jesus*, 158–70; and Koester, *Ancient Christian Gospels*, 127–28.

standing that characterized the identity of the seeker includes a discovery that the world remains a lifeless enclosure, and such a discovery provides the seeker a status superior to the world. These images and metaphors inflate the status of the seeker over that of the world, while at the same time providing negative images that warn the seeker away from involvement in the mundane world. The negative images abound. This world remains a place of conflict and destruction where Jesus may say, "it is dissension which I have come to cast upon the earth: fire, sword, and war" (Saying 16). This saying further demonstrates the dissension within the normative family structures that the mundane world promulgates: "For there will be five in a house: three will be against two, and two against three, the father against the son, and the son against the father." The *Gospel of Thomas* advances a theory of disengagement from the world not simply because the newly reconstructed world of the seekers holds positive associations, but also because the known and inherited world remains destructive, strife-torn, and lifeless. These sayings metaphorize the two worlds (the common one and the newly emergent one created by the seekers) with strong language intended to force a decision, to enhance the status of the seekers, to negate the value of the mundane world, and to draw stark and clear distinctions between the mundane world and the newly emergent understanding.

These three types of performances (those oriented toward discovery, to social relationships, and to shaping the symbolic universe) operate at the most basic level of human action and decision. The sayings address the seekers' lives at a number of different levels: they speak to the mind and its understanding of the human condition; they address the practicalities of reorganizing social relationships and rejecting existent arrangements; and they conceive of new actions that act out a new way of living in the world and of understanding the self. The ascetical theology of the *Gospel of Thomas* sets out a clear and practical program for the development of a new identity. That new identity demands a realignment of social relationships and a new understanding of the nature of the world and life lived in it. This constitutes a performative or practical theology that guides the seeker through practices that carefully articulate an alternative way of living in the world.

Subjectivity

These three types of performances inaugurate a particular understanding of the truly enlightened human subject. The performances retain their function as a means to an end; that is, as a means to the inauguration of a new subjectivity: the performances do not constitute the final product. These performances organize and energize the construction of a new identity, so that the desire to become someone new, to achieve a new identity, draws out particular performances that begin to realize that yet non-existent identity. But what "new identity" does the *Gospel of Thomas* promulgate?

Saying 22 provides the starting point for describing the content of this new identity:

> Jesus saw infants being suckled. He said to his disciples, "These infants being suckled are like those who enter the kingdom." They said to him, "Shall we then, as children, enter the kingdom?" Jesus said to them, "When you make the two one, and when you make the inside like the outside, and the outside like the inside, and the above like the below, and when you make the male and the female one and the same, so that the male not be male nor the female female; and you fashion eyes in place of an eye, and a hand in place of a hand, and a foot in place of a foot, and a likeness in place of a likeness; then you will enter [the kingdom]."

This list presents a very precise set of criteria for the new identity. That identity revolves about four primary elements: singularity ("make the two one"), consistency ("when you make the inside like the outside . . ."), a new gender ("that the male not be male . . ."),[47] and bodily transformation (the fashioning of the eye, hand, and foot).[48] Arrival at the goal (metaphorized as entry into the kingdom) depends upon achievements in these four areas. The strong verbs indicate that these achievements result from the activity of the seeker. The performances directly result in the transformation and refashioning of the person with very concrete and well-articulated actions leading to the encompassing goal of entering the kingdom.

47. Early in the history of scholarship about the *Gospel of Thomas*, Walter Till ("New Sayings of Jesus") argued that in Saying 22, "all differences, including that of the sexes, must disappear" (455).

48. This receives fuller explanation in my *Gospel of Thomas*, 95–96.

The *Gospel of Thomas* describes this new subjectivity in great and rich detail in many different sayings. One major task of the collection of these sayings lies precisely in the metaphorization of this new identity. The second part of Saying 3, for example, presents self-knowledge as an important aspect of this new identity:

> When you come to know yourselves, then you will become known, and you will realize that it is you who are the sons of the living father. But if you will not know yourselves, you dwell in poverty and it is you who are that poverty.

The refashioning of the self revolves about self-knowledge understood as a great wealth. Poverty exists when the seeker does not search, discover, or realize knowledge of the self. This self-knowledge and its implied opposite, ignorance of the self, articulate the contest between the received and the emergent identity at the heart of asceticism. Self-knowledge stands at the center of the new subjectivity.

Other sayings complete the picture of this new subjectivity. The seekers achieve immortality, an immortality graphically metaphorized as not tasting death. Saying 18 connects the theme of immortality with the theme of discovery:

> The disciples said to Jesus, "Tell us how our end will be." Jesus said, "Have you discovered, then, the beginning, that you look for the end? For where the beginning is, there will the end be. Blessed is he who will take his place in the beginning; he will know the end and will not experience death.

This interweaving of the major themes (discovery, self-knowledge, knowledge of the world, personal activity) with immortality displays the complexity that marks the development of this subjectivity. Immortality as a goal connects with all the major themes in such a way that the subjectivity may be seen in rich detail. Even without precise knowledge about the referent to such things as "the end" and "the beginning," it is possible to understand the contours of this new life.[49] Other sayings connect immortality to other themes: Saying 19 relates immortality to a myth of five

49. I resist the tendency to connect such phrases to a Greco-Roman or biblical myth of creation, but I am in a minority on this question. Buckley, for example, writes (about Saying 75): "I propose that the solitary is the prototype of Adam who needs to be re-united with himself" in the nuptial chamber ("Interpretation of Logion 114," 266). I do not find evidence for such mythologizing warranted by the sayings themselves.

trees in Paradise; Saying 1 connects it to the process of interpretation of the sayings; Saying 111 links immortality with a relationship to "the living one." The immortality of the new subjectivity has depth, which it receives through its connections with other dimensions of the new subjectivity articulated in these sayings.

Perhaps the metaphor for the new subjectivity most perplexing to scholars is that of singularity.[50] Saying 22 cited above presented one aspect of it: one cannot enter the kingdom until one has made the two into one. In one set of descriptions, then, singularity stands in opposition to duplicity: Saying 47 argues that a person cannot ride two horses or serve two masters; Saying 11 posits a day when the singular person became double; Saying 30 maintains Jesus' presence with the two or the one; Saying 48 describes two people making peace in a single house. Again, there is no clarity about the precise referent to these elements, but clearly the activity of playing with the transformation of one into two and two into one forms an important part of the self-understanding and activity of the newly emerging subjectivity. Singularity also describes the interior state of the new identity. Saying 49 states: "Blessed are the solitary and elect, for you will find the kingdom. For you are from it, and to it you will return." Singularity, however, does not relate only to the interior life of the person. Saying 38 describes the connection of singularity with election: "I shall choose you, one out of a thousand, and two out of ten thousand, and they shall stand as a single one." Some sayings emphasize the relational dynamic of singularity: Saying 4 describes the old man and the child who will "become one and the same" in the dependency of the old man upon the very young child; Saying 16 describes the singularity achieved by opposing members of a household; Saying 105 connects singularity with the redefinition of family life. The relational aspect of singularity connects also to the most enigmatic function of the bridal chamber as Saying 75 relates: "Many are standing at the door, but it is the solitary who will enter the bridal chamber." It can categorically be stated that the new subjectivity promulgated in these sayings revolves about singularity and duplicity even when it is not clear to what these categories refer. The pervasive thematizing of this subject as a single person, a solitary, and one who has passed from duplicity to singularity in a community of oth-

50. Sidney Griffith "Asceticism in the Church of Syria" has the best explanation. But see also M. Harl, "A Propos des *Logia* de Jésus; and A. F. J. Klijn, "'Single One' in the *Gospel of Thomas.*"

ers who have done the same, clearly emphasizes the importance of this aspect of the new identity.

The sayings describe other attributes of this subjectivity as well. The seekers imaged in these sayings experience an increment of freedom from worry (Saying 36), and will find rest (Sayings 50 and 90). The sayings describe the new subject as full of light (Saying 24), as having a clear vision of God (Saying 37), and as a person producing good works (Saying 45). Because the subjects promulgated in these sayings possess an eternal and invisible image (Saying 84), they are more worthy than Adam (Saying 85) and John the Baptist (Saying 46) and the prophets and angels bestow upon them things that are proper to their high status (Saying 88). The subjectivity promoted in these sayings remains a highly articulated and complex one.

The description of the subjectivity could continue. Enough has been said both to describe it and to indicate its centrality to the work of the *Gospel*. The subjectivity promulgated in this *Gospel* may be summarized as including singularity, consistency, a new gender, bodily transformation, self-knowledge, immortality, freedom, and origin in the light. It is highly valued, distinct from the identities existent in the world, and a result of purposeful action. It enables the person to enter the kingdom. The *Gospel of Thomas* points the way toward the development of that subjectivity. The performances constitute an ascetical system designed to bring it into existence with all its attendant glory and wealth. The images the *Gospel* employs to articulate the new identity are compelling, complex, dramatic, and sufficiently enigmatic to engage the reader continually in wanting to learn and understand more.

Summary of the *Gospel of Thomas*'s Asceticism

The positive agenda to create an alternative subjectivity so evident in the *Gospel of Thomas* points to its ascetical orientation. What makes the *Gospel* ascetical revolves not about particular renunciatory patterns but rather about a strategy of refashioning the self through specific, intentional activities. The exploration of the elements of those activities displays the complexity of that ascetical program. The diverse elements of the new subjectivity demand a total reorientation of the seeker to self-understanding, social relationships, and theological knowledge. The new identity slowly comes into being as specific performances enact it.

These performances remain subordinate to the task of refashioning the self; they are not in themselves the focus of attention but instrumental elements in a larger process. The gradual and sustained performances incrementally construct a new identity, slowly building up a new way of understanding self, society, and world. They build the new identity part by part, starting first with one element then moving to other seemingly unrelated elements. For example, singularity may come into being either through conflict in the family (Saying 16), or through being chosen by Jesus (Saying 49), or through making peace in a household (Saying 48), or by remaining alone and entering the bridal chamber (Saying 75). The practices remain subordinate to the goal, and yet they function as the primary means of enacting that goal in concrete human living. The same may be said of social relationships. Family continues to exist even though the received biological model is rejected. New social relationships, figured sometimes as a family and at other times as new economic and political associations,[51] build up a social network that enables the new subject to be related to other social groups. Living in those new types of relationship builds the identity. The alternative social arrangements call into being the new subject capable of living them, but the heart of the social relationships remains subordinate to the goal of constructing a new identity. The *Gospel of Thomas* certainly envisions new social relationships, but those new relationships act out a new way for a person to live in society and the world.

The conflict of two selves was the starting point for exploring the ascetical dimension of the *Gospel*. Very quickly, that conflict of selves resulted in specific performances designed to build the emergent self in relationship to the rejected received identity. The *Gospel of Thomas* gradually unfolds a very dramatic goal that includes singularity, immortality, transformation, and many other descriptors. The elements of this subjectivity find their articulation in small bits of information, in occasional metaphors, in specific actions, and in a myriad of other fine details. The seeker, reading and responding to the direction of the sayings, gradually begins to act out that identity in mind, social relations, and images of the world. The new person emerges from the relationship with the liv-

51. I specifically reject the notion of initiation into various levels of spiritual community propounded by Bruce Lincoln ("Thomas-*Gospel* and Thomas-Community") and by Buckley (*Female Fault*, 85–87). I see no justification to argue a sacramental system, or even a liturgical system, underlying these sayings.

ing Jesus who is speaking the sayings and who guides the seeker into a very specific set of actions that enable the new person to thrive. In the end, a new person has emerged, living with different social relationships, and understanding the world from a totally new perspective. Intended to create a new subjectivity, the *Gospel of Thomas* is ascetical because it promotes performances within the more dominant religious environment at the turn of the first and second centuries. The *Gospel* also fosters new social associations of people imaged as a group of solitaries (Saying 38) standing together with power as a new kind of family and living in a world full of light and immortality. The *Gospel* promotes a complete ascetical system for the refashioning of the self.

Revisiting an Old Problem with a New Theory

Gedaliahu G. Stroumsa argued for a significant transition in the understanding of the human person in Late Antiquity resulting from particularly Christian interests and theology.[52] Christian anthropology, in contrast to both the pagan and the Jewish world, came to value both the human body and soul as equally reflecting God's image. He argues that "the discovery of the person as a unified composite of soul and body in late antiquity was indeed a Christian discovery,"[53] and that "the maturing corpus of Christian thought, from the second to the fourth centuries, culminated with the notion of a radical reflexivity of the self."[54] Stroumsa establishes "the emergence of the new subject" as linked simultaneously to an enlargement of the understanding of the human subject as created in the image of God and to the breaking down[55] of that enlarged subject through an understanding of "original sin and . . . the radical asceticism appearing on a grand scale in the fourth century."[56] Stroumsa's instincts are correct: a radical reconstitution of the human person attends the development of formative Christianity, and asceticism founds that new

---

52. Stroumsa, "*Caro salutis cardo.*"

53. Ibid., 44.

54. Ibid., 27.

55. Bruce Malina calls this a shrinking of the self; see his "Pain, Power, and Personhood." But note the criticism by Elizabeth Castelli, "Asceticism—Audience and Resistance," in the same volume.

56. Stroumsa, "*Caro salutis cardo,*" 31.

understanding of the human subject. Stroumsa's argument[57] correctly and thoroughly develops the emergence of this new self in relationship both to Hellenistic and Classical Greek philosophy and to Judaism, but incorrectly locates that new self in encratism and later patristic theology. The question of the emergence of this new understanding of the human subject arose earlier in the sayings tradition of Jesus and finds clear expression in the *Gospel of Thomas* at the turn from the first to the second century, if not earlier in the first century C.E.[58]

When the presence of particular themes or actions defined asceticism, the task of interpretation remains descriptive and the goal revolves about a proper categorization of the text within other Greco-Roman or Late Antique texts and religious movements. The *Gospel of Thomas* would be aligned with the encratites, or with a group of encratites moving toward gnosticism, or with an early form of monastic lifestyle and community organization. However, when the presence of an agenda of self-reformation defines asceticism, the task of interpretation broadens significantly. The interpretative task now revolves about the conflict of selves in a social and religious setting and the struggle to articulate a new understanding of human subjectivity in newly designated social arrangements and theological constructions. The performances intended to create that new subjectivity emerge as important windows into the conflict of identities operative in the text and in the society. The designation of the *Gospel of Thomas* as an ascetical text forces the investigation of the differences between the rejected and the emergent self, the old and the new social arrangements, the old and the new understanding of the world. The ascetical question of the refashioning of the self demands that the conflicting selves of the text be explored, compared, and documented.

In the case of the *Gospel of Thomas*, the sayings promulgate a particular refashioning of the self through advocating specific performances. Such practices as discovery, or of stomping on one's clothes in the field, or of practicing to murder a powerful man, or of rejecting the biologi-

57. Ibid.

58. This is not the place to argue the case for the early dating of some of the sayings of the *Gospel of Thomas* because they are clear parallels to the Synoptic Sayings Source Q. These overlapping sayings, however, do seem to indicate the *Gospel of Thomas* has preserved sayings of Jesus from the earliest times of their collection, and many of these early sayings are at the heart of the ascetical agenda of the *Gospel of Thomas*. See Patterson, *Gospel of Thomas and Jesus*, 17–93; Koester, *Ancient Christian Gospels*, 86–107; and MacRae, "*Gospel of Thomas—Logia Iesou*?"

cal family, or of entering the bridal chamber, or of becoming singular, display the energy of creating a new kind of person who has entered into the Kingdom of God and who has a very different view of the mundane world. The *Gospel* promulgates an intriguing, articulate, and sophisticated understanding of the self through practices intended to bring it into being.

The ascetical dynamic of the *Gospel of Thomas* also addresses another difficult issue: the coherence of the sayings within the *Gospel*. The *Gospel of Thomas* consists of 114 sayings that display no system of coherence. Some scholars have attempted to find patterns among all 114 sayings,[59] others have attempted simply to show the cohesion of particular sets of sayings within the larger whole.[60] The attempts at defining an overall structure have failed, while some smaller collections of sayings may have been gathered into units either in the sources for the *Gospel of Thomas* or by its writer. Again, these attempts seek to impose structure from outside the text or by an intricate system of passages linked by verbal association.

The ascetical dynamic of the *Gospel of Thomas* makes a case for another kind of cohesion in the text, one based not on these former criteria but on the application of an interior one. The practice of discovery and the impetus to interpretation hold these sayings together. The loose and seemingly haphazard sequence of sayings forces the reader or hearer to embark on the interpretative process.[61] The rambling movement from one saying to another demands that the person begin to practice the central performance mandated by the text by seeking the meaning or the point at which these sayings cohere. In an ascetical text like the *Gospel of*

59. See, for example, Appendix I in Davies, *Gospel of Thomas and Christian Wisdom.* The most carefully reasoned and balanced argument remains Patterson, *Gospel of Thomas and Jesus,* 94–110. The latest attempt (still unconvincing) is that of Allan Callahan, "'No Rhyme or Reason.'" Here Callahan refers to Koester's statement in *Ancient Christian Gospels* (81) that the sayings in the *Gospel* show no "rhyme or reason." Koester uses the phrase as he rejects attempts by other scholars to find a system of organization.

60. See Doran, "Complex of Parables."

61. To Callahan's credit (even though I do not believe his argument), he finds an alliterative verbal and sometime stylistic connection between sayings that shows how a modern reader creates a thread through the sayings; "'No Rhyme or Reason,'" 425–26. A better and more convincing argument may be found in Patterson, *Gospel of Thomas and Jesus,* 99–102. But Gärtner (*Theology,* 28–29) claims that the lack of order indicates that the compiler did not want to present systematic material. These positions indicate the range of options.

Thomas, the interpretation and exploration of meaning of opaque sayings provides the cohesion. The sequence of sayings force the reader to create the metasystem(s) that holds them all together. The practice of seeking creates the cohesion of the sayings in the mind of the seeker. The genre of a sayings *Gospel* [62] demands such a construction of a metasystem that enables the sayings to cohere. In the synoptic Gospels that used collections of sayings (Matthew and Luke), the narrative replaced this metasystem by providing the interpretative link not in the mind of the reader or seeker but in the events of the life of Jesus. The narrative provided an interpretative context. Collections of sayings, however, remain dangerous in that they cannot be controlled by external forces: each reader or seeker must discover and create the structures of meaning. Ironically, in seeking the coherence of the individual sayings, the reader invokes the ascetical agenda and begins the performances that lead to a new subjectivity. [63] The very act of seeking coherence activates and inaugurates the ascetical agenda of the text.

Reading the *Gospel of Thomas* through this ascetical lens also addresses another formidable problem: how this *Gospel* relates to gnosticism, encratism, other ascetical texts, and other texts of the period. In earlier scholarship the question of whether the *Gospel of Thomas* represented gnosticism or wisdom traditions or encratism was based upon the question of the proper categorization of themes. Stevan Davies rejected the gnostic orientation of the *Gospel* in favor of wisdom, [64] while Gilles Quispel rejected gnosticism in favor of encratism, [65] while others interpreted the *Gospel* as clearly gnostic or proto-gnostic. [66] The issue has

62. See Koester's definitive examination of the *Gospel of Thomas* as a sayings *Gospel* in his *Ancient Christian Gospels*, 75–128 and his "Q and Its Relatives." Ron Cameron provides a good summary of Koester's findings on pages 384–88 of his "*Gospel of Thomas* and Christian Origins."

63. Frend argues that the *Gospel of Thomas* has value because it points to the ascetical reading of the sayings of Jesus "among the rural and semi-rural Christian" people in Syria, Palestine, and Egypt who would prepare the way for monasticism and also reject the Greek philosophical orientation of Chalcedon ("*Gospel of Thomas*," 25–26). I agree with him about the relationship of interpretation of asceticism, but I question the assumptions about the relationship of asceticism, monasticism, and non-Chalcedonian Christianity, to say nothing of his late dating of the *Gospel of Thomas*.

64. Davies, *Gospel of Thomas and Christian Wisdom*, 1–17. April D. De Conick also interprets some sayings as primarily wisdom; see her "Yoke Saying."

65. Quispel, "*Gospel of Thomas* Revisited."

66. See Gärtner, *Theology*, 77–210 and Grobel, "How Gnostic is the *Gospel of Thomas*?"

never been decided. With the theoretical lens presented here, however, it is possible to look at the structure of subjectivity in the *Gospel of Thomas* and to compare it with those subjectivities developed in wisdom circles, orthodox Christian circles, sectarian Jewish movements, Greco-Roman philosophical writings, as well as the wide variety of gnostic communities represented by both the heresiological literature and the newly discovered documents representing alternative Christianities. The contours of subjectivity in each of these bodies of literature will probably display many commonalities; the differences will enable researchers to articulate and compare the wide diversity of divergent expressions. The process of comparing different subjectivities and the performances that enact and inaugurate them provides the basis for comparing the religious dynamics and values of widely divergent expressions.

By visiting an old problem with a new theory, this paper attempted to unmask the complexity of these sayings and to expose the underpinnings that hold the individual sayings together. The cohesiveness of the *Gospel of Thomas* remains hidden so long as the approaches to it and to its asceticism remain merely descriptive of its content. Only when the interpreter of the *Gospel* takes into account its ascetical orientation does the *Gospel* begin to cohere. The vitality of the *Gospel of Thomas* emerges not as the *Gospel* is placed in the proper category ("gnostic" or "encratite") but in the gradual unfolding of the new way of being a person and in the incremental building of new social relationships and of a new view of the world. The ascetical agenda manifested in the complex and rich performances intended to construct a new self makes the *Gospel of Thomas* alive with concrete and describable particulars that fill out a dramatic and new way of living, thinking, exploring, organizing life, and orienting the self to the universe. This ascetical agenda, as I have argued here, however, has followed the lines the text itself enjoins for its readers, first by finding the interpretation of the sayings, then by being troubled, astonished, ruling, and finding rest. The true nature of the asceticism of the *Gospel of Thomas* may only be discovered by looking into the deep structure of its meaning and not by remaining on the surface in categories that do not resonate with the text. It has taken a new theory to confirm an old instinct about the *Gospel of Thomas*, that at its core, it is an ascetical text.

Koester moderates these opinions by describing the theology as esoteric, see his *Ancient Christian Gospels*, 124–28.

CHAPTER 10

Competing Ascetic Subjectivities
in the Letter to the Galatians

INTRODUCTION

IN 1989, VICTOR PAUL FURNISH COULD REPORT ABOUT THE STATE OF
Pauline studies that the analysis of the Pauline congregations had finally
displaced "biographical" questions about Paul. He wrote:

> Although the standard "biographical" questions about Paul are
> still debated, these have in general been subordinated to questions
> about the Pauline congregations and his interaction with them as
> apostle. One may judge this to be an altogether proper and indeed
> overdue refocusing of questions about Paul's life and ministry. It
> is Paul's interaction with his congregations, after all, for which
> his letters supply primary data—not for the reconstruction of his
> pre-Christian life, or for his theology in some systematic sense, or
> even, in the first instance, for his missionary preaching.[1]

A few years later in his SBL Presidential address of 1993, Furnish continued to emphasize how difficult it was to put Paul in his proper place in
the historical context of the first century. Furnish argued that the more
scholars learn about nascent Christianity, Rabbinic Judaism, and the
Hellenistic and Greco-Roman worlds, the more difficult it has become
to place Paul precisely in any one of these categories. In addressing this
persistent problem, Furnish proposed both an historical and a theological interpretation of the Pauline letters in which the specificity of their

---

1. Furnish, "Pauline Studies," 329.

historical context and theological content receive correlative and serious attention.[2]

Neither of these suggestions has yet been able to break through the persistent tradition of Pauline scholarship: neither the discursive practices of the community to which the letters stand as witness, nor the theological statements outside the parameters of later theological categories, have received primary scholarly attention. Pauline studies seem to revolve about the same scholarly questions without any attempt to shift the investigation or adjust the categories of research. The work of Daniel Boyarin, E. P. Sanders, James D. G. Dunn, and Alan F. Segal as well as the SBL Paul Group attests to this situation:[3] Paul holds scholarly fascination because he seems to beg to be explicated as the constructed "mind" or "personality" or "perspective" behind the letters. Pauline scholarship, even when oriented toward uncovering the historical context or the rhetorical strategies of the letters, has focused on the person, the mental processes, or the attitudes and theology of Paul in relationship to others.[4] "Paul," as constructed person, has remained the operative category of research. Furnish himself, in evaluating the scholarly production of Pauline studies, returns to the historical and theological investigation of *Paul* as the primary factor in understanding the historical context of the letters. This paper accepts Furnish's assessment and responds to his call for refocusing attention by moving in yet another direction, away from the psycho-theological construction of the person Paul, and toward the analysis of the discursive practices embedded in the Pauline letters.

Let me further explain my perspective. I wish to move the focus from Paul to the letters so that the center of attention revolves not about "what Paul thought" but on the evident and material discourse inscribed within the letters. This shift in focus emphasizes the discursive interaction of a community by contextualizing the narrative voice as only one

2. Furnish, "On Putting Paul in His Place," 3–17.

3. Of all of these scholars, the work of Daniel Boyarin in *A Radical Jew* stands out as the most significant attempt to restructure Pauline scholarship, although it continues in the tradition of discovering the Pauline mentality. See also Segal, *Paul the Convert* and Sanders, *Paul and Palestinian Judaism*. The work of the Pauline Theology Group of the SBL has begun the shift in paradigm, although many of the resulting papers remain connected to the older patterns of scholarship; see *Pauline Theology*, vols. 1 and 2, edited by Jouette M. Bassler and David M. Hay respectively.

4. See, e.g., Georgi, *Opponents of Paul*, who in constructing Paul's opponents still relates them primarily to Paul's own attitudes.

aspect of the discursive field. I am interested in the Pauline letters as sites of discourse, as *loci* of conversation recorded in the early period of formative Christianity, in which the narrative voice of the author opens out discursively with the lives and interests of the recipients of the letters as one factor among many. The narrative voice, not the personality or thought of Paul, receives the attention that focuses on the discourse that this voice articulates.[5] Here, in this discursive practice, not in the mind of Paul, will scholars discover the dynamic of formative Christianity.

So far I have presented the problem and the method of analysis: the problem revolves about redirecting the attention of the Pauline epistles away from the psychological and religious characterization of the author; and the method uses a kind of discourse analysis to investigate the dynamic discursive practices that these letters embody.[6] There is, however, one more factor in this discourse analysis that will aid me in my project of recovering the discursive practices of these early Christian communities—a theory of asceticism.

I have been intrigued over the years with the peripheral suggestion by scholars of the connection between early Christian literary traditions and asceticism. This connection has been proposed regarding the early Syrian traditions of the sayings of Jesus, the trajectory of the *logoi sophon* (sayings of the wise) into the *apophthegmata patrum* (the sayings of the fathers) of the desert monks, the theological orientation of the *Gospel of Thomas*, and many other sites of suspected ascetical influence.[7] My recent research and publication revolves about the definition and role of asceticism in the religious literature of first-century Christianity, Second Temple and Pharisaic Judaism, and Greco-Roman religions and philoso-

5. The strategy exactly parallels the strategy in the study of the historical Jesus in which the narrative voice of the evangelists has been problematized in order to understand the underlying perspectives of the original source material separate from that of the evangelists.

6. To accomplish this analysis of discourse deflected from the traditional constructions of Pauline theology, I have purposefully chosen non-theological language from modern discourse to explain the discursive practices in this Pauline letter; the language of "Law and Faith" or "Judaism and Christianity" has been suppressed from my discourse in order to highlight more vividly the discourse the letters themselves develop.

7. The Syrian tradition of asceticism has been located at the very earliest tradition of the Jesus movement, so that the early itinerant followers of Jesus were considered ascetic; see Koester, *Introduction to the New Testament* 2:156; Patterson, *Gospel of Thomas and Jesus,* 166–68; Griffith, "Asceticism in the Church of Syria;" Richardson, " Gospel of Thomas"; and Vööbus, "History of Asceticism in the Syrian Orient."

phy. I propose that what made Christianity advance so quickly through the first century revolves about a complex interaction of formative and ascetical practices, social and political experimentation, religious redefinition, and theological and biblical ingenuity focused upon the teaching and work of Jesus Christ. It is not primarily personality cult, either of Jesus or of Paul, although certainly such cannot be ruled out, but the performance of a new way of living inaugurated by Jesus and extended by those captivated by the alternative that Jesus offered. The performances of formative Christianity, I argue, established an alternative way of living that included both a subversive set of redefined social relationships and an alternative way of thinking about the world.[8]

I have offered the following definition of asceticism: "performances within a dominant social environment intended to inaugurate a new subjectivity, different social relations, and an alternative symbolic universe."[9] Within the scope of this definition, the performances of Christianity, which set it apart from the dominant social and religious cultures of both first-century Judaism and the Greco-Roman world, demanded the formation of a new kind of person, living in an alternative society with its own standards and ordering of social relationships, and in a symbolic universe that emerged to support both this alternative kind of person and these new social arrangements. I call this whole process "asceticism."[10] The theory explains four elements: intentional performances, the articulation of a new subjectivity, the reorganization of social relationships, and the reorientation of the symbolic universe.

The term "subjectivity" probably requires some preliminary discussion. By "subjectivity" I refer to the person that a society authorizes and designates as an agent, an actor, and a subject. A "subject" is the socially designated and authorized person within a cultural frame. I use this for-

8. I would also argue that Pharisaic Judaism developed in a parallel fashion with the asceticism of the observance of the law constructing an alternative to the temple cult after the destruction of the Temple in 70 C.E.

9. See chapter 2, "Constructions of Power in Asceticism," p. 38. But see also chapter 1, "Theory of the Social Function of Asceticism," pp. 3–13, and chapter 8, "Ascetical Withdrawal," pp. 169–84.

10. Although my theory emerged from an analysis based entirely on Greco-Roman and Late Antique literature, it does not purport to be a definition from antiquity, but a modern scholarly focus through which to interpret the ascetical activities of ancient people. It provides a critical framework through which to define what is ascetical and to define categories through which to compare various ascetical trends or activities.

mal (and somewhat foreign) term to stress that people (especially ancient people and people from different modern cultures) are "not the same;" that is, social and political agency and authorization differ in every concrete circumstance, so that it becomes necessary to construct the authorized agents of a given society both historical and modern. "Subjectivity" denotes the historically and culturally determined status of human identity. A construction of such a subjectivity includes those people who are considered capable of being agents in a particular society (on the analogy of the subject of a sentence being capable of relating to a verb), as well as those who have a unified psychological identity (although that psychology does not imply that it is according to modern or western psychology), and those who participate in systems of the mediation of power (as in a political subject, or someone subject to the law). [11] I understand asceticism as the means of creating alternatives to the subjectivities promulgated by dominant social groups.

Of all of the Pauline letters, the Letter to the Galatians most directly and persistently raises the question of the promulgation of a new subjectivity.[12] If, however, one begins with the usual categories of identity (Paul the Christian, fighting the Jewish-Christian missionaries about the role of the Jewish Law for the newly emergent Christian sectarians), one very quickly (as the secondary literature attests) becomes enmeshed in a hopeless morass of conflicting categories attempting to explain the relationship of Law to Faith and Jew to Christian to Jewish-Christian. The point of the Letter to the Galatians begins with the articulation of a "new creation" in contradistinction to those who are circumcised and those who are not: "for neither is circumcision anything, nor is uncircumcision, but (only a) new creation" [6:15]. The construction of this new person, this new identity, defined against the background of the these two

11. My description of subjectivity summarizes probably too simply an extensive scholarly discussion focused on Michel Foucault's Order of Things. For our purposes here, Elizabeth A. Castelli has worked through this concept in reading Foucault for Pauline studies; she writes: Foucault's "very use of the name 'subject' for the modern individual is a play on the various significations associated with this word: one is a subject in the grammatical sense (as in the subject of a sentence), in the psychological sense (as possessing a unified identity), and in the political sense (as being subject to dominant powers)"; Castelli, Imitating Paul, 40.

12. Beverly Gaventa has argued similarly that Galatians articulates "a new identity in Christ" that "results in the nullification of previous identifications"; Gaventa, "Singularity," 149. Our endpoints are similar while our methods of interpretation vary.

alternatives organizes the rhetoric and discourse of the letter.[13] Galatians articulates the relationship of these three subjectivities.

My thesis, stated simply and boldly, then, is that this letter organizes three different sorts of subjectivities: the first defines the natural subject;[14] the second defines the culturally dominant subjectivity of first-century Judaism; and the third develops the spiritual or pneumatic subjectivity of a Jewish sectarian group within the larger dominant Jewish religious and social culture. In this letter, the character Paul functions as an exemplar[15] of the third (or spiritual) category in an argument intended to solidify the continuing development of this subjectivity among people who cannot distinguish it properly from the perspective of the culturally dominant and Jewish subjectivity. These subjectivities compete because they are organized into a hierarchy in which the natural and traditional Jewish subjectivities must be left behind in order to develop the spiritual and because there is conflict within the community itself as to the understanding of these subjectivities. Inasmuch as that "new creation" becomes real through the exercise of freedom, it constitutes an ascetical process intended to bring into existence the pneumatic person.

The "Natural" Subjectivity

Two factors hinder the definition of the "natural" subject: first, the writer says very little about it, and second, what the writer says about it betrays his objections to it and bias against it. So, this subjectivity must be defined as from a "hostile witness." Only one section of the letter (4:8–11)

13. Gaventa ("Singularity," 149) calls this discourse a "Christocentric" one because the new subjectivity revolves about a particular understanding of Christ. I argue here that the pneumatic subjectivity is the emergent one, but I agree with Gaventa that this pneumatic subjectivity, particularly in its corporate dimension, revolves about Christological theologoumena.

14. I call this the "natural" subjectivity because I want to set it in contrast to the "traditional Jewish" subjectivity that carefully and clearly distinguishes itself from those with foreskins (the translation "uncircumcised" already prejudices a perspective) and in contrast to the Jesus Christ sectarians of Jews who also embraced both those with and without foreskins. I am aware that this characterization has serious gender implications that identify women with those without foreskins (that is, circumcised Jews). In fact, Boyarin (*Radical Jew*, 224–27) argues the identification of "women" and "Jew" in western discourse.

15. On this aspect of Pauline writing see Castelli, *Imitating Paul*, 119–36.

provides information regarding it and what it conveys can only provide us with the contours of the subjectivity.

The reference to this subjectivity emerges from a comparison. The writer describes it as the recipients' "former" one. Paul, the narrator of the letter, does not participate in this subjectivity because he uses the second person plural ("you") as referring only to the recipients of the letter. We can, therefore, conclude definitively that this subjectivity does not reflect the customary Judaism of the day, nor the Christian sect of Judaism that Paul advocates.[16] This subjectivity functions as a point of comparison with these others.

Three rather sketchy characteristics define this subjectivity: these people (1) submit to "beings that are by nature not gods," (2) they are oriented toward "elements" (*stoicheia*), and (3) they "observe (*paratereisthe*) days, months, seasons, and years." The last two factors, the "elements" and the cyclical kalendrical observations, seem to imply a deterministic symbolic universe in which the person is subject to cyclical determinative interactions of the cosmic elements.[17] This assumption of the cosmic dimension has guided Betz to include the descriptor "elements *of the world*" in his translation.[18] From the narrator's perspective, this kind of subjectivity constitutes an enslavement: the deterministic perspective that I perceive here relates to that characterization of this "former" subjectivity as "slaves," of people "enslaved" to "beings that are by nature not gods." This subjectivity, then, articulates a kind of person who reverences

16. James D. G. Dunn ("Echoes of Intra-Jewish Polemic") understands this reference to refer to specifically Jewish customs: "Paul clearly has particularly Jewish festivals in mind" (470). His argument is that everything except the years has a clear reference to contemporary Jewish practice (470–73). Because he views the entire letter within the context of intra-Jewish polemic, he fails to see the sorts of contrasts in practices which the letter displays. Troy Martin ("Apostasy to Paganism") argues that the primary problem with the Galatians is their supposed return to paganism. Martin's argument proceeds through an analysis of the rhetoric (stasis theory) of the letter, but his argument fails to convince me that the Galatians are indeed apostatizing. As will be seen in this analysis, the natural subjectivity does not receive sufficient attention to pose a real threat to the primary two subjectivities the letter develops.

17. Martin ("Apostasy to Paganism," 449–50) argues for the "pagan nature of this list" and refers the reader to a newer article entitled "Pagan and Judeo-Christian Time-Keeping Schemes in Gal 4:10 and Col 2:16." Betz, *Galatians*, 217 observes that "the cultic activities described in v 10 are not typical of Judaism (including Jewish Christianity), though they are known to both Judaism and paganism" and are akin to pagan superstition (218).

18. Betz, *Galatians*, 215–17.

the cosmic deities, who observes the kalendrical and cyclic organization of the universe and the effect these cycles have on the "elements" which constitute creation.[19] Betz concludes that "the opponents [of Paul] understand their religion as a cultic-ritualistic system of protection against the forces of evil."[20]

Although the narrator's perspective portrays the chronology of this subjectivity negatively in relationship to the recipients' current way of living, the distinction between this former and their current understanding is based also upon their knowledge of God. The narrator insists that this subjectivity chronologically preceded the time when they knew God and remains chronologically distinct from their current knowledge of God and God's knowledge of them. Its status as "former" and "prior" relates also to a quality or level of theological understanding. This former way of life, their chronologically prior way of living, was marked as theologically deficient, so that their current status in another subjectivity includes an increment of theological formation involving both knowing and being known by God.

Sketchy as this characterization remains, the writer does present us with enough information to outline the subjectivity. These persons, in a kind of subjectivity characterized as primitive or natural, acknowledge the cosmic elements and forces of the universe as deterministic of their lives, and they worship these elements according to the natural cycle of months, days, and years. So, this first subjectivity may be called a natural subjectivity, whose "natural" status becomes clearer in relationship to the next subjectivity.

THE "TRADITIONAL" OR CULTURAL SUBJECTIVITY

The natural subjectivity just defined stands in distinction to a one characterized by a relationship to "law" (*nomos*). Although the word "law" also has a specific bifocal reference to the Torah and to the customs of

---

19. Ibid., 214–15. Betz rightly observes that the enslavement to beings that are not gods emerges from two potential discourses, Hellenistic Judaism or Euhemerism, and that, in any event, it articulates the perspective of the narrator and does not provide in fact a unbiased description of this subjectivity. This element may positively be understood: this subjectivity finds its orientation to the subservience to gods who are believed to be gods by nature, at least by the people who fit into this category.

20. Ibid., 217.

Jewish religion,[21] I will employ periphrastic phrases and circumlocutions in order to avoid the technical theological language that has become the mainstay of both theologians and Pauline scholars.

In its dictionary meaning *nomos* denotes habitual practice or custom(s), as well as statute and ordinance, or generally "law."[22] In order for *nomos* to have the force of law, it must dominate within its social environment. It connotes, therefore, the prescription of cultural dominance; that is, it suggests the hegemony of custom, practice, habit, the legislated and regulated ways of the majority or dominant group of people in a given cultural frame.

This culturally dominant subjectivity revolves about the engagement with *nomos* or (as I will call it here) "performing dominant religious culture."[23] In the context of Galatians, in order to become and remain a participant in this cultural subgroup, the person must perform the dominant religious culture in its entirety: a person may not choose parts of the custom and ignore others, but must perform it all. Speaking to those who are circumcised, the narrator writes "he is obliged to perform the entire law" (5:3). The requirement of complete observance and performance enforces the totalizing thrust of the cultural systems. Cultural hegemony is precisely that, hegemonic power, so that this subjectivity defines itself in relationship to this dominant perspective and acts fully in accord with it, without the leeway either to ignore or to transgress its prescriptions.

This cultural dominance of religious habit encloses all things under the rule of "trespass," (3:22). "Trespass" or sin establishes the limit of acceptability, a move that enforces dominance within the religious system. In this letter strong boundaries produce clear delineations of acceptability and propriety, and these culturally dominant patterns are clearly delineated because "the writings enclosed all things under the category of sin"

21. See *TDNT* and Stendahl, *Paul among Jews and Gentiles*.

22. See LSJ, s.v. *nomos*.

23. My conceptualizing of "performing dominant religious culture" stands in marked contrast to what E. P. Sanders calls "covenantal nomism" in his *Paul and Palestinian Judaism*, 75, 420, 544. See also Dunn, "Theology of Galatians." Although I think that their cultural construction of Judaism at the time of Paul may have validity, I want to bracket the explicitly theological interpretation that both these scholars have placed on the "law." This is not because I reject their theological interpretation, but because I want to start fresh in understanding the theology present in the letter without the necessity of beginning with an artificially constructed theological category gleaned from all of the Pauline corpus, as well as from first-century Judaism.

(3:22). The combination of a complete system and a clear articulation of boundaries creates an inflexibility about the cultural performances. The inflexibility relates not so much to specific performances, but rather to the need carefully and clearly to define and sustain cultural dominance.

This inflexibility finds expression in the dual role of the curse in this discourse. First, Paul invokes the curse upon those who would follow any other gospel than the one that he preached to them (1:8–9). The curse in the *exordium* of the letter expresses the clear and inflexible limits of the narrative perspective. This inflexibility mirrors the inflexibility within the dominant cultural subjectivity that the narrator opposes, because the penalty for trespass against the dominant perspective is a curse. Everyone who does not conform to the dominant perspective and who does not perform all the elements of the customs is cursed: "For as many as exist from deeds of custom (*ex ergon nomou*), live under a curse" (*hypo kataran eisin*) (3:10).

The customs provide the education and induction of the person in the cultural sphere and provide guidance for the person living the traditional life in order to preserve the subject safe within the confines of the dominant sphere (*hypo nomon ephrouroumetha sygkleiomenmoi*) (3:23). This subjectivity emerges, then, from some sort of education in which the subject learns the culturally dominant performances. Teaching inducts subjects into the dominant culture, and it is to this teaching that Paul objects, saying that he did not learn his gospel from anyone (1:12). By distancing himself from those who receive agency by teaching, Paul suggests that he distinguishes himself from this subjectivity. The centrality of the educative function to the articulation of this subjectivity emerges also from the mocking statement "all I want to learn from you" (3:2): the process of teaching and learning (although not the perspective advocated in the letter) characterizes this subjectivity.[24]

This traditional Jewish subjectivity with its observance of cultural and religious codes stands in marked contrast with the natural subjectivity and with the pneumatic subjectivity that Paul develops (and to which

24. The theorists who have most assisted me in understanding these systems of cultural formation are Hodge and Kress in *Social Semiotics*. The process of such cultural formation has in itself been studied. Hodge and Kress have documented the formative interaction of dominant and minority culture in Australia. It does not surprise to find such a process of teaching and learning, whether oriented toward schools or just passed on through living in a society, present in a subjectivity oriented toward a specific, dominant culture.

I will turn shortly). The traditional subjectivity orients itself toward the culturally dominant religious perspective in which the subject embraces the traditions or customs as a sure guide to living and in becoming subject to the habitual mode of living. The hegemonic system guards the subject from trespass in that it functions as enclosure, as protector, and as guide. It remains a complete system that must be accepted fully in order to insure the success and fulfillment to the subject and, therefore, personal freedom and creativity are subordinated to the dominant construction and understanding.

The Pneumatic or Spiritual Subjectivity

This last subjectivity, the spiritual subjectivity, operates in a decidedly different way from these first two. The difference relates to two important shifts. In the first place, the person, the subject, receives definition only as part of a larger body of people, so that the individual becomes a member of a corporate body. In the second place, this corporate body becomes the place in which God dwells.

Baptism, apparently a ritual inaugurating the new corporate subjectivity, defines the spiritual subject: "As many as have been baptized into Christ have been clothed with Christ" (3:27). Baptism bestows identity, and the reference to "clothing" signifies the social markers for that identity. The corporate identity is that of Christ, into whose identity the subject has been incorporated. Moreover, that corporate identity leaves behind the old markers of ethnicity, social status, and gender, in order precisely to create a new corporate and unified subjectivity: "There is not Jew or Greek, there is not slave nor free person, there is not male and female, for all of you (plural) are one in Christ Jesus" (3:28).[25] This subjectivity exists as a plural unity, as a multiple one, whose unity destroys the traditional distinctions of ethnicity, social status, and gender. The corporate Christ-identity unites the plural membership into one, a unity that displaces old markers of identity.

This corporate subjectivity expresses a particular relationship with God: on the one hand, these corporate ones understand themselves as children of God, and, on the other hand, God's own Spirit is made to dwell within them. The metaphor employed to define the new subject's

---

25. Wayne A. Meeks, ("Image of the Androgyne") explores the performative basis of this. See also the creative work of Boyarin, *A Radical Jew*, on gender and the androgyne.

relationship to God is that of parent to child, as stated in 3:26: "You are all sons of God through the confidence found in Jesus Christ." The familial relationship maintains a hierarchy of parent to child, of God to God's children. Through that hierarchical relationship, however, the distance between the child and God collapses. Precisely because the hierarchical relationship has been familiarized, the Spirit of God enters into the person: "And because you are sons, God sent his spirit into our hearts crying, 'Abba, Father'" (4:6, reading with P46, which does not designate the spirit as the spirit of the Son but as the spirit of God). This strategy both collapses the hierarchy through the work of God's spirit by locating the spirit within the subject and also maintains the transcendence of God outside the corporate subject by metaphorizing the conferral of the spirit through a hierarchical family relationship.

The instrument of this new subjectivity comes as a revealed confidence in Jesus Christ. Faith (*pistis*), or as I call it, "confidence," is something revealed. The letter explains the revelatory quality of this confidence in the following way: "Before the coming of this confidence, we, being enclosed (in them), were guarded by the customs until the coming confidence should be revealed" (3:23). This confidence, or faith, comes by revelation, and it chronologically follows the traditional subjectivity that operates through the dominant cultural modes. In fact, this confidence stands in marked contrast, if not opposition, to the culturally dominant subjectivity, because vindication[26] will come to this subject through this confidence, not through any cultural performance: "We are Jews by nature and not trespassers from the other cultures, and we know that a human being is not (finally) vindicated (*ou dikaioutai anthropos*) from cultural performance (*ex ergon nomou*), but through the confidence (based upon) Jesus Christ (*ean me dia pisteos Iesou Christou*), and we came to believe in Christ Jesus so that we might be (finally) vindicated out of Christ's confidence (*hina dikaiothomen ek pisteos Christou*) and not from cultural performance (*kai ouk ex ergon nomou*), because all flesh is not (finally) vindicated from (its) cultural performance" (*hoti ex ergon nomou ou dikaiothesetai pasa sarx*) (2:15–16). In the discourse of this letter, the revelatory basis of the subjectivity follows upon the educative basis, so that revelation follows teaching. Baptism inaugurates the corporate Christ-subjectivity and confidence based in Jesus Christ accompanies it.

26. Here I am following Boyarin's explanation of the term in *A Radical Jew*, 117–18.

Three performances construct this subjectivity: God's provision of the spirit to the subject, God's performance of mighty acts among them, and freedom. The first two performances receive passing treatment while the third, freedom, receives extensive treatment. According to 3:5, God provides the spirit to this subjectivity and also performs mighty acts among them not by virtue of cultural performance, but by virtue of the subject's confidence in hearing about Jesus Christ (*ex ergon nomou ē ex akoes pisteos*). Although God performs these activities, the subject is filled with the spirit and experiences mighty deeds. Both of these become guarantors of the new subjectivity as people both spiritual and powerful; power and spiritual fullness characterize the corporate Christ-subjectivity.

The most significant performance of this subjectivity, however, relates to the performance of freedom. This freedom emerges as the primary marker of those who have withdrawn from the dominant culture in order to create, as written in the postscript, "a new creation" (6:15). "Christ has set you free for freedom, so stand up and do not again be engaged with the yoke of slavery" (5:1). This statement marks slavery as everything not performative of freedom and underscores that the Christ-subject lives without any customary constraint. In this context, freedom posits a hierarchy in which the natural and the cultural subjectivities take a lower place, because both the cosmic elements of the natural subjectivity and the cultural requirements of the traditional subjectivity enslave, while the higher subjectivity, the one found to be "clothed in Christ," has freedom.

The performance of freedom also undergirds the development of new social relationships: "For you were called to freedom, brethren, only [do] not [let] the freedom [become] a starting point for the flesh, but through love become slaves to one another" (5:13). This performance of freedom gathers all the elements of the *exhortatio* of the letter: freedom means, among other things, rejecting vices (5:16–21) and developing virtues (5:22–26), helping those who have fallen (6:1–5), guiding one another in the new life and mores (6:6), and positively developing other performances indicative of this new subjectivity (6:7–10). The Christ-subject exercises freedom precisely to redefine the social, ethical, and religious living of the community, and since this Christ-subject exists as a corporate body, such ethical and moral elements establish the interior dynamic of corporate relations.

The pneumatic subjectivity developed in the discourse of this letter, then, portrays the person as a member of a corporate body beyond the limits of race, class, or gender. The touchstone for this subject revolves about a dual performance of freedom and confidence in which the freedom activates the new status of the subject and the confidence enables the subject to live outside the dominant cultural sphere. The confidence and freedom testify to the presence of Jesus Christ within the subject and confirm the corporate coinherence of subjects within a larger body. This subjectivity would eventually become the one marked as "Christian," while the traditional would be marked as "Jewish" and the natural as "pagan."

THE RELATIONSHIP OF THESE SUBJECTIVITIES

How are these subjectivities related to one another? Although the narrator portrays himself as primarily oriented toward Gentiles (2:7–9), he expends little discursive energy on the articulation of the "former" or natural subjectivity. It seems as though this understanding of subjectivity stands as a foil to the articulation of the other two subjectivities (the traditional and the pneumatic) and does not really represent a viable subjectivity in the discourse of the letter. The narrator even characterizes the return to this subjective stance in the world as a return to "enslavement" to these "weak and poor elements" (4:9). Discursively, this subjectivity does not play an important role in the letter.

The next two subjectivities (the traditional and the pneumatic) have a specific relationship to one another. First, both of these subjectivities originate in the promise to Abraham. Both originate in a gospel (note the language) announced previously to Abraham: "The writings, seeing in advance that the other cultures are being vindicated by their confidence, announced the gospel in advance to Abraham that 'in you all the cultures will be blessed'" (3:8–9). This common origin receives allegorical treatment in the children of the two wives of Abraham, Sarah and Hagar (4:21–31). Both the common origin and the allegory of Abraham's sons imply an increment of equality in their difference. The narrator recognizes, on the one hand, that the promise to Abraham precedes the establishment of the cultural system and that the same father had two different, but equal children, based in an agreement that God made with all humanity and that cannot be annulled (3:15–18).

This second aspect of the relationship of these two subjectivities significantly disrupts this relative equality. The traditional subjectivity stands in a chronologically subordinate position to the pneumatic. The narrator posits the relationship in questioning the function of the traditional customs: "Why then the custom of performances? Until which time the seed to whom it was announced should come."[27] The customary subjectivity functioned provisionally until the pneumatic subjectivity could develop; that is, until the Christ whose identity marks the corporate body should come. As indicated above, the traditions and customs provided the guardianship, the parameters, and the revelation that established the pneumatic subjectivity. So, although these subjectivities find equality in their origins, they do not find equality in their chronology. The pneumatic subjectivity takes precedence over the customary.

The references to the various gospels preached support this simultaneous equality and subordination of the traditional to the pneumatic subjectivity. The letter's discourse actually differentiates three gospels: one gospel announced in the scriptures beforehand to Abraham (3:8); the gospel to the uncircumcised to which Paul was called and authorized by the other apostles to fulfill (1:15–16); and the gospel to the circumcised for which Peter was responsible (2:7–9) and that seems to have captivated the Galatians. Their inherent equality finds expression in their mutual concern for the poor (2:10); the subordination of one to the other finds expression both in the allegory of the slave son persecuting the free (4:29–30) and in the apostolic conflict in Antioch. Despite their equality and the problems inherent in it, however, the discourse in this letter emphasizes the subordination of the customary ways to the pneumatic. The provisional status of the traditional subjectivity receives constant attention: although it is equal to the pneumatic subjectivity, final vindication does not come through cultural performance, but through

---

27. There are a number of interesting textual and translation problems here. I am reading, as I consistently do, with P46, which has a significant variant merely acknowledged by Betz and Metzger, 594. P46 simply reads: *ti oun ho nomos ton praxeon*, which I have translated above. This reading with the addition of *etethe* is supported by other witnesses as well. Betz interprets the sense of the verse in relationship to a parallel in Romans. I am unwilling to make that assumption.

The second problem relates to the translation in the passive of *diatassō*, which properly should mean "bequeath," not "ordain," which is its active meaning. It certainly implies a "setting in order" or in the passive, a kind of "having been set in order and passed on" or "bequeathed" into the hand of an intermediary.

the confidence inspired by Jesus Christ. Paul further emphasizes his own perspective in the *exordium* of the letter by placing a curse on those who follow any other gospel except the one he advocates (1:6–9).

PAUL AS THE EXEMPLUM

Paul's autobiographical example demonstrates this peculiar relationship of the two primary subjectivities.[28] He expressed his own relationship to them in two different ways. First, Paul emphasizes the revelatory aspect of his own pneumatic subjectivity; second, he establishes himself as a fully entitled member of the traditional, Jewish variety of subjectivity.

Most interpreters understand Paul's reference to these revelations as part of his apology for his apostolic ministry, so that he is understood to be promoting the validity and authority for his own ministry. Given the distinctions made above between the traditional and pneumatic subjectivity, however, it seems more consistent that Paul wants a clear distinction drawn between the Paul formed in the traditional subjectivity and the Paul living in the pneumatic. Paul emphasizes the revelatory quality of his message in order to underscore that it is the pneumatic Paul speaking: "It is not based on human things," he writes, "nor did I receive it from any human, nor was I taught (it), but (I received it) through a revelation of Jesus Christ" (1:11–12). Here the threefold subjectivities (the natural one received from a human being; the traditional one taught to its members; and the revelatory one) are distinguished one from another. Paul's was not the first two, but only the third. His particular pneumatic subjectivity may be more properly described as pneumatic-revelatory, because within the sort of pneumatic subjectivity he commends to his readers, he emphasizes that he is guided by the revelations. These revelations, that is, not only provide the origin of his apostolic mission ("Paul, an apostle not from human beings nor through any human being, but through Jesus Christ and God the Father" [1:1]), but also guides his major activities ("I went up [to Jerusalem] according to a revelation" [2:1]). One subjectivity, for Paul, functions around education, being taught something, and the other subjectivity operates according to revelation. For Paul, this clearly marks the distinction between one subjectivity and the next, for "confi-

---

28. Please note that I am using Paul to demonstrate the different subjectivities: this is the reverse of most of the Pauline literature, which try to define Paul by the evidence of his discursive practice.

dence," or "faith," is something revealed to those who were "guarded and enclosed by the customs until the coming confidence should be revealed" (3:23). Revelation here distinguishes itself from education or cultural formation. Paul establishes himself solidly in the camp of the pneumatic subjectivity.

This same set of distinctions emerges in the second factor that Paul develops about himself: his credentials both in the traditional subjectivity and in the pneumatic. After characterizing himself as a persecutor of the assembly of God who wanted to destroy it (1:13), he establishes himself as one well-versed in the tradition: "I succeeded in Judaism beyond many of the people of my own age in my ethnic race, having a greater zeal for the traditions of my fathers" (1:14). This defines the traditional subjectivity for Paul as one that is caught up in the cultural dominance and cultural performance that younger people may learn. But Paul distinguishes it from the emergent subject constructed through revelation: "God was pleased ... to reveal his son in me" (1:15–16). The reference to "revealed in me" no longer sounds problematic: like the revealed confidence and the internalized presence of the deity, the revelation becomes internal, and that internal quality differentiates it from the external one that needs to be learned. In this section, Paul emphasizes that, until his revelation, he had all the necessary credentials for the traditional subjectivity; now that the revelation has come, however, that subjectivity no longer applies to him. His autobiography exemplifies the relationship of subjectivities in the letter.

THE COMPETING ASCETICAL SUBJECTIVITIES

Betz has rightly claimed that the "hermeneutical key" to the letter may be found in the epistolary postscript (6:11–18)[29] where Paul writes in his own hand. Three elements in this postscript stand out: (1) the conflict between representatives of the different missionary groups, (2) Paul's personal attestation that he boasts only in the cross of his Lord Jesus Christ through which "the world has been crucified to me, and I to the world," (6:14) and (3) his affirmation that the "new creation" takes precedence over circumcision and uncircumcision. All three of these elements point to an ascetical discourse within this letter.

---

29. Betz, *Galatians*, 313.

Asceticism can only emerge from conflict with a dominant perspective. This relationship with a dominant perspective provides the impetus, the yearning or desire, to create "someone" different. The ascetic impulse begins when the person discovers that the "old way," the "former way" no longer satisfies and something else begins to draw the person forward into another mode of existence. This means that asceticism begins not with withdrawal itself, but with the dissatisfaction with the dominant perspective that leads to withdrawal. Asceticism, that is, begins when the *desire* for some alternative way of living emerges. The performances that create that new identity constitute asceticism, so that asceticism may be understood as the means of creating a subversive subjectivity within the dominant sphere. Without the strongly articulated dominant subjectivity, an ascetical alternative cannot be defined. But as the person begins to live into the new understanding of self, society, and world, that is, as the person begins to "perform" that new subjectivity, the new person begins actually to come to life, to exist. The performances (intellectual, ritual, social, political, or of any nature) call that subjectivity into being, define its social dimension, and construct the symbolic universe that will legitimize and explain the new being.

The conflict of perspectives on subjectivities and their proper performances in the Letter to the Galatians portrays the simultaneous affirmation of the dominant perspective and dissatisfaction with it that characterizes Paul's letter. Another way of saying this is that the discursive problem of the Letter to the Galatians revolves about the clear delineation of these subjectivities with a demand that the recipients choose which one they will follow. The pneumatic subjectivity, however, does not emerge in a vacuum: as the subversive subjectivity within a dominant culture, it expresses the conflict between the traditional articulation of the Jewish subjectivity and the emergent subjectivity of the ascetical pneumatic. The curse in the *exordium*, invoking the curse that accompanies all those who do not perform all of the cultural prescriptions (as stated in 3:10), demands just such a choice based not so much on the question of the variety of Judaism that will be lived out, but based upon the desire, if not the need, to create an entirely different subjectivity than the one advocated by the traditionalists. The choice, that is, revolves about the commitment to a subversive asceticism that constructs an alternative subjectivity. The conflict in the Letter to the Galatians, then, does not relate primarily to Paul, or to his theology, or even to his relationship with the traditional

Judaism of his day, but to the right articulation of the pneumatic subjectivity among a group of people in Galatia who seem (to Paul, at least) not properly to understand it. In language typical of all ascetical literature, Paul insists that the old self must die in order for the new subject to be born: he "mortifies" himself, killing the world to him and him to the world, even bearing Jesus' stigmata on his body.[30] The old self must be repudiated, mortified, so that the new one may come to existence, and conflict remains endemic to this process.

I should be clear, however: the distinction between the old self and the new self finds clear articulation and delineation, but it does not imply an outright rejection or condemnation of the dominant view. One need only look at the relationship of monastic cultural withdrawal to the "great Church" to see that "difference" does not mean "repudiation." The difference expresses the subject's disillusion and dissatisfaction with the dominant perspective, a perspective without which the ascetical subject could not exist. Paul wants the church in Galatia to follow his way, but his way cannot exist divorced from the dominant perspective, and he affirms this coexistent interdependence in the allegory of Hagar and Sarah while posting his own preference in the hostile relations of their sons.

The difficulty is that the alternative subjectivity advocated in this letter may only be sustained by the performances proper to it. Tradition and the new subjectivity do not mix easily. To establish "the new creation" beyond circumcision or uncircumcision (here Paul lays out the three subjectivities clearly), the ascetic must live freely. The performance of freedom from traditional hegemonic Jewish practice inaugurates the pneumatic Christ-subjectivity of their Jewish sectarian subgroup organized around the confidence they experience through Jesus Christ, a confidence that comes to them by revelation, not by any dominant cultural performance or teaching.

The performance of freedom also reorganizes their social lives.[31] Their new identity emerges from performances structured in their becoming "slaves" to one another (5:13) as opposed to being slaves either of the cosmic elements or of the dominant culture. Their reorganized social life, moreover, demands that they live in the spirit (5:22–26) and reject the works of the flesh (5:19–21), while carrying one another's burdens

---

30. On the stigmata see Riley, *Resurrection Reconsidered*.

31. See Hays, "Christology and Ethics."

and helping one another live the new life (6:1–10). The rejection of social vices, the development of social virtues, and the embracing of weaker members of the community pattern the new social organization. The confidence found in Jesus Christ frees them to structure a new society, a new ethic, and a new way of living.

The symbolic universe, which explains and legitimizes the subversive identity, receives significant attention. The discussion of the promise made to Abraham, and of Abraham's two wives and the sons of each wife, redefines the theological perspective away from the dominant and traditional categories of the Law in order to provide the space for another understanding. Three gospels (one proclaimed in the scriptures to Abraham, one to the circumcised, and one to the uncircumcised) also explains the difference and locates the pneumatic subjectivity in relationship both to the past and to the future. The promise to Abraham confirms the relationship of the two major subjectivities by providing them with a common origin, and, these subjectivities get organized into (as Boyarin argues convincingly) a hierarchy of spirit over flesh, of freedom over slavery, so that, although both are vindicated by the promise, priority of the pneumatic subjectivity is maintained.

The formation of this Christ-identity locates as primary the ascetical project found in the Letter to the Galatians. It also mirrors the ascetical agenda of formative Christianity. The often conflicting literature of formative Christianity, like Galatians, exposes the energetic experimentation and reconsideration of human subjectivity, social relations, and theological formulations. Christian literature from even before the creation of the texts enshrined in the canon forcefully posits the question of human existence and human social relationships. Wandering prophets, purveyors of wisdom, apocalyptic seers, healers and magicians, and even heroes and divine figures point to the extensive range of human possibilities explored and modeled in formative Christianity. When the social context of this experimentation is considered—all varieties of Judaism, Samaritans, Romans, peoples of Phoenicia, Palestine, Arabia, Egypt, as well as people from all around the known world—this experimentation reaches monumental proportions. At the heart of the experimentation stands the consideration of a new subjectivity in Jesus Christ; at the heart of the experimentation stands asceticism.

The alternatives presented to the earliest followers of Jesus were complex and involved a wide spectrum of possibilities, each demanding its own formative processes. Each formative process, however, meant clear delineation and definition of its distinctiveness from the other options. The means that conflict and conflicting articulations form an essential aspect of the process. This is what we find in Paul's Letter to the Galatians: three options, clearly articulated and compared, but with a strong affirmation and choice of only one. With that choice and affirmation develop systems for the creation of people in the subjectivity; that is to say, with each choice comes an ascetical system that enables the new subjectivity, the yearned-for subjectivity, to become real. Asceticism, enshrining the conflict of differences, pervades the discourse of this letter and of all other aspects of early Christian formation.

part three

ROMAN ASCETICISM

CHAPTER 11

Nag Hammadi and Asceticism: Theory and Practice

I BEGAN STUDYING THE NAG HAMMADI DOCUMENTS UNDER THE GUID-
ance of a great scholar and teacher, Fr. George MacRae, SJ.[1] Fr. MacRae
enthusiastically supported my interest in moving the study of these Nag
Hammadi texts from the first phase, establishing the texts and circulat-
ing accurate translations, to the second, integrating these texts into the
theological and historical discourses concerning formative Christianity.
Early in our relationship, he guided me in publishing my first article,
which correlated the construction of the body in the two versions of the
Apocryphon of John with a similar interest in the transcript of a contem-
poraneous conversation between Origen and Heraclides.[2] In that article,
I speculated that certain of the Nag Hammadi documents betrayed an
ascetical orientation in a decidedly esoteric context. It is to that complex
of questions that I wish to return, now after a goodly number of years of
work on my own; in returning to those questions, my mind turns again
to my mentor and professor to whom I dedicate this essay.

Early in my reading of these Nag Hammadi texts, I wholeheartedly
embraced the view held by Henry Chadwick and other leading early
Church historians, and by Fredrick Wisse and other historians of religion, that these texts were produced and preserved by ascetical monks,
probably from a Pachomian monastery.[3] The rationale for reading these

1. In memory of George W. MacRae, SJ.

2. See "Uncovering Adam's Esoteric Body," chapter 6, pp. 119–33.

3. See Chadwick, "Domestication of Gnosis"; and Frederik Wisse, "Gnosticism
and Early Monasticism." This view is supported by Charles W. Hedrick; see "Gnostic
Proclivities." These early positions are reviewed by James E. Goehring (*Ascetics, Society,
and the Desert,* 162–86) and Armand Veilleux, "Monachisme et gnose" and "Monasticism

texts ascetically was a syllogistic one: the monks produced the texts, the monks were ascetics, and therefore the texts must reflect an ascetical community. Although it is generally known, as Michael Williams has summarized clearly,[4] that the Nag Hammadi Library's texts contain few if any references to the commonly known ascetical categories of fasting and sexual renunciation, many scholars have posited that these texts reflect and support an ascetical perspective. The fact that most of these texts were read as "gnostic" only supported the view that ascetics oriented themselves more toward orthopraxy than toward orthodoxy,[5] so that the Pachomian monks would presumably promulgate any text that supported its commitment to ascetic renunciation and discipline.[6] James Goehring has shown that the idealized literary descriptions of Pachomian monasticism and the documentary evidence show wide divergence, leading to his conclusion that the Pachomian monasteries were much more diverse than suspected by earlier scholars.[7] I myself had long recognized that in ascetical literature the boundaries between orthodoxy and heresy are permeable so that concepts such as divinization or the indwelling of the divine light[8] might sound heretical in one generation, but become part of the mainstream of ascetical thinking in later generations.[9] I was con-

---

and Gnosis in Egypt." The origins of this collection in Pachomian monastery was proposed based on the work of J. W. B. Barns ("Greek and Coptic Papyri") and then corrected by J. C. Shelton ("Introduction"). For other perspectives, see Torgny Säve-Söderbergh, "Holy Scriptures" and Clemens Scholten, "Die Nag-Hammadi-Texte." These sources fully explore the relationship of the Nag Hammadi Library to the Pachomian monasteries.

4. Williams, *Rethinking "Gnosticism,"* 139–50.

5. See Wisse, "Gnosticism and Early Monasticism," 437.

6. I am actually turning on its side a statement made by Wisse ("Gnosticism and Early Monasticism," 439) regarding Hieracas and his ascetical devotees: "The only standard of orthodoxy which remained was whether a theologumenon could be interpreted to have ascetic implications." Henry Chadwick ("Domestication of Gnosis," 4–5) justifies this standing on its side: "The dominant ethical proposition of the new texts is strenuously ascetic and encratite. The gnostic way in these documents is to learn to suppress the evil appetites that the maleficent Creator of this material world has inserted into or attached to the bodies of the elect." This has all been carefully analyzed and critically reevaluated by Williams, *Rethinking "Gnosticism,"* 139–88.

7. Goehring, *Ascetics, Society, and the Desert*, 187–95.

8. Here I am thinking of John Climacus on divinization and Gregory Palamas on the divine light.

9. See my early and largely exploratory "Eastern Church's Theme of Deification" and the more comprehensive "Daemons," chapter 7, pp. 134–68.

vinced that such was the case with the so-called heretical Nag Hammadi Library:[10] these texts would display the fully developed esoteric ascetical theology of a later period in an earlier, more problematic form and time. Although I am less naive today than I was then, these questions still merit attention.

The Nag Hammadi texts led me to study spiritual guidance and spiritual guidance in turn led me to explore asceticism. Here I return to the Nag Hammadi texts, but now with a different question. Rather than addressing the question from the perspective of the producers of the text, I would like to explore the question of the ascetical impulse of the Nag Hammadi texts from within the ascetical tradition of the Greco-Roman and Late Antique religious practitioners. I put aside the question of whether these texts were produced by monks in a Pachomian monastery, and redirect the question toward the resonance, or intertextuality, of these texts with the state of asceticism as we know it in the second, third, and fourth centuries of the Common Era. My question is this: given what is currently known about asceticism, what relationship exists between these Nag Hammadi texts and the varied understandings of asceticism among coeval religious practitioners? This question shifts from the producers of the text to the readers to explore the ascetical readers' response to and interest in the subject matter of these documents.[11]

This shift in interest about the asceticism of the Nag Hammadi texts, however, begs the question of the definition of asceticism and of the manner in which asceticism finds expression in the extremely varied religions and texts of the period. It is ultimately a question of reading. I am asking not only "Can a modern scholar read this library ascetically?" but also "Did an ancient person interested in asceticism find anything of interest

10. I should say that I do not consider these texts to be a library in the sense of a collection of clearly related treatises. George MacRae ("Nag Hammadi and the New Testament") cautioned: "we should also avoid treating the Nag Hammadi Library as a homogeneous collection. Here the issue is compounded by the fact that we really do not know the purpose of the collection in the first place" (150–51). I do not assume that this collection of treatises is a gnostic library, or any sort of library at all for that matter.

11. This takes up the question posited by Veilleux, ("Monasticism and Gnosis in Egypt," 304): "Once the origins and the development of Christian asceticism in general and Egyptian Christian asceticism in particular are better known, it will be possible to compare each one of the aspects of that ascesis with the gnostic ascesis." I do not compare monastic asceticism to gnostic asceticism, but rather take up the question of asceticism in general.

in these texts?" The task at hand demands that we fuse that ancient reader with a modern reader of asceticism.

Methodologically, I must first construct a sophisticated ascetical reader's perspective (both ancient and modern) in order to establish whether the Nag Hammadi documents would have provided interesting material to enhance the ascetic's practices. The construction of such a sophisticated reader is a difficult task. A 1996 conference on asceticism in the New Testament failed to reach any consensus about the definition of asceticism or the signs indicating an ascetical agenda in the early Christian period.[12] I have elected in this essay to address this problem both expansively and directly. The ideal ascetical reader has been constructed through four distinct (and yet correlated) ways of reading asceticism in the second through the fourth centuries: a theoretical reading, a social scientific definition, a classical studies exploration, and a patristic orientation. These four ways of reading asceticism summarize the various approaches that scholars have used in recent studies of asceticism and provide a broad, even inclusive, perspective on the definition and signs of asceticism. The four lenses also replicate the ascetical corpus in its widest possible construal. They will provide the most expansive perspective on asceticism, which will serve as the background for surveying the Nag Hammadi literature. Since it is not the object of this essay to define asceticism,[13] I will use the following scholars' work metonymically for the larger corpus of similar works.

FOUR PERSPECTIVES ON ASCETICISM

Over the past decade I have been working toward a definition of asceticism that would assist me in detecting an ascetical agenda as well as in comparing various types of asceticism, ancient and modern. In its current articulation, my definition of asceticism is this: "performances within a dominant social environment intended to inaugurate a new subjectivity, different social relations, and an alternative symbolic universe."[14] My goal

12. The international conference, organized by Vincent Wimbush and Leif Vaage, was held at Emmanuel College, University of Toronto, October 3–5, 1996. The revised papers from the conference have been published as Vaage and Wimbush: *Asceticism and the New Testament.*

13. See chapter 1 for a theoretical discussion of asceticism.

14. Valantasis, "Constructions of Power in Asceticism," chapter 2, p. 38. See also "Theory of the Social Function of Asceticism," chapter 1, pp. 3–13.

is simply to understand the way in which ascetical activities construct an identity through various regimes of discipline. As one of the lenses for this essay, this theory provides the broadest and most abstract approach to the ascetical dimension of the Nag Hammadi Library.

The social-scientific biblical scholar Anthony Saldarini has proposed a less abstract and more "vague"[15] definition because he does not find my definition "flexible enough" to "bear the weight of the varied phenomena that create new subjectivities, social relations, and symbolic worlds."[16] Saldarini proposes ten points (some of which only apply to biblical literature) of which the most significant are summarized here: intentional behavior both individual and corporate, worked out in a variety of social relationships, and which manifest power relationships. This constitutes a "social construction of the self or a subjectivity." Asceticism also includes some form of discipleship, education, and disciplined behavior. Asceticism often self-designates its own activity as ascetical.[17] For the purposes of this paper, I accept both Saldarini's criticism and his approach as one lens through which to read the Nag Hammadi Library.

Peter Brown[18] and Teresa Shaw[19] best illustrate the patristic orientation to the study of asceticism. Brown explored the question of sexuality and sexual renunciation in early Christian texts, while Shaw studied fasting and eating regimens. The traditional scholarly view of understanding of early Christian *enktrateia* primarily relates to questions of sexual continence and fasting.[20] These scholars, however, look not simply to the presence (or absence) of these particular ascetical practices, but to the wider anthropological, theological, sociological, medical, and political discourses surrounding these specific practices. Brown surveys the entire field of early Christian ascetical teaching about sexuality, both Eastern and Western. He traces the varying perspectives of Mediterranean sexual

15. Vaage and Wimbush, eds., *Asceticism and the New Testament*, 1–7, reference to p. 6.

16. Saldarini, "Asceticism and the Gospel of Matthew," 16.

17. Ibid., 17–18. I must apologize for the very short description of Saldarini's work here. In this paper, my intention is simply to indicate a wide variety of useful approaches of which this is one. I refer the readers to the article for more complete and thorough understanding.

18. See Brown, *Body and Society*.

19. See Shaw, *Burden of the Flesh*.

20. On *enkrateia* see Bianchi, *Tradizione dell' Enkrateia*.

renunciation, highlighting the differences and exploring the nuances differentiating one perspective from another. Shaw likewise exposes the medical, exegetical, mythological, and theological dimensions surrounding the ancient Christian understanding of fasting and its effect on the ascetic, especially the ascetic woman's body. Each of these scholars provides the rich description of ascetical practices, and each exemplifies one set of perspectives in the mind of my theoretical sophisticated ascetic reader.

The Late Antique Christian interest in asceticism did not arise in a vacuum. The discourse had involved classical Greek and Roman pagan authors for a number of years. The work of James Francis explores the classical pagan discourse concerning asceticism that arose in the Stoic and Cynic philosophical movements of the first century C.E. and flowered in the second century.[21] Francis locates the second-century discourse in the context of the stoicism of Musonius Rufus and Epictetus. Then Francis explores the conflicting perspectives about asceticism exemplified in Marcus Arelius, Lucian, Apollonius of Tyana, and Celsus. The pagan argument about asceticism revolved about the question of social accommodation, the attitude toward deviance (particularized in the ascetic), the centrality of traditional education and formation (*paideia*), the issue of authority (both personal and imperial), the significance of miracles and other wondrous deeds, and the boundary between acceptable religion and magic. The broad range of this discourse forms another lens through which to view asceticism and by which to construct our ideal reader of asceticism.

The Evidence for Ascetical Agendas in the Nag Hammadi Texts

With these four lenses firmly in my mind, I read the Nag Hammadi Library[22] codex by codex from the perspective of my ideal ascetical reader. The evidence for the relationship of this collection of texts to asceticism follows.

21. Francis, *Subversive Virtue.*
22. I have used Robinson, *NHLE.*

The Tripartite Tractate (1, 5)

The Tripartite Tractate is a theological treatise with only oblique references to asceticism. The first part of the treatise "describes the emanation of all supernatural entities from their primal source."[23] A theory of
emanation of spiritual and supernatural entities lacks an ascetical agenda
unless the emanations become a means by which a seeker may "return"
to the primordial source. Although the tractate refers to such a return,[24]
the return itself, described as a searching, remains a peripheral concern.
Emanation as a theological modality remains too static seriously to en-
tertain asceticism as a proper activity.[25]

The second part of the tractate holds the most promise for an ascetical reading. In explaining the creation of the material world and of
humanity, the tractate presents an educational model of formation:

> the entire preparation of the adornment of the images and repre-
> sentations and likenesses, have come into being because of those
> who need education and teaching and formation, so that the
> smallness might grow, little by little, as through a mirror image.
> For it was for this reason that he created mankind in the end, hav-
> ing first prepared and provided for him the things which he had
> created for his sake. (104:18–30)

This educational model reflects on the human level a phenomenon in the
cosmic spheres in which the Logos explains the purpose of the fall of the
aeons:

23. Attridge and Pagels, "Introduction," 58.

24. See, e.g. 71:7–18 ("The entire system of the aeons has a love and a longing for
the perfect, complete discovery of the Father and this is their unimpeded agreement.
Though the Father reveals himself eternally, he did not wish that they should know him,
since he grants that he be conceived of in such a way as to be sought for, while keeping
to himself his unsearchable primordial being."); and 72:3–9 ("and it gives them an idea
of seeking after the unknown one, just as one is drawn by a pleasant aroma to search for
the thing from which the aroma arises, since the aroma of the Father surpasses these
ordinary ones.").

25. A statement that contradicts this theory is found at 73:23–29 ("Rather, their [the
Totalities] begetting is like a process of extension, as the Father extends himself to those
whom he loves, so that those who have come forth from him might become him as
well."), but I would argue that the statement, though admitting of a transformation of
supernatural entities, explains a series of correlations rather than setting an agenda for
human transformation.

> The stumbling, which happened to the aeons of the Father of the
> Totalities who did not suffer, was brought to them, as if it were their
> own, in a careful and non-malicious and immensely sweet way. [It
> was brought to the] Totalities so that they might be instructed
> about the [defect] by the single one, from whom [alone] they all
> [received strength] to eliminate the defects. (85:33—86:4)

Educational formation, which can be construed as a form of asceticism,
in the explanation of the creation of the material world mirrors an educational motif in the emanations of the spiritual entities. The cosmology
prepares the way for the educational orientation.

This educational asceticism, however, does not apply to all humans.
At the same time that the treatise posits an increment of ascetical thinking, it is corrected by a static view of human agency:

> Mankind came to be in three essential types, the spiritual, the
> psychic and the material, conforming to the triple disposition of
> the Logos, from which were brought forth the material ones and
> the psychic ones and the spiritual ones. Each of the three essential
> types is known by its fruit. And they were not known at first but
> only at the coming of the Savior, who shone upon the saints and
> revealed what each was. (118:14–28)

The spiritual race did not need to work for its revelation, but rather "It
suddenly received knowledge in the revelation" (118:35–36). And the
material race "will receive destruction in every way, just as one who resists him [the Savior]" (119:18–20). These two races are, for different and
opposing reasons, beyond asceticism. The education exists for the benefit
of the psychics:

> The psychic race, since it is in the middle when it is brought forth
> and also when it is created, is double according to its determina-
> tion for both good and evil. (119:20–24)

> They will be saved completely [because of] the salvific thought.
> As he was brought forth, so, [too], were these brought forth from
> him, whether angels or men. In accordance with the confession
> that there is one who is more exalted than themselves, and in ac-
> cordance with the prayer and the search for him, they also will
> attain the salvation of those who have been brought forth, since
> they are from the disposition which is good. (119:33–120:8)

The psychics alone need the educational asceticism outlined in the treatise, the others remain statically fixed in their appointed and predetermined place with no means of self-transformation for the material race and with no need of change for the spiritual.

In the end, the *Tripartite Tractate* advocates asceticism only for the psychic Christians. The theological interest in the emanations has put everyone in their place at the two extremes, the spiritual Valentinians and the material Hebrews and Greeks,[26] leaving space for education and formation only for those in the middle. The theology creates just enough space to accommodate the weaker, middling humans, but in the main seems more oriented toward the static categories and theological structures that defy movement, growth, and change.

The Apocryphon of John (II,1, III,1, IV,1, BG 8502,2)

The *Apocryphon of John* does not present any recognizable ascetical system, although it contains material that would interest ascetics and it presents themes and topics that interested ascetical Christians particularly. The interesting ascetical themes are varied. In another article, I made the arguments about the possible ascetical function of the formation of Adam's body (15:1–19:14) and do not need to repeat them here.[27] The *Apocryphon of John* further describes the humors, which play so important a role in the medical and ascetical theories of fasting, as specifically named demons dwelling in the body:

> And the origin of the demons, which are in the whole body, is determined to be four: heat, cold, wetness, and dryness. And the mother of all of them is matter. And he who reigns over the heat (is) Phloxopha; and he who reigns over the cold is Oroorrothos; and he who reigns over what is dry (is) Erimacho; and he who reigns over the wetness (is) Athuro. And the mother of all of these, Onorthochrasaei, stands in their midst since she is illimitable, and she mixes with all of them. And she is truly matter, for they are nourished by her. (18:2–14)

26. The section describing the varieties of theology is very interesting in this regard: "Now, as for the things which came forth from the <race> of the Hebrews, things which are written by the hylics who speak in the fashion of the Greeks . . . ." (110-22-25).

27. See "Uncovering Adam's Esoteric Body," chapter 6, pp. 119–33.

This sort of detail, consistent with all the other elements in the creation of the human person, could enable a practitioner to manipulate magically or ritually the various demonic elements to balance or to change the consistency of the body.[28]

Although I would not want to push this correlation too far, there is resonance between the figure of the "virginal Spirit who is perfect" (4:35) and who is "the thrice-named androgynous one" (5:9) and the discourse concerning virginity for women. Shaw has shown that one effect of the intense fasting regime of young girls was the reduction of female physical attributes and she documents that regime in the medical literature.[29] The concept of a perfect virginal Spirit and androgyny would not be out of place in this particular ascetical discourse.

A common ascetic discourse revolves about the implications of the Genesis account of creation and of sinning for the regulation of fasting and sexual desire. Throughout the explication of the Genesis text,[30] the *Apocryphon of John* connects the mythology of the double creation of Adam (spiritual and physical) to the fact of human sexuality:

> Now up to the present day sexual intercourse continued due to the chief archon. And he planted sexual desire in her who belongs to Adam. And he produced through intercourse the copies of the bodies, and he inspired them with his counterfeit spirit. (24:26–31)

In the context of discussing the rectification of this physical replicating of the body, the *Apocryphon of John* sets forth what is its only specifically articulated ascetical agenda:

> Those on whom the Spirit of life will descend and (with whom) he will be with the power, they will be saved and become perfect and be worthy of the greatness and be purified in that place from all wickedness and involvements in evil. Then they have no other care than the incorruption alone, to which they direct their attention from here on, without anger or envy or jealousy or desire

28. This also seems to operate on the cosmic level in a kind of cosmic episteme, or a psychic geography in the cosmos at 7:30–8:28.

29. Shaw, *Burden of the Flesh*, 220–53.

30. See also the following sections: about the tree and the mystery of life (21:26–22:2); about the serpent and his work (22:9–21); and about Adam's first sighting of his counterpart (23:4–20).

and greed of anything. They are not affected by anything except the state of being in the flesh alone, which they bear while looking expectantly for the time when they will be met by the receivers (of the body). Such then are worthy of the imperishable, eternal life and the calling. For they endure everything and bear up under everything, that they may finish the good fight and inherit eternal life. (25:16—26:6)

Here the text combines such ascetic themes as focused attention, the passions (anger, envy, jealousy, desire, and greed), the passionless state in the body, and endurance. Although it suggests a thematic connection with asceticism, it does not in fact articulate an ascetical regime of any magnitude or substance.

The Gospel of Thomas (II,2)[31]

I have explored the ascetical dimension of this *Gospel*, and I argue that the *Gospel of Thomas* "promotes a complete ascetical system for the refashioning of the self" through a relationship established "with the living Jesus who is speaking the sayings and who guides the seeker into a very specific set of actions that enable the new person to thrive."[32]

The Gospel of Philip (II,3)

Like the *Gospel of Thomas*, the *Gospel of Philip* manifests a particular interest in asceticism. Unlike the *Gospel of Thomas*, that ascetical agenda stands more peripherally to the content of the *Gospel*; without the benefit of the consistency provided the sayings gospel genre, the *Gospel of Philip* presents its material in a more random fashion. But the *Gospel of Philip* presents its ascetical agenda, present in the articulation of a regime of formation, in the very first saying:

> A Hebrew makes another Hebrew, and such a person is called proselyte. But a proselyte does not make another proselyte [. . .] just as they [. . .] and make other like themselves, while [others] simply exist. (51:29—52:1)

The *Gospel of Philip* differentiates between various kinds of subjectivity and promotes the development of a particular one. This duality of sub-

---

31. See Veilleux, "Monasticism and Gnosis," 299–301.

32. See "Is the *Gospel of Thomas* Ascetical?" chapter 9, p. 207, pp. 206–7.

jectivity, which calls for a choice and for direct effort to construct it, takes a variety of forms. One description distinguishes the common person ("man in the world") from the ideal reader of the *Gospel*:

> It is not possible for anyone to see anything of the things that actually exist unless he becomes like them. This is not the way with man in the world: he sees the sun without being a sun; and he sees the heaven and the earth and all other things, but he is not these things. This is quite in keeping with the truth. But you (sg.) saw something of that place, and you became those things. You saw the spirit, you became spirit. You saw Christ, you became Christ. You saw [the father, you] shall become father. So [in this place] you see everything and [do] not [see] yourself, but [in that place] you do see yourself—and what you see you shall [become]. (61:20–35)

In this instance the dual subjectivity relates to vision, but other references construct this dual subjectivity in terms of the inner and outer person (67:31—68:16), in the difference between a slave and a free person and their access to the bridal chamber (72:17–29), and difference between worldly and spiritual farming where the primal, physical elements (earth, air, fire, and water) relate to the spiritual elements (faith, hope, love, and knowledge) in generating a good harvest (79:19–34).

The *Gospel of Philip* also acknowledges that the cultivation of this spiritual subjectivity requires serious effort. In sayings reminiscent of the *apophthegmata patrum*[33] regarding monastic labor (*ponos*) and progress (*prokope*), the *Gospel of Philip* relates the following parable:

> An ass that turns a millstone did a hundred miles walking. When it was loosed it found that it was still at the same place. There are men who make many journeys, but make no progress towards any destination. When evening came upon them, they saw neither city nor village, neither human artifact nor natural phenomenon, power nor angel. In vain have the wretches labored. (63:11–21)

The labor for the spiritual person in the *Gospel of Philip* has a specific referent:

> As for ourselves, let each one of us dig down after the root of evil which is within one, and let one pluck it out of one's heart from

---

33. For example: "Fear not the flesh nor love it. If you (sg.) fear it, it will gain mastery over you. If you love it, it will swallow and paralyze you." (66:4–6)

the root. It will be plucked out if we recognize it. But if we are ignorant of it, it takes root in us and produces its fruit in our heart.
It masters us. We are its slaves. It takes us captive, to make us do
what we do [not] want; and what we do want we do [not] do. It
is powerful because we have not recognized it. While [it exists] it
is active. Ignorance is the mother of [all evil]. Ignorance will result in [death, because] those that come from [ignorance] neither
were nor [are] nor shall be. (83:18–35)

The *Gospel of Philip* clearly promulgates an ascetic agenda focused upon
the purging of ignorance from the person.

A few other elements of the *Gospel* correlate to the wider corpus
of ascetical literature. The *Gospel of Philip* takes up the Late Antique
discourse regarding marriage and sexual intercourse.[34] The discussion
about sexual intercourse and marriage, while resonating with the arguments found in pagan and Christian authors, does not condemn them,
but seeks to understand and to spiritualize them. The *Gospel of Philip*
also promotes the important ascetical skill of discernment, which assists
the spiritual seeker in understanding the limits and uses of each human
function:

There was a householder who had every conceivable thing, be it
son or slave or cattle or dog or pig or corn [or] barley or chaff
or grass or [...] or meat and acorn. [Now he was] a sensible fellow and he knew what the food of each one was. He served the
children bread [...]. He served the slaves [... and] meal. And [he
threw barley] and chaff and grass to the cattle. He threw bones
to [the] dogs, and to the pigs he threw acorns and slop. Compare
the disciple of God: if he is a sensible fellow he understands what
discipleship is all about. The bodily forms will not deceive him,
but he will look at the condition of the soul of each one and speak
with him. There are many animals in the world which are in human form. When he identifies them, to the swine he will throw
acorns, to the cattle he will throw barley and chaff and grass, to
the dogs he will throw bones. To the slaves he will give only the
elementary lessons, to the children he will give the complete instruction. (80:23—81:14)

34. For adultery and intercourse see 60:34—61:13; on the union of man and woman
see 76:6–17; on the meaning of sexual intercourse see 81:14—82:25. For a thorough
reading of these texts, see Williams, *Rethinking "Gnosticism,"* 147–50.

As this example suggests, the ascetical dimension of the *Gospel of Philip* is fairly well developed and clearly taking place in the context of conflicting understanding of asceticism and its place in the religious life. Unfortunately, the content of the *Gospel* is not presented in any comprehensive or systematic manner.

The Book of Thomas the Contender (II,7)

The *Book of Thomas the Contender* displays no particular ascetical agenda. Some themes found in the wider ascetical corpus, however, find reference. The strongest case could be made that the treatise's exhortations to avoid lust (139:40—140:5) and other bodily passions (145:8–16) indicate an ascetic orientation. This exhortation connects with the treatise's systematic problematizing of sexual intercourse (144:9–10) as bestial (139:1–10). In fact, the *Book of Thomas the Contender* has more to say about avoiding a bestial human nature (139:24–31; 141:25—142:2) than about the alternative understanding of the human condition. It is mostly a negative treatise about avoiding certain behaviors, purporting to give the perfect teaching (140:9–14) to a seeker eager to know the self (138:7–20) and, therefore, only minimally ascetical, because it does not propose a more directive agenda for the formation or development of the person.

The Acts of Peter and the Twelve Apostles (VI,1)

It is not surprising to find an ascetical agenda in one of the apocryphal acts of the apostles. What surprises the reader of this treatise is the asceticism that is promulgated for the active leadership of the church. The narrative of *The Acts of Peter and the Twelve Apostles* presents an allegory of the empowering of true, healing leaders for the church. The asceticism of church leaders is likened to a voyage to the city in which Jesus lives. The hardships on the way outline the asceticism necessary for "arriving" at that city:

> And also (concerning) the road to the city, which you asked me about, I will tell you about it. No man is able to go on that road, except one who has forsaken everything that he has and has fasted daily from stage to stage. For many are the robbers and wild beasts on that road. The one who carries bread with him on the road, the black dogs kill because of the bread. The one who carries a costly

> garment of the world with him, the robbers kill [because of the] garment. [The one who carries] water [with him, the wolves kill because of the water], since they were thirsty [for] it. [The one who] is anxious about [meat] and green vegetables, the lions eat because of the meat. [If] he evades the lions, the bulls devour him because of the green vegetables. (5:19–6:9)

This asceticism involves renunciation and strict fasting in some sort of graded system of advancement ("daily from stage to stage").

This treatise presents this renunciation and fasting as a model to be imitated by church leaders:

> I hurried and went and called my friends so that we might go to the city that he, Lithargoel [=Christ], appointed for us. In a bond of faith we forsook everything as he had said (to do). We evaded the robbers, because they did not find their garments with us. We evaded the wolves, because they did not find the water with us for which they thirsted. We evaded the lions, because they did not find the desire for meat with us. [We evaded the bulls ... they did not find] green vegetables. (7:19–8:3)

The renunciation and fasting enables the leader to enter into contemplation and rest:

> A great joy [came upon] us [and a] peaceful carefreeness [like that of] our Lord. We [rested ourselves] in front of the gate, [and] we talked with each other [about that] which is not a distraction of this [world]. Rather we continued in contemplation of the faith. (8:4–11)

All the elements of a simple ascetical system cohere in the narrative: renunciation and fasting constitute a process leading to rest and contemplation for the leaders of the church.

Authoritative Teaching (VI,3)

The *Authoritative Teaching* bears all the markings of a treatise of ascetical theology. The end of the treatise presents a distinction between the ignorant souls, who "do not seek after God" (33:5) and who is contrasted with the pagan, and the rational soul, who has "learned about God" (33:36). The treatise characterizes the ignorant soul as "more wicked than the pagans" (33:10) because "even the pagans give charity, and they know that God who is in the heavens exists, the Father of the universe, exalted over their idols, which they worship" (33:27–33). The problem with the pagans, however, is simply that "they have not heard the word, that they should inquire about his [God's] ways" (33:34–35). On the other hand, "the senseless man hears the call, but he is ignorant of the place to which he has been called" (34:3–7). The natural ways of the pagan surpass the ineffective effort of the ignorant person. The treatise graphically describes the affect of this ignorance on the soul:

> The result is that the substance of hardness of heart strikes a blow upon his mind, along with the force of ignorance and the demon of error. They do not allow his mind to rise up, because he was wearying himself in seeking that he might learn about his hope. (34:24–33)

In portraying the darkening of the mind and the debilitating of the will, the treatise presents the affect of ignorance in psychological language. The description of the rational soul provides the counter-affect and image:

> But the rational soul who (also) wearied herself in seeking—she learned about God. She labored with inquiring, enduring distress in the body, wearing out her feet after the evangelists, learning about the Inscrutable One. She found her rising. She came to rest in him who is at rest. She reclined in the bride-chamber. She ate of the banquet for which she had hungered. She partook of the immortal food. She found what she had sought after. She received rest from her labors, while the light that shines forth upon her does not sink. (34:32—35:19)

The careful delineation of alternative and opposing subjectivities, described in terms of the performances (eating, resting, inquiring, enduring, learning, finding), points to the central role of asceticism in this treatise.

The treatise shows particular interest in the affect and procedure that desire has on the soul of the seeker. The dramatic narrative of the fisherman and the bait describes the intricate entrapment that desire accomplishes:

> For man-eaters will seize us and swallow us, rejoicing like a fisherman casting a hook into the water. For he casts many kinds of food into the water because each one of the fish has his own food. He smells it and pursues its odor. But when he eats it, the hook hidden within the food seizes him and brings him up by force out

of the deep waters. No man is able, then, to catch that fish down in the deep waters, except for the trap that the fisherman sets. By the ruse of food he brought the fish up on the hook. (29:18—30:5)

That food here operates both at the literal and the symbolic level, the treatise continues:

In this very way we exist in this world, like fish. The adversary spies on us, lying in wait for us like a fisherman, wishing to seize us, rejoicing that he might swallow us. For [he places] many foods before our eyes, (things) which belong to this world. He wishes to make us desire one of them and to taste only a little, so that he may seize us with his hidden poison and bring us out of freedom and take us into slavery. For whenever he catches us with a single food, it is indeed necessary for <us> to desire the rest. Finally, then, such things become the food of death. (30:4–26)

And then the treatise presents the inner workings of desire and points toward the arenas for vigilance by the ascetic:

Now these are the foods with which the devil lies in wait for us. First he injects a pain into your heart until you have heartache on account of a small thing of this life, and he seizes <you> with his poisons. And afterwards (he injects) the desire of a tunic so that you will pride yourself in it, and love of money, pride, vanity, envy that rivals another envy, beauty of body, fraudulence. The greatest of all these are ignorance and ease. (30:26—31:24)

The subtle conflating of the significance of spiritual and physical food while at the same time portraying the real dangers to the ascetic practitioner underscores the sophistication of this ascetical teaching. But the teaching relates not only to the avoidance of desire and wealth; it also presents a positive model for the ascetic to imitate:

But the soul—she who has tasted these things—realized that sweet passions are transitory. She had learned about evil: she went away from them and she entered into a new conduct. Afterwards she despises this life, because it is transitory. And she looks for those foods that will take her into life, and leaves behind her those deceitful foods. And she learns about her light, as she goes about stripping off this world, while her true garment clothes her within, (and) her bridal clothing is placed upon her in beauty of mind, not in pride of flesh. And she learns about her depth and runs

> into her fold, while her shepherd stands at the door. In return for
> all the shame and scorn, then, that she received in this world, she
> receives ten thousand times the grace and glory. (31:24—32:16)

This is very sophisticated ascetical theology and compares positively to
the ascetical theorizing of both John Cassian and his teacher Evagrius
Pontikos.

The Discourse on the Eighth and Ninth (VI,6)

I am not sure that I should include this treatise among the ascetical
treatises, partly because I do not know how to treat this sort of mystical ascent literature in relationship to ascetic practice.[35] The sections of
the Discourse on the Eighth and Ninth that most clearly reflect themes
resonant with the wider ascetical corpus relate primarily to the preparation for the mystical ascent. The prayer before the initiation describes a
process of renunciation preparatory to receiving the revelation:

> Lord, grant us a wisdom from your power that reaches us, so that
> we may describe to ourselves the vision of the eighth and the
> ninth. We have already advanced to the seventh, since we are pi-
> ous and walk in your law. And your will we fulfill always. For we
> have walked in [your way, and we have] renounced [. . .], so that
> your [vision] may come. Lord, grant us the truth in the image.
> Allow us through the spirit to see the form of the image that has
> no deficiency, and receive the reflection of the pleroma from us
> through our praise. (56:23—57:9)

The notions of advancement (54:3–18 and 63:9–14) accompany this interest in preparation. At some level this liturgical or cultic preparation does
indeed constitute an ascetical stage prior to enlightenment, although it
remains always very preliminary.

The Teachings of Silvanus (VII,4)

There is a particular affinity between ascetical literature and the Hellenistic
wisdom literature. The monastic ascetical tradition, at least, continued
to develop the wisdom genres, particularly in the sayings of the wise.
The apophthegmata patrum witness to this continuous tradition. The
Teaching of Silvanus, thus, forms a part of the living ascetical tradition

---

35. But see Swartz, Scholastic Magic.

of the second, third, and fourth centuries C.E.[36] The wisdom espoused would have been readily accessible to an ascetic either living in a monastery withdrawn from society or living the ascetical life in the city.

The exhortations to live the pious and holy life alert the reader to the presence of an active ascetical agenda. The *Teaching of Silvanus* ends with the following ascetical instruction:

> My son, prepare yourself to escape from the world-rulers of darkness and of this kind of air which is full of powers. But if you have Christ, you will conquer this entire world. That which you will open for yourself, you will open. That which you will knock upon for yourself, you will knock upon, benefiting yourself. Help yourself, my son, (by) not proceeding with things in which there is no profit. My son, first purify yourself toward the outward life in order that you may be able to purify the inward. (117:13–28)

This exhortation sets the stage for a struggle to develop a particular kind of person, exemplified between the choice either to follow the divine essence within the person (91:20—92:10) or to act as a foolish person (89:26—90:29). The language articulating that struggle revolves about certain specific activities, for example:

> Abolish every childish time of life, acquire for yourself strength of mind and soul, and intensify the struggle against every folly of the passions of love and base wickedness, and love of praise, and fondness of contention, and tiresome jealousy and wrath, and anger and the desire of avarice. Guard your (pl.) camp and weapons and spears. Arm yourself and all the soldiers which are the words, and the commanders which are the counsels, and your mind as a guiding principle. (84:16—85:1)

In addition to advocating these activities or ascetic performances, the treatise also discusses other typically ascetic themes: the problematizing of sexual intercourse as fornication and lust (104:32—105:25), becoming godlike or divine (108:25–32; 111:9–21), and resisting the fall into an animal nature (105:6–7).

36. See Veilleux, "Monasticism and Gnosis in Egypt," 293–99.

Zostrianos (VIII,1)

Zostrianos, like the *Discourse on the Eighth and Ninth*, presents asceticism as a form of preparation for a heavenly vision.[37] Both these treatises present their visions in a first-person narrative voice that presents the ascetical preparation as personal experience. Zostrianos' experience is described in this way:

> After I parted from the somatic darkness in me and the psychic chaos in mind and the feminine desire [. . .] in the darkness, I did not use it again. After I found the infinite part of my matter, then I reproved the dead creation within me and the divine Cosmocrater of the perceptible (world) by preaching powerfully about the All to those with alien parts. (1:10–21)

The tractate describes the psychological beginning point for the asceticism and the desire for the vision:

> I pondered these things to understand them; according to the custom of my race I kept bringing them up to the god of my fathers. I kept praising them all, for my forefathers and fathers who sought found. As for me, I did not cease seeking a resting place worthy of my spirit, since I was not yet bound in the perceptible world. Then, as I was deeply troubled and gloomy because of the discouragement which encompassed me, I dared to act and to deliver myself to the wild beasts of the desert for a violent death. (3:14–28)

This troubled mind that led to his dramatic action, which is thematized as doing battle with the beasts in the desert, resulted eventually in his becoming angelic: Zostrianos constructs himself as one who left the body behind ("I cast my body upon the earth," 4:23–24) in order to become an angel (7:1–22) capable of moving through the cosmic spheres.

The revelation, which Zostrianos receives, also contains a reference to this preparatory asceticism:

---

37. Turner, ("Typologies of the Sethian Gnostic Treatises," 169–217) links *Allogenes, Three Steles of Seth, Zostrianos,* and *Marsanes* as texts exhibiting "a graded series of visionary ascents initiated by the Gnostic" (188). He does not link this ascent to asceticism, but to a contemplative process: "salvation . . . occurs through the Gnostic's contemplative ascent through ever higher levels of the divine realm" (191). I think he is correct in locating this ascent in philosophical anthropology. See also, *idem,* "Gnosticism and Platonism," 425–59.

Now concerning the man in the Exile; when he discovers the truth in himself, he is far from the deeds of the others who exist [wrongly] (and) stumble. (Concerning) the man who repents: when he renounces the dead and desires those things which are because of immortal mind and his immortal soul, first he [...] makes an inquiry about it, not about conduct but about their deeds.... and the man who can be saved is the one who seeks him and his mind and who finds each one of them. (43:13—44:6)

The specific practices (discovering, renouncing, and inquiring) articulate an ascetical orientation similar to the *Gospel of Thomas* in Saying 2, for example:

Jesus said, "Let him who seeks continue seeing until he finds. When he finds, he will become troubled. When he becomes troubled, he will be astonished, and he will rule over the all."

This asceticism, geared as it is to equip a person capable of receiving divine revelation, remains preparatory.

The Testimony of Truth (IX,3)

The *Testimony of Truth* displays some interest in ascetical themes, but does not advocate any particular ascetical program. The primary ascetical activity discussed in the treatise advocates the struggle against the passions. The treatise's description of an ideal believer (42:21—44:30) begins with this: "[But] he struggled against their passions [. . .] he condemned their error. He cleansed his soul from transgressions" (42:28—43:2). These passions render intercourse suspect and worthy of rejection because they cause pleasure (38:27—40:8), a pleasure advocated by the Law for the procreation of children (29:22—30:17). The Law advocates marriage,[38] which is a form of bondage to the world, while this treatise advocates virginity (40:2—41:4), one form of renunciation of the world (41:4-13; 68:9-12) that brings knowledge and salvation. This treatise sets up a contrast between John the Baptist, "the archon of the womb," who is portrayed as the fulfillment of the Law by advocating sexual pleasure and sexual intercourse (30:30—31:6; 45:6-8) with Jesus, who was born of Mary, a virgin, (44:30—45:22) and who represents a life of continence.

---

38. Williams, *Rethinking "Gnosticism,"* 150–62.

Allogenes (XI,3)

Allogenes, like the *Discourse on the Eighth and Ninth* and *Zostrianos*, contains references to an ascetical system preparatory for receiving revelation. The treatise does not describe ascetical preparation itself, but merely refers to it as a hundred-year deliberation with the self (57:24–58:6) and a response to the reception of the revelation ("And at first I received them in great silence and I stood by myself, preparing myself" 68:31–34). In the context of the first-person description of receiving the revelation, Allogenes describes himself as becoming divine (52:10–12) and withdrawing (60:28–37) and he is instructed by the revealer to seek for knowledge (56:15–17).

The Sentences of Sextus (XII,1)

The *Sentences of Sextus* would have been of great interest to an ascetic (whether urban or monastic), as is most of the gnomic, wisdom literature.[39] The section of sayings preserved here thematize restraining the body (Saying 320), developing prudence and self-sufficiency (Sayings 332/334), and pious works (Saying 359). There is no specific ascetical program advocated here.

CONCLUSIONS

The results of this study surprised me. When I began, I expected to find interesting intertextual connections to the wider ascetical tradition. By expanding the purview of asceticism to incorporate all the current study of asceticism through the construction of my ideal ascetical reader, I thought the library would appear to have an even more ascetical orientation than I had initially thought. But that has not been the case.

The Nag Hammadi Library consists of forty-six different titles, which does not include the titles of treatises such as the *Apocryphon of John* or *Eugnostos the Blessed*, which have multiple attestations. Of these forty-six treatises only four display a thorough-going ascetical agenda: the *Gospel of Thomas*, the *Gospel of Philip*, the *Acts of Peter and the Twelve Apostles*, and *Authoritative Teaching*.[40] Of these four clearly ascetical treatises,

---

39. See Veilleux, "Monasticism and Gnosis in Egypt," 292–93.

40. My findings differ from Veilleux, "Monasticism and Gnosis in Egypt," 291–301, who found only three texts of relevance to monastic asceticism: the *Sentences of Sextus*, the *Teachings of Silvanus*, and the *Gospel of Thomas*.

three come from Christian apocryphal literature (two apocryphal gospels and an apocryphal act of the apostles) and one represents an asceticism not identified with any particular religious tradition (*Authoritative Teaching*).

Again, of the forty-six treatises, two represent a genre of wisdom literature, the sayings of the wise, which has formed an important part of the wider ascetical literary production: the *Teaching of Silvanus*, and the *Sentences of Sextus*. Both of these treatises display an interest in ascetical subjects, and both would have provided important teaching to anyone interested in pursuing asceticism. They remain, however, treatises that would assist ascetics or that advocate the pursuit of ascetical virtues.

Of the forty-six treatises, three treatises refer to an ascetical preparation for receiving divine revelations: *Zostrianos*, the *Discourse on the Eighth and Ninth*, and *Allogenes*. The central concern of these treatises rests with the reception and transmittal of revelations from a variety of divinities, but the preparation for the reception of these revelations also receives significant attention. In themselves, then, they are not ascetical treatises, but contain references to ascetical preparation for revelation.

Finally, among the forty-six treatises in the Nag Hammadi Library, four refer more vaguely to ascetical themes without advocating to any significant degree an ascetical agenda: the *Testimony of Truth*, *Tripartite Tractate*, the *Apocryphon of John*, and the *Book of Thomas the Contender*. It is surprising that the *Book of Thomas the Contender* has so little to relate about asceticism because the other books of the Thomas tradition (the *Gospel of Thomas* and the *Acts of Thomas*) both display significant interest in ascetical subjects. The other treatises refer to subjects of interest to ascetics, but these references tend to be peripheral to the primary content of the treatise: the *Tripartite Tractate* advocates an ascetical formation for the psychics only because the material and spiritual people both stand beyond change; and the *Apocryphon of John* has one particular interest in the formation of Adam's body, the humors, and the protology of Genesis.

Taken together, only thirteen treatises refer to asceticism in any way. Those thirteen treatises comprise less than one-third of the entire library. The vast majority of the treatises found at Nag Hammadi (thirty-three treatises in all) do not intersect with the ascetical tradition of Late Antiquity in any way at all. Even among the thirteen treatises that do refer to asceticism, only six (the four clearly ascetical treatises and the two wisdom collections) resonate with the ascetical tradition in any significant way; that represents only roughly thirteen percent of the treatises. This sort of reading indicates that the Nag Hammadi Library treatises display little or no interest in asceticism from the most broad construal of asceticism. Not only are there few treatises that discuss the traditional topics of asceticism (the sexual renunciation, fasting, social withdrawal, and fighting with the demons), but few that advocate a system for reforming the self. These treatises on the whole (with the exceptions noted early) display little interest in the reconstruction of the human person—the goals and performances aimed to achieve them—that marks out an ascetical agenda from a more theoretical perspective.

The mythological orientation of most of the cosmology in these texts presents the most difficulty for reading the collection ascetically. The intense interest in the exegesis of the protological texts of the Bible found in patristic authors and the theological anthropology developed through that exegesis focus primarily on a narrowly conceived set of issues regarding the significance of embodiment and its relationship to sexual identity and fasting. The closest patristic analogue to the Nag Hammadi's mythological explorations is the theology of the "double creation" articulated by the Cappadocian fathers.[41] Nonetheless, the intensity and degree of orientation toward the mythology of creation does not resonate with the ascetical tradition. Asceticism, oriented as it is toward the development of human subjectivities, needs the wider mythological and theological frame to give content to a theological anthropology and context to the construction of a new subjectivity, but the mythologies of the Nag Hammadi texts do not focus sufficiently on the formation or reformation of the self to betray an ascetical dimension to the mythmaking. The Nag Hammadi library expends too many lines exploring the development and evolution of the material world from the spiritual and not enough lines on the articulation of a new subjectivity.

In the face of this sort of evidence, one cannot argue that the Nag Hammadi Library has a demonstrable ascetical focus or interest. There is simply too little to do with asceticism as it is currently known to maintain that characterization of the library as a whole. The people who read and who produced these treatises would not have been doing so primarily for their ascetical content or usefulness.

41. On the concept of the double creation, see Gasparro, "Asceticism and Anthropology," 127–46.

This conclusion does not necessarily mean that monks, even Pachomian monks, did not produce these texts. James Goehring[42] has argued that early monasticism appears very different when described from the evidence of its literary productions (histories, *apophthegmata*, and hagiographies) and from the evidence of its documentary evidence. The literary evidence tends toward idealization and strict delimitation of monastery from city and world. The documentary evidence, however, shows active involvement of monks in most worldly activities: trading, renting and owning property, buying and selling necessary food items, selling monastic handiwork, among many others. It is quite conceivable that the production of these texts was important to a monastery, not because they were of intellectual or spiritual interest to the monks, but because they represented part of the intellectual trade of the monastic community with the wider intellectual life of their society.[43] The evidence from the Nag Hammadi library could support that kind of relationship with the ascetical and academic communities.[44] In the end, however, we will need to look elsewhere, away from ascetical seekers and communities, for the community that found these treatises interesting.[45] Both in theory and in practice, the Nag Hammadi library shows very little interest in asceticism.

42. Goehring, "Encroaching Desert," 73–88.

43. Two kinds of religious association have possibilities. Ewa Wipszycka ("Les confréries dans la vie religieuse de l'Egypt chrétienne," 511–25) lays out the evidence for *philoponoi* and *spoudaioi* as lay, urban sodalities throughout Egypt; David Brakke (*Athanasius*, 58–75) explores the groups he calls "academic" Christians in Egypt. It is clear from both of these studies that the intellectual horizon of Egypt (and of Late Antique Christianity in general) is broader than usually portrayed by scholars.

44. This argument will force a reconsideration of the intellectual environment of the Nag Hammadi Library. It will effect the phases for the transmission of texts, especially as Frederik Wisse has proposed for the *Apocryphon of John* ("After the *Synopsis*," 138–53). His "Coptic Monastic Phase" will need to be located in a different environment because his argument is based primarily on the ascetical orientation of the treatises: "The generally ascetic outlook of this diverse collection of tractates also fits the monastic setting" (147), and "It is likely that the monks cherished these unorthodox books . . . mainly for their ascetic and esoteric value" (148).

45. Michael Williams (*Rethinking "Gnosticism,"* 235–62) takes up this question. He also rejects the Sethian sectarian origins of the "library" as well as the monastic ascetic origins. He posits instead an orderly and intentional structure to each of the codices, reminiscent of the organization and structure of the Septuagint or the New Testament. His arguments will need to be more extensively evaluated by the scholarly community. See also idem, "Interpreting the Nag Hammadi Library," 3–50.

CHAPTER 12

Demons, Adversaries, Devils, Fishermen

The Asceticism of Authoritative Teaching *(NHL, VI, 3)*
in Roman Perspective

ROMAN ASCETICISM,[1] DEVELOPED BY SUCH IMPORTANT PHILOSOPHICAL
and intellectual leaders as Musonius Rufus, Epictetus, and the Cynics,
comes to center stage in the first and second centuries C.E.[2] The particular varieties of Roman asceticism developed during the imperial period
hold many things in common:[3] a typically Roman interest in what modern scholars would call lived religion,[4] that is, a concern for the practice
as well as the theory of ethical and philosophical living;[5] an orientation
toward the practice of virtue and the avoidance of vice; a problematizing of the dominant social and political society and a resistance to full
participation in normative society; a use of a wide variety of literary and

---

1. In Memoriam: George W. MacRae, SJ, mentor, scholar, teacher, and friend.

2. There is as yet no history of Roman asceticism. Some older preliminary studies
exist. See Swain, "Hellenic Origins of Christian Asceticism"; and Dressler, "*Usage of*
ΑΣΚΕΩ."

3. The elements in this list are my own compilation based on a reading of original
documents. My thinking has been particularly influenced by Goulet-Cazé's *L'Ascése*
Cynique, and her "Le cynism à l'époque impériale." Although I do not fully endorse the
perspectives and conclusions, I have also benefited from Pierre Hadot's, *Philosophy as a*
Way of Life.

4. See Hadot, *Philosophy as a Way of Life,* 49–70.

5. Musonius Rufus, Discourse V, on theory and practice; Epictetus Discourse III:12,
on asceticism.

philosophical genres (such as diatribes,[6] biographies,[7] *chreiai*,[8] epistles,[9] *gnomologia*[10]) to develop their ascetical systems; and a yoking of ascetical practice and education of youths (often both male and female). Immersed in Roman practicality and Greek philosophical traditions, Roman intellectual leaders of the imperial period energetically turned their minds to ascetical concerns.

The central role of asceticism in Roman religious and philosophical life has often been obscured by scholars of western civilization who assume that asceticism is primarily a Christian phenomenon in the West. Long before the emergence of Christian asceticism, however, many Roman philosophers of a wide variety proposed sophisticated systems of ascetical formation. The ascetical agenda of the Cynics is well attested both in ancient and modern literature.[11] But there were other systems as well. Musonius Rufus and Epictetus, his student, both present diatribes "concerning asceticism" in which they lay out their own system of asceticism. James Francis's study of the Roman ascetics of the second century[12] shows the pervasive interest in matters ascetical among a wide variety of Romans, including the Roman emperor Marcus Aurelius. The later Roman philosophical ascetics Plotinus, Porphyry, and Iamblichus build on this long tradition of Roman ascetical theory and further develop systems of asceticism by blending Stoic and Cynic interests in Neo-Platonic philosophical categories. These all attest to the emergence and development of Roman ascetical systems long before the more thoroughly researched Late Antique Christian systems.

The Nag Hammadi treatise *Authoritative Teaching* is part of this Roman tradition of ascetical speculation. Although the treatise was dis-

6. Preeminently those of Musonius Rufus and Epictetus, among many others.

7. See, e.g., Porphyry's "Life and Works of Plotinus," Philostratus's biography of Apollonius of Tyana, and Lucian's biography of Peregrinus.

8. Diogenes Laertius's compendium is replete with *chreiai*. For the sources, see Hock and O'Neill, *Chreia in Ancient Rhetoric*.

9. I am thinking especially of the Cynic epistles; see Attridge, *First-Century Cynicism*; and Malherbe, *The Cynic Epistles*.

10. See Chadwick, *Sentences of Sextus*, especially ix–xii and 97–106.

11. See the works already cited by Goulet-Cazé, as well as the superb collection of essays in Branham and Goulet-Cazé: *Cynics*, especially 1–27; Navia, *Classical Cynicism*, 145–92; the various essays in Goulet-Cazé and Goulet, *Cynism Ancien*; and, of course, Dudley, *History of Cynicism*.

12. Francis, *Subversive Virtue*.

covered as part of a collection of texts probably produced in a Christian monastery, the *Authoritative Teaching* is not (as will be discussed) a Christian nor even a Gnostic text. It is one of the few Nag Hammadi treatises of Roman philosophical and literary texts, which include a translation of a selection of Homer and a selection of the *Sentences of Sextus*. Because of its association with this so-called Gnostic library,[13] the *Authoritative Teaching* has received scant recent study. It has never been studied as part of the Roman ascetical tradition.

A summary of scholarly work on the *Authoritative Teaching* indicates how little this treatise has been incorporated into the religious and philosophical literature of the first three centuries C.E. George MacRae, to whose memory this essay is dedicated, was the first scholar thoroughly to present this treatise to the academic world. He understood his work of establishing the text and rendering an initial translation as the foundation for future scholars' work in integrating this and other Nag Hammadi treatises into the intellectual and scholarly mainstream of early Christian and Late Antique religious studies. He himself began this integrative function by correlating his own research on the *Authoritative Teaching* to the literature on the soul that A.-J. Festugière, the great scholar of the history of religions, outlined in his third volume of *La Révélation d'Hermès Trismègiste*.[14] R. van den Broek continued this scholarly tradition in his important article about the connection of the *Authoritative Teaching* with Platonic thought.[15] Jacques Ménard provided another critical edition and the first complete commentary on the treatise.[16] All of these initial investigations attempted to understand the *Authoritative Teaching* by comparison with parallel literature of the Roman Hellenistic period.

This essay builds on earlier scholarship and attempts to locate the *Authoritative Teaching* in the context of Roman ascetical theorizing. First, I will develop the ascetical theology articulated in the treatise with general reference to the first recorded ascetical theorist, Musonius Rufus.[17] This part simply provides an ascetical reading of the text with

13. The whole question of Gnosticism has been called into question by Michael Williams in *Rethinking "Gnosticism."* Also see chapter 11, pp. 235–59.

14. MacRae, "Nag Hammadi Tractate," 478–79.

15. van den Broek, "Authentikos Logos."

16. Ménard, *L'Authentikos Logos*, 45–62.

17. Throughout this article, I use the text and translation of Musonius's corpus by Cora E. Lutz, *Musonius Rufus*. The quotations, unless otherwise annotated, are taken

some reference to an earlier Roman ascetical theorist in order to establish general connections between the *Authoritative Teaching* and earlier
ascetical traditions. Then I will develop a general scheme for the gradual
development of Roman ascetical theory in the first three centuries C.E.,
and locate the *Authoritative Teaching* within that evolving ascetical theoretical discourse.

The Ascetical Theology
of the *Authoritative Teaching*

The ascetical theology of the *Authoritative Teaching* may be developed
from three different perspectives: the structure of the treatise and the way
that arguments have been located in sequence; the content of the treatise
with its emphasis on the ascetical contest and the program of ascent of the
mind; and the negative function, which describes the ascetical program
from the perspective of impediments to progress. Each of these perspectives will be explored and then compared where possible to the ascetical
theorizing of Musonius Rufus.

The content of the treatise, despite its seams, displays a coherent pattern. Overall, it moves from the question of the embodiment of the soul
of righteousness, through the establishment by the Father of a contest to
a description of the state of the contestants, and it ends with a description
of the fate of the successful contestant. In this broad overview, the ascetical dimension of the treatise seems obvious.

A closer look at the unfolding of the argument in the treatise confirms this observation. The treatise begins with a description of the embodiment of the soul of righteousness (22:8—23:34), which presents a
variety of themes such as the soul's root and family and the role of the
vices and materiality to the soul. Here the *Authoritative Teaching* emphasizes that the materiality of the soul makes it subject to lust and "the
outsiders—for the possessions of the outsiders are proud passions," the
pleasures of life, hateful envies, vainglorious things, nonsensical things,
accusations." A lacuna in the text ends the list of vices. Musonius also

---

from Discourse VI, "On Training," which are found on pages 52–57 (an enface edition
with the Greek text on the even pages). Since we have nothing from Musonius's own pen,
Lutz's edition and translation brings together all of the discourses of Musonius summarized by Lucius, as well as the fragments preserved in Epictetus, Plutarch, Aulus Gellius,
and Aelius Aristides. Discourse VI is part of the collection written down by Lucius and
preserved in Stobaeus's *Anthology* (III, 29, 78).

takes up the question of embodiment, arguing that "the human being is not soul alone, nor body alone, but a kind of synthesis of the two," [18] with the proviso that the ascetic must attend to both. His virtues, however, come from the philosophical tradition: the ascetic must practice to be temperate, just, courageous, and prudent. Both of these ascetical systems revolve about the attainment of specific and articulated virtues through physical training, a training made necessary by the human condition of embodiment.

The second section of the *Authoritative Teaching* describes the contamination of the soul (24:6—25:6a) through a variety of different metaphors such as being placed in a brothel, falling into drunken debauchery, falling into bestiality, and the mixing of wheat and chaff, a curious metaphor for the contamination of good with evil. Musonius Rufus also describes the contamination of the human being that comes through evil socialization. Musonius speaks of "the depravity which has become implanted in us straight from childhood because of the evil habits engendered by this depravity."[19] He argues as well that the philosopher in particular needs to retrain the self from this depravity: "men who enter the other professions [i.e., medicine and music] have not had their souls corrupted beforehand and have not learned the opposite of what they are going to be taught, but the ones who start out to study philosophy have been born and reared in an environment filled with corruption and evil."[20] Again, both these systems postulate a depraved human condition that forms the basis for ascetical activity.

The third section (25:26b—26:19) of the *Authoritative Teaching*, for which the first two sections carefully prepare, describes the appearance of the Father and his setting up a contest, an *agōn* for the people.[21] The contestants are required to progress beyond existent things and advance toward the Inscrutable One. This section, which will be discussed in more detail later, sets the stage for the ascetical effort of those established as contestants. Although Musonius does not develop a system based upon a theology of the work of the Creator of the universe as do many later Neo-Platonists, he nevertheless puts a contest at the center of his ascetical

18. Lutz, *Musonius Rufus*, 53, 55, 54 [lines 2–3].

19. Ibid., 53, 452 [lines 28–32].

20. On Musonius's doctrine of moral illness see Lutz, *Musonius Rufus*, 27–28.

21. This section begins at what appears to be a seam in the text; see MacRae, "Nag Hammadi Tractate," 473.

system. Musonius's contest revolves about the destruction of evil habits to which the ascetic has been socialized from his youth and to the acquiring of habits consistent with his virtuous goals. He recognizes the role of bodily training, on the model of training for an athletic exercise, as a suitable means of ascetical formation: "For obviously the philosopher's body should be well prepared for physical activity, because often the virtues make use of this as a necessary instrument for the affairs of life."[22] Both these systems have their foundation in a personal contest, and both promulgate systems for understanding both the theory or theology of the contest and the practices necessary to succeed in it.

The rest of the treatise deals with the contestants from a variety of perspectives. Section four (26:19—27:29) describes the state of the contestants' knowledge, their relationship to the world, their shame, their response to hostility, and their desire for permanence. Musonius also discusses similar subjects in the course of his teaching: that enduring hardship for the sake of the good is valuable (Discourse VII), that exile is not evil because philosophers are citizens of the City of God (Discourse IX), and that human transformation is both desirable and possible (Fragment XLII). Musonius's philosophical teaching does not, however, include a high valuation of permanence. Although there are differences of perspective on these subjects between Musonius and the *Authoritative Teaching*, similar topics are addressed in each of these philosophical and ascetical systems.

The fifth section (27:30—29:2) specifically addresses the state of the contestants' soul with the description of the anointing of the eyes with *logos* to see better and to enable the contestants to contend effectively. The sixth section (29:3—31:24) explicates the vigilance necessary for the contestants through an elaborate allegory of the fishnet, which entraps and ultimately destroys the fish and the fisherman, who baits the contestant with a small desirable item that leads to their capture and death. The seventh section (31:24—33:3) describes the work of the successful contestant. The last section contrasts the fate of the ignorant who do not seek God (33:4—34:31) with the fate of the rational soul (34:32—35:18). These three sections take up material unique to the *Authoritative Teaching* and do not have parallels in earlier Roman ascetical theory. They represent

---

22. Lutz, *Musonius Rufus*, 55, 54 [lines 7–8].

the particular and significant contribution of the *Authoritative Teaching* to ascetical theory.

The structure of the argument of the treatise, gathered as it probably is from a number of different sources and environments,[23] points to a sophisticated ascetical agenda. That structure begins with the state of embodiment of the soul and its potential for contamination, then it sets up the contest that enables the soul to contend with vices and temptations, and ends with a description of the rewards granted to the successful contender. Such a description of content, however, does not replicate the sophistication and subtlety of the treatise. The *Authoritative Teaching* uses metaphor extensively to give depth and substance to the argument. The treatise aligns metaphoric structures from a variety of sources within the structure of the ascetical argument in order precisely to create a unified ascetical theology. It is precisely this extensive use of metaphor that distinguishes the *Authoritative Teaching* from the work of earlier ascetical theorists, not only Musonius Rufus, but also Epictetus and the Cynics.

The structure of the treatise, pointing as it does toward asceticism is the first perspective from which to articulate the ascetical agenda in the *Authoritative Teaching*.[24] The content of the treatise itself provides the second. Here we find a number of elements that together make up a complete ascetical system. The content of the treatise centers on the description of a contest[25] established by the Father:

> He, then, the Father, wishing to reveal his [wealth] and his glory, brought about this great contest in this world, wishing to make the contestants appear, and make all those who contend leave behind the things that had come into being, and despise them with a lofty, incomprehensible knowledge, and flee to the one who exists. (26:8–20)

---

23. Again, see the commentary in Ménard, *L'Authentikos Logos*, 45–62.

24. The text and translation used throughout is that of George W. MacRae, SJ, to whose memory this article is dedicated: MacRae, "Authoritative Teaching," 257–89. I have included some of the Greek loan words from the Coptic text. See also, Ménard, *L'Authentikos Logos*, 7–35 for another edition and French translation; and the evaluation of that edition by Funk, "Der verlorene Anfang," 59–65.

25. Ménard acknowledges the ascetical nature of the combat and the ascetical dimension to the anointing of the eyes with *logos* for the combat: Ménard, *L'Authentikos Logos*, 2.

The embodiment of the soul in materiality (22:13–16 and 23:12–20) and its potential contamination by its embodiment occasions this contest. Ascetical systems commonly describe ascetical efforts under two correlative metaphors that are not mutually exclusive: a contest or endurance of hardship, both of which metaphorize the efforts of an athlete to prepare the body for engagement in sporting event. Both metaphors present the overall scheme of ascetical effort: the *Authoritative Teaching* presents the metaphor of the contest, while Musonius Rufus prefers the metaphor of enduring hardships.[26]

The *Authoritative Teaching* develops a number of subordinate metaphors to describe the potential contamination that form the center of the ascetical contest: the mixing of wheat and chaff (25:12–23), a falling into bestiality (24:20–26), entering into prostitution (24:7), the contamination of a virgin man by lust (25:6–9), the contamination that the secure storehouse prevents (25:24–26), and the general contamination brought on by desires (30:28—31:24). In light of her embodied state and potential for contamination, the soul must contend and she must pursue the goal that will result in the achievement of a number of goals: her fruitful search and knowledge of the Inscrutable One; her reclining in the Bridal Chamber and partaking of the immortal food of the banquet; her rest from her labors; and her dwelling in unending light (34:32—35:18). As will be demonstrated more fully below, the negative functions in the ascetical system express a positive goal: to have the mind ascend to the One, to which end *logos* is applied to the eyes to enable them to see and to assist their knowledge so that the mind may ascend to the One. These subordinate metaphors do not have parallels in Musonius's corpus; they represent the particular ascetical perspective of the *Authoritative Teaching*.

The *Authoritative Teaching* presents the positive goal of ascetical effort in this way:

> But the soul—she who has tasted these things—realized that sweet passions are transitory. She had learned about evil; she went away from them and she entered into a new conduct. Afterwards she despises this life because it is transitory. And she looks for those foods that will take her into life, and leaves behind her those deceitful foods. And she learns about her light, as she goes about

26. This is found in Discourse VII, immediately following upon the discourse on asceticism.

> stripping off this world, while her true garment clothes her within, (and) her bridal clothing is placed upon her in beauty of mind, not in pride of flesh. And she learns about her depth and runs into her fold, while her shepherd stands at the door. In return for all the shame and scorn, then, that she received in this world, she receives ten thousand times the grace and glory. (31:24—32:16)

The *Authoritative Teaching* does not simply present the ascetical goal, the ascent of the mind, but it also describes the specific activities that enable the soul to achieve her goal. Those activities, enumerated in the preceding quotation, include tasting the passions and recognizing their impermanence, changing her way of life from evil to something good, despising the world, searching for life-giving food, stripping off this world, and putting on a bridal garment. These activities establish for the soul a sophisticated ascetical system, articulated not only in the positive activities, but also through the careful and nuanced description of the negative functions.

Some of these themes in the Nag Hammadi treatise reflect ascetical issues explored by Musonius. At the heart of the Musonian ascetical system stands a project of redefining what is good and evil: the asceticism that pertains to the soul only revolves about "seeing that the proofs pertaining to apparent goods . . . and likewise those pertaining to apparent evils as not being real evils, and in learning to recognize the things which are truly good and in becoming accustomed to distinguish them from what are not truly good" (Discourse VI). Eating (Discourse XVIII A and B), clothing (Discourse XIX), and shelter (Discourse XX) all are arenas in which the ascetic discerns true and false good and exercises moderation. Musonius also emphasizes the importance of new conduct according to virtue in his discourse on asceticism (Discourse VI), especially as it manifests the ascetic's citizenship in a more noble city. Discourse IX, on the subject of exile, specifies that the ascetic is a citizen of the city of God, which means that the ascetic may embrace political exile, with the scorn, hardship, and shame that it brings, as an apparent evil and not as a real one.

The Negative Function within the Contest

Within most ascetical systems, the articulated positive goals call forth a correlative description of the hindrances to their achievement. This is certainly the case in Musonius Rufus's system where the impediments of social habituation and philosophical delusion play a central role in the ascetical process. Ascetical systems depend for the most part on the exercises and activities in overcoming those impediments in order to work toward the mastery necessary for the attainment of the goal.[27] In this way the negative function, often metaphorized as contest with demons, defines the asceticism.[28]

This ascetical system of the *Authoritative Teaching* addresses a basic problem: the mind of the senseless person has been so affected by the negative function that it cannot rise to a proper knowledge of God. This concluding section of the treatise describes the problem succinctly:

> But to this senseless man the word has been preached, teaching him: "Seek and inquire about the ways you should go, since there is nothing else that is as good as this thing." The result is that the substance of hardness of heart strikes a blow upon his mind, along with the force of ignorance and the demon of error. They do not allow his mind to rise up, because he was wearying himself in seeking that he might learn about his hope. (34:18–32)

These ignorant people do not seek God, nor do they seek their resting place, and their lives are determined by their own hardness of heart. Notice that the mind is distracted from seeking and finding the true good by a kind of intellectual confusion, which stands at the center of Musonius's system as well, confounded with ignorance and demonic delusion. The negative function within the ascetical system points to what prevents them from achieving their goals.

The treatise characterizes this demonic function with a number of different descriptors. As just quoted above, the negative function is a "hardness of heart," a "force of ignorance and the demon of error" (34:24–28). It is also a beguiling devil set upon ensnaring the eager ascetic:

> Now these are the foods with which the devil lies in wait for us. First he injects a pain into your heart until you have heartache on account of a small thing of this life, and he seizes <you> with his poisons. And afterwards (he injects) the desire of a tunic so that you will pride yourself in it, and love of money, pride, vanity, envy

27. See chapter 2, pp. 14–59, "Constructions of Power in Asceticism."
28. Chapter 7, pp. 134–68, "Daemons."

that rivals another envy, beauty of body, fraudulence. The greatest
of all these are ignorance and ease. (30:26—31:7)

This analysis of the negative function develops a psychology of socially constructed desire habituated to a series of vices (e.g., pride, vanity, envy) and it describes the debilitating hold that such desire exercises on the ascetic. The process describes psychologically what Musonius treats philosophically on these same topics of food, clothing, and shelter.[29]

The *Authoritative Teaching* also characterizes the demonic function as an adversary to the soul. In the section immediately following upon the description of the work of the devil, the treatise describes the adversary's effect upon the soul:

> Now all such things the adversary prepares beautifully and spreads out before the body, wishing to make the mind of the soul incline toward one of them and overwhelm her, like a hook drawing her by force in ignorance, deceiving her until she conceives evil and bears fruit of matter and conducts herself in uncleanness, pursuing many desires, covetousnesses, while fleshly pleasure draws her in ignorance. (31:8–24)

This adversary is one among the other adversaries in the Father's contest who are "those who contend with us, being adversaries, who contend against us" (26:20–22). The adversarial role psychologizes the negative function of desire, while simultaneously personifying it and relating it to the evil effect of vices (specifically covetousness and pleasure). Again, the *Authoritative Teaching* seems to present the psychological perspective to issues developed philosophically by Musonius.

In addition to the characterization as a demon, a devil, and an adversary, the *Authoritative Teaching* adds the dramatic description of the demonic function as a body merchandiser:[30]

> She [the soul] gave the body to those who had given it to her, and they were ashamed, while the dealers in bodies sat down and wept because they were not able to do any business with that body, nor did they find an (other) merchandise except it. They endured great labors until they had shaped the body of this soul, wishing to strike down the invisible soul. They were therefore ashamed

29. See Musonius's Discourses XVIII–XXI.
30. See MacRae, "Nag Hammadi Tractate," 475–76.

of their work; they suffered the loss of one for whom they had endured labors. (32:16–30)

This characterization as a body merchandiser is unique to this treatise. The image mirrors the positive ascetical reformation of the body to conform to the soul, but it develops the opposite and negative function, namely, a body that is formed in order to thwart the soul. The image, metaphorically and somewhat allegorically presented here, seems to reflect a similar concern found in Musonius Rufus where he discusses the need for asceticism among those training for philosophy: "the ones who start out to study philosophy have been born and reared in an environment filled with corruption and evil," which is "the depravity which has become implanted in us straight from childhood"[31] that engender evil habits.

These diverse characterizations of the negative function in the ascetical system do not build upon one another in a progression, because the characterizations do not relate to a coordinated and logical field of metaphors. No logical connection exists between the various characterizations as hardness of heart, force of ignorance, demon of error, devil, contesting adversary, and body merchandiser. No overarching conceptual frame links them. Rather they develop particular aspects of the negative dimension of the ascetical program in tandem in a kind of piling of images.

This piling of images creates the depth of the negative function in the ascetical system. Each one of the longer descriptions develops an aspect of the system. The hook of desire, planted by the devil through a small pain in this life, drags the ascetic into the morass of debilitating worldly desires. This characterization of the negative function explores the impact and negative effect of desire. The beauty of somatic things, set forth by the adversary through the presentation of beautiful bodies, draws the soul away from the higher things to pursue more and more of the lesser, somatic graces of the world. This characterization explains the seduction of bodily senses and their entrapment of the soul. The destructive formation of the soul, conducted by the body merchandisers through their effort to fashion the body into a commodity, thwarts the soul's desire to attain higher things. This characterization of the negative function explores the objectification of the soul through worldly engage-

---

31. Lutz, VI, 55, 54 [lines 35–37]

ment. Each of these characterizations adds depth to the understanding of the ascetical program by investigating various dimensions of the negative function within the ascetical system. By placing these various investigations side by side, they are associated with one another as elements of one, single, and comprehensive ascetical system.

In addition to these aligned characterizations of the demonic function, two other images presented in the treatise and unique to it add depth to the ascetical system by sustained metaphorization: the metaphor of the fishing net and the metaphor of the fisherman.[32] These metaphors explain the impact of the negative function on the ascetic seeker.

The metaphor of the net describes a process of drowning:

> For this reason, then, we do not sleep, nor do we forget [the] nets that are spread out in hiding, lying in wait for us to catch us. For if we are caught in a single net, it will suck us down into its mouth, while the water flows over us, striking our face. And we will be taken down into the dragnet, and we will not be able to come up from it because the waters are high over us, flowing from above downward, submerging our heart down in the filthy mud. And we will not be able to escape from them. (29:3–17)

The negative function within the ascetical system is like a dragnet that submerges the soul, pulling it down under water until it sticks in the mud and dies. It is a troubling metaphor, graphic in its description and frightening in its effect. The metaphor articulates dramatically the impact of the negative functions on the soul.

That dragnet metaphor introduces the next metaphor of a man-eating fisherman:

> For man-eaters will seize us and swallow us, rejoicing like a fisherman casting a hook into the water. For he casts many kinds of food into the water because each one of the fish has his own food. He smells it and pursues its odor. But when he eats it, the hook hidden within the food seizes him and brings him up by force out of the deep waters. No man is able, then, to catch that fish down in the deep waters, except for the trap that the fisherman sets. By

---

32. MacRae, "Nag Hammadi Tractate," 473–74. MacRae provides parallel literature in which the fisherman are sinister characters from Hab 1:13–17 and from *Hodayoth* 3:26 and 4:7–8, but concludes: "The metaphor in *Authoritative Teaching* is virtually unique in that the adversary fishes in his own interest" (474).

> the ruse of food, he brought the fish up on the hook. In this very
> way we exist in this world like fish. (29:18—30:6)

Here the image of fishing supplants the image of being drowned in the
dragnet, but with the same impact. The dragnet emphasized the overwhelming helplessness of the soul enmeshed in the world, while the image of the fisherman describes the process whereby the world overwhelms
and captures the soul. The work of the fisherman transforms this metaphor into an allegory of the fate of the soul and the manner of its capture.
The man-eating fisherman baits a hook with food particular to the kind
of person he desires to catch. The particularity of the bait suggests that
not all ascetics will be captured by the same bait, but that each ascetic's
capture differs according to the ascetic's temperament and tastes.[33] Once
the bait has been thrown before the ascetic, temptation and desire take
hold and the ascetic is captured. This allegory defines the way ascetics
live in the world, constantly tempted by food and other desires that have
been baited by the various demonic functions. Both of these metaphors
describe in psychological terms the social debilitation and habituation,
which Musonius Rufus describes and for which he promulgates his system of moral reformation. The attitude toward the overwhelming deca-
dence and destructive effect of the world on the person remains similar,
while the way of describing these influences diverge.

The treatise further develops this metaphor and its allegory by connecting it to many of the themes presented in the ascetical system:

> The adversary spies on us, lying in wait for us like a fisherman,
> wishing to seize us, rejoicing that he might swallow us. For [he
> places] many foods before our eyes, (things) which belong to
> this world. He wishes to make us desire one of them and to taste
> only a little, so that he may seize us with his hidden poison and
> bring us out of freedom and take us into slavery. For whenever
> he catches us with a single food, it is indeed necessary for <us>
> to desire the rest. Finally, then, such things become the food of
> death. Now these are the foods with which the devil lies in wait
> for us. (30:6–27)

The linking here of desire, food, slavery, death, entrapment, and the work
of the devil displays the intricate interconnection of elements in the as-

---

33. In Discourse I and II Musonius also differentiates levels of learning for different
people.

cetical system. The negative function characterized in a variety of ways and placed side by side explicates carefully the entire ascetical movement in the treatise.

The negative function in the ascetical system described in the *Authoritative Teaching* articulates a number of different perspectives on the impediments to the achievement of the ascetical goal. Although each of the various perspectives differs from one another and could stand on its own, the treatise makes them cohere by associating them with the other elements in the ascetical system. All the characterizations of the negative function—as a hardened heart, and an ignorant force, and a demon of error, and a variety of adversaries, and a body merchandiser, combined with the more allegorical descriptions of fish caught in a dragnet and fish caught by bait—create a systematic and thoroughly explained set of impediments to the soul's life and well-being. The piling of these images identify them with the others in order to add depth to the ascetical process.

THE *AUTHORITATIVE TEACHING* IN ITS ROMAN CONTEXT

Authoritative Teaching presents a fully articulated ascetical system. The soul's embodiment and its potential for contamination provide the occasion for the explanation of the system. The negative function within the system—that is, the demonic ascetical function—gathers various metaphors, unrelated by any inherent system or logic, to dramatize and to explain in great detail and with rich nuance the ascetical contest. This ascetical system resonates with psychological insight and understanding. A significant contribution of this treatise to the literature of asceticism lays precisely in its mode of piling metaphors as a means at once of combining elements from a variety of religious and philosophical circles and simultaneously adding depth and richness to the ascetical system it promulgates. The *Authoritative Teaching* takes an interest in the development of virtues and the avoidance of vices, complementary in conception to the earlier ascetical system of Musonius Rufus, while at the same time developing a richly textured psychology of ascetical formation, also resonant with the philosophical theory of social dishabituation found in Musonius Rufus. The independent parts and metaphors relate to an overarching plan to which each part becomes an elaboration and explanation. The system developed here emerges from the constellation of images, metaphors, and concepts juxtaposed to one another in an orderly ascetical system.

The *Authoritative Teaching* is significant to ascetical literature because it represents as well a serious effort at systematizing and syncretizing[34] philosophical and religious ascetical practice. Stoic ethics, Platonic doctrines, Jewish and Christian scriptural references and images, and Hermetic doctrines combine in a system not identified with any one religious or philosophical tradition, but with a depth that could speak to any one of them. This is to say that the more generic ascetical system of the *Authoritative Teaching* emerges from many traditions and potentially may address any number of them in turn without prejudice.

The comparison with the asceticism of Musonius Rufus establishes the *Authoritative Teaching* as a treatise recognizably in the tradition of earlier Roman ascetical theorizing. It is possible now in very broad strokes to trace the history of Roman asceticism from the second century until the fourth century C.E. through the significant work of a number of scholars in order to situate the *Authoritative Teaching* more precisely.

The first century witnessed a development of the earliest traditions of ascetical writing, first with Musonius, then in Epictetus, Musonius's influential student and successor. And, of course, the first century includes the Cynic epistles and the letters of Heraclitus. Although Cynicism did not develop the same sort of theoretical base as did the Stoics Musonius and Epictetus, nonetheless their literary output in the first century witnessed to the central role of critical Cynicism in the philosophical scene. The question of the living out of a morally responsible life was firmly established in practice and in theory in the first century C.E.

For the second century, James Francis provides a thorough analysis of Roman asceticism beginning with the Stoic asceticism of Musonius Rufus and Epictetus, and ending with Celsus's criticism of Christian practice.[35] Francis begins with the interior asceticism of Marcus Aurelius, which constitutes a direct inheritance from the ascetical teaching of Epictetus. Pierre Hadot explicates the ascetical tradition embodied in the work of Epictetus taken up by the emperor Marcus Aurelius.[36] Marcus Aurelius does indeed follow the tradition of Musonius Rufus and Epictetus in de-

---

34. Ménard, *L'Authentikos Logos*, 3.

35. See especially Francis, *Subversive Virtue*, 181–89.

36. Hadot, *Inner Citadel*, 54–100.

veloping a mode of action, of asceticism, that molds and forms the intellectual, social, religious, and political aspects of the individual's life. This early stream of Roman asceticism represents an intellectual and moral asceticism of comprehensive dimensions.

After Marcus Aurelius, however, Francis explores the largely literary productions of second-century asceticism. The modality of ascetical exploration moves from ethical ascetical theory (as in Musonius Rufus, Epictetus, and Marcus Aurelius) to biography. Later second-century writers explore ascetical issues through literary biography, such as Lucian's *Peregrinus*,[37] which represents Cynic asceticism, and Flavius Philostratus's *Apollonius of Tyana*,[38] which represents a more thaumaturgic and charismatic ascetical figure. These biographies explore asceticism in the lives of these personages. Biography enables Lucian and Philostratus to explore the manifold dimensions of asceticism (e.g., wonderworking, ascetical practice, magic, psychological orientation, social implications) and their social reception by Roman audiences.

This biographical tradition of ascetical exploration reaches new heights in the work of Diogenes Laertius. Marie-Odile Goulet-Cazé has devoted special attention to Diogenes Laetius's compendium of the doctrines and teachings of Cynic philosophers.[39] Diogenes combines an interest in both biographical detail and doctrine in his work to the point that Goulet-Cazé believes that she can extract historical information about the life and teaching of the historical Diogenes, the reputed founder of Cynicism.[40] What is of significance in this context is the combination of ascetical theory and biographical detail as an incremental development in Roman asceticism.

Roman asceticism takes a different turn in other more philosophical circles. Here the work of Anthony Meredith[41] comes to the fore. Meredith studied the relationship of Christian and Roman asceticism in the later third and early fourth centuries C.E. primarily in philosophical and theological categories. Meredith relates the philosophical asceticism of Plotinus, Porphyry, and Iamblichus to the Christian ascetical masters

37. Francis, *Subversive Virtue*, 53–81.

38. Ibid., 83–129.

39. See Goulet-Cazé, "Le cynism à l'époque impériale"; and her *L'Ascèse Cynique*.

40. Goulet-Cazé, *L'Ascèse Cynique*, 11–14.

41. Meredith, "Asceticism—Christian and Greek," 313–32.

Athanasius, Basil, and Gregory of Nyssa. He concludes that there exists "a common tradition of popular morality, to which many similarities owe their existence"[42] and there are philosophical agreements, while noting that there are also significant differences. The common moral tradition to which Meredith refers presumably reaches back to the ethical asceticism of Musonius and Epictetus and their ethical successors. The philosophical system gathers up elements from "platonized Stoicism,"[43] neo-Platonism, and later Cynicism.

In broadest strokes, Roman asceticism in the first four centuries C.E. begins with the theory and practice of Stoic and Cynic moral virtue.[44] While this moral tradition continues to develop as witnessed by Marcus Aurelius, ascetical systems find articulation in literary biography in which the moral and religious dimensions of religious practice are both displayed and debated. By the third century, asceticism has developed also in neo-Platonist and later Stoic traditions into fully articulated theological and philosophical systems that crossed over into most every religious environment (Roman philosophy, Christianity, Judaism, Manicheaism, Gnosticism, among others). These articulated systems also continue to explore ascetical aspects of personal development and personal sanctity, as witnessed in Porphyry's "Life and Works of Plotinus" and in the many biographies of the saints that begin to emerge in Christian circles. Roman asceticism was both highly developed and widely attested.

Within the spectrum of asceticism just outlined, the *Authoritative Teaching* seems best to fit as a point of transition between the pure ethical systems of the moralists of the first century and the neo-Platonist philosophical and theological traditions of the early third century. The *Authoritative Teaching* displays an interest in the way that passions and embodiment affect the individual; in other words, there are biographical interests, but explained through psychological, moral, and intellectual concepts. The use of metaphors bridges the moral and philosophical interests of the early moral ascetical theorists and the literary structure of the biography of later writers. From the asceticism of *Authoritative Teaching* asceticism may be seen to develop more intensely into biography (as in Peregrinus, Apollonius, and even the Christian Antony of Egypt)

42. Ibid., 331.
43. Ibid., 330.
44. Ibid., 331 and Francis, *Subversive Virtue*, 1–19.

and into the great ascetical systems of the later third and early fourth centuries (Iamblichus, Proclus, and the Christian Cappadocian fathers). The ascetical tradition found in the *Authoritative Teaching* suggests that it was composed sometime between Lucian and Diogenes Laertius, that is, sometime between 150 and 250 C.E., during a shift in interest from ethical and philosophical theory to the role and function of asceticism in personal psychology and formation.

This study had two goals: first to explain the ascetical system of the Nag Hammadi treatise; and second to locate this treatise within the context of Roman asceticism. Roman asceticism, eclipsed as it has been in the West by Christian asceticism, has a long and vital history that promotes practices of theological and philosophical values and virtues. By the end of the Roman period, this asceticism has had wide influence in every religious system. The *Authoritative Teaching* is an example of an author who engages with the Roman ascetical tradition and who begins to analyze the psychological and social implications of earlier writers. It is perhaps this experimentation with the psychology of living in the habituated and deadening social environment that attracted the Christian ascetics to this treatise: the Roman ascetical psychology resonated with the Christian monastic experience of the world. So the monks preserved the *Authoritative Teaching* as part of their secular literature that furthered their ascetical agenda.

CHAPTER 13

Musonius Rufus and Roman Ascetical Theory

FOR GENERATIONS, ASCETICISM HAS BEEN A CENTRAL INTEREST FOR scholars in the study of religion. In more recent years, however, as inter-disciplinary studies have brought together often divergent disciplines,[1] asceticism has emerged as a significant topic in the study both of religion and of philosophy in antiquity, especially in Late Antiquity.[2] The study of religion, history of philosophy, and classics converge particularly well for studying the history of Western asceticism. This essay explores the inter-section of those interests by exploring the ascetical theory of the Roman philosopher Musonius Rufus.

Musonius Rufus (ca. 30–102 C.E.), born in Volsinii, was an Etruscan by birth and an *eques* by status. His influence as a philosopher, however, emerged from his teaching and political involvement in Rome. Cora Lutz, an English translator of Musonius's treatises, maintained that "he was at the height of his influence in the time of Nero," while his politi-cal interactions included banishment by Nero, involvement in political activity during the reign of Vespasian, who also banished him, and rein-statement by Titus. His intellectual influence in the imperial period and following extended far: among others he influenced Pliny, Artemidorus, and Clement of Alexandria; and he taught the influential philosophers

1. This is best shown by the international conference on asceticism sponsored by Union Theological Seminary in New York City and Saint Louis University, which brought together classicists, philosophers, historians of religions, church historians, pa-trologists, anthropologists and sociologists. The papers of this conference were published in Wimbush and Valantasis, *Asceticism*.

2. There is a vast bibliography for asceticism in Late Antiquity. See especially Brown, *Body and Society*; Cameron, *Christianity and the Rhetoric of Empire*; Clark, "Women and Asceticism in Late Antiquity," 46–48; and idem, *Women in Late Antiquity*.

Dio Chrysostom and Epictetus.[3] Both in antiquity and in modern times, Musonius has been characterized as the Roman Socrates.[4] He is generally acknowledged as an important philosopher of the imperial Stoa.[5]

Musonius is the first Western author from whom we have a recorded discourse on asceticism.[6] Granted, the concept of ascetical formation, verbally designated by the Greek words *meletaō*, *gymnazō* and *askeō* and their cognates,[7] was part of the philosophical tradition prior to Musonius, and many earlier philosophers spoke of ascetical activity as part of philosophical and civic life, some of whom may even have written treatises on asceticism.[8] From the perspective of religious studies, the life and teachings of the Cynics from their founding through Late Antiquity provides an important witness to this prolonged interest and orientation toward asceticism.[9] Additionally, the therapeutic moral literature of the

3. This biographical information is based on Lutz, *Musonius Rufus,* 13–20, quotation on 14. Lutz provides all the documentation for Musonius's biography and influence. See also Houser, " Philosophy of Musonius Rufus," 1–11, Wiens; "Musonius Rufus and Genuine Education," 1–16 and von Fritz, "Musonius," 894.

4. Lutz, *Musonius Rufus,* 3–4 cites the sources and discusses the comparison. Jagu, *Musonius Rufus Entretiens et Fragments* provides an overview of his life and thought with a French translation of the discourses; for an Italian introduction, overview of life and thought, and translation of the discourses, see Guidotti, *Gaio Rufo Musonio e lo Stoicismo Romano.*

5. Musonius's Stoic credentials are difficult to establish. Houser, "Philosophy of Musonius Rufus," 12–48 documents Musonius's philosophical connections with known Stoics. Musonius's emphasis on practice resembles Cynicism. My argument is that the question is not whether Musonius was Cynic or Stoic, but that he, like both Cynicism and Stoicism, turns toward asceticism as a primary modality and concern of philosophy. For further discussion, see the conclusions below.

6. Musonius did not leave any of his own writings. I accept the reliability of the textual witnesses to his diatribes as edited by Hense, *Musonius Rufus Reliquae* and revised by Lutz, *Musonius Rufus.* On the question of the reliability of the texts, see Lutz, *Musonius Rufus,* 6–13; Houser, "Philosophy of Musonius Rufus," 2–7; Wiens, "Musonius Rufus," 1–18.

7. See Dressler, *Usage of ΑΣΚΕΩ and its Cognates.*

8. See Swain, "Hellenic Origins of Christian Asceticism"; also the section on pagan asceticism by Olphe-Galliard in the *Dictionnaire de Spiritualité* s.v. "Ascèse, Ascétism."

9. The best collection of essays on Cynicism that spans the whole history is that of Branham and Goulet-Cazé, *Cynics.* See also Goulet-Cazé, *L'Ascése Cynique* and her "Cynism á l'époque impériale." Another important collection of essays is Goulet-Cazé and Goulet, *Cynisme Ancien et ses Prolongements.* The history of Cynicism may be consulted (though with care) in the now classic Dudley, *History of Cynicism,* as well as the more recent Navia, *Classical Cynicism.*

Hellenistic and Roman period, read with ascetical theory in mind, points toward the pervasive nature of the ascetical question.[10] But none of these writings on the theory of asceticism has survived from a period earlier than Musonius.

The first tangible articulation of an ascetical theory[11] emerges from the summaries written by Lucius, a student or follower of Musonius Rufus.[12] From Musonius and his student Epictetus, as James Francis demonstrates, Roman asceticism flourishes in the second century C.E.[13] The most influential form of Roman ascetical theory[14] develops during the third and fourth centuries in the work of Plotinus, Porphyry, Iamblichus, and Proclus.[15]

10. Nussbaum, in *Therapy of Desire,* explores Hellenistic ethics and underscores the performative dimension of ethics, but nowhere refers to asceticism. Her references to Musonius are scant. But see Houser, "Philosophy of Musonius Rufus," 12–48.

11. It is possible to document a corpus of theoretical treatments of asceticism in western philosophy and religion beginning with the first century C.E. We know of two treatises from the Roman imperial period: Discourse VI of Musonius Rufus and Discourse XII of Epictetus. These treatises inaugurate a very long literary tradition of works developing ascetical theory that gathers up all the major religions of the Greco-Roman period and Late Antiquity and that include such significant figures as Clement of Alexandria, Plotinus, Iamblichus, Porphyry, Proclus, the Cappadocians Basil and Gregory of Nyssa, Evagrius of Pontus, John Cassian, and John Climacus, among many others. There is a wide diversity of sources. Among the most helpful, see Clark, *Origenist Controversy;* Elm, '*Virgins of God*'; Harpham, *Ascetic Imperative;* Rousseau, *Ascetics, Authority, and the Church;* Rousselle, *Porneia.* For sources and texts, see Wimbush, *Ascetic Behavior in Greco-Roman Antiquity.*

12. For a general overview of Musonius's asceticism from a religious studies perspective see Shaw, *Burden of the Flesh,* 33–37.

13. Francis, *Subversive Virtue.*

14. Parallel to the development of ascetical theory stands various other genres of literature that apply ascetical theory without discussing the theory itself. These applied ascetical writers include Marcus Aurelius (see Francis, *Subversive Virtue,* 21–52; Hadot, *Inner Citadel,* 183–231); Philo of Alexandria (See Harrison, "Allegorization of Gender," 520–34; and more peripherally, Satlow, "Shame and Sex," 535–43); Lucian's *Peregrinus* (See Francis, *Subversive Virtue,* 53–81); the *Sententiae* of Sextus (See Chadwick, *Sentences of Sextus,* 97–106); and the sayings collection in the *Gospel of Thomas* (see chapter 9, pp. 185–211; "Is the Gospel of Thomas Ascetical?); perhaps the gospels of the New Testament (see Saldarini, "Asceticism and the Gospel of Matthew," 11–27; Tolbert, "Asceticism and Mark's Gospel," 29–48; Garrett, "Beloved Physician of the Soul?," 71–96; Rensberger, "Asceticism and the Gospel of John," 127–48); the apocryphal acts of the New Testament (see Cooper, *Virgin and the Bride,* 20–67); as well as the biographies of Diogenes Laertius (see, e.g., Goulet-Cazé, *L'Ascèse Cynique* among many other texts).

15. See Meredith, "Asceticism—Christian and Greek," 313–32; and on the Platonist

Although Musonius provides the earliest extant ascetical theory, few scholars have noticed, explored, or explained his theory in relationship to his philosophy. A. C. van Geytenbeek's *Musonius and Greek Diatribe*, for example, reviews the major doctrines of Musonian ethics and philosophy and intends to locate Musonius's teaching in the context of the diatribe, the popular philosophy of the Hellenistic and Roman period. A chapter entitled "The Problems of Asceticism"[16] discusses Musonius's teaching with regard to the regulation of food, clothing, footwear, household living conditions, furniture, and the personal hygiene of the philosopher without discussing Discourse VI, which is entitled "On Asceticism." Van Geytenbeek treats Discourse VI primarily under the rubric of "Practical education to virtue" where *askesis* relates principally to the practice and enactment of ethical principles.[17] Van Geytenbeek rejected Musonius's own categorization and systematization in exploring asceticism and analyzed only the applied categories of Musonius's asceticism. Two unpublished dissertations display the same tendency. Delbert Wiens's 1970 dissertation, "Musonius Rufus and Genuine Education" treats asceticism as part of the education of adults as distinct from the education of children. Joseph Houser's 1997 dissertation, "The Philosophy of Musonius Rufus: A Study of Applied Ethics in the Late Stoa," also explores tantalizingly "applied ethics" and approaches Musonius's philosophy from its pervasive practical application. While valuing Musonius's applicability and even his theory of *askesis*, Houser never expressly studies Musonius's practicality as part of the larger philosophical and theological discourse about asceticism. For Houser Musonius's practicality remains an expression of a philosophical disposition rather than as a reformulation of philosophy itself towards ascetical theory and practice.[18] Indeed asceticism in the classical period was a function of education at least beginning with Aristotle, but it cannot be assumed that such an educational formation was the only application of asceticism particularly among philosophers exploring the moral life. Especially when Musonius addresses the question of ascetical theory directly, that ascetical theory must be taken

---

traditions, see Dillon, "Rejecting the Body," 80–87 and Milhaven, "Asceticism and the Moral Good," 375–94.

16. van Geytenbeek, *Musonius*, 96–123.

17. Ibid., 40–50.

18. A similar academic treatment regarding Epictetus occurs in Hijmans, *ΑΣΚΗΣΙΣ*.

seriously as central to a description and analysis of his asceticism, and that ascetical theory ought to be integrated into an understanding of the author's philosophy and ethics. This has not been the case with those studying Musonius's asceticism.

The evidence for Musonius's ascetical theory is very strong.[19] Lucius, Musonius's student, transmits the teaching of his teacher by summarizing teaching that he heard from Musonius over a period of time.[20] Discourse VI is presented as a set of arguments reconstructed by Lucius about a subject upon which Musonius frequently spoke: "He always vigorously urged his students toward asceticism using arguments such as these."[21] This introductory statement makes two important points. First, asceticism was central to Musonius's teaching. Second, the arguments presented in Discourse VI, therefore, are summary arguments, not a recording of an argument as Musonius made it. Musonius presented the case for asceticism to his students frequently and consistently using a variety of arguments.

Musonius, however, has remained a peripheral figure to the history of western asceticism. By explicating Musonius's theory of asceticism, this essay will attempt to locate Musonius as part of the mainstream of Greco-Roman and Late Antique Roman and Christian ascetical authors. This essay develops a four-part argument. First, I will argue that Musonius Rufus's ascetical theory begins in a particular understanding of the human condition and its attendant debilitation by negative socialization. Second, within the context of the bad habits inculcated by socialization, Musonius advances the cardinal virtues as the goal of ascetical effort, constructing in the process dual subjectivities, a rejected one that remains in the state of negative socialization and an embraced one that strives to understand and to practice the virtues. Third, in this context Musonius's two systems of asceticism, one for the soul and body together and one for the mind alone, give substance and direction to the effort to practice

19. Francis, *Subversive Virtue*, 11–19 provides a general and helpful introduction to Musonius's and Epictetus's ascetical teaching.

20. See Lutz, *Musonius Rufus*, 8–13 for a description of the two sources (Lucius and Pollio) for summaries of Musonius's teaching.

21. This is my translation. Unless otherwise noted, I use the text and translation of Lutz, *Musonius Rufus* and I identify each passage according to the page and first line number in the Greek text. This quotation begins at page 52, line 8.

the virtues. Fourth, Musonius's ascetical theory will be connected to his philosophy and ethics.

PHILOSOPHICAL ANTHROPOLOGY AND NEGATIVE SOCIALIZATION

Musonius's ascetical teaching originates in his philosophical anthropology. Outside Discourse VI on asceticism, Musonius's anthropology revolves about two elements: an innate propensity for virtue and a correlative capacity for becoming like gods. In Discourse II, Lucius explains that Musonius argued that "All of us, he used to say, are so fashioned by nature that we can live our lives free from error and nobly."[22] He underscores that this capacity to live well and blamelessly is for all and not simply for a few, and he attributes this to the fact that "Clearly, then, there is no explanation for this other than that the human being is born with an inclination toward virtue."[23] This is a very positive orientation toward the human condition and its innate inclination toward virtue.

Musonius also argued that "it is necessary for us to become of one mind with God" [fragment XXXVIII])[24] with respect to human actions. This similarity of opinion with God (*sympsēphou toi theoi*) demands that humans accomplish that which is in their control and that they entrust the things outside their control to the benevolence of the cosmos. This high regard for human capacity again underscores Musonius's positive attitude toward human effort.

This positive construction of philosophical anthropology contrasts markedly, however, with the perspective on the human condition described in Discourse VI on asceticism. Here Musonius's ascetical theory problematizes human activity and capacity in order precisely to articulate a basis for ascetical activity.[25] Musonius's anthropology in this discourse on ascetical theory has three elements. The first is a rather benign observation that human beings consist of a composite (*ti suntheton*) of both

22. Lutz, *Musonius Rufus*, 36, line 16.

23. Ibid., 38, line 1.

24. Ibid., 136, line 4 (my translation).

25. Houser, "Philosophy of Musonius Rufus," 12–48 discusses the medical analogy and therapeutic model in relationship to Stoic teaching. My perspective here is different, but not contrary to Houser's.

soul and body,[26] each of which must be addressed fully in any ascetical activity. Musonius will use these constituent elements of human existence as the basis for developing two distinct types of ascetical systems (this will be taken up more fully later). Musonius argues that the ascetic must attend to both (*anangke ton askounta amphoin epimeleisthai*),[27] without neglecting or denigrating either part. This anthropology remains consistent with the very positive view of the human's capacity to incline toward virtue and the human's ability to cooperate with the divine mind.

The positive perspective on anthropology ends there, however, because the next two elements of Musonius's ascetical anthropology in Discourse VI take a decidedly negative turn. Musonius contrasts the necessity for training in philosophy with medical and other training:

> And moreover such practical exercise is the more important for the student of philosophy than for the student of medicine or any similar art, the more philosophy claims to be a greater and more difficult discipline than any other study. The reason for this is that men who enter the other professions have not had their souls corrupted beforehand and have not learned the opposite of what they are going to be taught, but the ones who start out to study philosophy have been born and reared in an environment filled with corruption and evil, and therefore turn to virtue in such a state that they need a longer and more thorough training.[28]

Musonius argued that the social and political environment corrupts the soul. This corruption does not impede those who pursue training in medicine and other practical arts, but has a debilitating effect on those pursuing philosophy because this environment in fact teaches the opposite of the virtues pursued by the philosopher. Doctors and musicians may learn their arts without reference to this depravity, but this environmental depravity forces the philosopher to pursue virtue with vigorous ascetical training. This environmental depravity functions as the springboard to asceticism, the starting point for the pursuit of virtue.

The third element of Musonius's ascetical theory builds upon this theory of environmental depravity:

26. Lutz, *Musonius Rufus*, 54, line 4.
27. Ibid.
28. Ibid., 52, line 23.

> It is true that all of us who have participated in philosophic discussion have heard and apprehended that neither pain nor death nor poverty nor anything else which is free from wrong is an evil, and again that wealth, life, pleasure, or anything else which does not partake of virtue is not a good. And yet, in spite of understanding this, because of the depravity which has been implanted in us straight from childhood and because of evil habits engendered by this depravity, when hardship comes we think an evil has come upon us, and when pleasure comes our way we think that a good has befallen us; we dread death as the most extreme misfortune; we cling to life as the greatest blessing, and when we give away money we grieve as if we were injured, but upon receiving it we rejoice as if a benefit had been conferred.[29]

Musonius presented this depravity as implanted from youth onward. Depravity comes through socializing, not through the ontology of the human condition (an ontology described in neutral, if not positive terms in other discourses as discussed above). Negative socialization hardens into bad habits that impede philosophical progress by habitually interpreting hardship as evil, pleasure as good, death as misfortune, life as a blessing, monetary benefaction as loss, and monetary gifts as gain. Musonius summarized this habituation to false thinking succinctly: "Similarly with the majority of other things, we do not meet circumstances in accordance with right principles, but rather we follow wretched habit."[30] These habitual responses to the impulses of daily life delude and degrade human reactions by impeding the principled response required by philosophy. Habit, precisely as recrudescent evil socialization, puts a barrier between right thinking and response and the true virtue of the philosopher. The proper philosophical response to this situation is the philosophical development of proper habits:

> Since, then, I repeat, all this is the case, the person who is in training must strive (*dei ton askounta zētein*) to habituate himself not to love pleasure, not to avoid hardship, not to be infatuated with living, not to fear death, and in the case of goods or money not to place receiving above giving.[31]

29. Ibid., 54, line 30.
30. Ibid., 56, line 5.
31. Ibid., line 7.

The contrary ascetical discipline, oriented toward indifference to pleasure, endurance of hardship, honesty about living, bravery with respect to death, and giving money rather than receiving it, establishes the values of the true philosopher.[32]

In general, Musonius's anthropology remained positive. Human beings consist of a composite of soul and body that inclines toward virtue and may agree with the mind of God. Only when the issue turned to asceticism did Musonius introduce the negativity of destructive socialization and evil habits. Without this evil against which humans struggle there can exist no correlative good for humans to develop. His theory needed the negative habituation as a platform for positive philosophical effort. Musonius's positive articulations about human ontology and potentiality set the goal for ascetic practice: to acquire virtue and to become god-like despite the habits instilled by society that impede those goals.

VIRTUES AS THE GOALS OF ASCETICAL EFFORT

Musonius's ascetical system promulgates the four cardinal virtues as goals: the good person must display temperance, justice, courage, and prudence. He presents these virtues not as abstractions, but as fully embodied practices.[33] Of temperance, for example, he writes:

> How, indeed, could a person immediately become temperate if he
> only knew that one must not be overcome by pleasure, but was
> quite unpracticed in withstanding pleasure.[34]

The practices associated with a particular virtue give the virtue substance and authenticity. Justice requires not only knowing what is fair, but practicing to avoid selfishness and greed; courage requires not only knowing not to fear, but positively practicing courage in the face of fearful things; prudence does not simply list what is good and bad, but must also practice scorn for what appears on the surface to be good. The goal of the good life revolves about the practices associated to each of the four cardinal virtues. Musonius summarized his perspective: "Therefore upon the learning of the lessons appropriate to each and every excellence

32. Wiens, "Musonius Rufus," 38–46 explicates well the Musonian concept of *ethos*.
33. See Houser, "Philosophy of Musonius Rufus," 83–93.
34. Lutz, *Musonius Rufus*, 52, line 15.

(*arêtê*), practical training (*askesis*) must follow invariably."[35] Musonius yoked virtue to ascetical training. These ascetical practices of virtue, however, require special toil (*ponos*)[36] precisely because people have been socialized and habituated in an opposite direction from birth, a depravity implanted early and seriously impeding progress.

Musonius argued that the theory of virtues and their practice mutually develop the person. Like musicians and doctors, theory must be performed: doctors and musicians "not only must master the theoretical side of their respective arts but must also train themselves to act according to their principles."[37] It is not the specific vocation of philosopher who must practice the theory of virtues, but any person who would become good (*ton esomenon agathon andra*).[38] For anyone who seeks the good life and who desires to become good, that person must know both the theory and the practice of virtue. They must be trained in virtue to perform their skills as admirably as a good doctor and an accomplished musician. The person striving toward becoming good must display and perform the virtues in their daily lives. Musonius argued that "Virtue is not simply theoretical knowledge, but it is practical application as well, just like the arts of medicine and music."[39] The analogy with other arts implies that the acquisition of virtue is also an art. Not only is the acquisition of virtue a performance, like the offering of a musician or the therapy of a doctor, but also the end result is a work of art, a fabrication of an artifact of the good person.[40] The virtuous art produces a person who displays the theory of virtues in the events of daily living, the finished product of an artistic endeavor of creation. The following summary presents this argument succinctly:

> Therefore, as the physician and the musician not only must master the theoretical side of their respective arts but must also train themselves to act according to their principles, so a man who wishes to become good (*ton esomenon agathon andra*) not only must be thoroughly familiar (*gymnazesthai*) with the precepts which

35. Ibid., line 24.
36. This is discussed explicitly in Musonius's Discourse VII.
37. Lutz, *Musonius Rufus,* 52, line 10.
38. Ibid., line 12.
39. Ibid., line 8.
40. See Gleason, *Making Men.*

are conducive to virtue but must also be earnest (*philotimōs*) and
zealous (*philoponōs*) in applying (*gymazesthai*) these principles.[41]

The acquisition of virtue stands as a goal toward which humans may apply themselves energetically. The achievement of the goal will refashion
and recreate the person fully, making them not only an artisan but also
an artifact of virtue as well.

In Musonius's theory two distinct subjectivities may be understood
to function for each person: the first person is that one into whom depravity has been implanted from youth onwards; the second person is the
one who aims toward becoming good and who becomes good through
practice of the virtues. These subjective options are implicit in his treatment of the human condition and the role of the virtues. The second
person, the one who strives for the good, receives deliberate training in
rejecting the habits formed from childhood onward—negative habits
that inhibited the ability to understand the virtues and to perform them
accordingly. The person striving toward living the virtuous life rejects
the normatively socialized person. The rejection of the socially received
subjectivity forms the foundation for the construction of the ascetically
virtuous subjectivity. The struggle for the ascetic revolves about the construction of an alternative subjectivity oriented toward the understanding and performance of virtues.[42]

MUSONIUS'S TWO INTERRELATED ASCETICAL SYSTEMS

Musonius presents two interrelated systems of asceticism[43] to assist the
seeker in understanding the steps toward the construction of this alternative and preferred subjectivity: "Now there are two kinds of training, one
which is appropriate for the soul alone, and the other which is common
to both soul and body."[44] Musonius describes the asceticism common to
both soul and body:

> We use the training (*askēsis*) common to both when we discipline
> ourselves (*synethizomenōn hemōn*) to cold, heat, thirst, hunger,

41. Lutz, *Musonius Rufus*, 52, line 10.

42. The theory undergirding this reading of Musonius's asceticism comes from my
essay "Constructions of Power in Asceticism." See chapter 2, pp. 14–59.

43. Francis, *Subversive Virtue*, 12–13; Shaw, *Burden of the Flesh*, 34–35; Wiens,
"Musonius Rufus," 73–85.

44. Lutz, *Musonius Rufus*, 54, line 10.

> meagre rations, hard beds, avoidance of pleasures, and patience
> under suffering. For by these things and others like them the
> body is strengthened and becomes capable of enduring hardship,
> sturdy and ready for any task; the soul too is strengthened since
> it is trained for courage by patience under hardship and for self-
> control by abstinence from pleasures.[45]

Musonius based the ascetical system for both body and soul upon the accommodation and endurance of physical hardship. By training the body
to endure a variety of negative physical circumstances, the ascetic develops physical strength while at the same time training the soul to manifest
two of the four primary virtues: courage and self-control.

There is no suggestion here of denigration or rejection of the body.[46]
Nor is there any sense that bodily practices are secondary to spiritual
practices. The focus on the performance of specific acts of endurance
allows Musonius to integrate body and soul in one common ascetical
formation that benefits the whole person. In other words, the body-soul
distinction reiterates the distinction between theory of virtue and the
practice of virtue discussed earlier: the theory only has validity when it
is put into practice, so that the practice, the physical actions, perfect and
complete the theoretical formulation.

The second ascetical system engages the mind and adapts practices
to intellectual discernment:

> Training which is peculiar to the soul consists first of all in see-
> ing that the proofs pertaining to apparent goods as not being real
> goods are always ready at hand and likewise those pertaining to
> apparent evils as not being real evils, and in learning to recognize
> the things which are truly good and in becoming accustomed to
> distinguish them from what are not truly good. In the next place
> it consists of practice in not avoiding any of the things which only
> seem evil, and in not pursuing any of the things which only seem
> good; in shunning by every means those which are truly evil and
> in pursuing by every means those which are truly good.[47]

The second ascetical system describes a set of intellectual practices correlative and parallel to the physical practices of the asceticism appropri-

45. Ibid., line 11.

46. Francis, *Subversive Virtue*, 12–13.

47. Lutz, *Musonius Rufus*, 54, line 18.

ate to the body and the soul. These intellectual practices strive to exercise the mind in right judgment and to lead the person to good living in a fully integrated system. This second ascetical system revolves about three steps.

The first step is insuring that proofs are ready at hand.[48] The proofs, presumably drawn from Musonius's school lessons, indicate that apparent goods are not really good and apparent evils are not necessarily evil. The proofs thereby undercut the received reality that depends upon appearances and they probe further to establish what is indeed good and evil within the system that Musonius propounds. This step hinges on mastering the principles that undercut appearances and having them available for easy use. These appearances in all likelihood reproduce the depraved reality of the wider culture that impedes philosophic pursuit of the good and that result in deadening habits.

The second step follows more explicitly on the first. In addition to the proofs, the ascetic must recognize and distinguish what is truly good, while at the same time developing a familiarity and comfort with the understanding that follows from that recognition and distinction. The second step, then, consciously redefines the good and establishes the redefined goods as patterns of response in daily circumstances. It is not only that the ascetic must master the classroom understanding, but that the ascetic must also learn personally to understand and distinguish the truly good things. This step describes a process of accommodation to the redefined and re-articulated concept of the good central to the development of a subjectivity oriented toward the development of virtue.

The third step, keeping to Musonius's emphasis on the full integration of theory and practice, advocates the practice of acting on the basis of the newly redefined reality. Here the ascetic practices the refusal to act on the wider culture's wrongly conceived and false fantasy of reality of the good and evil. Positively put, the ascetic embraces the pursuit of a good and the avoidance of evil articulated in the reality reconstructed away from the deadening habits of action and thought promulgated in the wider culture.

It is possible now in summary to describe Musonius's system from all the parts that have been explored. Musonius developed a fully articu-

---

48. On the role of arguments and proofs in the Stoic context, see Houser, "Philosophy of Musonius Rufus," 93–96.

lated ascetical theory that integrates every facet of human existence—the personal and the social, as well as the intellectual and the physical. His ascetical system, the integrated system of theory and practice, recognizes that social habituation ruins an otherwise healthy human inclination toward the development of virtue and the conforming of the mind to the divine. Asceticism seeks to reverse this debilitating social habituation by the intentional pursuit of virtues. This reversal requires two strategies of reconstruction. The first encompasses the redefinition of what is good and what is evil away from their socially received definitions and the construction of what is truly good and truly evil based on an understanding of the virtues. The second strategy involves the reconstruction of reality that follows from this redefinition of good and evil so that the person learns to live naturally and habitually in a world that at once deviates from the surrounding received and common social world and manifests the newly articulated morals and values. The ascetic must learn not only to redefine good and evil, but to live a life based on this redefinition and rehabituation. The strategies of reconstruction provide the foundation for the practice of what has been theoretically presented. The center of this ascetical system remains the fabrication of the truly good person as an artifact, an embodiment, of virtue. The reality of the good person's life will be known to exhibit the redefined understanding of the world based upon the pursuit of truly good things and the avoidance of evil things. In short, the lived religion of the person will display the ethical, spiritual, and intellectual understanding of the person. Two related kinds of ascetical programs lead to the development of this fabricated personality: the intellectual formation of the soul and the ethical (or practical) formation of the soul and the body together. The person, a composite of soul and body in this system, receives complete transformation of mind and body in concrete experiences both mental and physical. This ascetical system does not rest on a bifurcation of physical and spiritual, but upon their mingling in the life of the person. Through this complete ascetical system, the problem that arose for the person through debilitating habituation is resolved: by dual ascetical work on soul and body, and on the soul, the person is freed again to attain the virtuous life that communicates the mind of God.

ASCETICISM IN MUSONIUS'S PHILOSOPHY

Musonius's ascetical system does not diverge from his philosophical agenda. His ascetical system in fact explains much about what has been recorded about his thought and his concerns. Van Geytenbeek's analysis of Musonius's specific practices makes sense only in relationship to this articulated ascetical system. The ultimate goal in Musonius's system includes the regulation of food, clothing, footwear, living conditions, furniture, and personal hygiene, not as separate activities unrelated to one another, but as practical elements displaying, or embodying, particular virtues. These practices, both physical and intellectual, become ascetical for Musonius precisely because they become arenas for the struggle against received socialization and toward the attainment of virtue in the practice of everyday living. Divorced of the system, these practices seem quaint and common, but aligned with the ascetical system they become the concrete places where reality is reconstructed and where the person gains mastery of a new self.

These seemingly unrelated topics such as food and clothing are central, not peripheral, elements of his ascetical system. Musonius's system expands the conceptual mold of ascetical concerns to include a wide variety of practices not normally associated with asceticism by modern scholars. Here we can include also the following as ascetic disciplines: exile (Discourse IX), freedom from prosecuting others (Discourse X), farming (Discourse XI), disobedience (Discourse CVI), marriage (Discourses XII and XIII A and B),[49] and the education of women (Discourse III).[50] Musonius purposefully connects theory and practice in every domain of human existence in which humans might cultivate the life of virtue. For Musonius, every human activity, not just a select few, holds the potential for ascetic endeavor.

An analysis of a one of these ascetical disciplines according to Musonius's own system will illustrate its ascetical modality and the way Musonius's system operates. Discourse IX[51] takes up the question of

49. Ibid., 135–36.

50. Ibid., 158–96. Here Houser explores this fully in the context of Roman moralizing.

51. Lutz, *Musonius Rufus*, 68–77. Lutz argues that this treatise may in fact reflect an actual letter by Musonius and may reflect his own thinking and writing. Her opinion has received little support; see Houser, "Philosophy of Musonius Rufus," 2–3 and note 11. I find the treatise a curious mixture of direct address (see the summary argument

whether or not exile is an evil. After a brief argument that a person in exile still has access to the physical world, since exile "does not in any way deprive us of water, earth, air, or the sun and the other planets, or indeed even the society of other people,"[52] the treatise presents the simple principle to be applied readily to exile:

> For such [an exiled person] does not value or despise any place as the cause of his happiness or unhappiness, but he makes the whole matter depend upon himself and considers himself a citizen of the city of God which is made up of humans and gods.[53]

This is, of course, a familiar Stoic teaching, which is not peculiar to Musonius, but he employs it as the basis for analyzing a life situation. There follows a series of propositions that explores what is really good (or only apparently good) and what is really bad (or only apparently bad): that one may acquire virtue in any place; that exile provides the leisure for discerning and practicing the good; that (contrary to wider opinion) exile may be a blessing to some, as with Diogenes for personal transformation; that exile provides an opportunity to live simply and healthily and that it "helps rather than hinders health both of body and of spirit";[54] that virtuous people thrive wherever they are; that some exiled people have even acquired large fortunes, as with Odysseus and Themistocles; that there is no opprobrium involved because the errors of the judicial system are well known; and finally, that any restriction of freedom of speech results not from exile but from the exiled person's fear of reprisal.[55] These propositions redefine the substance of good and evil, and they provide a new way of understanding exile, the world, and the opportunities presented. By engaging in the mental exercise, the ascetic comes to understand exile as an occasion of personal, social, and intellectual growth. The centrality of the virtues is made clear in this summary argument:

---

that follows) to the reader and Lucius's summary arguments. In agreement with Lutz, I suggest that an original letter may have served as the basis for the incorporation of other summary materials by Lucius.

52. Ibid., 68, line 6 (translation slightly revised).

53. Ibid., 68, line 19.

54. Ibid., 70, line 21.

55. I consider these summary arguments to be the product of Lucius's work that have been incorporated into Musonius's earlier and original letter.

The reflections which I employ for my own benefit so as not to be irked by exile, I should like to repeat to you. It seems to me that exile does not strip a person entirely, not even of the things which the average man calls good, as I have just shown. But if he is deprived of some or all of them, he is still not deprived of the things which are truly goods. Certainly the exile is not prevented from possessing courage and justice simply because he is banished, nor self-control, nor understanding, nor any of the other virtues which when present serve to bring honor and benefit to a man and show him to be praiseworthy and of good repute, but when absent, serve to cause him harm and dishonor and show him to be wicked and of ill repute. Since this is true, if you are that good man and have his virtues, exile will not harm or degrade you, because the virtues are present in you which are most able to help and to sustain you. But if you are bad, it is the evil that harms you and not exile; and the misery you feel in the exile is the product of evil, not of exile. It is from this you must hasten to secure release rather than from exile.[56]

Musonius develops a compelling argument that redefined the nature of reality with respect to apparent and real good and evil, while at the same time opening avenues for the exiled person to grow, develop, and become healthy of mind and body. The ascetical program has combined physical and intellectual labor into a comprehensive program for reform. For Musonius, exile is an ascetical practice.

Musonius presents a bold and consistent plan for transforming members of his society through rigorous ascetical activity, a personal transformation in direct conflict with the prevailing mores of the majority culture. It is not surprising that Musonius's project, and that of other philosophers of his day, sufficiently threatened the established order that they were at various time persecuted by emperors of Rome.[57] Their ascetical formation was understood as a subversive program.[58] Exile, banishment, and sometimes death were the cost of pursuing these ascetical aims.

56. Lutz, *Musonius Rufus*, 74, line 20. I consider this summary statement to be part of Musonius's original letter.

57. Harris, "Stoic and Cynic Under Vespasian," 105–14. More generally, see Brunt, "Stoicism and the Principate," 7–35.

58. This has been fully explored, and convincingly argued, by Houser, "Philosophy of Musonius Rufus," 53–96. He argues that both philosophy and the philosopher could be viewed as subversive.

CONCLUSIONS

From the perspective of a religious studies scholar, classicists and historians of philosophy have missed the heart of his philosophical agenda
by not addressing the ascetical dimension of his teaching. His ascetical
project, that is, forms not a peripheral, but a central part of his program and his life. By rejecting the traditional subjects of philosophical
discourse and teaching and by taking up asceticism as the center of his
philosophical program, Musonius placed ethical and religious practice in
the fore of philosophical activity. To be a philosopher meant to practice
and manifest philosophical articulated virtues. As Pierre Hadot describes
it, philosophy became a way of life.[59] The instrument of that philosophy,
however, was not the ethical tradition alone, not the theoretical study
of good and evil, but the ascetical formation of people capable of living
according to values and mores divergent from the normative culture and
expressive of an alternative world and its understanding. That new way of
life was thoroughly ascetical.

The existence in Rome of a philosopher with a fully articulated ascetical system generations before the so-called flowering of asceticism in Late
Antique Christianity demands a rewriting of the scholarly reconstruction
of the history of Western asceticism. Not only must that history begin in
Roman philosophical circles of the imperial era, but it must also begin to
explore the Roman philosophical interaction with Christian asceticism.
Musonius's ascetical theory, as well as his emphasis on asceticism in his
philosophy, shifts attention both earlier in time to the first century and
further West to Rome and the western Mediterranean basin.

Religious scholars also have much to learn from Musonius. His theory of asceticism was developed during the critical period during which
most New Testament literature was being written. His theory circulated
in Rome and the Mediterranean basin at the time of the writing of the
Gospel of Mark and was disseminated during the revisions of Mark produced by Matthew and Luke. His theory was in circulation during the
collection of the sayings of Jesus, a collection not unlike the collection
of the sayings of Musonius by his followers. The skeptical reception of
Musonius's project by those in authority possibly sheds light on the poor
reception of Pauline theology in incipient Christianity.

---

59. See Hadot, *Philosophy as a Way of Life*; this is a revision and expansion of *Exercices
Spirituels et Philosophie Antique*.

In the face of Musonius's ascetical project, scholars of early Christianity cannot seek to define asceticism by first looking to the fourth-century Christian ascetics and working backward in time,[60] but now they must look across to Roman and Jewish contemporaries of Christian writers to seek a different understanding of ascetical theory and practice in the first century.[61] The definition of asceticism, dependent as it has been on Late Antique models, must now shift to authors and projects of the imperial period as models and systems of asceticism that preceded and perhaps even produced the later and more familiar asceticism of Late Antique Romans, Jews, and Christians.[62] Above all, Musonius's ascetical project places in the center of scholarly attention the critical question of systems of formation in classical antiquity, the curious place where theory and practice meet to produce subjects empowered to live and to act in their own society either as a member of the dominant society or as members who withdraw from that dominant society to produce an alternative social grouping. All of this formative interest may not have begun with Musonius, but Musonius provides the first documented instance of a Roman ascetical project that has theological, philosophical, and certainly political implications then and now.

There is, however, more to say about the larger picture of religion and philosophy in the imperial period. It is difficult to know how to categorize Musonius Rufus in terms of the history of philosophy. His thought certainly resembles, and often develops from, Stoic philosophy. Yet his emphasis on practice seems to align him more with the Cynicism of the imperial period. The style of his teaching, the diatribe, was certainly common to both, so much so that it has been called by New Testament scholars, the Cynic-Stoic diatribe.[63] This attempt at categorization in known philo-

60. Shaw, *Burden of the Flesh*, 5–10 also argues that asceticism must be contextualized more widely.

61. There is serious resistance to looking at Roman asceticism as a model for early Christian practice; see, e.g., Tolbert, "Asceticism and Mark's Gospel," 29–48. Here Tolbert uses later Christian monastic asceticism as the model for interpreting the Gospel of Mark despite the existence of coeval Roman ascetical writings. A more interesting and engaging study of ancient Greek models of asceticism and their potential for interpreting early Christianity is displayed in the same volume by Patterson, "*Askesis* and the Early Jesus Tradition," 49–69.

62. For the most valuable exploration of these issues, including the question of cross-cultural ascetical studies, see Clark, "Ascetic Impulse in Religious Life," 505–10.

63. See the classic study by Bultmann, *Der Stil der Paulinischen Predigt und die*

sophical movements does not seem to account for the kind of thinking that begins to take place in the first century C.E. Among at least a few of these philosophers like Musonius Rufus, Epictetus, and Marcus Aurelius, the distinguishing characteristic seems to revolve about an interest and pursuit of ascetical activity as the heart of philosophy and religion. Such authors seem more appropriately to be identified with their asceticism than with specific philosophical schools. Musonius Rufus leads the way in this movement, providing both a complete ascetical system central to his philosophy and a set of applications of these principles in the daily life of his followers. This is precisely where Houser has correctly identified the heart of Musonius's philosophy.[64]

My argument goes further than Houser's to argue an ascetical orientation, not only in Musonius Rufus, but also in a variety of philosophical environments. For example, some scholars who study the early Christian interaction with Hellenistic and Roman religion and philosophy have argued that Jesus was a Cynic[65] and that Paul was a Stoic.[66] The Cynic-Stoic alignment of formative Christianity has been commonplace for over a century. All such arguments attempt to locate their principals in known philosophical categories based on reconstructions of real and distinct Stoicism and Cynicism in the imperial period. The definitions of Stoicism and Cynicism both include an orientation toward asceticism. Perhaps what is needed, and this follows from my argument about Musonius, is not a redefinition of the philosophical schools, but a recognition that asceticism emerged as a major factor in philosophical and religious life. It is precisely this turn to asceticism witnessed in Musonius Rufus that may also be detected in the emergence of Rabbinic Judaism, Pauline Jewish-Christianity, and formative Christianity. The list of ascetically oriented religious leaders and philosophical teachers gathers up many of the leading minds of the period. Musonius Rufus documents the emergence of this ascetical orientation and, through his influence, set the agenda for philosophers and theologians of generations to follow.

Kynisch-Stoische Diatribe and also Stowers, *Diatribe and Paul's Letter to the Romans.*

64. See Houser, "Philosophy of Musonius Rufus," 101–57.

65. See Downing, *Cynics and Christian Origins* and *Christ and the Cynics.*

66. There are many studies, including Engberg-Pedersen, *Paul and the Stoics.*

Bibliography

Airaksinen, Timo. "The Rhetoric of Domination." In *Rethinking Power*, edited by Thomas E. Wartenberg, 102–20. Albany: State University of New York Press, 1992.

Althusser, Louis. *Lenin and Philosophy and Other Essays*. Translated by Ben Brewster. New York: Monthly Review Press, 1971.

Althusser, Louis and Étienne Balibar. *Reading Capital*. Translated by Ben Brewster. London: NLB, 1970.

Apophthegmata Agion Pateron. Athens: Aster, 1970.

Attridge, Harold W. *First-Century Cynicism in the Epistles of Heraclitus*. HTS 29. Missoula, MT: Scholars, 1976.

Attridge, Harold W., and Elaine Pagels. "Introduction." In *NHLE*, edited by James M. Robinson. 3rd ed. San Francisco: Harper & Row, 1988.

Bachrach, Peter and Morton S. Baratz. "Decisions and Non-decisions: An Analytical Framework." *American Political Science Review* 57 (1963) 641–51.

———. "Two Faces of Power." *American Political Science Review* 56 (1962) 947–52.

Ball, Terence. "New Faces of Power." In *Rethinking Power*, edited by Thomas E. Wartenberg, 947–52. Albany: State University of New York Press, 1992.

Bammel, Ernst. "Rest and Rule." *VC* 23 (1969) 88–90.

Barns, J. W. B. "Greek and Coptic Papyri from the Covers of the Nag Hammdi Texts." In *Essays on the Nag Hammadi Codices in Honour of Pahor Labib*, edited by Martin Krause, 9–18. NHS 6. Leiden: Brill, 1975.

Basil, Saint. *St. Basil: The Letters, 1:6–25*. Translated by Roy J. Deferrari. LCL 190. Cambridge: Harvard University Press, 1972.

Bassler, Jouette M., editor. *Pauline Theology Volume I: Thessalonians, Philippians, Galatians, Philemon*. Minneapolis: Fortress, 1991.

Berger, Peter L., and Thomas Luckmann. *The Social Construction of Reality: A Treatise in the Sociology of Knowledge*. Garden City, NY: Doubleday, 1966.

Betz, Hans Dieter. *Galatians: A Commentary on Paul's Letter to the Churches in Galatia*. Hermeneia. Minneapolis: Fortress, 1979.

Bhabha, Homi K. *The Location of Culture*. London: Routledge, 1994.

Bianchi, Ugo, editor. *La Tradizione dell' Enkrateia: Motivazione Ontologiche e Protologiche, Atti del Colloquio Internazionale Milano, 20–23 aprile 1982*. Rome: Ateneo, 1985.

Biblia Patristica: Index des citations et allusions bibliques dans la litterature patristique. Vol. 3. Paris: Centre National de la Recherche scientific, 1980.

Bien, Peter. *Kazantzakis: Politics of the Spirit.* 2 vols. Princeton Modern Greek Studies. Princeton: Princeton University Press, 1989.

Boulding, Kenneth E. *Three Faces of Power.* Newbury Park, CA: Sage, 1989.

Bowersock, G. W. *Julian the Apostate.* Cambridge: Harvard University Press, 1978.

Boyarin Daniel. *A Radical Jew: Paul and the Politics of Identity.* Contraversions 1. Berkeley: University of California Press, 1994.

Brakke, David. *Athanasius and the Politics of Asceticism.* Oxford Early Christian Studies. Oxford: Clarendon, 1995.

Branham, R. Bracht, and Marie-Odile Goulet-Cazé, editors. *The Cynics: The Cynic Movement in Antiquity and Its Legacy.* Hellenistic Culture and Society 23. Berkeley: University of California Press, 1996.

Broek, R. van den. "The Authentikos Logos: A New Document of Christian Platonism." *VC* 33 (1979) 260–86.

Brown, Peter. *The Body and Society: Men, Women, and Sexual Renunciation in Early Christianity.* New York: Columbia University Press, 1988.

———. *The Cult of the Saints: Its Rise and Function in Latin Christianity.* Chicago: University of Chicago Press, 1981.

Brunt, P. A. "Stoicism and the Principate." *Papers of the British School at Rome* 43 (1975) 7–35.

Buckley, Jorunn Jacobsen. "A Cult-mystery in the *Gospel of Philip*." *JBL* 99 (1980) 569–81.

———. *Female Fault and Fulfillment in Gnosticism.* Chapel Hill: University of North Carolina Press, 1986.

———. "An Interpretation of Logion 114 in *The Gospel of Thomas*." *NovT* 27 (1985) 245–72.

Bultmann, Rudolf. *Der Stil der Paulinischen Predigt und die Kynisch-Stoische Diatribe.* FRLANT 13. Göttingen: Vandenhoeck & Ruprecht, 1910. Reprinted, 1984.

Burkert, Walter. *Greek Religion.* Translated by John Raffan. Cambridge: Harvard University Press, 1985.

Butler, Judith. *Giving an Account of Oneself.* New York: Fordham University Press, 2005.

Callahan, Allan. "'No Rhyme or Reason': The Hidden Logia of the *Gospel of Thomas*." *HTR* 90 (1997) 411–26.

Cameron, Averil. *Christianity and the Rhetoric of Empire.* Sather Classical Lectures 55. Berkeley: University of California Press, 1990.

Cameron, Ron. "The *Gospel of Thomas* and Christian Origins." In *The Future of Early Christianity: Essays in Honor of Helmut Koester,* edited by Birger A. Pearson, 381–92. Minneapolis: Fortress, 1991.

Castelli, Elizabeth A. "Asceticism—Audience and Resistance." In *Asceticism,* edited by Vincent L. Wimbush and Richard Valantasis, 178–87. New York: Oxford University Press, 1995.

——. *Imitating Paul: A Discourse of Power.* Louisville: Westminster John Knox, 1991.

——. "Pseudo-Athanasius, *The Life and Activity of the Holy and Blessed Teacher Syncletica.*" In *Ascetic Behavior in Greco-Roman Antiquity: A Sourcebook,* edited by Vincent L. Wimbush, 265–311. SAC. Minneapolis: Fortress, 1990.

Chadwick, Henry. "The Ascetic Ideal in the History of the Church." In *Monks, Hermits and the Ascetic Tradition,* edited by W. J. Sheils, 1–23. Ecclesiastical History Society Papers. Oxford: Blackwell, 1985.

——. "The Domestication of Gnosis." In *The Rediscovery of Gnosis: Proceedings of the Conference at Yale, March 1978,* edited by Bentley Layton, 2 vols., 1:3–16 Leiden: Brill, 1980.

——.*The Sentences of Sextus: A Contribution to the History of Early Christian Ethics.* Texts and Studies 5. Cambridge: Cambridge University Press, 1959.

Chadwick, Henry, and John Ernest Leonard Oulton. *Alexandrian Christianity.* LCC. Philadelphia: Westminster, 1954.

Clark, Elizabeth A. "The Ascetic Impulse in Religious Life: A General Response." In *Asceticism,* edited by Vincent L. Wimbush and Richard Valantasis, 505–10. New York: Oxford University Press, 1995.

——. *Ascetic Piety and Women's Faith: Essays in Late Ancient Christianity.* Studies in Women and Religion 20. Lewiston, NY: Mellen, 1986.

——. "Devil's Gateway and Bride of Christ: Women in the Early Christian World." In *Ascetic Piety and Women's Faith: Essays on Late Ancient Christianity,* 23–94. Lewiston, NY: Mellen, 1986.

——. "Foucault, The Fathers, and Sex." *JAAR 56* (1988) 619–41.

——. "John Chrysostom and the Subintroductae." In *Ascetic Piety and Women's Faith: Essays on Late Ancient Christianity,* 265–90. Lewiston, NY: Mellen, 1986.

——. "New Perspectives on the Origenist Controversy: Human Embodiment and Ascetic Strategies." *CH* 59 (1990) 145–62.

——. *The Origenist Controversy: The Cultural Construction of an Early Christian Debate.* Princeton: Princeton University Press, 1992.

Clark, Gillian. "Women and Asceticism in Late Antiquity: The Refusal of Status and Gender." In *Asceticism,* edited by Vincent L. Wimbush and Richard Valantasis, 33–48. New York: Oxford University Press, 1995.

——. *Women in Late Antiquity: Pagan and Christian Lifestyles.* Oxford: Clarendon, 1993.

Climacus, John. *The Ladder of Divine Ascent.* Rev. ed. Translated by Holy Transfiguration Monastery, based on a translation by Archimandrite Lazarus Moore. Boston: Holy Transfiguration Monastery. 1978.

Cooper, Kate. *The Virgin and the Bride: Idealized Womanhood in Late Antiquity.* Cambridge: Harvard University Press, 1996.

Corrington, Gail Paterson. "Anorexia, Asceticism, and Autonomy: Self-Control as Liberation and Transcendence." *JFSR* 2 (1986) 51–61.

―――. "Philo, *On the Contemplative Life: Or, On the Suppliants* (The Fourth Book on the Virtues)." In *Ascetic Behavior in Greco-Roman Antiquity: A Sourcebook,* edited by Vincent L. Wimbush, 134–55. SAC. Minneapolis: Fortress, 1990.

Cullman, Oscar. "The Gospel of Thomas and the Problem of the Age of the Tradition Contained Therein." Translated by Balmer H. Kelley. *Int* 16 (1962) 418–38.

Dahl, Robert."The Concept of Power." In *Political Power: A Reader in Theory and Research*, edited by Roderick Bell, et al., 79–93. New York: Free Press, 1969.

―――. "A Critique of the Ruling Elite Model." In *Political Power: A Reader in Theory and Research*, edited by Roderick Bell et al., 36–41. New York: Free Press, 1969.

Davies, Stevan L. *The Gospel of Thomas and Christian Wisdom.* New York: Seabury, 1983.

Dechow, Jon F. *Dogma and Mysticism in Early Christianity: Epiphanius of Cyprus and the Legacy of Origen.* Patristic Monograph Series 13. Macon, GA: Mercer University Press, 1988.

De Conick, April D. "The Yoke Saying in the *Gospel of Thomas.*" *VC* 44 (1990) 280–94.

Desjardins, Michel. "Where Was the Gospel of Thomas Written?" *TJT* 8 (1992) 121–31.

Dillon, John M. "Rejecting the Body, Refining the Body: Some Remarks on the Development of Platonist Asceticism." In *Asceticism,* edited by Vincent L. Wimbush, and Richard Valantasis. 80–87. New York: Oxford University Press, 1995.

Dodds, E. R. *The Greeks and the Irrational.* Berkeley: University of California Press, 1951.

―――. *Pagan and Christian in an Age of Anxiety.* Cambridge: Cambridge University Press, 1965.

Doran, Robert. "A Complex of Parables: GTh 96–98." *NovT* 29 (1987) 347–52.

Downing, F. Gerald. *Christ and the Cynics: Jesus and Other Radical Preachers in First-Century Tradition.* Sheffield: JSOT Press, 1988.

―――. *Cynics and Christian Origins.* Edinburgh: T. & T. Clark, 1992.

Dressler, Hermigild. *The Usage of ΑΣΚΕΩ and its Cognates in Greek Documents to 100 A.D.* The Catholic University of America Patristic Series 73. Washington, DC: Catholic University of America Press, 1947.

Dudley, Donald R. *A History of Cynicism From Diogenes to the 6th Century A.D.* 1937. Reprinted, New York: Gordon, 1974.

Dunn, James D. G. "Echoes of Intra-Jewish Polemic in Paul's Letter to the Galatians." *JBL* 112 (1993) 459–77.

―――. "The Theology of Galatians: The Issue of Covenantal Nomism." In *Pauline Theology Volume I: Thessalonians, Philippians, Galatians, Philemon,* edited by Jouette M. Bassler, 125–46. Minneapolis, Fortress, 1991.

Elm, Susanna. *Virgins of God: The Making of Asceticism in Late Antiquity.* Oxford Classical Monographs. Oxford: Clarendon, 1994.

Engberg-Pedersen, Troels. *Paul and the Stoics.* Louisville: Westminster John Knox, 2000.

Fagan, Livingstone. "Mount Carmel: The Unseen Reality." Appendix B: "Intuition—the Emerging Soul." http://www.parascope.com/articles/1296/faganful.htm (accessed August 7, 2004).

Ferguson, Everett. *Backgrounds of Early Christianity*. Grand Rapids: Eerdmans, 1987.

Flood, Gavin. *The Ascetic Self: Subjectivity, Memory, and Tradition*. Cambridge: Cambridge University Press, 2004.

Foerster, Werner. "Daimōn." In *TDNT* 2 (1964) 1–20.

———, editor. "The Apocryphon of John." In *Gnosis: A Selection of Gnostic Texts*. Vol. 1. Oxford: Clarendon, 1972.

Foucault, Michel. "Afterward: The Subject and Power." In *Michel Foucault: Beyond Structuralism and Hermeneutics*, by Hubert L. Dreyfus and Paul Rabinow, 208–26. 2nd ed. Chicago: University of Chicago Press, 1983.

———. "The Ethic of Care for the Self as a Practice of Freedom: An Interview with Michel Foucault on January 20, 1984." Interview by Raúl Fornet-Betancourt, Helmut Becker, and Alfredo Gomez-Müller. Translated by J. D. Gauthier, SJ. In *The Final Foucault*, edited by James Bernauer and David Rassmussen, 1–20. Cambridge: MIT Press, 1994.

———. *The Hermeneutics of the Subject: Lectures at the Collége de France 1981–1982*. Edited by Frédéric Gros. Translated by Graham Burchell. New York: Picador, 2005.

———. *The History of Sexuality: An Introduction*. Vol. 1. Translated by Robert Hurley. New York: Vintage, 1980.

———. *The History of Sexuality: The Use of Pleasure*. Vol. 2. Translated by Robert Hurley. New York: Vintage, 1985.

———. *The History of Sexuality: Care of the Self*. Vol. 3. Translated by Robert Hurley. New York: Vintage, 1988.

———. "On the Genealogy of Ethics: An Overview of Work in Progress." In *The Foucault Reader*, edited by Paul Rabinow, 340–72. New York: Pantheon, 1984. First published in Michel Foucault: *Beyond Structuralism and Hermeneutics*, 2d ed., edited by Hubert L. Dreyfus and Paul Rabinow. Chicago: University of Chicago Press, 1983.

———. *The Order of Things: An Archaeology of the Human Sciences*. New York: Pantheon, 1970.

———. *Power/Knowledge: Selected Interviews and Other Writings 1972–1977*. Edited by Colin Gordon. Translated by Colin Gordon, Leo Marshall, John Mepham, and Kate Soper. New York: Pantheon, 1980.

Fowden, Garth. "The Pagan Holy Man in Late Antique Society." *JHS* 102 (1982) 33–59.

Fox, Robin Lane. *Pagans and Christians*. New York: Knopf, 1987.

Francis, James A. *Subversive Virtue: Asceticism and Authority in the Second-Century Pagan World*. University Park, PA: Pennsylvania State University Press, 1995.

Frend, W. H. C. "The Gospel of Thomas: Is Rehabilitation Possible?" *JTS* 18 (1967) 13–26.

———. *The Rise of Christianity*. Philadelphia: Fortress, 1984.

Fritz, K. von. "Musonius." In *RE* 15 (1973) 894.

Funk, Wolf-Peter. "Der verlorene Anfang des Authentikos Logos." *APF* 28 (1982) 59–65.

Furnish, Victor Paul. "Pauline Studies." In *The New Testament and Its Modern Interpreters*, edited by Eldon Jay Epp and George W. MacRae, 321–50. Philadelphia: Fortress, 1989.

———. "On Putting Paul in His Place." *JBL* 113 (1994) 3–17.

Garrett, Susan R. "Beloved Physician of the Soul? Luke as Advocate for Ascetic Practice." In *Asceticism and the New Testament*, edited by Leif E. Vaage and Vincent L. Wimbush, 71–96. New York: Routledge, 1999.

Gärtner, Bertil E. *The Theology of the Gospel of Thomas*. Translated by Eric J. Sharpe. New York: Harper, 1961.

Gasparro, Giulia Sfameni. "Asceticism and Anthropology: *Enkrateia* and 'Double Creation' in Early Christianity." In *Asceticism*, edited by Vincent L. Wimbush and Richard Valantasis, 127–46. New York: Oxford University Press, 1995.

Gaventa, Beverly. "The Singularity of the Gospel: A Reading of Galatians." In *Pauline Theology Volume I: Thessalonians, Philippians, Galatians, Philemon*, edited by Jouette M. Bassler 147–59. Minneapolis: Fortress, 1991.

Geertz, Clifford. *The Interpretation of Cultures*. New York: Basic Books, 1973.

Genet, Jean. *Our Lady of the Flowers*. Translated by Bernard Frechtman. New York: Grove, 1976.

Georgi, Dieter. *The Opponents of Paul in II Corinthians*. Philadelphia: Fortress. 1986.

Geytenbeek, A. C. Van. *Musonius Rufus and Greek Diatribe*. Rev. ed. Assen: Van Gorcum;, 1963.

Gleason, Maude. *Making Men: Sophists and Self-Representation in Ancient Rome*. Princeton: Princeton University Press, 1995.

Goehring, James E. *Ascetics, Society, and the Desert: Studies in Early Egyptian Monasticism*. SAC. Harrisburg, PA: Trinity, 1999.

———. "The Encroaching Desert: Literary Production and Ascetic Space in Early Christian Egypt." In *Ascetics, Society, and the Desert: Studies in Early-Egyptian Monasticism*, 73–88. SAC. Harrisburg, Pa: Trinity, 1999.

———. "New Frontiers in Pachomian Studies." In *Ascetics, Society, and the Desert: Studies in Egyptian Monasticism*, 162–86. SAC. Harrisburg, PA: Trinity, 1999.

———. "Theodore's Entry into the Pachomian Movement (Selections from the *Life of Pachomius*)." In *Ascetic Behavior in Greco-Roman Antiquity: A Sourcebook*, edited by Vincent L. Wimbush, 349–56. SAC. Minneapolis: Fortress, 1990.

Gordon, Colin. "Afterward." In *The History of Sexuality: An Introduction*, vol. 1. by Michel Foucault. Translated by Robert Hurley. 229–59. New York: Vintage, 1980.

Goulet-Cazé, Marie-Odile. *L'Ascése Cynique: Un commentaire de Diogène Laërce VI 70–71*. Histoire des Doctrines de l'Antiquité Classique 10. Paris: Librairie Philosophique J. Vrin, 1986.

———. "Le cynism à l'époque impériale." In *ANRW* II, 36.4: 2720–833.

———, and Richard Goulet, editors. *Le Cynisme Ancien et ses Prolongements: Actes du Colloque International du CNRS (Paris, 22–25 juillet 1991)*. Paris: Presses Universitaires de France, 1993.

Grant, Robert M. "The Mystery of Marriage in the *Gospel of Philip*." *VC* 15 (1961) 129–40.

———. editor. *Gnosticism*. New York: Harper & Row, 1961.

Griffith, Sidney. "Asceticism in the Church of Syria: The Hermeneutics of Early Syrian Monasticism." In *Asceticism,* edited by Vincent L. Wimbush and Richard Valantasis, 220–45. New York: Oxford University Press, 1995.

Grobel, Kendrick. "How Gnostic Is the Gospel of Thomas?" *NTS* 8 (1961–62) 367–73.

Guidotti, Sante. *Gaio Rufo Musonio e lo Stoicismo Romano*. Bolsena: Libreria Antonini, 1979.

Hadot, Pierre, *Exercices Spirituels et Philosophie Antique*. 2nd ed. Paris: Études Augustiniennes, 1987.

———. *The Inner Citadel: The* Meditations *of Marcus Aurelius*. Translated by Michael Chase. Cambridge: Harvard University Press, 1998.

———. *Philosophy as a Way of Life: Spiritual Exercises from Socrates to Foucault,* edited by Arnold I. Davidson. Translated by Michael Chase. Oxford: Blackwell Publishers, 1995.

Haraway, Donna. "The Biopolitics of Postmodern Bodies: Determinations of Self in Immune System Discourse." In *Differences: A Journal of Feminist Cultural Studies* 1 (1989) 3–43.

Hardman, O. *The Ideals of Asceticism: An Essay in the Comparative Study of Religion*. New York: Macmillan, 1924.

Harl, M. "A Propos des *Logia* de Jésus: Le sens du mot MONAXOS." *REG* 73 (1960) 464–74.

Harpham, Geoffrey Galt. *The Ascetic Imperative in Culture and Criticism*. Chicago: University of Chicago Press, 1987.

Harris, B. F. "Stoic and Cynic Under Vespasian." *Prudentia* 9 (1977) 105–14.

Harrison, Verna E. F. "The Allegorization of Gender: Plato and Philo on Spiritual Childbearing." In *Asceticism,* edited by Vincent L. Wimbush, and Richard Valantasis, 520–34. New York: Oxford University Press, 1995.

Hartsock, Nancy C. M. "Gender and Sexuality: Masculinity, Violence, and Domination." In *Rethinking Power,* edited by Thomas E. Wartenberg, 249–76. Albany: State University of New York Press, 1992.

Harvey, Paul J., Jr. "Jerome, *Life of Paul, The First Hermit*." In *Ascetic Behavior in Greco-Roman Antiquity: A Sourcebook,* edited by Vincent L. Wimbush, 357–69. SAC. Minneapolis: Fortress, 1990.

Harvey, Susan Ashbrook. *Asceticism and Society in Crisis: John of Ephesus and "The Lives of the Eastern Saints."* Berkeley: University of California Press, 1990.

Hassan, Nasra. "An Arsenal of Believers." In *The New Yorker* (November 19, 2001); cited at http://www.newyorker.com/fact/content/?011119fa_FACT1 (accessed August 7, 2004).

Hay, David M., editor. *Pauline Theology Volume II: 1 & 2 Corinthians*. Minneapolis: Fortress, 1991.

Hays, Richard B. "Christology and Ethics in Galatians: The Law of Christ." *CBQ* 49 (1987) 268–90.

Hedrick, Charles W. "Gnostic Proclivities in the Greek Life of Pachomius and the *Sitz im Leben* of the Nag Hammadi Library." *NovT* 22 (1980) 78–94.

Hense, O. *Musonius Rufus Reliquae*. Leipzig: Teubner, 1905. Reprinted, 1990.

Hijmans, Jr, B. L. *ΑΣΚΗΣΙΣ: Notes on Epictetus' Educational System*. Wijsgerige Teksten en Studies 2. Assen: Van Gorcum, 1959.

Hock, Ronald F., and Edward N. O'Neil, editors and translators. *The Chreia in Ancient Rhetoric. Volume I: The Progymnasmata*. SBL Texts and Translations 27. Graeco-Roman Series 9. Atlanta: Scholars, 1986.

Hodge, Robert and Gunther Kress. *Social Semiotics*. Ithaca, NY: Cornell University Press, 1988.

Horsley, Richard A. "Spiritual Marriage with Sophia." *VC* 33 (1979) 30–54. Reprinted in idem, *Wisdom and Spiritual Transcendence at Corinth: Studies in First Corinthians*, 39–64. Eugene, OR: Cascade, 2008.

Houser, Joseph Samuel. "The Philosophy of Musonius Rufus: A Studied of Applied Ethics in the Late Stoa." Ph.D. diss., Brown University, 1997.

Isaac, Jeffrey C. "Beyond the Three Faces of Power: A Realist Critique." In *Rethinking Power*, edited by Thomas E. Wartenberg, 32–55. Albany: State University of New York Press, 1992.

Jagu, Amand, *Musonius Rufus Entretiens et Fragments: Introduction, Traduction, et Commentaire*. Hildesheim: Olms, 1979.

Jones, Alan W. *Soul Making: The Desert Way of Spirituality*. San Francisco: Harper & Row, 1985.

Jung, Carl Gustav. "Foreword to Werblowsky's 'Lucifer and Prometheus.'" In *Collected Works*, vol. 11: *Psychology and Religion: West and East*. Bolligen Series 20. Princeton: Princeton University Press, 1958.

Kaelber, Walter O. "Asceticism." In *ER* 1 (1987) 441–45.

Kaestli, Jean-Daniel. "L'Evangile de Thomas: son importance pour l'étude des paroles de Jésus et du gnosticisme Chrétien." *Études théologiques et religieuses* 54 (1979) 375–96.

Kazantzakis, Nikos. *ΑΣΚΗΤΙΚΗ: Salvatores Dei*. Athens: Eleni Kazantzakis, n.d; English translation: *The Saviors of God: Spiritual Exercises*. Translated by Kimon Friar. New York: Simon and Schuster, 1960.

Kelly, Henry Ansgar. *The Devil, Demonology and Witchcraft: The Development of Christian Beliefs in Evil Spirits*, Rev. ed. New York: Doubleday, 1974.

Kelsey, Morton. *Discernment: A Study in Ecstasy and Evil*. New York: Paulist, 1978.

———. *Healing and Christianity: Healing in Ancient Thought and Modern Times*. New York: Harper & Row, 1973.

Kirschner, Robert. "The Vocation of Holiness in Late Antiquity." *VC* 38 (1984) 105–24.

Kittel, Gerhard, and Gerhard Friedrich, editors. *Theological Dictionary of the New Testament*. 10 vols. Translated by Geoffrey W. Bromiley. Grand Rapids: Eerdmans, 1964–76.

Klijn, A. F. J. "The 'Single One' in the Gospel of Thomas." *JBL* 81 (1962) 271–78.

Klinz, Albert. *Hieros Gamos: Quaestiones Selectae ad Sacras Nuptias Graecorum Religionis et Poeseos Pertinentes*. Halle: Halis Saonum, 1933.

Koester, Helmut. *Ancient Christian Gospels: Their History and Development*. Philadelphia: Trinity, 1990.

——. *Introduction to the New Testament.* Vol. 2. Philadelphia: Fortress, 1982.

——. "Q and Its Relatives." In *Gospel Origins and Christian Beginnings: In Honor of James M. Robinson,* edited by James E. Goehring, Charles W. Hedrick, and Jack T. Sanders, 49–63. Forum Fascicles 1. Sonoma, CA: Polebridge, 1990.

——. "The Story of the Johannine Tradition." *STRev* 36 (1992) 17–32.

Kovalchuk, Fedor S., editor. *Abridged Typicon,* 2nd ed. South Canaan, PA: St. Tikhon's Seminary Press, 1985.

——. *The Church Kalendar,* South Canaan, PA: St. Tikhon's Seminary Press, 1947.

Krause, M. and P. Labib, editors. *Die Drei Versionen des Apokryphon des Johannes.* Wiesbaden: Harrassowitz, 1962.

Lakoff, George and Mark Johnson. *Metaphors We Live By.* Chicago: University of Chicago Press, 1980.

Lambdin, Thomas O. *The Gospel of Thomas, Nag Hammadi Codex II, 2–7 Together with XIII.2, Brit. Lib. OR.49261(1), and P.Oxy 1, 654, 655.* Vol. 1., edited by Bentley Layton, 53–93. NHS 20. Leiden: Brill, 1989.

Layton, Bentley. *The Gnostic Scriptures.* Garden City, NY: Doubleday, 1987.

Liddell, H. G., R. Scott, and H. S. Jones, *A Greek-English Lexicon.* 9th Edition, with revised supplement. Oxford: Oxford University Press. 1996.

Lincoln, Bruce. *Holy Terrors: Thinking About Religion after September 11.* Chicago: University of Chicago Press, 2003.

——. "Thomas-Gospel and Thomas-Community: A New Approach to a Familiar Text." *NovT* 19 (1997) 65–76.

Luke, Timothy W. *Screens of Power: Ideology, Domination, and Resistance in Informational Society.* Urbana: University of Illinois Press, 1989.

Lukes, Steven. "Power and Authority." In *A History of Sociological Analysis,* edited by Tom Bottomre and Robert Nisbet, 633–76. New York: Basis Books, 1978.

——. *Power: A Radical View.* London: Macmillan, 1974.

Lutz, Cora E. *Musonius Rufus: "The Roman Socrates."* Yale Classical Studies 10. New Haven: Yale University Press, 1947.

Macarius the Egyptian. *Pseudo-Macarius: The Fifty Spiritual Homilies and the Great Letter.* Translated by George A. Maloney, SJ. CWS. New York: Paulist, 1992.

MacRae, George W., SJ. "Authoritative Teaching VI, 3:22, 1–35, 24." In *Nag Hammadi Codices V,2–5 and VI with Papyrus Berolinensis 8502, 1 and 4,* edited by Douglas M. Parrott, 257–89. NHS 11. Leiden: Brill, 1979.

——. "The Gospel of Thomas—*Logia Iesou?*" *CBQ* 22 (1960) 56–70.

——. "Nag Hammadi and the New Testament." In *Gnosis: Festscrift für Hans Jonas,* edited by Barbara Aland, 144–57. Göttingen: Vandenhoeck & Ruprecht, 1978.

——. "A Nag Hammadi Tractate." In *La Révélation d'Hermès Trismégiste: III Les Doctrines de l'Ame,* edited by A.-J. Festugière. Paris: Belles Lettres, 1983.

Malherbe, Abraham J. *The Cynic Epistles: A Study Edition.* SBLSBS 12. Missoula, MT: Scholars, 1997.

Malina, Bruce J. "Pain, Power, and Personhood: Ascetic Behavior in the Ancient Mediterranean." In *Asceticism,* edited by Vincent L. Wimbush and Richard Valantasis, 162–77. New York: Oxford University Press, 1995.

Martin, Troy. "Apostasy to Paganism: The Rhetorical Stasis of the Galatian Controversy." *JBL* 114 (1995) 437–61.

———. "Pagan and Judeo-Christian Time-Keeping Schemes in Gal 4:10 and Col 2:16." *NTS* 42. (1996) 105–19.

Maxius the Confessor. *The Ascetic Discourse.* Translated by Polycarp Sherwood. ACW 21. New York: Newman, 1955.

———. *Maximus the Confessor: Selected Writings.* Translated by George C. Berthold. CWS. New York: Paulist, 1985.

McGuckin, J. A. "Christian Asceticism and the Early School of Alexandria." In *Monks, Hermits and the Ascetic Tradition,* edited by W. J. Shiels, 25–39. Ecclesiastical History Society Papers. Oxford: Blackwell, 1985.

McGuire, Anne. "Virginity and Subversion: Norea Against the Powers in the *Hypostasis of the Archons.*" In *Images of the Feminine in Gnosticism,* edited by Karen L. King, 239–58. SAC. Philadelphia: Fortress, 1988.

Meeks, Wayne A. "'The Image of the Androgyne': Some Uses of a Symbol in Earliest Christianity." *HR* 13 (1974) 165–208.

Ménard, Jacques. *L'Authentikos Logos.* Quebec: Les Presses de l'université Laval, 1977.

Meredith, Anthony. "Asceticism—Christian and Greek." *JTS* 27 (1976) 312–32.

Metzger, Bruce M. *A Textual Commentary on the Greek New Testament.* 3rd ed. London: United Bible Societies, 1971.

Meyer, Marvin. "Making Mary Male: The Categories of 'Male' and 'Female' in the Gospel of Thomas." *NTS* 31 (1985) 554–70.

Michie, Helena. *The Flesh Made Word: Female Figures and Women's Bodies.* New York: Oxford University Press, 1987.

Miles, Margaret R. *Fullness of Life: Historical Foundations for a New Asceticism.* 1981. Reprinted, Eugene, OR: Wipf & Stock, 2006.

Milhaven, J. Giles. "Asceticism and the Moral Good: A Tale of Two Pleasures." In *Asceticism,* edited by Vincent L. Wimbush and Richard Valantasis, 375–94. New York: Oxford University Press, 1995.

Miller, Jean Baker. "Women and Power." In *Rethinking Power,* edited by Thomas E. Wartenberg, 240–48. Albany: State University of New York Press, 1992.

Miller, Patricia Cox. "Desert Asceticism and 'The Body from Nowhere.'" *JECS* 2 (1994) 137–53.

Mills, C. Wright. *The Power Elite.* Oxford: Oxford University Press, 1956.

Moore, Archimandrite Lazarus, translator. *The Ladder of Divine Ascent.* Rev. ed. Translated by Holy Transfiguration Monastery. Boston: Holy Transfiguration Monastery. 1978.

Nautin, Pierre. *Origene: Sa vie et son oeuvre.* Christianisme antique 1. Paris: Beauchesne, 1977.

Navia, Luis E. *Classical Cynicism: A Critical Study.* Contributions in Philosophy 58. Westport, CT: Greenwood, 1996.

Nietzsche, Friedrich. "Untimely Meditations." In *Schopenhaurer as Educator,* edited by Daniel Breazeale, 125–94. Translated by R. J. Hollingdale. Cambridge Texts in the History of Philosophy. Cambridge: Cambridge University Press, 1997.

Nouwen, Henri J. M. *The Way of the Heart: Desert Spirituality and Contemporary Ministry*. New York: Seabury, 1981.

Nussbaum, Martha C. *The Therapy of Desire: Theory and Practice in Hellenistic Ethics*. Martin Classical Lectures, New Series 2. Princeton: Princeton University Press, 1994.

O'Laughlin, Michael. "Origenism in the Desert: Anthropology and Integration in Evagrius Ponticus." Th.D. diss., Harvard University, 1987.

Olivelle, Patrick. "Deconstruction of the Body in Indian Asceticism." In *Asceticism*, edited by Vincent L. Wimbush and Richard Valantasis, 188–210. New York: Oxford University Press, 1995.

Olphe-Galliard, M. "Ascèse, Ascétism." In *Dictionnaire de Spiritualité* 1 (1937) 941–60.

Pagels, Elaine. "Exegesis and Exposition of the Genesis Creation Accounts in Selected Texts from Nag Hammadi." In *Nag Hammadi, Gnosticism, and Early Christianity*, edited by Harold W. Attridge, Charles W. Hedrick, and Robert Hodgson, 257–85. 1986. Reprinted, Eugene, OR: Wipf & Stock, 2005.

———. *The Johannine Gospel in Gnostic Exegesis: Heracleon's Commentary on John*. Nashville: Abingdon. 1973.

———. "The Politics of Paradise: Augustine's Exegesis of Genesis 1–3 versus that of John Chrysostom." *HTR* 78 (1985) 67–99.

Patterson, Stephen J. "*Askesis* and the Early Jesus Tradition." In *Asceticism and the New Testament*, edited by Leif E. Vaage and Vincent L. Wimbush, 49–69. New York: Routledge, 1999.

———. *The God of Jesus: The Historical Jesus and the Search for Meaning*. Harrisburg, PA: Trinity, 1998.

———. *The Gospel of Thomas and Jesus*. Sonoma, CA: Polebridge, 1993.

Peters, Greg. "Spiritual Marriage in Early Christianity: 1 Cor 7:25–38 in Modern Exegesis and the Earliest Church." *TJ* 23 (2002) 211–24.

Pseudo-Athanasius. *The Life and Activity of the Holy and Blessed Teacher Syncletica*. PG 28: cols. 1487–558.

Quispel, Gilles. "L'Évangile selon Thomas et les origines de l'ascèse chrétienne." In *Aspects du Judéo-Christianism (Colloque de Strasbourg 23–25 avril 1964)* 35–52. Paris: Presses Universitaires de France, 1965.

———. "Gnosticism and the New Testament." *VC* 19 (1965) 65–85.

———. "The *Gospel of Thomas* Revisited." In *Colloque International sur les textes de Nag Hammadi, 1*, edited by Bernard Barc, 218–66. Quebec: Les Presses de l'université Laval, 1981.

Reitzenstein, Richard. *Hellenistic Mystery-Religions: Their Basic Ideas and Significance*. Translated by John E. Steely. Pittsburgh Theological Monograph Series 15. Pittsburgh: Pickwick, 1978. German ed., Stuttgart: Teubner, 1927.

Rensberger, David. "Asceticism and the Gospel of John." In *Asceticism and the New Testament*, edited by Leif E. Vaage and Vincent L. Wimbush, 127–48. New York: Routledge, 1999.

Richardson, Cyril. "The Gospel of Thomas: Gnostic or Encratite?" In *The Heritage of the Early Church: Essays in Honor of Georges Florovsky,* edited by David Neiman and Margaret Slatkin. OrChrA 195. 65–76. Rome: Ponti. Institutum Studiorum Orientalium, 1973.

Riley, Gregory J. "The Gospel of Thomas in Recent Scholarship." *Currents in Research* 2 (1994) 227–52.

———. *Resurrection Reconsidered: Thomas and John in Controversy*. Minneapolis: Fortress, 1995.

Robinson, James M., editor. *The Nag Hammadi Library in English*. 3rd edition. San Francisco: Harper & Row, 1988.

Rouselle, Aline. *Porneia: On Desire and the Body in Antiquity*. Translated by Felicia Pheasant. Oxford: Blackwell, 1988.

Rousseau, Philip. *Ascetics, Authority, and the Church in the Age of Jerome and Cassian*. Oxford: Oxford University Press, 1978.

———. *Pachomius: The Making of a Community in Fourth-Century Egypt*. The Transformation of the Classical Heritage 6. Berkeley: University of California Press, 1985.

Rudolph, Kurt. *Gnosis*. Translated by Robert McL. Wilson. New York: Harper & Row, 1983.

Russell, Burton. *The Devil: Perceptions of Evil from Antiquity to Primitive Christianity*. Ithaca, NY: Cornell University Press, 1977.

———. *Lucifer: The Devil in the Middle Ages*. Ithaca, NY: Cornell University Press, 1984.

———. *The Prince of Darkness: Radical Evil and the Power of Good in History*. Ithaca, NY: Cornell University Press, 1988.

———. *Satan: The Early Christian Tradition*. Ithaca, NY: Cornell University Press, 1981.

Saldarini, Anthony J. "Asceticism and the Gospel of Matthew." In *Asceticism and the New Testament*, edited by Leif E. Vaage and Vincent L. Wimbush, 11–27. New York: Routledge, 1999.

Sanders, E. P. *Paul and Palestinian Judaism: A Comparison of Patterns of Religion*. Minneapolis: Fortress, 1977.

Satlow, Michael L. "Shame and Sex in Late Antique Judaism." In *Asceticism,* edited by Vincent L. Wimbush, and Richard Valantasis, 535–43. New York: Oxford University Press, 1995.

Säve-Söderbergh, Torgny. "Holy Scriptures or Apologetic Documentations?: The 'Sitz im Leben' of the Nag Hammadi Library." In *Les Textes de Nag Hammadi*, edited by Jacques-E. Ménard, 3–14. NHS 7. Leiden: Brill, 1975.

Schechner, Richard. *The Future of Ritual: Writings on Culture and Performance*. London: Routledge, 1993.

———. "Magnitudes of Performance." In *The Anthropology of Experience,* edited by Victor W. Turner and Edward M. Bruner. Urbana: University of Illinois Press, 1986.

———. *Performance Theory*. Rev. ed. London: Routledge, 1988.

Scherer, Jean. *Entretien d' Origene*. Cairo: Institute Francais d'Archeologie Orientale, 1949.

Scholten, Clemens. "Die Nag-Hammadi-Texte als Buchbesitz der Pachomianer." *JAC* 31 (1988) 144–72.

Segal, Alan F. *Paul the Convert: The Apostolate and Apostasy of Saul the Pharisee.* New Haven: Yale University Press, 1990.

Segelberg, Eric. "The Coptic-Gnostic Gospel According to Philip and Its Sacramental System." *Numen* 7 (1960) 189–200.

Shaw, Teresa. *The Burden of the Flesh: Fasting and Sexuality in Early Christianity.* Minneapolis: Fortress, 1998.

Shelton, J. C. "Introduction." In *Nag Hammadi Codices: Greek and Coptic Papyri from the Cartonnage of the Covers,* edited by J. W. B. Barnes, G. W. Browne, and J. C. Shelton, 1–11. NHS 16. Leiden: Brill, 1981.

Spivak, Gayatri Chakravorty. "More on Power/Knowledge." In *Rethinking Power,* edited by Thomas E. Wartenberg, 149–73. Albany: State University of New York Press, 1992.

Stander, Hendrik F. "Encratites" In *EEC,* 2nd ed., 370–71.

Stendahl, Krister. *Paul Among Jews and Gentiles and Other Essays.* Minneapolis: Fortress, 1977.

Stroumsa. Gedaliahu G. "*Caro salutis cardo*: Shaping the Person in Early Christian Thought." *HR* 30 (1990) 25–50.

Stowers, Stanley K. *The Diatribe and Paul's Letter to the Romans.* SBLDS, 57. Chico, CA: Scholars, 1981.

Swain, Joseph Ward. "The Hellenic Origins of Christian Asceticism." Ph.D. diss., Columbia University, 1916. (privately printed).

Swartz, Michael D. "*Hêkâlôt Rabbâtî* 297–306: A Ritual for the Cultivation of the Prince of the Torah." In *Ascetic Behavior in Greco-Roman Antiquity: A Sourcebook,* edited by Vincent L. Wimbush, 227–34. SAC. Minneapolis: Fortress, 1990

———. *Scholastic Magic: Ritual and Revelation in Early Jewish Mysticism.* Princeton: Princeton University Press, 1996.

Tanquerey, Adolphe. *The Spiritual Life: A Treatise on Ascetical and Mystical Theology.* Translated by Herman Branderis. 2nd ed., revised. Tournai: Desclée, 1920.

Theodora, Amma. *To Gerontikon ētoi apophthegmata agiōn gerontōn,* edited by P. B. Paschou. Athens: Astir, 1987.

Till, Walter. "New Sayings of Jesus in the Recently Discovered Coptic 'Gospel of Thomas.'" *BJRL* 41 (1958–59) 446–56.

———, and Hans-Martin Schenke, editors. *Die Gnostischen Schriften des koptische Papyrus Berolinensis 8502.* Texte und Untersuchungen zur Geschichte der altchristlichen Literatur 60. Berlin: Academic Verlag, 1972.

Tolbert, Mary Ann. "Asceticism and Mark's Gospel." In *Asceticism and the New Testament,* edited by Leif E. Vaage and Vincent L. Wimbush, 29–48. New York: Routledge, 1999.

Turner, John D. "Gnosticism and Platonism: The Platonizing Sethian Texts from Nag Hammadi in their Relation to Late Platonic Literature." In *Neoplatonism and Gnosticism,* edited by Richard T. Wallis and Jay Bregman, 425–59. International

Society for Neoplatonic Studies. Albany: State University of New York Press, 1992.

———. "Typologies of the Sethian Gnostic Treatises From Nag Hammadi." In *Les Textes de Nag Hammadi et le Probéme de Leur Classification: Actes du Colloque Tenu à Québec du 15 au 19 Septembre 1993*, edited by Louis Painchaud and Anne Pasquier, 169–217. Québec: Les Presses de L'Université Laval, 1995.

Vaage, Leif E., and Vincent L. Wimbush, editors. *Asceticism and the New Testament*. New York: Routledge, 1999.

Valantasis, Richard. "Adam's Body: Uncovering Esoteric Tradition in *The Apocryphon of John* and Origen's *Dialogue with Heraclides*." *SecCent* 7 (1989) 150–62.

———. "Asceticism or Formation: Theorizing Asceticism After Nietzsche." In *The Subjective Eye: Essays in Honor of Margaret R. Miles*, edited by Richard Valantasis, 157–75. Princeton Theological Monograph Series 59. Eugene, Ore.: Pickwick, 2006.

———. "Asceticism as a Sacred Marriage." In *Sacred Marriages: The Divine-Human Sexual Metaphor from Sumer to Early Christianity*, edited by Martin P. Nilsson and Risto Uro. Eisenbrauns, 2008.

———. "Competing Ascetic Subjectivities in the Letter to the Galatians." In *Asceticism and the New Testament*, edited by Leif Vaage and Vincent L. Wimbush, 211–29. London: Routledge. 1999.

———. "Constructions of Power in Asceticism." *JAAR* 63 (1995) 775–821.

———. "Daemons and the Perfecting of the Monk's Body: Monastic Anthropology, Daemonology, and Asceticism." *Semeia* 58 (1992) 47–79.

———. "Demons, Adversaries, Devils, Fishermen—The Asceticism of *Authoritative Teaching*." *JR* 80 (2001) 549–65.

———. "The Eastern Church's Theme of Deification in Nicholas Cabasilas' *The Life in Christ*." *Studies in Formative Spirituality* 9 (1990) 89–101.

———. *The Gospel of Thomas*. New Testament Readings. London: Routledge, 1997.

———. "Is the Gospel of Thomas Ascetical? Revisiting an Old Problem with a New Theory." *JECS* 7 (1999) 55–81.

———. "Musonius Rufus and Roman Ascetical Theory." *GRBS* 40 (1999 [2001]) 207–31.

———. "Nag Hammadi and Asceticism: Theory and Practice." *StPatr* 35 (2000) 172–90.

———. "Praying the Bodies: Parish Communication, Liturgy, and Community Spiritual Growth." *STRev* 38 (1995) 313–28.

———. *Spiritual Guides of the Third Century: A Semiotic Study of the Guide-Disciple Relationship in Christianity, Neoplatonism, Hermetism, and Gnosticism*. HDR 27. Minneapolis: Fortress, 1991.

———. "The Stranger Within, the Stranger Without: Ascetical Withdrawal and the Second Letter of Basil the Great." In *Christianity and the Stranger: Historical Essays*, edited by Francis W. Nichols, 64–81. Atlanta: Scholars. 1995.

———. "A Theory of the Social Function of Asceticism." In *Asceticism,* edited by Vincent L. Wimbush and Richard Valantasis, 544–52. New York: Oxford University Press, 1995.

van Leeuwen, Theo. *Introducing Social Semiotics.* London: Routledge, 2005.

Veilleux, Armand. "Monachisme et gnose." In *LTP* 40 (1984) 275–94 and 41 (1985) 3–24.

———. "Monasticism and Gnosis in Egypt." In *The Roots of Egyptian Christianity,* edited by Birger A. Pearson and James E. Goehring, 271–306. SAC. Minneapolis: Fortress, 1986.

Venn, Couze. *Occidentalism: Modernity and Subjectivity.* London: Sage, 2000.

Viller, Marcel, editor. Dictionaire de Spiritualité ascétique et mystique, doctrine et histoire. Paris: Beauchesne, 1957.

Vööbus, A. *History of Asceticism in the Syrian Orient: A Contribution to the History of Culture in the Near East.* CSCO 184. vol. I. Louvaine: Secrétariat du Corpus SCO, 1958.

Ware, Kallistos. "The Way of the Ascetics: Negative or Affirmative?" In *Asceticism,* edited by Vincent L. Wimbush and Richard Valantasis, 3–15. New York: Oxford University Press, 1995.

Wartenberg, Thomas E. *The Forms of Power: From Domination to Transformation.* Philadelphia: Temple University Press, 1990.

———, editor. *Rethinking Power.* SUNY Series in Radical Social and Political Theory. Albany: State University of New York Press, 1992.

Weber, Max. *The Protestant Ethic and the Spirit of Capitalism.* Translated by Talcott Parsons. London: Unwin Hyman, 1930.

———. *The Sociology of Religion.* Translated by Ephraim Fischcoff. Boston: Beacon, 1963. German ed., Tübingen: Mohr/Siebeck, 1922.

White, Edmund. *Genet: A Biography.* New York: Knopf, 1993.

Wicker, Kathleen O'Brien. "Ethiopian Moses (Collected Sources)." In *Ascetic Behavior in Greco-Roman Antiquity: A Sourcebook,* edited by Vincent L. Wimbush, 329–48. SAC. Minneapolis: Fortress, 1990.

———. "'The Politics of Paradise' Reconsidered: John Chrysostom and Porphyry." In *Gnosticism and the Early Christian World: In Honor of James W. Robinson,* edited by James E. Goehring, Charles W. Hedrick, and Jack T. Sanders. Forum Fascicles 2. Sonoma, CA: Polebridge, 1990.

Wiens, Delbert L. "Musonius Rufus and Genuine Education." Ph.D. diss., University of Chicago, 1970.

Williams, Michael Allen. "Divine Image—Prison of Flesh: Perceptions of the Body in Ancient Gnosticism." Part I. In *Fragments for a History of the Human Body,* edited by Michael Feher, 129–47. 3 vols. New York: Zone, 1989.

———. *The Immoveable Race: A Gnostic Designation and the Theme of Stability in Late Antiquity.* NHS 29. Leiden: Brill, 1985.

———. "Interpreting the Nag Hammadi Library as "Collection(s) in the History of "Gnosticism(s)." In *Les Textes de Nag Hammadi et le Problèm de leur Classification actes due colloque tenu à Québec du 15 au 19 Septembre 1993,* edited by Louis

Painchaud and Anne Pasquier, 3–50. Bibliothèque copte de Nag Hammadi: Etudes 3. Québec: Presses de l'Université Laval, 1995.

———. *Rethinking "Gnosticism": An Argument for Dismantling a Dubious Category.* Princeton: Princeton University Press, 1996.

———. "Stability as a Soteriological Theme in Gnosticism." In *The Rediscovery of Gnosticism,* edited by Bentley Layton, 2:819–29. SHR 41. Leiden: Brill, 1981.

Wilson, R. McL. *Studies in the Gospel of Thomas.* London: Mowbray, 1960.

Wimbush, Vincent L., editor. *Ascetic Behavior in Greco-Roman Antiquity: A Sourcebook.* SAC. Minneapolis: Fortress, 1990.

———, and Richard Valantasis, editors. *Asceticism.* New York: Oxford University Press, 1995.

Wipszycka, Ewa. "Les conferéries dans la vie religieuse de l'Egypt chrétienne." In *Proceedings of the Twelfth International Congress of Papyrology,* edited by Deborah H. Samuel, 511–25. ASP 7. Toronto: Hakkert, 1970.

Wisse, Frederik. "After the *Synopsis*: Prospects and the Problems in Establishing a Critical Text of the Apocryphon of John and in Defining its Historical Location." In *The Nag Hammadi Library after Fifty Years: Proceedings of the 1995 Society of Biblical Literature Commemoration,* edited by John D. Turner and Anne McGuire, 138–53. Nag Hammadi and Manichaean Studies 44. Leiden: Brill, 1997.

———. "Gnosticism and Early Monasticism in Egypt." In *Gnosis: Festschrift für Hans Jonas,* edited by Barbara Aland, 431–40. Göttingen: Vandenhoeck & Ruprecht, 1978.

———. "Language Mysticism in the Nag Hammadi Texts and in Early Coptic Monasticism I: Cryptography." *Enchoria* 9 (1979) 101–20.

Wyschogrod, Edith. *Saints and Postmodernism: Revisioning Moral Philosophy.* Chicago: University of Chicago Press, 1990.

Young, Iris Marion. "Five Faces of Oppression." In *Rethinking Power,* edited by Thomas E. Wartenberg, 174–95. Albany: State University of New York Press, 1992.

p 8 – original def. of asceticism